Milton's Moving Bodies

Rethinking the Early Modern

Series Editors
Marcus Keller
Ellen McClure
Feisal Mohamed

Milton's Moving Bodies

~

Edited by
Marissa Greenberg and
Rachel Trubowitz

Northwestern University Press
Evanston, Illinois

Northwestern University Press
www.nupress.northwestern.edu

Copyright © 2024 by Northwestern University. Published 2024 by
Northwestern University Press. All rights reserved.

Printed in the United States of America

10 9 8 7 6 5 4 3 2 1

Library of Congress Cataloging-in-Publication Data

Names: Greenberg, Marissa, 1976– editor. | Trubowitz, Rachel, editor.
Title: Milton's moving bodies / edited by Marissa Greenberg and Rachel
   Trubowitz.
Description: Evanston, Illinois : Northwestern University Press, 2024. |
   Series: Rethinking the early modern | Includes index.
Identifiers: LCCN 2024019891 | ISBN 9780810147409 (cloth) | ISBN
   9780810147416 (ebook)
Subjects: LCSH: Milton, John, 1608–1674. Paradise lost.
Classification: LCC PR3562 .M57 2024 | DDC 821/.4—dc23/eng/20240506
LC record available at https://lccn.loc.gov/2024019891

For Paul Stevens
with gratitude

CONTENTS

A Note on Texts   ix

List of Abbreviations   xi

List of Illustrations   xiii

Acknowledgments   xv

Introduction
Milton's Moving Bodies   3
Marissa Greenberg and Rachel Trubowitz

Chapter 1
Be Still: Milton's Poetry of Motion   23
John Rumrich

Chapter 2
That "Strange / Desire of Wandring": Physical and
  Ideological Movement in *Paradise Lost*   47
Sydney Bartlett

Chapter 3
Extraterrestrial Eden: The Migration of Paradise in the
  Early Modern European Imagination   71
Erin Webster

Chapter 4
Milton's Moving Bodies at the Border: Kinopolitics in
  Paradise Lost and *Samson Agonistes*   99
Rachel Trubowitz

Chapter 5
Moving Jewish Bodies, Moving Jewish Souls: Milton's *Paradise
  Regain'd*, the Jewish (Readmission) Question, and John Toland   127
Achsah Guibbory

Chapter 6
Decomposing Milton: Romantic Reading and Demotic Dispersal   159
  Jennifer Wallace

Chapter 7
Shapes of Things to Come: Milton, Evolution, and the Afterlife
  of Species in Tennyson's *In Memoriam, A. H. H.*   181
  Ryan Hackenbracht

Chapter 8
Anon They Move: Two Hispanoamerican Translations of
  Paradise Lost, Book 3   213
  Mario Murgia

Chapter 9
Presencing the Author: Illustrations of Milton in
  Hispanoamerican Publications   233
  Angelica Duran

Chapter 10
Moved and Surprised by White Sin: Milton's Satanic Influence
  in Part 1 of Pauline E. Hopkins's *Hagar's Daughter*   259
  Reginald A. Wilburn

Chapter 11
Snaking the Path: Disability, Pedagogy, Justice   283
  Marissa Greenberg

Afterword
Moving in and with Milton   311
  Stephen M. Fallon

List of Contributors   319

Index   321

A NOTE ON TEXTS

To ensure greatest accessibility and inclusion of readers, the editors have opted for online editions of texts whenever possible.

All in-text citations of Milton's poetry and most of his prose refer to *The John Milton Reading Room*, gen. ed. Thomas H. Luxon, Trustees of Dartmouth College, 1997–2021, https://milton.host.dartmouth.edu/reading_room/contents/text.shtml.

Where *JMRR* does not include Milton's prose, in-text citations refer to *The Complete Poetry and Essential Prose of John Milton*, ed. William Kerrigan, John Rumrich, and Stephen M. Fallon (New York: Modern Library, 2007).

All biblical references are to *The Holy Bible, conteyning the Old Testament, and the New: Newly Translated out of the Originall tongues: & with the former Translations [Tyndale's, Matthew's, Coverdale's, Cranmer's, Parker's, and the Genevan] diligently compared and reuised by his Maiesties speciall Comandement* (London, 1611), https://archive.org/details/1611TheAuthorizedKingJamesBible.

All references to the plays of William Shakespeare are to *Shakespeare's Plays, Sonnets and Poems from The Folger Shakespeare*, ed. Barbara Mowat, Paul Werstine, Michael Poston, and Rebecca Niles, Folger Shakespeare Library, https://folger.edu/explore/shakespeares-works/all-works.

ABBREVIATIONS

Areo.   *Areopagitica* (1644)

CPEP   *The Complete Poetry and Essential Prose of John Milton*, ed. William Kerrigan, John Rumrich, and Stephen M. Fallon (New York: Modern Library, 2007)

JMRR   *The John Milton Reading Room*

Nativity Ode   *On the Morning of Christ's Nativity* (composed 1629; published 1645)

PL   *Paradise Lost*, 2nd ed. (1674)

PR   *Paradise Regain'd* (1671)

SA   *Samson Agonistes* (1671)

Tenure   *The Tenure of Kings and Magistrates*, 2nd ed. (1650)

ILLUSTRATIONS

Fig. 3.1. Psalter *Mappa Mundi*, or London Psalterkarte
(ca. 1265)   76

Fig. 3.2. Ebstorf *Mappa Mundi* (ca. 1235)   77

Fig. 3.3. Detail of Eden from Ebstorf *Mappa Mundi*
(ca. 1235)   78

Fig. 9.1. Portrait of John Milton, *101 Famous Poems
with a Prose Supplement* (1929)   235

Fig. 9.2. Paperback book cover, *El Paraíso perdido* (1957)   236

Fig. 9.3. Portrait of John Milton, *El Paraíso
recobrado* (1889)   240

Fig. 9.4. Portrait of John Milton, *La Ilustración
mexicana* (1852)   242

Fig. 9.5. Portrait of John Milton, *El Paraíso perdido* (1967)   242

Fig. 9.6. "Reconciliación de Milton con su esposa,"
El Paraíso perdido (1967)   249

Fig. 9.7. "Milton dictando su poema a sus hijas,"
El Paraíso perdido (1967)   249

Fig. 9.8. "Milton secretario de Cromwell," *El Paraíso
perdido* (1967)   250

Fig. 9.9. "Milton enfermo," *El Paraíso perdido* (1967)   250

ACKNOWLEDGMENTS

Milton's Moving Bodies is the result of passion and compassion, grit and grace. It began as a Milton Society of America–sponsored panel of the same name at the 2019 Renaissance Society of America Meeting. Originally composed of Marissa Greenberg, Achsah Guibbory, and Rachel Trubowitz, with Paul Stevens as respondent, the panel pivoted to include a paper by Professor Stevens when Professor Guibbory was unable to attend the conference in Toronto. About a year later plans for the collection needed to adapt again when the COVID-19 pandemic impacted everyone's capacity to perform scholarly work. Even as the world returned to a new normal, health issues and family obligations required we prioritize our and contributors' well-being over punctuality. Together with wandering steps and slow we continued to make progress, energized by a shared belief in the important contributions of this collection to Milton studies and early modern literary studies.

This belief is shared by not only the collection's editors and contributors but also a community of advocates. Paul Stevens has supported this collection from the beginning and offered invaluable input throughout its evolution. Our experience with Northwestern University Press has been characterized by clear communication and patient persistence, which allowed us to extend the same to contributors. We are grateful to Marcus Keller, Ellen McClure, and Feisal Mohamed, the series editors of Rethinking the Early Modern, for championing the collection and to Faith Wilson Stein, Senior Editor for Scholarly Titles, for shepherding it through review amid a global pandemic that brought many presses to a standstill. We also wish to thank the two anonymous readers whose comments spurred us to refine and clarify key elements of the collection, in particular its attention to the diversity of bodies in Milton's writings, their afterlives, and their scholarly study.

xv

Milton's Moving Bodies

INTRODUCTION

Milton's Moving Bodies

Marissa Greenberg and Rachel Trubowitz

Motion, Stasis, Flow

The opening stanza to book 3 of *Paradise Lost* is all about return. Often referred to as "The Ode to Light," the fifty-five-line invocation describes how blindness precludes the Miltonic speaker's renewed encounter with the rising and setting sun and with anything and everything that it illuminates. Yet the repetition of "return . . . returns" (*PL*, 3.41) invites a critical return to the dynamics of this famous passage. While physical light "not to me returns" (*PL*, 3.41), a metaphysical light does arrive dynamically on the epic scene in response to the speaker's invocation: "Celestial light / Shine[s] *inward* . . . all mist from thence the [speaker's] mind and [inner] eyes . . . *disperse*" (*PL*, 3.51–54, emphasis added). Light flows in, while mist flows out. The consequence is a new understanding of return as nonidentical recursivity.[1]

This personal sense of return must be paired with a cosmological one: in the Copernican world system, the sun does not move to usher in "the sweet approach of . . . Morn" or the change of "Seasons" (*PL*, 3.42, 41). No longer the steadfast center of the universe, the earth now orbits around the sun. Although Milton never completely gives up on the old Aristotelian-Ptolemaic model, he nonetheless entertains the idea of a heliocentric universe in which "The Planet Earth" "dance[s] around [the sun] various rounds" (*PL*, 8.129, 125).[2] Elsewhere in *Paradise Lost* and throughout his writings, Milton does more than recognize that the earth moves.[3] Everything on it—from the great (oceans, mountains, towers, and temples) to the small (ants, bees, leaves of grass, and grains of sands)—also moves, even when they seem to stand still.

We begin with the invocation to book 3 of Milton's epic because it draws critical attention to the many bodies and their motions that

4   Introduction

motivate *Milton's Moving Bodies*. These diverse moving bodies inspire the contributors to this volume to "revisit," as Milton's epic-speaker terms it, critical concepts in Milton's writings and their legacy and to "wander" in new fields of inquiry (*PL*, 3.13, 21, 23, 27). "Though hard and rare," this critical "return" does not presume to supersede established scholarship (*PL*, 3.21, 41); instead, *Milton's Moving Bodies* unfolds adjacent to these conversations and thereby participates in their dynamic continuation and change. Moreover, in "aftertimes," to borrow the poet's term in *The Reason of Church Government*, Milton's moving bodies change direction and range anew in ways that, until recently, have been underappreciated.

Principal among these conversations is Milton's monism. Milton's kinetic sensibility is essentially if not absolutely monistic.[4] Bodies in Milton's poetry and prose move not only externally in physical space and time but also internally as mental, affective, and spiritual motions. The imaginative "descent, and . . . ascent" (*PL*, 3.20) of Milton's epic-speaker, for instance, follows Satan's intertwining physical and spiritual trajectory. After his authorized departure from Hell, Satan passes through Chaos's realm, at first "ascending," but on "meet[ing] / A vast vacuitie," "plumb down he drops / Ten thousand fadom deep" (*PL*, 2.930–34). The epic-speaker asserts that "ill chance" reverses Satan's physical fall (*PL*, 2.932). Yet, lest readers conclude that Milton's God plays dice with the universe, they are told that "The strong rebuff" that halts Satan's physical plummeting does not cease his spiritual, moral, and affective "Down . . . falling" (*PL*, 2.936, 935).[5] Satan's famous declaration that "Which way I flie is Hell; my self am Hell" (*PL*, 4.75) is most often read as Satan's identification with the place of damnation. Just as importantly, we argue, these lines cue Satan's internal hell as a dynamic state.[6] This monist continuity between the material and immaterial forms of Satan's downward movement finds an instructive analogy in what physicists term "change of state."[7] Take, for example, the substances of "Fire and Nitre" (*PL*, 2.937). Flame and gas are characteristic of both Hell and Chaos. In the former, they are source and symptom of damnation: fire and "vapors noxious" (*PL*, 2.216) torment the fallen. In the latter, however, they are morally neutral yet vitally charged: they inflame ("Instinct"; *PL*, 2.937) the "tumultuous cloud" that "hurr[ies]" Satan "aloft" (*PL*, 2.936–38). Despite such alterations in location, condition, and effect, these substances remain elementally identical. So too, Satan's fall never ceases, even if it undergoes a change of state.

Not even chance can alter such divinely ordained laws in Milton's epic—laws that determine the material-spiritual movements of all bodies. Because in Milton's monistic cosmos God's physical laws are inseparable from his moral laws, bodies that move in accordance with God's will inherently exert the just and the good. In the "Father's harmoniously balanced material universe," as John Rogers cogently argues, "material processes [including, or especially, the motions of bodies] exercise their own highly moral form of justice as they follow inexorably the laws of nature which the Father has established."[8] So, despite the chance reversal of Satan's freefall through the vacuum in Chaos, God's physical and moral laws remain unaltered. Approaching Earth, "Still" (*PL*, 4.77) Satan falls from "the lowest deep" to "a lower deep" (*PL*, 4.76) through the abysmal Hell that is "[him]self" (*PL*, 4.75). Chance might seem to interfere with divine will, but, as Satan learns, all creatures endowed with free will inevitably pay for their premeditated crimes against God and Nature: "God and Nature bid the same" (*PL*, 6.176), as Abdiel informs Satan.[9] No one, even, or especially, those who sit "High on a Throne of Royal State" (*PL*, 2.1), is above God's law and (as) natural law.

Happily, for humanity, salvation in Milton's epic is governed by the same physical-moral laws of motion. Grace proves a powerful force of ascent. The stairway "mysteriously . . . meant" (*PL*, 3.516) by which angels ascend to Heaven is also, as Raphael explains, available to humanity, "If [they] be found obedient" (*PL*, 3.516; 5.501, cf. 5.512–14). So too, if humanity "hear[s]" and freely chooses to answer God's "call," made audible through Christian scripture and godly conscience, the faithful will "safe arrive" in Heaven (*PL*, 3.185, 197). More than metaphysical metaphors, Milton's imagery of scaling and hearing is part of a holistic monism that takes seriously the connections among physical, affective, cognitive, and spiritual movements. As Ryan Hackenbracht contends, in *Paradise Lost* pre- and postlapsarian walking is "a physical register for the growth or decline of a character's self-knowledge" necessary for salvation.[10] Seth Herbst similarly argues that, long before *Paradise Lost*, Milton underscores music's "effectual agency" to move body, mind, and soul.[11] This same kinetic sensibility extends to Milton's understanding of the created universe in his epic.[12] Animal and elemental bodies also move. In book 5 of *Paradise Lost* we learn how the physical motions of Edenic bodies serve God: from "Aire, and ye Elements" that "in quaternion run / Perpetual Circle," to the "Rising [and] falling" of mists and rain, to "Fountains and yee, that warble, as flow," joining with the birds and "all ye living Souls" that "tune his praise" (*PL*, 5.180–96). Running and tuning, rising and falling, warbling and flowing—these motions characterize humanity's oneness with and movement through an equally dynamic cosmos. What *matters* to Milton, both as pressing topics of theological, philosophical, scientific, and historical inquiry and debate and as the material stuff of existence, is not if human and nonhuman bodies move but how and why they do so.

Surprisingly perhaps, universal physical-moral laws of motion also govern bodies at rest. In *Paradise Lost* Adam and Eve's primal "happy State," like God's perfect bliss prior to creation, is a "Rest[ing]" state (*PL,* 1.29, 7.91).[13] Yet neither human nor divine rest is in opposition to movement. In Milton's epic universe, as in Galileo's physical universe, stasis is motion with a velocity of zero. Prelapsarian Adam and Eve thus move not only during their manual labor but also in their spiritual obedience.[14] Indeed, for Milton, stillness is perhaps the most challenging and important motion of all. When Jesus stands "on the highest Pinacle" of the temple in Jerusalem (*PR,* 4.549), he models and anticipates humanity's "renew[ed]" capacity to "stand / On even ground against his mortal foe" (*PL,* 3.175, 178–79). Significantly, though, Jesus's stillness has the efficacy of a blow or kick that sends Satan falling.[15] In this revision of his biblical sources, Milton draws on two seventeenth-century models of motion's embodiment: mechanism, which ascribes the motions of bodies to outward forces, and vitalism, which ascribes motions to the bodies themselves.[16] Without disputing the crucial distinctions between mechanism and vitalism (including their very different political implications, respectively, authoritarian and liberal), we contend that Milton's lifelong commitment to right use of reason and liberty of choice cannot be separated from his emphasis on bodies moving in accordance with God's inexorable laws.[17] Whether celestial or terrestrial, linear or looping, observable or imperceptible— motion is, for Milton, primary to the operations of a divinely created universe and all the bodies in it.

For Milton, it is not stasis but stagnation that interrupts grace. This distinction is evident in *Areopagitica,* where Milton defines "flow" as Truth's most salient feature: "Truth is compar'd in Scripture to a streaming fountain; if her waters flow not in a perpetuall progression, they sick'n into a muddy pool of conformity and tradition" (*Areo.*). The best way to ensure the ongoing flow of Truth, Milton argues, is to ensure liberty of expression through books unencumbered by preprint censorship. This dynamic view of Truth also forms the context for his well-known, if controversial, version of the book-as-body metaphor:

> For Books are not absolutely dead things, but doe contain a potencie of life in them to be as active as that soule was whose progeny they are; nay they do preserve as in a violl the purest efficacie and extraction of that living intellect that bred them. I know they are as lively, and as vigorously productive, as those fabulous Dragons teeth; and being sown up and down, may chance to spring up armed men. (*Areo.*)

According to Stanley Fish, in this passage Milton acts quite out of character. Fish argues that, in claiming that books "doe contain a potencie of life in them," Milton animates an inanimate object in ways analogous to the Eucharist: turning wine and bread into Christ's blood and body. Milton "could not have really meant" to elevate books to such a high status, Fish insists, because Milton would never locate "value and truth in a physical object."[18] In our view, Fish's reading misunderstands the dynamics in the passage.[19] Books appear static objects, yet they move and thus have agency in ways that reflect not only the vitalism documented by Stephen M. Fallon and John Rogers but also the kinetics explored in this volume.[20]

A youthful Milton meditating on how to "serve [God] best" wrote: "They also serve who only stand and wait" (Sonnet 19, lines 11 and 14). The words "also" and "only" protract an otherwise straightforward assertion—they serve who stand and wait—to convey the passion of patient obedience to divine, and poetic, stricture.[21] Nearing the end of his life, in the 1671 volume that contains *Paradise Regain'd* and *Samson Agonistes*, Milton would confirm that freely chosen yet hard-won stasis best serves not only God but also humanity.[22] By contrast, in *Paradise Lost*, Satan "Forthwith upright . . . rears from off the Pool" and "with expanded wings . . . stears his flight / Aloft, . . . till on dry Land / He lights" (*PL*, 2.221–28), yet for ten more books of epic poetry, not to mention Milton's brief epic, Satan remains spiritually stagnant, "in the fiery Gulfe / Confounded" (*PL*, 2.52–53). Such convolutions of diverse bodies resonate with the delirium that Gordon Teskey identifies as Miltonic: "a rapid oscillation between some apparently rational standard . . . and the experience of transport, of shamanistic flight into the heavens or into the depths of matter, that the very effort to adhere to the standard provokes."[23] They also spur the contributors to *Milton's Moving Bodies* to trace dynamism, flow, and stillness in Milton's poetry and prose and their afterlives across time and space.

Monism, Migration, Diversity

Focusing on Milton's moving bodies, this volume seeks to contribute to and intervene in several critical conversations ongoing in Milton studies and, more broadly, premodern literary and cultural studies. The first of these critical conversations concerns monism and vitalism. Monism, the heretical assumption that body and soul are one and the same, directs scholarly attention to "Milton's articulated conception of embodied human spirit," to borrow Stephen M. Fallon and John Rumrich's apt phrase. For Fallon and Rumrich, whose breakthrough work on animist materialism shaped a generation of Milton scholars, Milton's monist understanding of the body as "a pivotal site" anticipates "what Merleau-Ponty calls a 'chiasm,' of self and world woven together."[24] If Milton's monism recognizes the coexistence of matter and spirit, his vitalism ascribes active movement to the embodied soul. Milton and other seventeenth-century vitalists repudiate the mechanistic view of uniform matter as passively receiving and transferring motion according to mathematical laws of collision.[25]

Milton's Moving Bodies contributes to this rich scholarship on early modern monism and vitalism by discovering how the poet, as well as readers, comprehend and configure the complexities of embodiment and/in motion. Milton's monism may inform his examination of humanity's "ontological mobility" through bodily action, as Kevin J. Donovan and Thomas Festa have pointed out.[26] But monism does not account for the various other moving bodies of Milton's poetic universe. Neither does a vitalist lens. Vitalism's opening gambit is to separate nonliving entities from living organisms by assigning an animating principle, which some equate with the soul, solely to the living. In *Paradise Lost*, however, Milton advances the notion that animate and inanimate bodies are equally important because they all derive from the "all" of God's primal "matter" (*PL*, 5.472). "All things proceed" from God and to God all things "return" (a key word for our introduction) regardless of form or substance or, "in things that live, of life" (*PL*, 5.470–74). The critical point here is that, regardless of variations in kind and degrees of vitality, for Milton all of creation moves from and to the divine body. In this volume Ryan Hackenbracht and Mario Murgia nuance the dichotomy between these philosophical positions by exposing its theological foundations and highlighting its critical implications for embodied motion in *Paradise Lost* and its afterlives in nineteenth-century adaptation and translation.

Scientific developments in seventeenth-century Europe—the second critical conversation in which this volume participates—included but also exceeded debates about monism and vitalism.[27] We argue that Galileo's radical revision of Aristotelian principles of motion is crucial to understanding Milton's ideas and representations of moving bodies. Aristotle taught that the natural state of an object is at rest, that all objects seek this state, and that a constant outside action is required to keep an object in motion. By contrast, for Galileo, all bodies move, even when they stand still—an insight that he formalized as the law of inertia. That Galileo is the only modern thinker whom Milton cites by name in his epic underscores the poet's indebtedness to the "*Tuscan* Artist" (*PL,* 1.288). Moreover, in *Areopagitica*, Milton famously laments the injustice of Galileo's trial by the papal court that found him guilty of heresy and forced him to recant his life's work. Supposedly Galileo responded to his sentence by muttering "Eppur si muove" ("Still it [the earth] moves")—an early modern urban legend that nonetheless testifies to motion as a central issue of the era. Galileo's scientific innovations and insights prove essential for recasting our understandings of moving bodies in Milton's writings, as John Rumrich, Rachel Trubowitz, and Erin Webster show in their interrogations of the physics of stillness, border crossing, and space travel.

In his biography of Milton, Joe Moshenska imagines the poet's purported meeting with Galileo in 1638: "Two figures [walk] . . . , with inching slowness, around the perimeter path" of the courtyard of Villa Il Gioiello in Florence; perhaps they talk about "Galileo's most famous device, and the heavenly discoveries he had made within a quarter century before"; or perhaps they discussed the arts—Galileo's expertise extended to music, drawing, and poetry.[28] Intertwining the aging body and the eternal cosmos, opera and epic, text and image, Moshenska's flight of fancy points up the possible impact of Milton's experiences as a traveler on his thinking about bodies and movement. Following Milton's incomplete Grand Tour in 1638–39, he remained an avid armchair traveler, gleaning from personal correspondence, printed books and images, and popular newsprint information about the adventurers, colonists, merchants, and missionaries who "post o're Land and Ocean without rest" (Sonnet 19, line 13).[29] Attending to embodied movement as changes in physical locations and geopolitical conditions expands our understanding of seventeenth-century global exploration and imperial expansion.[30] This volume brings Milton studies into increasingly urgent conversations about migration and diaspora in premodern Europe and the Americas with Rachel Trubowitz's and Achsah

Guibbory's appraisals of Milton's border-crossing human bodies in his great, late-career verse and Mario Murgia's and Angelica Duran's analyses of his ocean-crossing textual bodies in translation.[31]

For more than a quarter century, scholars of premodern critical race studies have explored archives of medieval and early modern European constructions of somatic difference and exposed histories of systemic oppression, exclusion, and violence against Black, Brown, Indigenous, and other persons of color in both northern and southern hemispheres, "Old" and "New" Worlds.[32] By calling attention to the place of Amerindians in an imagined interstellar Paradise to which English Protestants might travel, Erin Webster reminds us that Milton and his contemporary (and later) readers understood race in intimate connection with Protestant evangelism and empire. Even as early modern science revised its theories of spiritual transmission through bodily fluids, including blood and humors, and through physical vision, following Johannes Kepler's paradigm-changing, intromission theory of light, early modern culture retained its palpable sense of essential difference among Protestant, Catholic, Muslim, and Jewish bodies and their motions, both internal and external, individual and collective.[33]

Such palpable ethnic and religious differentiation must be understood in the context of Milton's lifelong oscillations about the constitution of the nation. As Elizabeth Sauer argues, "Milton's own oeuvre reveals how his thinking about and his treatment of toleration were subject to historical contingencies of various kinds and shifted from positive to negative," culminating in *Samson Agonistes*, with its bluntly Hebrew (prot)agonist: "Configured as an ethnic body, the nation is marked by a common bloodline or genealogy, but as a civic construction, the nation is bound by laws, duties, and rights ideally designed to preserve the liberty of its citizens, and thus it is deemed less exclusionary than an ethnicity."[34] Focusing on actual ethnic bodies in motion attunes us to Milton's policing of the boundaries of the English national body. In reassessments of Milton's monism and religious toleration in *Paradise Regain'd* and *Samson Agonistes*, Achsah Guibbory and Rachel Trubowitz move beyond the poet's use of Hebraic texts and representation of biblical Hebrews to demonstrate his resistance to the (re)incorporation of Jews within the Commonwealth and communion of white Protestant England.[35] Roman Catholics, however, are the primary target of Milton's intolerance. In ways different if not separate from Milton's diasporic Jews, Catholics were unwelcomed in Milton's body of the Christian faithful not only because they too constituted racial-religious "others" but also because Catholic nations, like Spain and France, slaughtered Protestants from England and elsewhere. Curiously, Milton's antipathy toward Roman Catholicism did not put off Catholic Hispanoamerican writers and artists who keenly adapted his textual and physical bodies.[36] The transatlantic movement of Milton's writings and portraits yielded mixed bodies that provoked fears and aversions from white Protestants on both sides of the Atlantic Ocean, as Mario Murgia and Angelica Duran discover as colonial resistance in Miltonic translation and cultural hybridity in Miltonic illustration.

Milton was deeply invested in this project of translating—or carrying across—bodily motions. As Leah Whittington's study of "supplicatory gestures" in *Paradise Lost* shows, "patterns of ascent and descent, up and down, elevation and reduction" situate Milton's epic at the "crossroads of past literary tradition and present lived experience."[37] So too, when later writers and artists crossed paths with Milton, they adapted his moving bodies to conditions that he could not anticipate. Edited by Mary Nyquist and Margaret W. Ferguson, *Re-membering Milton* spurred generations of scholars to pursue how the limbs of Milton's bodies, like Truth, have been scattered through time and space and reassembled in manifold ways to advance alternative ideas and traditions.[38]

Indebted to *Re-membering Milton*, our volume moves beyond this storied antecedent by bringing new attention to Milton's kinetic sensibilities of embodied identity. We draw inspiration from the lived experience of moving through institutional, national, and global spaces in "other(ed)" bodies. Although Milton was proud that his "eys, . . . clear / To outward view, of blemish or of spot" rendered his disability invisible, his infirmity was exposed every time he needed to move from one place to another because he required use of a stick or a human aid to guide him.[39] Marissa Greenberg's chapter brings her experiential knowledge of mobility limited by chronic illness to her Milton scholarship and pedagogy. Milton's representations of Black bodies and comments on slavery are not historical artifacts, especially for readers of color, as Reginald A. Wilburn shows in his "pathbreaking work on engagements of Milton in African American literature," including in the present volume.[40] As self-identifying Jewish Miltonists, the editors of *Milton's Moving Bodies* along with Achsah Guibbory are likewise spurred by the legacies of premodern antisemitism. Ideologies of bodily difference are "at once situation-specific *and* resonant," meaning that Milton's representations of disability, Blackness, and Jewishness cannot be separated from more modern histories of violent oppression and inequity.[41] This legacy also presents powerful

12   Introduction

opportunities for solidarity, both academic and activist.[42] Naming the personal bases for Milton's and Miltonists' investment in embodied motion, we hope our volume will inspire future scholars to continue fleshing out "other(ed)" moving bodies.

More broadly, *Milton's Moving Bodies* aims to cultivate a more inclusive field. Indeed, contributors represent a range of career stages—from independent scholar, to established academic, to senior administrator—and institutional contexts in the United States and England. Miltonists' personal and professional trajectories, like Milton's, must be part of our conversations if we wish to understand fully the diversity of bodies (cosmic and creaturely, terrestrial and textual) and their movements (loops closed and unclosed, ebbs and flows, and changes of position with and without a singular or set destination) in Milton's writings and their legacies.

Dynamism, Contents, Structures

Although responsive to the entanglements of literature, location, and history, the kinetic sensibilities of Milton's poetry and prose resist being read through twentieth-century cultural poetics. As practiced by Stephen Greenblatt across numerous monographs and articles, cultural poetics presupposes a social and political dialectic that resolves in conformation with hegemonic power. Despite often lively turns of phrase, such as "circulation of social energies" and "a shift, a fault, a rift," Greenblatt perceives culture along Aristotelian lines, moving necessarily toward rest in accordance with dominant ideologies and centralized authorities.[43] Milton's moving bodies do not comply with such a restrictive model. Instead, resembling Galileo's radical revision of Aristotle, they are always moving, even if that movement has a velocity of zero. What this means for scholars of Milton is that the returns, flows, rolls, and flights in Milton's poetry and prose must be understood as taking new twists and turns when they encounter, and are encountered by, the embodied minds of readers, translators, illustrators, and adapters across the globe and at different moments in time. Put in the terms of vitalism and mechanism, Milton's moving bodies both move and are moved by many more and diverse bodies than the epic-speaker's "fit audience . . . [and] few" (*PL*, 7.31). For this reason, while Milton's moving bodies may be motivated by the specific spatiotemporal moment of early modern England, they do not remain isolated or unified then and there. Instead, they initiate, proliferate, and participate in diverse movements—intellectual, spiritual, aesthetic, political—across far-flung times and spaces.

The structure of this volume enacts this unrestricted flow. *Milton's Moving Bodies* rejects thematic divides in favor of dynamic rhythms that "take place in part in or through the body" throughout Milton's life, writings, and afterlives.[44] Following the new-scientific concept of "time as a measure of motion," as introduced in this volume by John Rumrich, we return to monism, migration, race, and adaptation as they appear again and again in Milton's moving bodies from the seventeenth to the twenty-first centuries. But this is not your father's chronology (to adopt an idiom that also gestures to the volume's social justice commitments). A structure that traces the linear movements of Milton's texts in time allows for thematic knots to form among the volume's eleven chapters, even as it moves geographically in looping fashion from England to the Americas to the United States.

The volume begins squarely if not exclusively in early modern England. In chapter 1 John Rumrich establishes Milton's fascination with moving bodies from his early Psalm translations and *Nativity Ode* to his grand epic and 1671 volume. In doing so, Rumrich traces Milton's poetics of "stillness" in relation to biblical sources and mathematical developments that precede and follow, respectively, Milton's situation in seventeenth-century England. In chapter 2 Sydney Bartlett spotlights the postlapsarian language of erroneous and regressive movement— "wandering," "creeping," "falling"—in Milton's political writings prior to the Restoration. This language reappears in the postlapsarian books of *Paradise Lost* where, for Milton, as Bartlett argues, although distant in time, humanity's loss of innocence after the Fall parallels England's loss of liberty following the collapse of the Commonwealth. In chapter 3 Erin Webster draws on medieval cartography and early modern science to historicize early modern European advancements in terrestrial and cosmic cartography and to show how those changes often led to anxious speculations about an extraterrestrial Eden. In *Paradise Lost*, as Webster demonstrates, Milton appropriates images of Amerindians and maps of the world to impose Christian space-time on the prospect of a lunar Paradise. In chapter 4 Rachel Trubowitz, revisiting the biblical sources and mathematical developments introduced by Rumrich, traces the dynamism of physical borders in *Paradise Lost* and the Pauline dynamics of racial-religious-national construction in *Samson Agonistes*. Trubowitz argues that representations of the ebb and flow of borders in Milton's epic and of inconvertible Jewish bodies, which are turned back at the border between the Judeo and the Christian in

14 Introduction

Milton's tragedy, anticipate Thomas Nail's theory of kinopolitics. This conceptual boundary between the Judeo and the Christian—and its historically specific relationship to the proposal for Jewish readmission to England in 1656—form the core of chapter 5 by Achsah Guibbory. In the Son's physical and spiritual distancing of himself from biblical Jewry in *Paradise Regain'd*, Guibbory discerns Milton's opposition to the readmission of the Jews to England proposed during Oliver Cromwell's tenure. Rather than allow Jews to return to England, Milton sought to keep them "still" or forever in a diasporic condition.

Guibbory concludes her chapter with a discussion of one of Milton's most energized interpreters, John Toland, and his more tolerant position on the so-called Jewish Question. This discussion brings the volume into the eighteenth and nineteenth centuries. In chapter 6 Jennifer Wallace discusses the historical and social context for *Digging Up Milton* (2015), her novelistic reimagining of Milton's body's disinterment and dismemberment by a group of working-class Londoners in 1790. The Romantics, whose reception of Milton's poetic corpus shapes Wallace's reading, and writing, of this infamous incident, set the stage for our transition to the Victorians in chapter 7. Here Ryan Hackenbracht examines the appropriation of Milton's *Paradise Lost* in one of the greatest religious poems of the Victorian age, Alfred, Lord Tennyson's *In Memoriam* (1850). Tennyson misreads Milton's materialism, Hackenbracht argues, in the service of a metaphysical dualism. In chapter 8 Mario Murgia examines a parallel theological appropriation in nineteenth-century Spanish-language translations of book 3 of Milton's epic. Murgia spotlights an emergent language of dynamic descent and situates that lexicon in the context of the needs of colonial Spanish Catholic writers and readers.

Having translated Milton's moving bodies from Europe to the Americas, the volume remains on this side of the Atlantic but moves to twentieth-century adaptations of Milton. In chapter 9 Angelica Duran attends to illustrations of Milton in twentieth-century Hispanophone editions of *Paradise Lost*. Imported from Spain and created in Latin America, these depictions of Milton's body—as male, variously disabled, and alternatively generally European and particularly British—shaped readers' reception of and response to his epic. Moving to the United States in chapter 10, Reginald A. Wilburn reads Pauline E. Hopkins's *Hagar's Daughter* (1901–2) as a narrative of racial passing that also documents the extent to which African Americans "marked" Milton as one of their own. *Milton's Moving Bodies* concludes with a chapter that transposes the ethnic and racial dynamics of the preceding two chapters into visual art, embodied identity, and disability. In chapter 11 Marissa Greenberg analyzes Alexis Smith's art installation *Snake Path* (1992) in the context of moving disabled bodies in *Paradise Lost* and the Milton classroom.

By ending on the topics of accessibility and pedagogy, the volume gestures intentionally to and beyond itself. *To itself* in terms of the choice of edition of Milton's writings: by opting to cite Milton's poetry and prose from *The John Milton Reading Room* (*JMRR*), this volume holds up open educational resources, like *JMRR*, as a model for accessibility in Milton studies. We, the community of Milton scholar-teachers, must cease standing at the gates and brandishing the two-handed sword of wealth and education. Both our justice-conscious present and Milton studies' intellectual, creative, and cultural future demand we welcome all bodies regardless of socioeconomic or first-generation college status. *Beyond itself* because we believe Miltonic motions are and can be part of our embodied routines and habits of thought.[45] The variety of movements engaged by the bodies in the oeuvre of Milton, both his own writings and their afterlives, are also available to those of us who read, teach, create, and study them. So, although this volume does not presume to cover all aspects of Miltonic kinesis, let alone supersede established scholarship on Milton and embodiment, it seeks to move current conversations about these issues in new directions: across historical periods, through geographical and linguistic borders, and among generic and bodily kinds. What *Milton's Moving Bodies* invites is nothing less than dynamic engagement in constructing the better future toward which we inexorably are moving.

Notes

1. On revolution as "nonidentical recursivity" in Milton's works, consult Marissa Greenberg, "Milton Much Revolving," in "Milton and the Politics of Periodization," ed. Rachel Trubowitz, special issue, *Modern Language Quarterly* 78, no. 3 (September 2017): 373–93.

2. Scholars who argue that Milton adheres to the old Aristotelian-Ptolemaic model include Arthur O. Lovejoy, *The Great Chain of Being: A Study in the History of an Idea* (Cambridge, MA: Harvard University Press, 1936), and "Milton's Dialogue on Astronomy," in *Reason and the Imagination: Studies in the History of Ideas, 1600–1890*, ed. Joseph A. Mazzeo (New York: Columbia University Press, 1962), 129–42; and Kester Svendsen, *Milton and Science* (Cambridge, MA: Harvard University Press, 1956). Scholars who argue that Milton entertains the idea of the new Copernican world system include Catherine Gimelli Martin, "'What If the Sun Be Centre to the World?': Milton's Epistemology, Cosmology, and Paradise of Fools Reconsidered," *Modern Philology* 99, no 2 (November 2001): 231–65; and Dennis Danielson, "*Paradise*

Lost" and the Cosmological Revolution (Cambridge: Cambridge University Press, 2014).

3. In book 8 of his epic, Milton merely speculates on the possibility of an Earth that moves: "what if sev'nth to these [planets] / The Planet Earth, so stedfast though she seem, / Insensibly three different Motions move?" (*PL,* 8.128–30). In his editorial note Thomas Luxon tells us that "the three motions are rotation, orbital revolution, and the very slow revolution of the earth's north pole around that of the ecliptic, causing the precession of the equinoxes or 'Trepidation' of 3.483" (*JMRR*).

4. On "the recurrent monist-dualist tension in [Milton's] writing," consult Rachel J. Trubowitz, "Body Politics in *Paradise Lost,*" *PMLA* 121, no. 2 (2006): 388–404.

5. John Rumrich, "Does Milton's God Play Dice with the Universe?" in *Milton and the New Scientific Age: Poetry, Science, Fiction,* ed. Catherine Gimelli Martin (New York: Routledge, 2019), 108–26.

6. In another potent example, Satan, gazing on the created universe, Satan *"falls into many doubts with himself"* (*PL,* 4, Argument). But this "much revolving" (*PL,* 4.31), which appears visibly in his shifting position, gaze, and facade, actually marks the continuation of physical and affective motions begun in Hell, where Satan "Lay . . . rowling in the fiery Gulfe," his thoughts turning over "lost happiness and lasting pain," as "round he throws his baleful eyes" (*PL,* 2.52–56). What Milton shows here and throughout *Paradise Lost* is damnation not simply in but *as* motion, both external and internal; see Greenberg, "Milton Much Revolving," 378–80.

7. Rachel Trubowitz, "The Fall and Galileo's Law of Falling Bodies: Geometrization vs. Observing and Describing Things in *Paradise Lost,*" in Martin, *Milton and the New Scientific Age,* 79–107.

8. John Rogers, "Milton and the Mysterious Terms of History," *ELH* 57, no. 2 (Spring 1990): 286.

9. Earlier in the epic narrative but later in its chronology, Satan registers Abdiel's lesson when, speaking to and about himself, he acknowledges that "curs'd be thou" because "against his thy will / Chose freely" (*PL,* 4.71–72).

10. Ryan Hackenbracht, "Milton on the Move: Walking and Self-Knowledge in *Paradise Lost,*" in *Milton, Materialism and Embodiment: One First Matter All,* ed. Kevin J. Donovan and Thomas Festa (Pittsburgh: Duquesne University Press, 2017), 61. Philippa Earle makes a similar argument about walking in *Paradise Regained,* in which "the progress of the Son's walking also appears proportional to that of his self-understanding"; Earle, "'Till Body Up to Spirit Work': Maimonidean Prophecy and Monistic Sublimation in *Paradise Regained,*" *Milton Studies* 62, no. 1 (2020): 168.

11. Seth Herbst, "Sound as Matter: Milton, Music, and Monism," in Donovan and Festa, *Milton, Materialism, and Embodiment,* 41. Also consult Marissa Greenberg, "Noise, the Great Fire, and Milton's *Samson Agonistes,*" in *Metropolitan Tragedy: Genre, Justice, and the City in Early Modern England* (Toronto: University of Toronto Press, 2015), 108–38.

12. Cf. Ross Lerner's discussion of the "shockwave" initiated by Eve's fall—a tremor felt by Adam, Earth, and readers—in "The Astonied Body in *Paradise Lost,*" *ELH* 87, no. 2 (2020): 433–61.

13. In chapter 2 of this volume Sydney Bartlett takes up the embodied and political dynamics of Adam and Eve's "happy State."

14. For a discussion of "rest" in relation to worldly activity, both pre- and postlapsarian, consult Daniel Ritchie and Jared Hedges, "Choosing Rest in *Paradise Lost*," *Christianity & Literature* 67, no. 2 (2018): 271–93. The authors' focus is, however, on emplacement rather than movement.

15. "But Satan smitten with amazement fell . . . Fell whence he stood to see his Victor fall" (*PR*, 4.562, 571). According to the *OED*, meanings of the verb "smite" from the fourteenth century onward included "Of the feet: to strike (the ground, a person, etc.) . . . Formerly also of a person: to strike with the feet or with spurs (*obsolete*)." This verb, which is significantly more forceful than either "departed" (Luke 4:13) or "leaveth" (Matt. 4:11), suggests that Jesus's embodied motion includes not only his act of standing still but also whatever acts on Satan's body to cause Satan to go from standing to falling.

16. As discussed later in this introduction, our understandings of mechanism and vitalism are indebted to Stephen M. Fallon, *Milton among the Philosophers: Poetry and Materialism in Seventeenth-Century England* (Ithaca, NY: Cornell University Press, 1991); and John Rogers, *The Matter of Revolution: Science, Poetry, and Politics in the Age of Milton* (Ithaca, NY: Cornell University Press, 1996).

17. As Milton argues vehemently in *Areopagitica*, for example, virtue must "sall[y] out" and be exercised if it is to be considered virtue.

18. Stanley Fish, "Driving from the Letter: Truth and Indeterminacy in Milton's *Areopagitica*," in *Re-membering Milton: Essay on the Texts and Traditions*, ed. Mary Nyquist and Margaret W. Ferguson (New York: Methuen, 1987), 236.

19. As Christopher Kendrick observes in "Ethics and the Orator in *Areopagitica*," *ELH* 50, no. 4 (1983), "Nowhere is the tract's profession of monism so clear" as in Milton's generative ("active," "lively," "vigorously productive," "spring up") depiction of the embodied motion of books (669). The passage also traces a progression that turns the book-as-body metaphor inside out: first, books are the progeny of men; then men are the progeny of books. This movement culminates in Milton's equation of books to "the pretious life-blood of a master spirit, imbalm'd and treasur'd up on purpose to a life beyond life" (*Areo.*). Cf. John Rumrich, "Flesh Made Word: Pneumatology and Miltonic Textuality," in *Immortality and the Body in the Age of Milton*, ed. John Rumrich and Stephen M. Fallon (Cambridge: University of Cambridge Press, 2018), which argues that Milton ascribes agency, vital extension, and generation of life to books that in turn plant a seed in readers, either through their eyes or their ears, in "the sort of aggressive takeover sometimes depicted in science fiction" (146). Responding to Rumrich's likening of books in *Areopagitica* to a "tomb containing a mummy of the author's spirit" (149), David A. Harper reads *Eikonoklastes* in terms of the book's violent, even executioner-like, assault on the bodies of the text and its author; Harper, "Milton Beyond Iconoclasm," in Rumrich and Fallon, *Immortality and the Body in the Age of Milton*, 153–67.

20. Fallon, *Milton among the Philosophers*; and Rogers, *The Matter of Revolution*. Also consult the contributors to Emma Depledge, John S.

Garrison, and Marissa Nicosia, eds, *Making Milton: Print, Authorship, After-lives* (Oxford: Oxford University Press, 2021), who "[embrace] the idea that Milton's reception did not follow a linear trajectory" but is "best understood within the rich, complex system in which he emerged as an author, including the workings of the book trade; social networks that first received his writing in academies, universities, and urban settings; and the adaptation and appropriation of Milton in literary circles" (5). On Milton's "metonymic relationship with his books," refer to Depledge, Garrison, and Nicosia, introduction to *Making Milton*, esp. 8–9.

21. This reading is inspired by Amrita Dhar, "When They Consider How Their Light Is Spent: On Intersectional Race and Disability Theories in the Classroom," in *Race in the European Renaissance: A Classroom Guide*, ed. Anna Wainwright and Matthieu Chapman (Tempe: Arizona Center for Medieval and Renaissance Studies Press, 2023), 161–83.

22. In addition to Jesus's "uneasie station" (*PR*, 4.584), which phrase cues the extraordinary effort required to sustain immobility atop the pinnacle amid the simultaneous pulls of gravity and temptation, the violent catastrophe of *Samson Agonistes* may be understood as a continuation of Samson's labor in the mill. Even as he grinds bones instead of grain, as Richard Halpern argues, effective political action eludes the erstwhile champion, as it did the republican poet in post-Reformation England; Halpern, "The Same Old Grind: Milton's Samson as Subtragic Hero," in *Eclipse of Action: Tragedy and Political Economy* (Chicago: University of Chicago Press, 2017), 159–80.

23. Gordon Teskey, *Delirious Milton: The Fate of the Poet in Modernity* (Cambridge, MA: Harvard University Press, 2006), 24.

24. Rumrich and Fallon, introduction to *Immortality and the Body in the Age of Milton*, 10.

25. Fallon, *Milton among the Philosophers*; Rogers, *Matter of Revolution*. Also consult Fallon's afterword in this volume.

26. Donovan and Festa, introduction to *Milton, Materialism, and Embodiment*, 6.

27. Consult Danielson, *"Paradise Lost" and the Cosmological Revolution*; Karen Edwards, *Milton and the Natural World: Science and Poetry in* Paradise Lost (Cambridge: Cambridge University Press, 1999); Martin, *Milton and the New Scientific Age*, and "'What If the Sun Be Centre to the World?': Milton's Epistemology, Cosmology, and Paradise of Fools Reconsidered," *Modern Philology* 99, no. 2 (November 2001): 231–65; and Joanna Picciotto, "Milton and the Paradizable Reader," in *Labors of Innocence in Early Modern England* (Cambridge, MA: Harvard University Press, 2010), 400–507.

28. Joe Moshenska, *Making Darkness Light: A Life of John Milton* (New York: Basic Books, 2021), 214, 215, 219–21.

29. On Milton's armchair travels, consult Elizabeth Sauer, "Studied for Action: Milton's Bookscape and *Communes Loci*," in *Locating Milton: Places and Perspectives*, ed. Thomas Festa and David Ainsworth (Clemson, SC: Clemson University Press, 2021), 37–58.

30. In addition to David Quint's influential study *Epic and Empire: Politics and Generic Form from Virgil to Milton* (Princeton, NJ: Princeton University Press, 1993), readers may wish to consult Angelica Duran and Elizabeth Sauer,

eds, "Milton in the Americas," special issue, *Milton Studies* 58 (2017); and Paul Stevens and Patricia Simmons, eds, "Milton in America," special issue, *University of Toronto Quarterly* 77, no. 3 (Summer 2008).

31. For example, Sydney Bartlett, "'Facile Gates': Walls and Identity across *Paradise Lost* and along the US-Mexico Border," in "Milton Today, Part I," ed. Stephen B. Dobranski, special issue, *Milton Studies* 62, no. 2 (2020): 294–305.

32. Recent contributions include Dorothy Kim, ed., "Race Before Race: Premodern Critical Race Studies," special issue, *Literature Compass* 18, no. 10 (October 2021); and Urvashi Chakravarty and Ayanna Thompson, eds, "Race and Periodization," special issue, *New Literary History* 52, no. 3/4 (Summer/Autumn 2021).

33. On blood and humors as the basis for early modern religious conversion, respectively, consult Dennis Austin Britton, *Becoming Christian: Race, Reformation, and Early Modern English Romance* (New York: Fordham University Press, 2014); and Kimberly Anne Coles, *Bad Humor: Race and Religious Essentialism in Early Modern England* (Philadelphia: University of Pennsylvania Press, 2022). On early modern optics, consult Erin Webster, *The Curious Eye: Optics and Imaginative Literature in Seventeenth-Century England* (Oxford: Oxford University Press, 2020).

34. Elizabeth Sauer, *Milton, Toleration, and Nationhood* (New York: Cambridge University Press, 2014), 9, 20. Among others, also consult Ben LaBreche, "*Areopagitica* and the Limits of Pluralism," *Milton Studies* 54, no. 1 (2013): 139–60; Sharon Achinstein and Elizabeth Sauer, eds, *Milton and Toleration* (Oxford: Oxford University Press, 2007); and Feisal G. Mohamed, "Donne, Milton, and the Two Traditions of Religious Liberty," in *A New Companion to English Renaissance Literature and Culture*, ed. Michael Hattaway (Malden, MA: Wiley-Blackwell, 2010), 1:289–303.

35. For scholarship on Milton and Judaism, consult Douglas A. Brooks, ed., *Milton and the Jews* (Cambridge: Cambridge University Press, 2008); Achsah Guibbory, *Christian Identity, Jews, and Israel in Seventeenth-Century England* (Oxford: Oxford University Press, 2010); Jason P. Rosenblatt, *Torah and Law in "Paradise Lost"* (Princeton, NJ: Princeton University Press, 1994); and Jeffrey S. Shoulson, *Milton and the Rabbis: Hebraism, Hellenism, and Christianity* (New York: Columbia University Press, 2001). For scholarship on Milton and Islam, the editors also direct readers to Islam Issa, *Milton in the Arab-Muslim World* (London: Routledge, 2017).

36. A partial bibliography includes Angelica Duran, "Mexican Miltons," in Depledge, Garrison, and Nicosia, *Making Milton*, 171–83, and, *Milton among Spaniards* (Newark: University of Delaware Press, 2020); Angelica Duran, Islam Issa, Jonathan R. Olson, and Gordon Campbell, eds, *Milton in Translation* (Oxford: Oxford University Press, 2017); Angelica Duran and Elizabeth Sauer, "Milton in the Americas"; and Mario Murgia, "Either in Prose or Rhyme: Translating Milton in(to) Latin America," in Duran et al., *Milton in Translation*, 279–92, and "Milton in Revolutionary Hispanoamerica," in Duran and Sauer, "Milton in the Americas," 203–22. Murgia has also published annotated Spanish editions of Milton's *Mask*, *Areopagitica*, and *Tenure*.

37. Leah Whittington, "Milton's Poetics of Supplication," *Milton Studies* 55 (2014): 114–15. Lara Dodds demonstrates similarly Milton's debt to Homer

for the gestural habitus of his angels, both fallen and unfallen, specifically changes of coloration that accompany "moments of transformation or particular emotional intensity"; Dodds, "Dark Looks and Red Smiles: Homeric Gesture and the Problem of Milton's Angels," in Donovan and Festa, *Milton, Materialism, and Embodiment*, 145. Cf. Judith H. Anderson, *Reading the Allegorical Intertext: Chaucer, Spenser, Shakespeare, Milton* (New York: Fordham University Press, 2011), which focuses on "Spenser's engagement in binarism—matter and spirit, in particular" and how Milton (and Shakespeare) "engage and develop" it (22). In this volume Erin Webster and Mario Murgia approach the dynamics of ascent and descent in *Paradise Lost* in relation to imperial expansion and linguistic translation, respectively.

38. Mary Nyquist and Margaret W. Ferguson, eds, *Re-membering Milton: Essays on The Texts and Traditions* (New York: Methuen, 1987). Also consult Lunger Knoppers and Gregory M. Colón Semenza, eds, *Milton in Popular Culture* (New York: Palgrave Macmillan, 2006); Depledge, Garrison, and Nicosia, *Making Milton*; and Mandy Green and Sharihan Al-Akhras, eds, *Women (Re-)writing Milton* (New York: Routledge, 2021).

39. Sonnet 22 ("Cyriack, this three years day"), lines 1–2. In this same poem Milton insists that he could have "no better guide" than "conscience" to "lead [him] through the worlds vain mask" (lines 14, 10, 13); yet, of course, he required human guides and other supports to navigate the world.

40. Feisal G. Mohamed, "On Race and Historicism: A Polemic in Three Turns," *ELH* 89, no. 2 (2022): 394. In addition to his award-winning monograph *Preaching the Gospel of Black Revolt: Appropriating Milton in Early African American Literature* (Pittsburgh: Duquesne University Press, 2014), Reginald A. Wilburn's most recent publications include "Getting 'Uppity' with Milton; or Because My Mom Politely Asked: 'Was Milton Racist?,'" *Milton Studies* 62, no. 2 (2020): 266–79; "Looking 'Foreword' to Milton in Toni Morrison's *Paradise*," *Religions* 11, no. 11 (2020): 562 (19 pages), https://doi.org /10.3390/rel11110562; and "Phillis Wheatley and the 'Miracle' of Miltonic Influence," *Milton Studies* 58 (2017): 145–65. Also consult Paula Loscocco, *Phillis Wheatley's Miltonic Poetics* (New York: Palgrave Macmillan, 2014).

41. Although writing about Jewish racialization in medieval England, Geraldine Heng's words also apply to constructions of "otherness" in premodern Europe and the Americas; Heng, *The Invention of Race in the European Middle Ages* (Cambridge: Cambridge University Press, 2018), 58, quoted in Dorothy Kim, "The Historiographies of Premodern Critical Race Studies and Jewish Studies," *Cambridge Journal of Postcolonial Literary Inquiry* 9, no. 1 (2022): 139.

42. For example, Magda Teter, "Blood Libel, a Lie and Its Legacies," in *Whose Middle Ages?: Teachable Moments for an Ill-Used Past*, ed. Andrew Albin, Mary C. Erler, Thomas O'Donnell, Nicholas L. Paul, and Nina Rowe (New York: Fordham University Press, 2019), 44–57; and Jonathan Hsy, "Plague: Toxic Chivalry, Chinatown Crusades, and Chinese/Jewish Solidarities," in *Antiracist Medievalisms: From "Yellow Peril" to Black Lives Matter* (Leeds, UK: Arc Humanities Press, 2021), 43–62.

43. Stephen Greenblatt, *Shakespearean Negotiations: The Circulation of Social Energy in Renaissance England* (Berkeley: University of California

Press, 1988), and *Learning to Curse: Essays in Early Modern Culture* (New York: Routledge, 1990).

44. Moshenska, *Making Darkness Light*, 62.

45. For example, Moshenska, *Making Darkness Light*; and Susannah B. Mintz, *Love Affair in the Garden of Milton: Loss, Poetry, and the Meaning of Unbelief* (Baton Rouge: Louisiana State University Press, 2021).

CHAPTER 1

Be Still

Milton's Poetry of Motion

John Rumrich

That Milton often represents states of being via descriptions of motion may seem blindingly obvious.[1] How could a mimetic literary artist do otherwise? Yet even as a young poet Milton seems intent on making a virtue of this necessity. A tendency to juxtapose motion and stasis, if not seizure, appears early on and becomes variously characteristic of his art. By the end of his career, his versatility and amplitude in using motion to express existential states (and straits) becomes astonishing. To cite the most imposing example, his epic rendition of humanity's fall from grace recounts an unstoppable sequence of unfortunate events. Yet the narrative often comes to halt unexpectedly, and anticipated actions are prevented.

Near the heart of his epic's inexorable yet halting process of speech, we learn that ceaseless but cyclic motion indwells at the very pinnacle of existence:

> There is a Cave
> Within the Mount of God, fast by his Throne,
> Where light and darkness in perpetual round
> Lodge and dislodge by turns. (*PL*, 6.4–7)

This do-si-do of light and dark informs the site that God describes as "our high place, our Sanctuarie, our Hill" (*PL*, 5.732). Yet all is not as it might seem. When the paternal deity utters this deliberately anticlimactic descriptive series, he is laughing derisively, ridiculing the very notion that God's "Hill" rather than God himself is a mighty fortress, or that his "high place" is a stationary site of authority that requires defensive measures to repel a rebel. Unaccommodated God may lie beyond any creature's understanding, but it seems safe to say that the security of his regime does not depend on a hill vulnerable to conquest. Satan and his followers have misconstrued a divine accommodation for the inconceivable reality it signifies.

"Psalm 114"

Before returning to the War in Heaven as a culminating example of the interplay of motion and stillness in Milton's poetry, this chapter will begin by noting how certain early lyrics illustrate his persistent evocations of motion and stillness. This inclination is evident from the first. The English *A Paraphrase of Psalm 114*, "don by the Author at fifteen yeers old," features shivering and fleeing seas, recoiling streams, shaking earth, gushing rills, and—presciently so far as the War in Heaven is concerned—mountains that skip.[2] Fascination with seemingly immovable mountains that nonetheless move stayed with the young poet. His subsequent poetry rarely evokes an imposing mountain or hill without also including some hint that it could indeed move.

In Psalm 114 not just mountains but also the entire landscape responds with animation to the eternal presence "Of him that ever was, and ay shall last"—the theologically inflected description that young Milton substitutes for "God" (*Psalm 114*, 16). The Hebrew original of this psalm is itself a strikingly kinetic song of praise, so the excitement attributed to earth and water in Milton's paraphrase is hardly his invention. Still, out of 150 psalms, the young student of Hebrew began his poetic career by choosing this one to paraphrase rather than another.[3] A decade later, he would translate it again, into Greek, and deploy similarly vivid Attic diction to represent miraculous motion as a natural response of creatures to their creator. Nineteen psalms were variously paraphrased or translated by Milton during his lifetime. Psalm 114 is the only one he revisited and the only one he translated into a language other than English. From the first, then, Milton honored scripture's insistence that the most inertial phenomena, even "unremoved" mountains, are movable and certainly shakable no matter how fixed and motionless they may appear (*PL*, 4.987). The psalm's representation of an animated landscape struck his poetic fancy and would figure into various moments in his poetry, most overtly in Raphael's narration of a cartoon-like War in Heaven, in which angels pound each other with flying mountains till the Son rumbles over the ruined terrain on a chariot, also animated, and summarily repairs it—"the uprooted Hills retir'd / Each to his place" (*PL*, 6.781–82). Everything in Heaven moves in harmonious obedience to the Son except the rebel forces, who remain stuck in their disobedience: "This saw his hapless Foes but stood obdur'd" (*PL*, 6.785).

Aside from Psalm 114's sheer spectacle, which plainly delighted this most serious child, its lyric exhilaration testifies to the impact of the Exodus narrative, which for Milton as for most Puritans—and Pilgrims—was the archetypal account of people on the move for the sake of constancy to their faith. The story of the Hebrew migration out of Egypt is generally accepted as the definitive narrative concerning Israel's formation as a nation. Relatively literal translations of the first verse of Psalm 114 thus adhere to the Hebrew original and confine their patriarchal register to Israel/Jacob: "In the going out of Israel from Egypt, the house of Jacob from a strange people."[4] Milton's paraphrase, however, refers to the chosen people as "the blest seed of *Terah's* faithful son" (*Psalm 114*, 1). Milton's substitution of the more inclusive patriarch Abraham for Jacob may reflect a generalizing Christian agenda, and the use of the patronymic "Terah's . . . son" to invoke Abraham may specifically reflect familial pride in the personal exodus of John Milton Sr. from his Roman Catholic and therefore Terah-like father.[5] As Achsah Guibbory observes in chapter 5 of this volume, although Milton is England's "most Hebraic writer," his embrace of Hebrew scripture does not necessarily imply philosemitism. Yet his enthusiasm for the Hebrew language and literary art begins early and is sustained throughout his writings. The budding student of biblical tongues thus likely knew that the word "Hebrew" first occurs in scripture as an epithet for Abraham, still referred to as "Abram" at that point and derives from a verbal root that means "crossing over or passing through" (Gen. 14:13).[6] The etymology thus associates Abraham, the original Hebrew, with this crossing movement.

Christian bias and familial interest may have shaped the beginning of Milton's paraphrase, but it seems likely that the young poet also had in mind the historically telescopic account of Abraham in the book of Joshua as the paradigmatic instance of the migratory impulse implicit in the word "Hebrew," a pattern that the Exodus from Egypt recapitulates on a grand scale:

> Your fathers dwelt on the other side of the flood in old time, even Terah, the father of Abraham, and the father of Nachor: and they served other gods. And I took your father Abraham from

26   Be Still

> the other side of the flood, and led him throughout all the land of
> Canaan, and multiplied his seed, and gave him Isaac. And I gave
> unto Isaac Jacob and Esau: and I gave unto Esau mount Seir, to
> possess it; but Jacob and his children went down into Egypt. I
> sent Moses also and Aaron, and I plagued Egypt, according to
> that which I did among them: and afterward I brought you out.
> (Josh. 24:2–5)

The nomadic Abraham described in Joshua 24 exemplifies the rooted
constancy of faith by moving in obedience to God. In fleeing Egypt
and renouncing its false gods, the nation of Israel hews to the original
Abrahamic pattern.[7]

If Milton can be said to put a Christian or familial spin on the Hebrew
psalm by invoking faithful Abraham's flight from his idolatrous father,
he does so by implying that Christians must make themselves akin to
Abraham just as the Hebrews fleeing Egypt did—crossing boundaries if necessary to remain constant to God. This is not to suggest that
transgression is itself a fixed moral imperative, any more than borders themselves are fixed and static, as Rachel Trubowitz explains in
chapter 4 in this volume. Passing through boundaries, however those
boundaries are construed, may be what God wants, as in the case of
Abraham crossing the Euphrates to enter Canaan. Or, as Jeffrey Shoulson observes, it may suggest an ethically challenging contention and
"something of an antagonistic relationship with the divine" as in the
case of Jacob's striving with an angel or perhaps with God himself.
The implication seems to be that Hebrews, like Abraham, are those
who "presume to face off with the divine," as Shoulson puts it.[8] If so,
Milton by attempting a genuine theodicy in his epic masterpiece also
may be said to have adopted a similarly Abrahamic identity.

In the Exodus narrative God himself becomes a Hebrew in the
sense that his movement conforms to the original Abrahamic pattern,
though with a difference. Before leading his people through the Red
Sea, he prepares the way for them to escape from Egypt by "pass[ing]
through to smite the Egyptians," killing all the firstborn males. The
description of God's motion as "passing through" derives from the
same root word as Abraham's epithet. But the Hebrew God does not
pass through Egypt indiscriminately. He adds a motion of his own by
also passing *over* the dwellings of the Hebrews (Exod. 12:23). One
meaning for the verb translated as "pass over"—the origin of the name
for the Passover festival—is "skip" or "jump," which suggests, from
an Egyptian perspective at least, that God, in a chilling, Joker-like

John Rumrich

variation on Milton's Mirth, "trip[s] it as he goes" (*L'Allegro*, 33), not simply passing through Egypt to kill all the firstborn males but "skipping" over the houses of the Hebrews, setting the stage for them to depart from Egypt and pass through the Red Sea, like Abraham writ large. It may seem indecorous if not blasphemous to refer to a comic book villain like DC's Joker in discussing the behavior of the Judeo-Christian deity, but scripture does represent God as unpredictable, as exhibiting a deliberate flair for the dramatic (especially in the Exodus narrative), and as one whose laughter portends the destruction of his enemies. Also, in Milton's view at least, God's omnific power derives from his substantial access to and identification with the infinite and eternal realm of Chaos.[9]

Constancy and Motion in Milton's Early Poetry

Milton's poetry subsequent to *Psalm 114* is similarly preoccupied with motion as a timely response to divine stimulus—and with God's own motions too. In *Nativity Ode*, for example, apprehensive Nature initially scrambles at the prospect of Christ's birth, wooing the winter air "to throw" a veil of "innocent Snow" and hide "her foul deformities" (*Nativity Ode*, 39–44). But prevenient Peace soothes her shame and "strikes a universal peace through Sea and Land" to prepare for the advent of the Christ child: "Kings sate still with awfull eye"; "The Windes, with wonder whist, / Smoothly the waters kist"; "Birds of Calm sit brooding on the charmed wave"; "The Stars with deep amaze / Stand fixt in stedfast gaze"; "the Sun himself with-held his wonted speed" (*Nativity Ode*, 52–79). Even the winged angels who attend the nativity scene "sit in order serviceable" (*Nativity Ode*, 244). The peace and quiet that descend on creation, however, skip over the false gods, who instead panic and flee: "the chill Marble seems to sweat, / While each peculiar power foregoes his wonted seat" (*Nativity Ode*, 195–96). The "old Dragon" seems like an exception because he does not run off (*Nativity Ode*, 168). Instead, his freedom to move is represented as now constrained "in straiter limits" (*Nativity Ode*, 169). Yet he writhes against this imposition like a crossed cat and "Swindges the scaly horrour of his foulded tail" (*Nativity Ode*, 172).

A creature's motion or stillness in relation to the will of God readily lends itself to metaphorical expressions of moral status. But as the preceding examples from Milton's early religious poetry indicate, the moral significance of any specific motion, and indeed, any particular boundary, is relative and context dependent. Milton's poetic interest in the moral significance of motion lies more in the opportunity it presents for vivid juxtaposition between states of motion and immobility, as in *Nativity Ode*. Most of creation occupies a state of suspended animation at the prospect of the Nativity, but the false gods scatter. By contrast, in the opening stanzas, prior to the hymn proper, the reverse is true. While "all the spangled host keep watch in squadrons bright," an image of sublime steadfastness, the "star-led wizards haste" toward Bethlehem, prompting the inspired poet into a fit of anxious emulation: "O run, prevent them with thy humble ode" (*Nativity Ode*, 23–24). The wizards and Milton rush to the nativity scene rather than flee from it as the false gods do.

Milton's artistic investment in the interplay and moral relativism of motion and stasis appears perhaps most obviously in his companion poems, which scholars regularly construe as young Milton's elaboration of the two paths of life that he might walk. Unlike *Psalm 114* and *Nativity Ode*, these poems are not overtly religious, nor does God play an overt role in them to inspire motion or arrest it. With the First Mover mostly absent from the poetic scene, these poems offer a rare theologically neutral example of Milton's poetry of motion. *L'Allegro* in particular takes notable pains to cordon off an autonomous zone for innocent, playful, pleasurable activity. The lively man's declared intention to live with Liberty and Mirth in "unreproved pleasures free," if Mirth can provide them, alludes to the first lines of Christopher Marlowe's "The Passionate Shepherd to His Love," a lyric that other Renaissance poets took as a provocation, one that they responded to with scornful rejection (*L'Allegro*, 40).[10] In this cultural context, Milton's attempt instead to negotiate a safe if straitened circuit for such pleasures comes as a surprise, even if he does evade explicit endorsement of them. Regardless of what logic says about double negatives, "unreproved" stops short of approval. On the contrary, "unreproved" consumes half the line's syllables in a prevenient hedge against the trailing description of the pleasures as "free."

For Freud, "un" is the prefix that bespeaks repression, but as used in *L'Allegro*, "unreproved" seems more interested in warding off the superego's inexorable drive, unusually powerful in mid-seventeenth-century English Puritan culture, to forbid, rebuke, condemn, and, generally, weigh every behavior down to a scruple.[11] There may be, as Hamlet says, "special providence in the fall of a sparrow" (*Hamlet*, 5.2.234), but Milton here, and elsewhere too, suggests that the infinitely sharp and intimately attentive eye of Providence is inclined to

John Rumrich

wink at some indulgences. Milton will even claim in *Tetrachordon* that such providential allowance is a main basis for marriage:

> We cannot . . . always be contemplative, or pragmatical abroad, but have need of some delightful intermissions, wherein the enlarged soul may leave off a while her severe schooling, and, like a glad youth in wandering vacancy, may keep her holidays to joy and harmless pastime. (*CPEP*, 998)

As Sydney Bartlett shows in this volume, "wander" often appears at ominous moments in Milton's works, yet it names a motion that also seems an inevitable concession to human frailty: "we . . . have need of some delightful intermissions."[12] The mutually exclusive posture of the companion poem's opening lines reinforces the tendency to take them as presenting an either/or, but these exorcisms can as easily be construed as evidence that transient moods and emotions, especially in youth, tend not to believe in one other. Milton seems to have been predominantly pensive, but as a youth he also embraced the mirthful encouragement of his friend Charles Diodati to seek out "sunshine and enjoyment, for the time at least": "the air and the sun and the river, and trees and little birds and earth and men will laugh and dance with us as we make holiday" (*CPEP*, 767). Later in life, though blind and plagued by gout, Milton continued to recommend occasional pleasurable indulgences, insisting that one who knows enough to indulge sparingly is—and again we find the double-negative hedge—"not unwise" (Sonnet 22, line 14).

Another explanation for the suspension of active moral judgment in *L'Allegro* is that Milton's portrayal of the lively man betrays very little by way of a subjectivity on which judgment might light. Although the poem is persistently first-person in its point of view, first-person pronouns appear only five times in the poem's 152 lines: "I" and "me" twice each and one "us." As a subject of moral judgment, the lively man offers very little to target, a mere observational point with which a steady pulse of unremittingly pleasant activity is coordinated. Verbs and verbals of motion conjure and convey him.[13] The imperative dictates of his invocations and the narrative transitions from pleasure to pleasure merely imply him. He is more mood than character, even if that mood initiates itself by imperatively invoking frolicking motion. Melancholy is banished to darkness and desolation, and Mirth conjured to hasten her approach along with her nodding, laughing, beckoning, and tripping entourage.

Although Mirth is expelled at the open of *Il Penseroso*, "retired leasure" quietly joins in Melancholy's retinue, taking an Eve-like pleasure "in trim Gardens" (*Il Penseroso*, 49–50). Similarly, even if the pensive man eschews "all resort of mirth," an aural remnant of mirthful pleasures—"the cricket on the hearth, / Or the bellman's drowsy charm"—remains unreproved (*Il Penseroso*, 81–83). The regiment of Mirth is by comparison a notably thorough government: *L'Allegro* purges heaviness more absolutely than *Il Penseroso* does lightness. "[W]rincled Care" tags along with Mirth it seems but only to supply an object for Sport's derision (*L'Allegro*, 31). Even labor is not allowed to be laborious.[14] The plowman "[w]histles" while he works, and the milkmaid "singeth blithe" (*L'Allegro*, 64–65). Only the drudging goblin breaks a sweat, and for his superhuman efficiency receives a trivial wage (though one fat in nourishment), further lightening the already unweary load of the music-making, story-telling, ale-drinking human laborers. In the rosy world of Mirth such distinct if subtle pleasures as Melancholy might afford have no standing. No change from major to minor is nodded to, no wistful nostalgic smiles are seen nor compelling sad songs heard, not even the one imagined to persuade Pluto to restore Eurydice to Orpheus without restraint (*L'Allegro*, 149–50).

Yet the lively man does at least concentrate on the goal of freeing Eurydice unconditionally. The attention of the pensive man, by comparison, is primarily drawn by the power of Orpheus's song to bend Pluto to his will rather than by the prospect of freeing the captive woman. *L'Allegro* raises, if only for a moment, the questionable moral implications of thorough dedication to the pursuit of innocent pleasures—pleasures generally taken in cheerful community with others. In *Il Penseroso*, by contrast, the moral dangers of the willfully isolated pensive man's ambition for power through forbidden knowledge, including necromancy, whether alone in a tower or alone in a hermitage, are more portentous than any of the unreproved pleasures pursued by the lively man. Yet these moral dangers are utterly elided.

The pensive man's ambition to encompass all is susceptible to the most extreme sort of moral failure, yet it also allows him to assimilate at least some muted vestiges of Mirth. The lively man by comparison comes to seem unrelenting in his smiley-faced progress from merriment to merriment. The following fully trochaic couplet with its long vowels quantitatively registers the happy pilgrim's progress from one appealing pastoral setting to the next: "Streit mine eye hath caught new pleasures / Whilst the lantskip round it measures" (*L'Allegro*,

69–70). Aside from metrically marking the transition, the couplet aptly illustrates the no regrets, forward-looking movement of *L'Allegro* from scene to scene. The extended quantitative duration of the distich may sound inconsistent with the poem's predominant aural breeziness, but the quick bright pace is slackened only to register a pause that refreshes before raising the prospect of an array of fresh pleasures from which to choose. This transitional downshift from the lively locomotion of *L'Allegro* has its complement within the slower moving lines of *Il Penseroso*. But here the alternative being considered, for once with aurally brisk efficiency, is a singular refuge in case of bad weather rather than an array of accommodating venues: "Or if the Ayr will not permit / Som still removed place will fit" (*Il Penseroso*, 77–78).

As compared to Mirth, the movements associated with Melancholy, her "eev'n step and musing gate," are generally more restrained, inhibited, and, when she is "held in holy passion still," prone to interruption (*Il Penseroso*, 38, 41). The seven-syllable headless lines that in *L'Allegro* urge on Mirth and her tripping followers with such pop and bounce occur about half as often in *Il Penseroso*. And when they do, the initial syllable, standing in for a full iamb, will sometimes invoke or describe motion (or distance and aversion), only to have the rest of the line apply the brakes: "Com, but keep thy wonted state" (*Il Penseroso*, 37). The caesura following the initial syllable brings the line to a halt and endows the lingering humming sound of "com" with a resonant, almost mantra-like quality in its splendid phonic isolation from the plosive "but." In the parallel truncated line in *L'Allegro*—"Com, and trip it as ye go" (*L'Allegro*, 33)—the initial syllable slides more easily into "and," which initiates a short-voweled insistence on spriteliness rather than a long-voweled demand for languid stateliness. Even without that resonating caesura, the strategic arrangement of consonants and vowels in *Il Penseroso*, illustrated by a truncated line like "Sober, steadfast, and demure," roll out in sibilant slow motion by comparison with the plosive thump of *L'Allegro*'s "Buxom, blithe, and debonair" (*Il Penseroso*, 32; *L'Allegro*, 24). Milton seems determined to demonstrate that number and pace are of distinct metrical houses and that in prosody, too, motion is relative. If the lively man is a low-profile creature who hurries along in almost perpetual motion, at least until Lydian airs dissolve what little self he seems to possess, the more self-involved pensive man somehow manages to make motion even over abbreviated distances seem like standing still.

The contrasting moods distinguished by the companion poems become if anything even more confused in Milton's *A Mask Presented at Ludlow Castle* (1634; hereafter *Mask*). The nomadic Comus, who has migrated from Italy to Wales, is Mirth's sinister half-brother, at least per the genealogy in *L'Allegro* that makes Bacchus her father. But as the Attendant Spirit observes, the enchanter favors his mother Circe more than his father and is practiced in her arts of deception. Like the melancholy man, Comus is learned in the lore of plants, knows how to mix a potion, and avoids light. His longest speech of the work invokes Night in octosyllabic couplets, predominantly truncated and highly reminiscent of the prosody of the companion poems. This brilliant passage, which sometimes echoes Ariel's song in William Shakespeare's *The Tempest*, ends with a call to dance that includes phrasing sampled from *L'Allegro*: "Com, knit hands and beat the ground / In a light fantastick round" (*Mask*, 143–44). The pensive, nunlike Lady, by contrast, who, like Melancholy, tends to move in stop-motion, believes that the disguised Comus will show her a villager's pastoral hospitality, something like that shown the lively man in *L'Allegro*. But the enchanter—and would-be rapist—instead of offering "Spicy Nut-brown Ale" and supernatural tales of a "drudging *Goblin*" sweating for a "cream-bowl," plies her with a magical potion intended to make a beast of her (*L'Allegro*, 100, 105). What is fascinating about the *Mask* is how many supernatural beings—Comus, the Attendant Spirit, Sabrina—percolate around the motionless, root-bound Lady. Given its compositional proximity to the companion poems, some have construed the *Mask*'s recombinant characters, along with the perplexing climax of its action, as symptomatic of Milton's identification with the Lady as a literary expression of his own latency and sense of paralysis for much of the 1630s.

The poems examined thus far indicate a persistent inclination to represent divine actions and creatures' spiritual conditions through metaphysically oriented metaphors of motion and stasis. We find a great variety of such instances among his early works, which, as in the introductory stanzas to the *Nativity Ode*, also include implicit or explicit references to the march of time as a source of psychological pressure on mortal creatures to meet their obligations while they have the chance. Pained awareness of time's passage is in early modern poetry a conventional characteristic of melancholy. Jacques in *As You Like It* serves as perhaps the most familiar exemplar. But Milton's references to time add an explicitly philosophical complication by endorsing the Aristotelian definition of time as the measure of motion, sometimes quite wittily. His second Hobson poem ("Another on the Same"), for example, entertains the paradoxical claim that in the case of the university carrier, motion became the measure of time rather than vice versa. How does one stand still in the midst of time, the medium of motion? So long as Hobson could "still jogg on, and keep his trot," he defied time by staying alive ("Another on the Same," 3). Only when his appointed rounds were interrupted and his motion arrested did he change, by ceasing to be: "Rest that gives all men life, gave him his death / And too much breathing put him out of breath" ("Another on the Same," 11–12). The same paradox of remaining unchanging while nevertheless always in motion animates the Latin lyric *Naturam non pati senium* (Nature is not subject to old age).

Milton is being playful in describing the death of an otherwise unageing Hobson, but a similar reversal of time and motion also animates the more personal and reflective Sonnet 7. Twenty-three years of his life have already elapsed, the young poet initially complains; his "hasting dayes flie on with full career" (Sonnet 7, line 3). Yet the corresponding effects of those fleeting days register in neither his appearance nor his achievements. Like old Hobson, young Milton remains the same despite the mounting total of elapsed days, belying the usefulness of time as a measure of motion. Time is relative; its pace unaccountable. Milton's lack of development, like Hobson's nonstop busyness, seems to measure time, or defy time's passage, rather than the other way around. The resolution of the sonnet, however, invokes the eternal stillness of God, and in that regard recalls the paraphrase of Psalm 114 and its invocation of "him that ever was, and ay shall last." Milton insists that regardless of whether his development is "soon or slow," from God's eternal perspective, everything remains "as ever," regardless of how much or how little motion is evidenced by his creatures. As many have observed, much the same resolution of time and motion into stillness appears in Sonnet 19, with its extraordinary use of enjambed lines to describe the busy thousands actively devoted to fulfilling God's will: "his State / Is Kingly. Thousands at his bidding speed / And post o're Land and Ocean without rest" (Sonnet 19, lines 11–13). Then follows the full stopped line that brings the sonnet to its arresting close: "They also serve who only stand and waite" (Sonnet 19, lines 14).

Motions Observed

The mutuality of time and motion in Milton's early works brings to mind three momentous scientific breakthroughs. Each of these famous epiphanies concerns the force of gravity, specifically as it affects motion measured by time. First was Galileo Galilei's observation that objects drop to earth at the same rate regardless of their mass. Decades later, Isaac Newton would propose that gravitational attraction is a function of mass. The third breakthrough came with Albert Einstein's realization that the physical sensation of a falling man hurtling toward earth would be, were it not for atmospheric effects, indistinguishable from that of a man floating weightless.

Milton claimed to have become personally acquainted with Galileo in the late 1630s when the great physicist was a prisoner of the Inquisition in Tuscany. Galileo would become the only contemporary of Milton's named in *Paradise Lost*, and his telescope had a great impact on the poet's imagination.[15] As for Newton, while it is doubtful that he and Milton ever met or that Milton would have been aware of him, the timing and setting of Newton's original epiphany concerning gravity are remarkable in their historical juxtaposition with the subject and publication of *Paradise Lost*. The first edition of Milton's epic was being prepared for the press when young Newton sitting in his mother's garden was prompted by the fall of an apple to theorize about the attractive force of gravity over distance. The history and cultural context that tie Milton to his two greatest scientific contemporaries is thus powerfully suggestive, and their experiments concerning motion are pertinent to Milton's poetic representations of it.

Galileo maintained that differences in mass do not affect the speed of falling objects.[16] Such differences had previously been deemed a fundamental organizational fact of creation, a notion whose classical and scriptural authority Milton, even with his commitment to mathematical analysis, recognizes.[17] Hence in *Paradise Lost* the scales that God displays when a mountain-like Satan opposes the angelic guard are the same as those he deployed during creation, "wherein all things created first he weighd" (*PL*, 4.999). Yet despite the importance that Milton attaches to the qualities of heavy and light, it is not clear that he endorsed the notion that the weight of an object affects the speed at which it falls. The moral fall of the rebel angels also involves a physical fall, but the rate of their descent hardly seems relevant though the narrative is not entirely silent about such concerns. Moloch's testimony related to this point is hardly reliable (see *PL*, 2.70–77).

Young Newton's breakthrough regarding gravitational attraction may seem more directly pertinent because of its highly suggestive setting—maternal garden, tree, fruit, the quest for scientific knowledge. But it is otherwise oblivious to falling as represented in Milton's epic.

John Rumrich

William Stukely's account makes it clear that no moral charge attaches to Newton's apple. It is merely a material object in motion:

> "why should that apple always descend perpendicularly to the ground," thought he to him self: occasion'd by the fall of an apple, as he sat in a comtemplative [*sic*] mood: "why should it not go sideways, or upwards? but constantly to the earths centre? assuredly, the reason is, that the earth draws it. there must be a drawing power in matter. & the sum of the drawing power in the matter of the earth must be in the earths center, not in any side of the earth. therefore dos this apple fall perpendicularly, or toward the center. if matter thus draws matter; it must be in proportion of its quantity. therefore the apple draws the earth, as well as the earth draws the apple."[18]

Newton concerns himself with the apple's fall solely as an example of how a certain parcel of matter moves in relation to the center of another larger parcel of matter, leading to the hypothesis of a "drawing power" in matter itself that pertains to both bodies in proportion to their material quantities. The line of scientific inquiry that Newton allegedly initiated in his mother's garden thus represents a pivotal moment in intellectual and cultural history. For Newton, an apple dropping toward Earth from a tree limb, impelled by the force of gravity, lacks any salient connection with Adam and Eve "fall[ing] off / From thir Creator" (*PL*, 1.30–31).

Surprisingly, though centuries removed from the theorizing of Galileo and Newton, Einstein's account of falling bodies appears more pertinent than those of Galileo and Newton to Milton's peculiar tendencies as a poet of motion in time. In the most famous thought experiment of the twentieth century, Einstein considered the phenomenon of falling abstractly, in space-time. Unlike Newton and Galileo, however, he imagined the fall not of an inanimate falling body—a ball or a piece of fruit—but of a human subject capable of conscious perception. Looking back at that moment in subsequent years, he repeatedly referred to the idea that arose as "the happiest thought of my life" (*der glücklichste Gedanke meines Lebens*):

> I was sitting in a chair in the patent office at Bern when all of sudden a thought occurred to me: If a person falls freely, he will not feel his own weight. I was startled. This simple thought made a deep impression on me. It impelled me toward a theory of gravitation.[19]

36   Be Still

Galileo and Newton certainly lurk behind the scene of Einstein's happy thought. But for Einstein the perception of the falling subject is crucial. The only way that his free-falling man could experience motion as measurable movement is through the accommodation of the abstract geometry of space-time to his senses, that is, through the mediation of an external frame of reference. If that man were falling in a dark vacuum, as Satan does in book 2 of *Paradise Lost*, for example, his sense of his condition would be the same as if he were floating weightless in outer space.

Neither Galileo nor Newton is concerned with the experience of motion in the way that both Milton and Einstein are. Milton for his part reveals an articulate understanding of how deceptive such experience can be when Raphael poses this hypothetical question: "what if . . . / The Planet Earth, so stedfast though she seem, / Insensibly three different Motions move?" (*PL*, 8.128–30). A state of motion that feels motionless is a phenomenon that fascinated Milton, as it did Einstein. It is further developed in Raphael's striking elaboration of the Copernican Earth's revolution around the sun:

> Or Shee from the West her silent course advance
> With inoffensive pace that spinning sleeps
> On her soft Axle, while she paces eev'n,
> And beares thee soft with the smooth Air along. (*PL*, 8.163–66)

In this scenario Mother Earth bears her children so softly as she revolves around the sun that they do not perceive their motion. Even without the institutional pressure brought on Galileo "to save appeerances," as Raphael puts it, modern physics still struggles to become incrementally more aware, typically through mathematics, of the difficulties and opportunities presented by our accommodating senses (*PL*, 8.82). Milton was similarly aware of this challenge. Had Einstein's thought experiment centered on an apple instead of a sentient being, it is unlikely that the fall he imagined would have been so scientifically fortunate.

Although Raphael refrains from answering questions about celestial motion, he does assure Adam and Eve that in Heaven as on Earth time measures motion, an assurance that grounds his historical narrative. This fundamental confirmation of narrative as a shared means of registering experience also illuminates Milton's outsized reliance on the small word "still," which in its import for his epic narrative approaches that of other small, plain, but critical words. Four of them—"one

John Rumrich   37

first matter all"—appear in sequence as Raphael explains the abiding ontological solidarity that underlies the natural "work" by which,
over time, material bodies develop spiritual capabilities (*PL*, 5.472).
"Work," too, belongs on the list of plain but conceptually rich terms
anchoring Milton's epic masterpiece.[20] But it is the modifying word
"still" that pertains most directly to the physical and moral relativism
of time and motion in Milton's epic poetry.

"Still" often occurs in Milton's epic to indicate the obligation of
creatures to commit unwaveringly to temporal process as a condition
of advancement. In its now obsolete adverbial sense of "constantly,
continually, invariably," "still" combines two of the word's more common, still extant meanings, which can otherwise seem at odds with
each other: the adjectival sense indicating absence of motion ("at rest,
quiet, calm"); and the adverbial sense indicating duration ("continuing till now"). When used in the obsolete adverbial sense denoting
constancy, "still" as applied to verbs of motion can seem paradoxical,
as if the motionless state associated with the adjective had infiltrated
the temporal persistence conveyed by the adverbial sense. Consider,
for example, the description of Satan in *Paradise Regain'd* "roving
still / About the world" (*PR*, 1.33–34). More commonly in Milton's
poetry, however, stillness, combining the ideas of stasis and duration,
is depicted in culminating triumph over busy motion: the presence "Of
him that ever was and ay shall last" makes mountains skip and earth
shake in *Psalm 114* (16); the Son as a baby, immobile "in his swaddling
bands," controls pagan gods (*Nativity Ode*, 228); the rapt Lady ter-
rorizes Comus with what she could but refuses to say; Jesus decisively
ends Satan's incessant temptations by standing; Samson, "patient but
undaunted," grips the fatal pillars "As with the force of winds and
waters pent / When Mountains tremble" and pulls destruction down
on his captors (*SA*, 1623, 1647–48). Milton is as concerned to express
the state of poised constancy as he is the variety of motion: not only the
type of stillness and standing that precludes motion but also standing
and being still while ineluctably in motion, like an extremely confident
and accomplished surfer riding a wave with regal bearing.

In *Paradise Lost*, on the other hand, especially when the syllable
"still" is metrically stressed and repeated, it can become ominously
expressive of frustration, as in Eve's disquiet over the burgeoning garden's mockery of their labors: "well may we labour *still* to dress / This
Garden, *still* to tend Plant, Herb and Flour" (*PL*, 9.205–6; my italics).
Satan, in the paradigmatic instance of this expressive power of "still,"
laments "The debt immense of endless gratitude, / So burthensome still

paying, still to ow" (*PL,* 4.52–53). In such examples "still" conveys the ineluctable terms of divine accommodation presented to finite, temporal creatures: the mortgage of our existence. King Lear in his madness similarly recognizes the basis of his plight as a state of *still* owing, as layers of "lendings" that he would like to "unbutton here" and strip so as to achieve the condition of "unaccommodated man" (*King Lear,* 3.4.115, 116, 113). Einstein's falling man, bodily unaware of his state of motion, is in this sense "unbuttoned." But the alternative to our buttoned-up situation in the world is no alternative, or, as Jean-Paul Sartre puts it, "no exit."[21] Given an eternal and omnipotent creator who establishes the forms of finite existence out of his own infinite material potency, the only alternatives to submission are either a return to Chaos or occupation of the foreclosed homelessness of Hell, which may still be recognized as a divine accommodation but one unpleasant enough that it tends to cast a pale and dreadful light on the terms of Milton's theodicy.

Paradise Lost

As observed at the beginning of this chapter, Satan's assumption that he can win the war by taking possession of the Mount of God betrays confusion over the nature of divine accommodation, which at its most basic level is an attempt to convey the eternal creator to temporal creatures. Our entire universe is also such an accommodation, a point on which Milton and Einstein would agree even though their ideas about God are quite distinct. Satan's confusion is not altogether absurd. Milton insists in book 1, chapter 2, of *A Treatise on Christian Doctrine* that we should think of God as he accommodates himself to us to "avoid vague subtleties of speculation" (*CPEP,* 1147). Raphael's account of Heaven thus confirms that the "Mount of God" is the official site of God's regal purview, with an interior that includes a natural chronometric mechanism governed by the circling hours: "For Time, though in Eternitie, appli'd / To motion, measures all things durable / By present, past, and future" (*PL,* 5.580–82). God in *Paradise Lost* is in effect "set on a clock-case," as young Milton evidently wanted his short lyric "On Time" to be.[22] The exalted location of the clockwork internal to the Mount of God implies that when it comes to creatures' observance of the almighty's accommodations, time is of the essence.

Unlike the domestic clock in Milton's household, the heavenly horologe is communally oriented rather than a private possession and does not depend on an artificial, mechanical operation. Instead, as with the naturally produced alternation of day and night on earth, God's clockwork measures motion via the succession of light and dark. In Heaven, that succession does not depend on celestial bodies in motion. Time in Heaven instead issues directly from the seat of deity in a dancing round of light and darkness. Raphael's narration makes it clear that angels submit to this temporal framework in various ways. They mark time's passage, for example, answering to God's imperial summons "on such day / As Heav'n's great Year brings forth," bearing "Ensignes high advanc'd, / Standards and Gonfalons" that display historical records: "Holy Memorials, acts of Zeale and Love / Recorded eminent" (*PL*, 5.582–83, 588–89, 593–94). Angelic conformity to the alternation of day and night also appears in their waking and sleeping in corresponding turns—"save those who in thir course / Melodious Hymns about the sovran Throne / Alternate all night long" (*PL*, 5.655–57). This last point of angelic duty—that some angels are assigned to adore God during the night shift—may seem relatively trivial, but the first clues indicating Satan's alienation from God are that he is awake when he should be sleeping and that he orders his followers to "dislodge, and leave / Unworshipt, unobey'd the Throne supream / Contemptuous" (*PL*, 5.669–71).

The depiction of Hell also includes a tableau representing something like clockwork, but not one integral to a monarchical high place or at the heart of the communal landscape. Nor do Hell's restless inhabitants enjoy anything approaching a natural "Grateful vicissitude, like Day and Night," disposing them to sleep or wake (*PL*, 6.8). Instead, as with the "lazy leaden-stepping hours" of the domestic timepiece Milton contemplates in "On Time," the hours endured in Hell are experienced privately and accompanied by eating cares ("On Time," 2).

Intimately connected with Satan and yet displaced from his seat of authority, the clockwork of Hell occupies the allegorical person of Sin. Hellhounds begotten by Death's rape of his mother gnaw at Sin's insides and then burst forth: "yelling Monsters that with ceasless cry / Surround me . . . hourly conceiv'd / And hourly born, with sorrow infinite" (*PL*, 2.795–97). The somber thoughts of mortality evoked by time's passage in Milton's youthful meditation on an artificial clock come nowhere near this savagery, and yet even with that poem's promise of salvation and individual consolation, Milton's intricately constructed lyric is more melancholic than the posies found on sundials. With "On Time" young Milton does not simply take the mini-genre associated with sundials and transfer it to a modern clock. He instead updates the chronometric genre to suit the psychological estrangement and malaise that often attend private possession of, and compulsive observations paid to, an artificial chronological mechanism. Like its heavenly counterpart, Hell's clock thus also operates by alternating between internal and external manifestations. But in Hell these manifestations horrify rather than gratify, alternating acoustic assault and embodied remorse rather than light and dark. The language Milton uses in the invocation to book 7 of *Paradise Lost* to describe the "evil dayes" on which he has fallen, echoes the description of Sin's hourly torment: "In darkness, and with dangers compast round," Milton implores the Muse for protection from the "barbarous dissonance" and "savage clamor" that threaten him (*PL*, 7.26, 27, 32, 36).

The rebellion in Heaven thus begins with blatant disregard of scheduled reverential duties and ends with the infernal experience of time's passage as cyclical alienation and torment. The initial defiance expressed by the rebels' neglect of their worship duties is bookended by God's announcement of their defeat, in which he reassures the loyal angels that even after the loss of one-third of the angelic host, a sufficient population nonetheless remains "this high Temple to frequent / With Ministeries due and solemn Rites" (*PL*, 6.148–49). God does not say that the quota of worship duties allotted to the remaining loyal angels will have to be proportionately increased to compensate for the diminished number of adorers, but Satan's repeated contempt for and mockery of such duties—the angry exchange with Gabriel in the garden is especially pointed—imply that it is not impertinent to wonder about the worship workload of the remaining angels and how it is divided (*PL*, 4.957–60).

Angels are conventionally depicted singing God's praises, but Raphael makes it plain that they also dance. The familiar image of angels strumming harps and hymning God with elevated gazes misses the animation that Milton insistently attributes to them. He might have scorned scholastics debating the number of angels that might fit on the head of a pin, but the notion of their dancing on one would not have made him blink. It is not only in *Paradise Lost* that Milton presents angels as dancing. "The solemn troops and sweet Societies" that entertain Lycidas "singing in their glory move" ("Lycidas," 180). This description may evoke thoughts of gentle music and stately, dignified gestures, approximating the somber atmosphere of a high-end funeral parlor. It is after all the consolation of a pastoral elegy. But such genre associations can be misleading. The concluding verses of Milton's *Epitaphium Damonis* (1645) represent heavenly consolation as being

John Rumrich

more along the lines of a jazz funeral procession at its wild culmination: "Cantus ubi, choreisque furit lyra mista beatis, / Festa Sionaeo
bacchantur & Orgia Thyrso" (Where there is singing and the lyre rages
in the midst of blessed dances, and orgiastic feasts have their Bacchic
celebration of the thyrsus of Zion) (*Epitaphium Damonis*, 218–19).

Similarly, in book 3 of *Paradise Lost*, after God announces his salvation plan and the instrumentality of the Son's death and resurrection,
angels "shout / Loud," bow low, cast down their crowns, and pick
them up again before they even begin to play their harps (*PL,* 3.345–
46). The rest of Milton's account of that angelic performance is mainly
devoted to articulating "their sacred song," but Raphael's narration
in book 5 of a similar scene insists on the mazelike intricacy of their
"Mystical dance":

> which yonder starrie Spheare
> Of Planets and of fixt in all her Wheeles
> Resembles nearest, mazes intricate,
> Eccentric, intervolv'd, yet regular
> Then most, when most irregular they seem,
> And in thir motions harmonie Divine
> So smooths her charming tones, that Gods own ear
> Listens delighted. (*PL,* 5.620–27)

Thomas Greene has elaborated how Raphael's account of the angelic
dance, itself intricate and intervolved, seems to "act out the physical
movements it evokes," a characteristic feature of early modern written accounts of "labyrinth dances."[23] The angels' inspired singing
and dancing give both reassurance and pleasure, Greene observes, as
they ecstatically intimate "the elusive order of a universe not easily
grasped."[24] Raphael's description of these musical solemnities recalls
the self-displacement produced by the soul-piercing and labyrinthine
"*Lydian* Aires" of *L'Allegro*, with their nearly oxymoronic "Wanton
heed, and giddy cunning, / The melting voice through mazes running"
(*L'Allegro*, 136, 141–42). "The full voic'd Quire" in *Il Penseroso* similarly dissolves the pensive man "into extasies, / And bring[s] all Heav'n
before [his] eyes" (*Il Penseroso*, 162, 165–66). These pleasures are not
merely unreproved by God but inclusive of him, too, as an audience at
once appreciated and appreciative.

Time is measured in Heaven without the mediation of celestial
bodies but by the dance of the "circling Hours" and the "perpetual
round" of day and night beneath God's throne (*PL,* 6.3, 6). Yet when

the angels sing and dance around God's throne, according to Raphael, their dancing evokes the celestial motions that accommodate time's passage to humanity. These motions are a source of bewilderment for Adam and Eve and their offspring, perhaps deliberately designed to generate amusing confusion for the entertainment of the creator, who, according to Raphael, "his Fabric of the Heav'ns / Hath left to thir disputes, perhaps to move / His laughter at thir quaint Opinions wide" (*PL,* 8.76–78). Celestial dynamics, dancing that appears most irregular when most regular, polyphonic harmonies at once eccentric and intervolved—all are, like debates over predestination and free will, comparable to mazes. Mazes are paradoxical fabrications built with the intention of eliciting a great deal of motion without a destination—a deliberate superimposition of wandering and stasis. Satan, too, as he moves toward Eve in the form of a serpent, conforms to this pattern, a "Circular base of rising folds, that tow'red / Fold above fold, a surging maze" (*PL,* 9.498–99).

Left to themselves, the fallen angels resist participating in any such accommodative motion and indeed work to subvert it. After blasting the loyal angels with artillery, Satan mocks the angels' resulting loss of bodily self-control as if "they would dance, yet for a dance they seemd / Somwhat extravagant and wilde" (*PL,* 6.615–16). The joy in angelic motion is in this case all Satan's as he exults over his invented weaponry, which has forcibly produced an involuntary loss of self-possession eerily reminiscent of angelic dances about the throne of God. (Satan's humor here is not too far distant from that of the villain in an old western movie who yells "dance" while shooting at his victim's feet.) The invention of the gunpowder that produces this effect explicitly negates the process of time in Heaven, by which the deity is accommodated to his creatures. In revealing the basis of his invention to his followers, Satan traces the florid beauties of Heaven's landscape to the potent materials of Chaos that lie beneath its "bright surface" (*PL,* 6.472). The extraction and concoction of gunpowder short circuits the natural process of maturation, tapping into what Dylan Thomas described as "[t]he force that through the green fuse drives the flower" to create a weapon of sufficient impact to coerce his opponents to dance.[25] This short-circuiting of temporal process, and thus of divine accommodation, is characteristic of Satan and lies at the heart of his temptation of Eve. By eating the fruit, he tells her, she will exalt her status immediately, bypassing "the tract of time" and transforming herself into a subject of adoration: "nor was God-head from her thought" (*PL,* 9.498, 790).[26]

Satan's punishment is suited to his impatience with divine accommodation and refusal to submit to timely expression of it. Only the Son of God accommodates his father's immense power fully, through a face-to-face expression and reception of God that renders the Son "Mightiest in [his] Fathers might" (*PL*, 6.710). Raphael reports that when he drove the rebels before him, Heaven's wall "Rowld inward" like a furling scroll, and "a spacious Gap disclos'd / Into the wasteful deep," a disclosure from which the rebels recoil (*PL*, 6.861–62). Although in inventing gunpowder Satan has shared his awareness of the potent depths below Heaven's surface, now, as the image of the rolled-up scroll suggests, they confront the thing itself, unaccommodated God in the infinitude of his material might.[27] Only the even more horrifying holy terror in pursuit of them compels them to hurl themselves headlong into the heart of that mystery. The rebels have no control of themselves as they fall, and once in Hell, after Satan's successful temptation of humanity, "some say," God annually inflicts humbling loss of control on them "certain number'd days," transforming them into a mosh pit of swarming, hissing, "complicated monsters" (*PL*, 10.575–76, 523). Perhaps this timely, intricate, and intervolved display of eternal God's transcendence is, like angelic music and motion, most regular when most irregular it seems. If it is comparable to dancing, it is a mixed dance divinely enforced. Otherwise left to themselves, fallen angels of their own initiative move in various ways expressive of their fallen or falling condition. They even march to music to express their military discipline. But they do not dance.

It bears repeating in conclusion that insofar as the true nature of God is concerned, time as a measure of motion is an accommodation. Raphael in narrating the days of creation informs Adam and Eve that the acts of God are "Immediate . . . more swift / Then time or motion" and that the entire history he will recount through "process of speech" is a figurative representation (*PL*, 7.176–77, 178). Because the essential reality of the deity, infinite and eternal, lies beyond creatures' limited understanding, as Milton the theologian concedes, we cannot conceive how the chronological structure of obedient or disobedient motions relates back to God. Yet accommodation, in the narrative process of *Paradise Lost* at least, does seem also to operate in reverse: time as a measure of motion not only mediates the ways of a synchronic God to diachronic creatures but also relates those same time-bound creatures back again to the transcendent deity. This reverse process of accommodation, moreover, in which motions measured by time seem to be received by the eternal deity as if they were news bulletins, is represented as having the incomprehensible effect of moving *him*. The God of holy scripture as Milton understands it relies on the accommodative temporal process of narrative to convey himself to creatures. Because God also endows those creatures with free will, he too apparently submits to that same accommodative process. Milton with excellent scriptural warrant represents him doing so in the guise of a terrifyingly passionate monarch who when offended can scarcely control himself. At such moments even creatures innocent of offense feel compelled to scatter, "least the wrauth / Impendent, raging into sudden flame / Distinguish not" (*PL*, 5.890–92).

Notes

1. This chapter has been shaped by the advice and insight of Marissa Greenberg and Rachel Trubowitz, as well as by comments of anonymous readers for the Northwestern University Press, to whose aid and insights I am indebted.

2. Headnote to *A Paraphrase on Psalm 114*, hereafter cited in text as *Psalm 114* with line number.

3. Milton probably began learning Hebrew by the age of ten, when Thomas Young became his tutor in 1617 or 1618; see Jeffrey Alan Miller, "Milton, Stock, Young, and Puritanism," in *Young Milton: The Emerging Author, 1640–1642*, ed. Edward Jones (Oxford: Oxford University Press, 2013), 84.

4. Robert Young, *Young's Literal Translation of the Holy Bible*, rev. 3rd ed. (Edinburgh: G. A. Young and Co., 1898).

5. Jack Goldman makes this case in "Milton's Intrusion of Abraham and Isaac upon Psalm 114," *Philological Quarterly 55*, no. 1 (Winter 1976): 119–21.

6. Goldman, "Milton's Intrusion," 120.

7. The teenaged Milton could have known the rabbinical commentaries that tie Abraham, Isaac, and Jacob to the Exodus and celebration of Passover. As Jeffrey Shoulson has argued, however, evidence of a direct link is lacking, and, more to the point, Jewish, Christian, and Hellenistic traditions had over centuries interacted to such an extent that it is difficult to distinguish when "an idea, theme, and emphasis" is "distinctively Judaic or Hebraic and when it is Christian." Jeffrey S. Shoulson, *Milton and the Rabbis: Hebraism, Hellenism, and Christianity* (New York: Columbia University Press, 2001), 4.

8. Jeffrey Shoulson, email message to author, January 3, 2021.

9. On the essential identification of chaos with God, see my "Milton's God and the Matter of Chaos," *PMLA* 110, no. 5 (October 1995): 1035–46.

10. Access Marlowe's poem on the Poetry Foundation website: https://www.poetryfoundation.org/poems/44675/the-passionate-shepherd-to-his-love.

11. Sigmund Freud, "The 'Uncanny' " (1919), in *The Pelican Freud Library*, vol. 14, trans. James Strachey, ed. Albert Dickson (Harmondsworth, UK: Penguin, 1985), 368.

12. Consult chapter 2 by Sydney Bartlett in this volume.

13. See Gordon Teskey's observations on the speaker's fugitive grammatical presence in *The Poetry of John Milton* (Cambridge, MA: Harvard University Press, 2015), 82–83.

14. On the suppression of labor in Milton's early poetry, see Annabel Patterson, "'Forc'd fingers': Milton's Early Poems and Ideological Constraint," in Claude J. Summers and Ted-Larry Pebworth, eds, *"The Muses Common-Weale": Poetry and Politics in the Seventeenth Century* (Columbia: University of Missouri Press, 1988), 9–22. See also Marshall Grossman, "The Fruit of One's Labor in Miltonic Practice and Marxian Theory," *ELH* 59, no. 1 (Spring 1992): 77–105.

15. See Marjorie Hope Nicholson's seminal articles, "The 'New Astronomy' and English Literary Imagination," *Studies in Philology* 32 (1935): 428–62, and "Milton and the Telescope," *ELH* 2 (1935): 1–32.

16. On Galileo's mathematical analysis of falling bodies and its relevance to Milton, see Rachel Trubowitz, "The Fall and Galileo's Law of Falling Bodies: Geometrization vs. Observing and Describing Things in *Paradise Lost*," in *Milton and the New Scientific Age: Poetry, Science, Fiction*, ed. Catherine Gimelli Martin (New York: Routledge, 2019), 79–107. As Trubowitz observes, "Milton claims that poetry, like mathematics, enhances our ability to see a great deal more than meets the eye. Both allow us, if only for an instant, to share in God's marvelous powers of infinite perception" (100).

17. On Milton's interest in the latest advances in mathematics, see Trubowitz, "The Fall and Galileo's Law," especially 79–81; Matthew Dolloff, "'Gabriel's Trumpet': Milton and Seventeenth-Century conceptions of Infinity," in *Locating Milton: Places and Perspectives*, ed. Thomas Festa and David Ainsworth (Clemson: Clemson University Press, 2021), 81–99; and, in the same collection, Christopher Koester, "Mathematical Milton: Number Theory and Nesting Infinities in *Paradise Lost*," 101–23.

18. William Stukely, *Memoirs of Sir Isaac Newton's Life* (1752), *The Newton Project*, published online September 2004, dir. Rob Iliffe (University of Oxford, 2023), https://www.newtonproject.ox.ac.uk/view/texts/normalized/OTHE00001.

19. Michio Kaku, *Einstein's Cosmos* (New York: Norton, 2005), 92.

20. William Kerrigan, *The Sacred Complex: One the Psychogenesis of Paradise Lost* (Cambridge, MA: Harvard University Press, 1983), coined the phrase "the enfolded sublime" to describe the arresting power of "one first matter all": "these four words alone, fully heard, comprehend a great poem with much to say; to have them before us in a meaningful syntactic sequence is to be made momentarily giddy with the plasticity of huge meaning" (235).

21. Jean-Paul Sartre, *No Exit (Huis Clos)* (1943), trans. Stuart Gilbert (New York: Alfred.A. Knopf, 1946).

22. In the Cambridge Manuscript of Milton's poems, "To be Set on a Clock Case" is written above the body of Milton's lyric (the first two words have been obscured) but are crossed out. The title "On Time" appears above it. The crossed-out heading may have originally been intended to serve as the lyric's title. If so, the phrase "On Time," the title we know it by, may be construed as an economical bit of wordplay.

23. Thomas M. Greene, "Labyrinth Dances in the French and English Renaissance," *Renaissance Quarterly* 54, no. 4, part 2 (2001): 1457.

24. Greene, "Labyrinth Dances," 1456–57.

25. Dylan Thomas, "The force that through the green fuse drives the flower," in *18 Poems* (London: Fortune Press, 1934), 17 (line 1).

26. "[T]he tract of time" becomes one of numerous allusions to *Paradise Lost* in Alfred, Lord Tennyson, *In Memoriam*, specifically canto 77; for a full discussion of Tennyson's engagement with Milton's moving bodies, see chapter 7 by Ryan Hackenbracht in this volume.

27. Rachel Trubowitz presents a complementary reading of these lines (pp. 105–6 in this volume).

CHAPTER 2

That "Strange / Desire of Wandring"

Physical and Ideological
Movement in *Paradise Lost*

Sydney Bartlett

Late in book 9 of John Milton's *Paradise Lost*, Adam and Eve awake
groggy and disoriented, "bare / Of all thir vertue" (*PL,* 9.1062–63),
after indulging in the Tree of Knowledge's forbidden fruit.[1] Reminiscent
of Satan and his fallen comrades following their expulsion from Heaven
(*PL,* 1.51–81), humankind grapples with the weight of its trespass in a
moment devoid of sound and motion: "Confounded long they sate, as
struck'n mute" (*PL,* 9.1064). While guilt washes over the pair, Adam initiates an intense bout of marital discord in which he lashes out at Eve's
"strange / Desire of wandring" (*PL,* 9.1135–36), an action that severs
the pair from the "happie State" (*PL,* 8.331) they previously enjoyed in
the garden of Eden.[2] What's noteworthy here is that, out of the myriad
ways to describe Eve's transgression, Adam defines her offense in terms
of "wandring." She ate the fruit, but first she pursued her "strange /
Desire" and moved toward the Tree of Knowledge, following Satan's
suggestive lead: "Hee leading swiftly rowld / In tangles, and made the
intricate seem strait" (*PL,* 9.631–32). Her husband's rhetoric indicates
that the two actions, walking toward the Tree of Knowledge and eating
that "Bad Fruit" (*PL,* 9.1073), remain inextricably linked, much like an
apple and its seed. As Eve strays from Adam, moving closer to the Tree
and her own trespass, she perverts Eden's divine order and divorces
humankind from the ideological and geographic "happie State" they
enjoyed in Eden. Indeed, throughout Milton's epic, the subtle, embodied
motions of creation remain connected to the larger ideological moves
that define not only Milton's poetry but also his prose.

47

This chapter connects *Paradise Lost* to Milton's political writings by focusing on movement as another expression of Milton's monism—as both physical activity and ideological expression. It suggests that this trend in Milton's great epic is rooted within his political writings. I shall examine the varied motions Milton employs, ranging from movements confined to bodily gestures to those that propel bodies across geographies, and suggest that the poet's lexicon of illicit movement is both expansive and connected to deeper ideological leanings. While the political significance of movement may be subtle within *Paradise Lost*, I aim to root the trend in Milton's earlier tracts. Indeed, by close reading motion's parts of speech—including verbs, nouns, and adverbs that indicate and describe movement—I hope to establish new connections between Milton's epic poem and political prose while inviting an expanded understanding of movement's implications within Milton's work.

Like Adam and Eve's position in the garden, the happy state of the English Commonwealth had grown increasingly unstable by the time Milton began writing the epic around 1658. In 1660, seven years before *Paradise Lost*'s publication, England abandoned its republic and restored the monarchy, and Charles II returned to the throne that his father lost to Oliver Cromwell's Parliamentarians. Milton's political tracts, notably *Second Defense of the English People* (1654) and *The readie and easie way to establish a free Commonwealth* (1660; hereafter *The Ready and Easy Way*), demonstrate Milton's fervent and—in 1660—final attempts to protect the failing prospect of an English republic. Under Oliver Cromwell, the poet served as the Secretary of Foreign Tongues, and even after Cromwell's death, Milton remained dedicated to the republican cause. For this chapter, the respective timelines of composition between Milton's late poetry and political prose are worth particular emphasis. Work on *Paradise Lost* overlaps with that of *The Ready and Easy Way*, with Milton likely initiating the epic's composition in 1658, two years before publishing either edition of *The Ready and Easy Way* in 1660. *Paradise Lost*, while several years away from meeting readers, was in process, absorbing the tumultuous world the poet and polemicist inhabited. Indeed, the first edition of *The Ready and Easy Way* appeared in February 1660 and the second, expanded and revised edition in April. In May of the same year, Charles II returned, and England walked away from the Commonwealth that Milton and other republicans dedicated decades to constructing. Milton spent years forgoing his poetic calling to dedicate his voice instead to the republican cause, only for its conclusion to result in profound

Sydney Bartlett 49

ideological disappointment and the threat of execution to the poet and other radicals.[3]

Typical approaches to establishing a connection between *Paradise Lost* and the English Commonwealth employ Milton's biography, his political works and occupations, and larger thematic examinations of the poem, emphasizing its particular tone of disillusionment and focus on failed rebellions.[4] None of these approaches is flawed, but I propose an additional method to connect Milton's epic to its political context: a closer reading of movement in *Paradise Lost* and the political tracts. Physical movement on minute and cosmic scales is rampant throughout *Paradise Lost*—Satan crosses Chaos to reach Earth in book 2, and Eve turns back to her own reflection in book 4—but potent physical actions also appear in Milton's political work.

This chapter is hardly the first work in Milton studies to map *Paradise Lost* onto England's short-lived republic. Christopher Hill's seminal 1977 book *Milton and the English Revolution* paints a detailed image of Milton's life during the Civil War. With a focus that ranges from Milton's early childhood to the poet's last years, Hill describes the tense political situation of Milton's youth and its eruption into a yearslong bloody conflict by the poet's early thirties. He also details the republican disillusionment that accompanied the English Commonwealth's swift demise. Discussing the Civil War's effects on *Paradise Lost*, Hill writes:

> Between February 1659 and April 1660 Milton moved from the revived optimism of *Civil Power* to the despair of the second edition of *The Ready and Easy Way*. Later in 1660 he was in prison, in danger of his life. When released he had to live in obscurity and fear of assassination. These are the years in which he was writing *Paradise Lost*. Even if Milton had been a much less political character, it is unlikely that such events would have left him unaffected. The calm and distanced effect of *Paradise Lost* is astonishing, remarkable testimony to Milton's art and sense of decorum; but it is also deceptive. Not to grasp the magnitude of the disaster which had overwhelmed the poet would be a serious failure of imagination.[5]

Hill captures the profound disappointment that would characterize Restoration England for someone as deeply involved in the Commonwealth as Milton. The political work that superseded his poetic ambitions led Milton to a prison cell and, even when inexplicably released, into a world where his name was reviled throughout England.[6] Such disappointment must, Hill contends, bleed into the work that Milton felt called to produce his entire life. Focusing on Milton's employment during the Civil War, Robert Thomas Fallon in *Divided Empire: Milton's Political Imagery* also rightly finds it impossible to divorce England's political atmosphere from the epic. Milton's position as England's Secretary of Foreign Tongues would have ensured that he remained keenly aware of the delicate and often tumultuous nature of diplomacy in early modern England and as presented in *Paradise Lost*.[7]

Like Hill and Fallon, David Loewenstein and Barbara K. Lewalski concentrate on *Paradise Lost* as an epic indebted to the Civil War but pay specific attention to the poem's relationship with classical epics. David Loewenstein's article, "Writing Epic in the Aftermath of Civil War: *Paradise Lost*, the *Aeneid*, and the Politics of Contemporary History," draws a connection between Milton's *Paradise Lost* and Virgil's *Aeneid* that extends beyond their rhetorical strategies and epic form.[8] These works are intimately connected in both style and genre, Loewenstein argues, because their authors composed their respective epics in the aftermath of intense and divisive political turmoil. For Barbara Lewalski, as well, the poetic resemblance between *Paradise Lost* and its classical predecessors remains less impressive than the striking, contentious political contexts that produced them.[9] In *Life of John Milton* Lewalski offers a persuasive perspective on the relationship between *Paradise Lost* and war-torn England. Observing the poem's employment of blank verse and rejection of "the contemporary norm of rhyme for heroic poetry and drama," she describes Milton's choice in the context of "an aesthetic debate that had political implications." In fact, she argues, Milton's epic remains "a more daring political gesture than we often realize, even as it is also a poem for the ages by a prophet-poet who placed himself with, or above, Homer, Virgil, Ariosto, Tasso, and the rest."[10] By its very nature, argues Lewalski, *Paradise Lost* is political. Indeed, in many ways—particularly the epic's descriptions of physical movement, I argue—its poetry both reveals and embodies Milton's politics even more than his classicism.

Although this chapter will not use strictly biographical evidence or classical tradition to understand *Paradise Lost*, it will nonetheless borrow from both historicism and formalism, looking closely at the epic's language to connect the movement present in Milton's poetry and his political writings. Close reading is not a novel approach to literary studies, but Sharon Achinstein in *Milton and the Revolutionary*

Reader describes the merits of close reading *Paradise Lost* in relation to contemporary politics. Milton's use of allegory and other literary devices created a clean division within the author's readership in early modern England: "those who read and understood and those who did not."[11] More broadly, Milton published *Paradise Lost* in "a literary culture that was intensely interested in political analysis."[12] Despite an increase in censorship following the Restoration, Thomas Tomkins licensed the poem though "the arguments of the regicide tracts were often perceived in *Paradise Lost*."[13] Even Milton's first audience illustrated "a peculiar sensitivity to how Milton's poetry might revive the sedition of his prose."[14] While not overt, Milton's political priorities found a home in the epic. "Veiled" as political allusions may be, they "are not indecipherable"—nor are they meant to be.[15]

This chapter begins with an examination of a selection of Milton's political tracts from the 1640s, 1650s, and 1660 to identify instances of physical motion and parse the corresponding ideological implications of that movement. Following the prose, it turns to Milton's epic, mapping movements within *Paradise Lost* onto the ideas Milton first posited in the political tracts. Together I intend those respective instances of motion in the political tracts and the epic to expand the lexicon of motion in Milton's work while emphasizing its intricate, politically radical nature.

England Enthralled

By the time Milton published *The Ready and Easy Way* in 1660, he had been composing *Paradise Lost* for two years. Yet, even before the composition of either work, Milton's early political tracts demonstrate a connection between humankind's fall and England's return to monarchy. This section will trace the association of England and Eden throughout Milton's political prose, and I will also pay particular attention to the types of movement that represent Milton's republican leanings—motions that often exist in conversation with humankind's biblical ancestors. Indeed, Milton's political prose illustrates an explicit, historical association between the English people and their biblical ancestors; but these tracts also paint motion as a morally suspect action first executed by Adam and Eve. Tracing these two trends throughout Milton's subsequent political prose, I show that *The Ready and Easy Way* crystallizes the relationship between England and Eden and the shared movements that their inhabitants adopt.

Beginning in *The Tenure of Kings and Magistrates* (1649), Milton delves into the history of monarchy, associating the act of acquiring a king with humankind's original sin. Milton creates a causal relationship between the two instances. To describe the "first beginning, the original of Kings," Milton starts with the Fall:

> No man who knows aught can be so stupid to deny that all men naturally were borne free . . . and that they liv'd so. Till from the root of *Adams* transgression, falling among themselves to doe wrong and violence, and foreseeing that such courses must needs tend to the destruction of them all, they agreed by common league to bind each other from mutual injury . . . Hence came Citties, Townes, and Common-wealths. And because no faith in all was found sufficiently binding, they saw it needfull to ordaine some authoritie, that might restrain by force and punishment what was violated against peace and common right. (*Tenure*)

Humankind's Fall thus introduces a constant state of "falling," a forceful, chaotic motion propelling humankind toward an intricate sequence of events that, beginning in cities and towns, eventually produces a monarchy. Indeed, the necessary "authoritie" Milton describes involves either a single leader, "whom for the eminence of his wisdom and integritie [men] chose above the rest," or multiple leaders, "more then one whom they thought of equal deserving," and "the first was call'd a King" (*Tenure*). Nearly a decade before initiating *Paradise Lost*'s composition, Milton roots monarchy's origin story squarely within Adam and Eve's transgression.

Later in *The Tenure of Kings and Magistrates* Milton turns his attention to Protestant divines and offers a strange, pointed understanding of movement. He critiques the divines' integrity, reviling what he considers their opportunistic relationship with "truth" and reluctance to perform "necessary self-defense" against a tyrant (*Tenure*). In his sharp condemnation Milton repurposes movement as a way both to identify and to denounce this group:

> For Divines, if ye observe them, have thir postures and thir motions no less expertly, and with no less variety then they that practice feats in the Artillery-ground . . . But if there come a truth to be defended, which to them, and thir interest of this world seemes not so profitable, strait these nimble motionists can finde no eev'n leggs to stand upon: and are no more of use to

Sydney Bartlett

> reformation throughly performd, and not superficially, or to the
> advancement of Truth . . . (*Tenure*)

Here, as Thomas Luxon observes, Milton "compares the spiritual 'motions' [of] Presbyterian divines to the military 'motions' of foot-soldiers on parade, except that he insists the divines don't know (or ignore) the difference between right and left."[16] In Milton's comparison the divines lose the active quality of the soldiers' "feats" practiced "in the Artillery-ground." Instead, he transforms such action into an identifying noun: "motionists." The problem for Milton is not a lack of available verbs to describe the divines. He spares no details when relating the variety of martial motions that they adopt. They "seem furiously to march on, and presently march counter; by and by they stand, and then retreat; or if need be can face about, or wheele in a whole body," perform "turnes and doublings," and "winde themselves by shifting ground" (*Tenure*). There is no lack of movement, but the sheer abundance of motion requires additional consideration for Milton. Ultimately, the constant movement cues a never-ending vacillation between states that requires not just the descriptions of action but also an entire identity defined by it. The noun "motionists" thus communicates Milton's disdain for the divines, along with his understanding of their ideological leanings, with more fervor than any specific verb that the divines enact. This identifying quality of motion is one that will reappear in both *The Ready and Easy Way* and *Paradise Lost*, but the active verbs employed in the later tracts enliven motion for Milton as he continues to solidify England's association with Eden and refine the actions that "nimble motionists" might adopt.

Published in 1654, Milton's *Second Defense of the English People* (hereafter *Second Defense*) again juxtaposes kingship with the Fall. In this instance, recalling England's biblical ancestors reveals Milton's own anxious preoccupation with the new Commonwealth's fragility. The work indicates that England's own "happie State" (*PL*, 8.331) within the Commonwealth remained as tenuous as that tranquil position that Adam and Eve occupy only briefly in Eden. Indeed, six years prior to Charles II's return to the throne, Milton writes in *Second Defense*:

> If the republic should miscarry, so to speak, and as quickly vanish, surely no greater shame and disgrace could befall this country. Finally, honor yourself, so that, having achieved that liberty in pursuit of which you endured so many hardships and

> encountered so many perils, you may not permit it to be violated
> by yourself or in any degree diminished by others . . . Honor
> itself, virtue itself will seem to have melted away, religious faith
> will be circumscribed, reputation will hereafter be a meager
> thing. A deeper wound than this, after that first wound, can
> never be inflicted on the human race. (*CPEP*, 1103)

Humankind's "first wound," eating from the Tree of Knowledge, is on par with the Commonwealth's demise, according to Milton. England took "the one direct road to true liberty," and straying from that path, he warns, would have drastic consequences (*CPEP*, 1075). Like *The Tenure of Kings and Magistrates*, the language of *Second Defense* demonstrates not only the gravity of England's potential retreat but also a key, early association between England and Eden—between the English people and their first biblical ancestors. When Milton considers England's potentially treacherous return to the monarchy, he thinks of humankind's first transgression; the two moments—and movements— occupy the same critical space.

With both a historical (*Tenure*) and metaphorical (*Second Defense*) connection established between the Fall and the Restoration, it follows that a rhetorical link between the two events might exist for Milton as well. In *Areopagitica* (1644), the powerful oration condemning censorship, Milton invokes two specific types of movement that are integral to the poet's ideologically charged lexicon of motion: "creeping" and "wandering." Beginning the tract with an overview of licensing's history, Milton writes, "this project of licencing crept out of the Inquisition, was catcht up by our Prelates, and hath caught some of our Presbyters" (*Areo.*). In this case, licensing is an active force, one with the power to move and to ensnare. Most notably, though, Milton writes that the project *creeps*—through the past and toward England's Presbyters—and a brief investigation into this term's history proves enlightening.

Creeping contains an important duality: the term remains reminiscent of the nonhuman, such as snakes, as well as the demonic and satanic.[17] In Genesis 1:26 God intends humankind to exercise authority over all living creatures, including "every creeping thing that creepeth upon the earth." In *Paradise Lost* Milton provides a nearly identical poetic account of this moment, as Raphael recounts God's command: "Let us make now Man in our image, Man / In our similitude, and let them rule / . . . every creeping thing that creeps the ground" (*PL*, 7.519–20, 523). Even before the Fall, it is clear that creeping is below

Sydney Bartlett

humankind's dignity, but in this first instance, creeping is not indicative of an inherently morally compromised state.

Nonetheless, in *Areopagitica*, Milton uses the verb to suggest its subject's nefarious nature. And in *Paradise Lost*, the epic's most menacing characters—including the Hell Hounds that "would creep . . . into [Sin's] womb" (*PL*, 2.656)—adopt the motion too. On Earth, creeping characterizes Satan's intentionally malicious mode and mission as well as marks the beginning of humankind's corruption. At the start of book 9, Satan, "like a black mist low creeping" (*PL*, 9.180), locates the sleeping serpent before entering it. That moment, even though the serpent is not yet implicated in Satan's action, offers a quick, rhetorical message to readers regarding what comes next. To tempt humankind successfully, Satan has no need for the serpent's mind but only its capacity for motion. The word "creeping" is thus a sinister precursor signaling humankind's impending Fall, just as to "creep back" signaled England's own return to monarchy in *The Ready and Easy Way*. Although both usages of "creep" are relevant to Milton's poetry, his prose—both *Areopagitica* and, as this chapter will soon demonstrate, *The Ready and Easy Way*—establishes the term's marked significance in Milton's work.

The term "wandering," like "creeping," also comes replete with ideological implications. Etymologically, "wander" finds its roots in the Latin verb *errare*, "to err," and by the early modern period, both Milton and his audience would have been familiar with the affiliation between the action of "wandering" and its implied immorality.[18] Take, for example, Milton's attitude in *An Apology for Smectymnuus* (1642) when he offers an ardent defense of his chastity: "Next (for hear me out now readers), that I may tell ye wither my younger feet wandered" (*CPEP*, 851). Notably, this sentence anticipates readers' assumptions through its parenthetical request. Of course, Milton does not detail any illicit affairs, instead describing his reading of "lofty fables and romances" as part of a program through which he

> learnt what a noble virtue chastity sure must be . . . So that even those books which to many others have been the fuel of wantonness and loose living . . . proved to me so many incitements, as you have heard, to the love and steadfast observation of that virtue which abhors the society of bordellos. (*CPEP*, 851)

Milton assures readers that his own experience with wandering remains fictional—as well as instructional.

Turning again to the later work, in *Areopagitica* the movement reappears as Milton considers the "high providence of God" (*Areo.*). He admits that the deity has "give[n] us minds that can wander beyond all limit and satiety" (*Areo.*). In this case, "wander[ing]" exists both "beyond" something—the (at times physical) boundaries of virtue—and toward something else—sin (*Areo.*). Milton expands on this capacity to wander as a choice without which humankind "had bin else a meer artificiall *Adam*, such an *Adam* as he is in the motions," or a puppet show (*Areo.*). As in the "nimble motionists" that Milton describes in *The Tenure of Kings and Magistrates*, here, too, "the motions" indicates inherent falsity. Yet in *Areopagitica* Milton contends that, despite humankind's propensity for straying from the "temperance, justice, [and] continence" that God commands, censorship is nonetheless unjustifiable (*Areo.*). Indeed, he writes, "How much we thus expell of sin, so much we expell of vertue: for the matter of them both is the same" (*Areo.*). Later, in *Paradise Lost*, after Eve wanders and eats the forbidden fruit, Adam will bemoan that humankind now knows "Both Good and Evil, Good lost, and Evil got" (*PL,* 9.1072). In a fallen world, parsing virtue and sin, dividing the act of wandering from abiding, is impossible. The qualities and actions exist in relation to each other.[19]

Milton's political tracts do, in fact, provide readers with notable, and perhaps ambitious, prescriptions that oppose sinister motions. The idea of steadfast endurance proves just as potent as that of illicit movements. Take, for example, Milton's brief essay *Of Education* (1644), in which he outlines a detailed, ideal curriculum for hypothetical English students. The essay indicates that the relationship between education and the state is a close one for Milton. After learning economics by reading "some choice Comedies . . . [and] Those Tragedies also that treat of Houshold matters," students should master studies that enhance the state's status:

> The next remove must be to the study of *Politicks* . . . that they may not in a dangerous fit of the Common-wealth be such poor, shaken, uncertain Reeds of such a tottering Conscience as many of our great Counsellers have lately shewn themselves, but stedfast pillars of the State. (*Of Education*)

By Milton's measure, ideal pupils should, in turn, become ideal citizens of the state: "stedfast" in their own right and at odds with the quick, tottering movements of uncertainty that threaten the Commonwealth's stability. Again, in *Eikonoklastes* (1649), written five years after *Of*

Education, the same sentiment echoes throughout Milton's defense of Charles I's execution. Milton criticizes "the rage and torrent of that boisterous folly and superstition, that possesses and hurries on the vulgar sort" (*Eikonoklastes*). He encourages the English people instead to "stand upright and stedfast in [God's] cause; dignify'd with the defense of truth and public libertie" (*Eikonoklastes*). In both these works, the idea of resisting hurried, irrational motion remains preeminent; yet, as with *Areopagitica*'s sin and virtue, Milton does not encourage the act of abiding without first detailing its irrational, hurried opposite.

By 1660 Milton's political tracts read with a tone as grim as the events that change his epic's "Notes to Tragic" in book 9 of *Paradise Lost* (*PL,* 9.6). When he published the second edition of *The Ready and Easy Way*, England's return to monarchy was no longer a potential, half-hearted retreat but a seemingly inevitable sprint back to traditional rule. Nonetheless, Milton persisted in his staunchly republican writing despite the significant risk of harm at the hands of new regime.[20] Milton's language in this tract is pointed. There is no longer the narrative distance contained in kingship's origin story, as in *The Tenure of Kings and Magistrates*, or the passive voice that *Second Defense* employs within its most potent metaphor ("A deeper wound . . . can never be inflicted"). Instead, it is Milton's word choice—specifically, choice in verbs and the subjects enacting them—that indicates England's dangerous new reality. The second edition of *The Ready and Easy Way* includes a new introduction, in which Milton reviles "those who are in power"—specifically, the readmitted members of the Long Parliament—for their "absolute determination . . . to enthrall [England]" in monarchical rule, when the country could "remain finally secure from the exasperated regal power and out of snares." Notably, the chaotic and intricate action of "enthrall[ing]" contrasts the implied tranquil stasis of "remain[ing] finally secure" in the Commonwealth—after, of course, facing the necessary "fears and difficulties" that England should "easily overcome" (*The Ready and Easy Way*).

Throughout *The Ready and Easy Way*, Milton articulates England's treacherous return to monarchy in terms of motion while emphasizing the supposed stability of the Commonwealth:

> After our liberty and religion thus prosperously fought for, gaind
> and many years possessd, except in those unhappie interruptions,
> which God hath remov'd, now that nothing remains, but in all
> reason the certain hopes of a speedie and immediate settlement
> for ever in a firm and free Commonwealth, for this extolld and

58   That "Strange / Desire of Wandring"

> magnifi'd nation, regardless both of honour wonn or deliverances
> voutsaf't from heaven, to fall back or rather to creep back so
> poorly as it seems the multitude would to thir once abjur'd and
> detested thraldom of Kingship . . . (*The Ready and Easy Way*)

Notably, Milton refines the passive phrase "fall back" with the more
infernal "creep back." Both terms contrast his description of the Commonwealth as "firm," but the distinction between them is revealing.
While "fall" is often used to describe human actions or tendencies—
particularly in Christianity's concept of humankind's Fall—"creep"
introduces a more sinister component to the passage. Indeed, "fall[ing]"
is human, but the motion feels almost accidental when compared to
the deliberate act of creeping. Despite their difference in connotation,
the two words share a notable adverb: "back." In both cases, the word
indicates an act of regression—one that grows only more abhorrent
when paired with "creeping." Together, the phrase "to fall back or
rather to creep back" underscores the English people's agency while
emphasizing the movement's negative connotation. Creeping back is
not only a deterioration of humankind's divinely ordained upright status but an active adoption of a more nefarious one.

The backward movement of return occurs elsewhere in this last
republican tract. In *The Ready and Easy Way* Milton mourns the
practical losses associated with reacquiring a king: "all the treasure
we have spent, not that corruptible treasure only, but that far more
precious of all our late miraculous deliverances; treading back again
with lost labour all our happie steps in the progress of reformation"
(*The Ready and Easy Way*). Again, moving backward is a regression,
but Milton is explicit here that such motion is not only illicit (as in
"creep back") but also antithetical to his concept of a state's happiness.[21] Just as Milton offers a clear portrait of what exactly England's
return to monarchy entails, he is explicit when describing the opposite.
Expanding on the happiness of the state, he writes that England "in
the midst of greater difficulties, courageously, wisely, constantly went
through with the same work, and are setl'd in all the happie enjoi-
ments of a potent and flourishing Republic to this day" (*The Ready
and Easy Way*). There is no rash movement in Milton's description
of a happy state, but there is the reliable and noble notion of with-
standing turbulence. Indeed, Milton insists: "The happiness of a nation
must needs be firmest and certainest in a full and free Council of thir
own electing, where no single person, but reason only, swaies" (*The
Ready and Easy Way*).[22] Once again, the joint concepts of firmness

and certainty articulate Milton's republican ideals—even in the face of certain monarchical return. These two qualities are necessary conditions of a happy state, and this particular notion in *The Ready and Easy Way* is consistent with the notions of abiding articulated earlier in *Eikonoklastes* and *Of Education*.

Milton concludes *The Ready and Easy Way* on a note of hope, albeit perhaps half-hearted. Should this piece, he writes, "seem strange to any, it will not seem more strange, I hope, then convincing to backsliders" (*The Ready and Easy Way*). Milton identifies his key audience in terms of motion (sliding), a verb that comes imbued with the direction (back) already derided as antithetical to happy action. Like *Tenure*'s "nimble motionists," the "backsliders" in *The Ready and Easy Way* perform both their ideology and its corresponding movement. The verbs, emboldened by the ideologies that animate them, transform into nouns—their subjects now embodying their actions in a notable display of Milton's ideas of monism. Like many aspects of language contained in the political tracts, this same metamorphic trend will reappear in *Paradise Lost*. The epic is already in its infancy when Milton publishes *The Ready and Easy Way* in the hopes that "backsliders" read it and adopt a different politics, a different motion, a different identity. When *Paradise Lost* reaches readers seven years later in 1667, it will feature movement—and motion-oriented nouns—first flexed in the political prose that Milton penned decades prior.

Terms That Move

Throughout Milton's prose and poetry, the physical and the ideological capacities of movement function in ways so identical that parsing them is not simply challenging but unproductive. Time and again, the epic, like the political tracts, demonstrates the dialectical relationship between changes in physical and ideological positions. Centering my discussion on specific terms within *Paradise Lost*, "wandring" (*PL*, 9.1136) and "happie State" (*PL*, 8.331), provides an acute demonstration of just how deeply an individual's—or a nation's—movements are intertwined with their moral choices.

Wander

In book 9 of *Paradise Lost*, Eve does not stride or walk toward the Tree of Knowledge; instead, Adam insists that she wanders, and the ideological consequences of that particular mode are as intentional in its immorality as it is serendipitous in physical direction. Humankind's mother, however, is hardly the first character in the epic to adopt the practice of wandering.[23] Following Hell's "great consult" (*PL*, 1.798), the fallen angels, "Disband[ed], and wandring, each his several way" (*PL*, 2.523), take up a myriad of fruitless activities in their new realm. Many seek entertainment in sports or music. Other fallen angels choose to preoccupy themselves with philosophy, engaging in discourses on "Fixt Fate, free will, foreknowledg absolute" in which they "found no end, in wandring mazes lost" (*PL*, 2.560–61). Wandering in Hell, it seems, is circuitous. With no further to fall or additional punishments yet available, the fallen angels adopt the mode in perpetuity, awaiting Satan's return from Earth.

Satan's most infamous action on Earth is also introduced in terms of wandering. Overjoyed by Eve's assent to "Lead then" (*PL*, 9.631), Satan—in the serpent—reacts bodily as they proceed toward the Tree of Knowledge. He shares the eerie glow of a will-o'-the-wisp, which the narrator describes "as when a wandring Fire . . . Misleads th' amaz'd Night-wanderer from his way" (*PL*, 9.634, 640). The mobility in this simile is notable for two reasons: first, it underscores the sinister nature of Satan's mission (the misled nocturnal traveler becomes "swallow'd up and lost, from succour farr"; *PL*, 9.642), and second, "wander" appears in gerundive and nounal forms that make it less an action than an identity. The fire is defined as much by its "wandring" as its brightness, and the hopelessly lost traveler by both his time and motion: "Night-wanderer." Enacting the monism of movement and identity, Satan's description as he leads Eve to the Tree of Knowledge embodies and foreshadows humankind's postlapsarian fate. They too will be misled "from [their] way" and "lost," though not "from succour farr."

While wandering drives the structure and narrative of *Paradise Lost*—from Satan's journey through the realm of Chaos to Adam and Eve's departure from Eden—there remains a particular location around which that movement revolves: the Tree of Knowledge. Satan, masquerading as the serpent, leads Eve, assuring her "the way is readie, and not long" (*PL*, 9.626), phrasing that suggests an intriguing though hardly subtle connection with Milton's *The Ready and Easy Way*. When describing how he himself happened upon the Tree, Satan tells Eve:

> Till on a day roaving the field, I chanc'd
> A goodly Tree farr distant to behold
> Loaden with fruit of fairest colours mixt,

Ruddie and Gold: I nearer drew to gaze . . .
. . . I resolv'd
Not to deferr; hunger and thirst at once,
Powerful perswaders, quick'nd at the scent
Of that alluring fruit, urg'd me so keene. (*PL*, 9.575–78, 585–88)

The physicality of the Tree—its distance from the observer—precedes discussion of the fruit because, before eating it, humankind must move toward it. And like Satan they rove: first Eve toward the Tree, and then Adam toward Eve.[24] Before criticizing Eve's "strange / Desire of wandring," Adam, with a sinking premonition ("Yet oft his heart, divine of somthing ill / Misgave him"; *PL*, 9.845–46) goes "forth to meet her" (*PL*, 9.847). On his way, "by the Tree / Of Knowledge he must pass" (*PL*, 9.848–49), and he discovers Eve not far from it, fruit in hand. Horrified, Adam drops the flower crown intended for Eve, and his hand is left empty. Eventually, he grabs the fruit and eats, but Eve's being led by the serpent and Adam's "meet[ing]" her—two kinds of roving that result in geographic movement and moral transgression—precede humanity's corruption.

After humankind eats the fruit and falls, Adam considers the pair's alternative fate bitterly, one in which Eve did not desire to wander and "we had then / Remaind still happie, not as now" (*PL*, 9.1137–38). Adam juxtaposes opposites: unhappiness and happiness, wandering and remaining. Adam's speech recognizes the "unhappie morn" (*PL*, 9.1136) as a sorrowful one, yes, but also as one marked by evil action.[25] He questions "whence possessd" (*PL*, 9.1137) Eve, who is taken aback at her husband's speech:

What words have past thy Lips, Adam severe,
Imput'st thou that to my default, or will
Of wandring, as thou call'st it, which who knows
But might as ill have happ'nd thou being by,
Or to thy self perhaps: hadst thou been there. (*PL*, 9.1144–48)

Adam's accusation as a whole is difficult for Eve to bear, but Eve's fixation on his diction indicates that one term—"wandring" (*PL*, 9.1146)—is worth specific critique. She too appears aware of the word's nefarious implications and avoids considering her trespass in the same way: "as thou call'st it," she retorts. Adam and Eve share a mutual understanding of the term's immoral implications, and although Eve does not accept "wandring" as an accurate description of her movement, she notably fails to offer an alternative. Instead, she replaces the sinister gerund with a decidedly vaguer pronoun, "it."

Regardless of Eve's perceived disdain toward the term, "wandring" continues to define humankind's newfound, fallen nature. In book 12 the angel Michael foretells the future, describing Jesus as he

> . . . who shall quell
> The adversarie Serpent, and bring back
> Through the worlds wilderness long wanderd man
> Safe to eternal Paradise of rest. (*PL*, 12.311–14)

By this time in humankind's story, wandering is not a fallen action but a fallen identity—an evolution hinted at in Satan's description as a will-o'-the-wisp in book 9 and reaching fruition by book 12.[26] Redemption does not uncouple movement and identity, but it alters the quality of their unity. Only when Jesus "bring[s] back . . . long wanderd man" will humankind return safely to an "eternal Paradise of rest," or enduring moral and physical security and stillness (*PL,* 12.311–14).[27]

This "bring[ing] back" is a form of return notably different from those in Milton's earlier prose—as in "to fall back, or rather to creep back so poorly" (*The Ready and Easy Way*)—and elsewhere in *Paradise Lost*, including when Satan for Eve "Waited with hellish rancour imminent / To intercept thy way, or send thee back / Despoild of Innocence, of Faith, of Bliss" (*PL,* 9.409–11). Through Christ's sacrifice alone, moving back becomes redemptive rather than regressive. Yet by insisting on Christ's agency, Michael seems to underscore the consequences of humankind's own transgressions; that is, Michael reminds us that without Christ, humankind's movement "back" is only possible as illicit and immoral motions. This much proved true for England, when in *The Ready and Easy Way* "back" becomes a term employed only to indicate the country's ill-fated return to monarchy. Ultimately, humankind—Adam and Eve along with the English people—becomes "long wanderd" only because they have first wandered along a way that was "readie, and not long" (*PL,* 9.626).

Happy State

From where humankind departs—its "happie State"—remains another point of ideological and physical convergence within *Paradise Lost*. The poem invokes the two definitions of "state" extant in Milton's time: (1) "A condition of mind or feeling; the mental or emotional condition

Sydney Bartlett

of a person at a particular time" and (2) "A community of people living in a defined territory and organized under its own government; a commonwealth, a nation. Also occasionally: the territory occupied by such a community."[28] Both understandings of "state" appear throughout *Paradise Lost* without contradiction and often in tandem. In book 8, for example, Adam recounts his creation to Raphael, describing in detail God's initial commands to him:

> But of the Tree whose operation brings
> Knowledg of good and ill . . .
> Remember what I warne thee, shun to taste,
> And shun the bitter consequence; for know
> The day thou eat'st thereof, my sole command
> Transgrest, inevitably thou shalt dye;
> From that day mortal, and this happie State
> Shalt loose, expell'd from hence into a World
> Of woe and sorrow. (*PL*, 8.323–24, 327–33)

God has provided humankind with a "happie State," but he is explicit concerning its fragility: if humankind eats of the Tree of Knowledge's fruit, they will die and be forcibly removed from Eden. Their punishment is physical—"expell'd from hence" (*PL*, 8.332)—and psychological—"woe and sorrow" (*PL*, 8.333)—a duality that contains both the early modern definitions of "state." Much like humankind's embodied fall as "long wander[ing]," so too does its "happie State" dictate how prelapsarian Adam and Eve move through the world and where they move to. When humankind strays from their divinely intended location and activities—for instance, by moving in accordance with "that strange / Desire of wandring"—they are physically removed from Eden and ushered into "a World" defined by mental anguish and physical insecurity.

In their first marital dispute, Adam and Eve indicate a shared preoccupation with the fragile nature of their "happie State." Preceding Eve's "wandring" in book 9, humankind's signature disagreement introduces—and comes to define—the risk that certain types of movement pose to their condition. Like God's command, Adam and Eve's dispute spotlights deviant motion as a threat to their peaceful existence and stable place. Eve initiates the dispute by attempting to convince Adam to separate for the day. Overwhelmed by the garden's unruly growth, Eve suggests that she and Adam "divide [their] labours . . . where choice / Leads . . . or where most needs" (*PL*, 9.214–15). Adam resists Eve's proposal, maintaining that, should the pair physically separate, their "happie State" will be vulnerable to the "malicious Foe" (*PL,* 9.253). Eve responds by pointing out the dubious merits of a "happie State" with boundaries etched by fear:

> If this be our condition, thus to dwell
> In narrow circuit strait'nd by a Foe . . .
> How are we happie, still in fear of harm? (*PL,* 9.322–23, 326)

While Eve acknowledges their state's vulnerability to an external enemy, she encourages Adam to trust in their strength to resist it: "Let us not then suspect our happie State / Left so imperfect by the Maker wise" (*PL,* 9.337–38). Adam counters Eve's argument of collective strength by testifying to the inherent goodness within all of God's creation: "Nothing imperfet or deficient left / Of all that he Created" (*PL,* 9.345–46); but then he expresses his opposition to separating in terms of his individual—and patriarchal—security: "*his* happie State" (*PL,* 9.347, emphasis added). Eve is uncertain about the integrity of humankind's happiness, whereas Adam is concerned not with the merits of the patriarchal state but with the inner strength of its inhabitants: "Secure from outward force; within himself / The danger lies" (*PL,* 9.348–49). Humankind's parents both admit to threats against their happiness, but they differ on the identity and location of these threats. While Eve argues that humanity's "integritie" (*PL,* 9.329)—the potential for "double honour gaine[d]" (*PL,* 9.332) by rebuking temptation—is a powerful protection against an external force, Adam finds the potential for fault within that very safeguard Eve proposes—that is, humankind's own strength. Adam and Eve agree on the potential for risk, but they fail to reach a consensus on what threatens—and thus is necessary to secure—their "happie State."

Yet, as Milton first outlines in his political prose, the threat to a "happie State" is inherent to the illicit movements of straying from it. Those movements, such as wandering and creeping, are indeed physical, but they are also ideological. And both components of motion are implied within Adam and Eve's argument. Indeed, Adam appears most concerned about battles "within himself" (*PL,* 9.348), much like the ideological "wandering" outlined in *Areopagitica,* yet Eve begrudges the physical limits, the "narrow circuit strait'nd by a Foe" (*PL,* 9.323), that preclude her happiness as independent motion. The dual qualities of motion and the state exist in tandem to precipitate humankind's fall. Ultimately, and much to their mutual regret, both Adam and Eve are

Sydney Bartlett

right. The physical consequences of humanity's movement remain connected to their ideological ones, just as the state's physical condition remains connected to its moral one.

Their unresolved argument, which ends in Adam's dull assent for Eve to "Go" (*PL,* 9.372), permits Eve's physical departure from Adam and, subsequently, from their "happie State" within Eden. Eve, who just that morning had derided the "narrow circuit strait'nd by a Foe," follows Satan who "made intricate seem strait" (*PL,* 9.632) on the path toward the Tree of Knowledge. And while she initially refers to the Tree's fruit as "Fruitless" (*PL,* 9.648), her mind—which "can wander" (*Areo.*)—changes. At noon, "She pluck'd, she eat" (*PL,* 9.781), and upon meeting her, Adam too takes the fruit and consumes it. Ultimately, it is God's understanding of a "happie State"—both mental and geographic—that applies to Adam and Eve's transgressive movements and transforms them into a fallen identity. Humankind's sin invokes the dual physical and ideological components of motion, and the consequences of that illicit motion embrace both of the available definitions of "state" in Milton's time. Although their marital dispute failed to reach a meaningful consensus, they were both right—and wrong. As Adam and Eve depart from Eden, "expell'd . . . into a World / Of woe and sorrow" (*PL,* 8.332–333), humankind takes a final look at "Paradise, so late thir happie seat" (*PL,* 12.642).

In Milton's own time, the English people, too, would forgo the republic's own happy state: the Commonwealth. In *Second Defense* Milton asks: "What nation, what state has displayed superior fortune or stouter courage in securing for itself such liberty?" (*CPEP,* 1074). The same nation, as he warns in *The Ready and Easy Way,* may lose the liberty it once secured, choosing instead to "[tread] back again with lost labour all our happie steps in the progress of reformation." The failure of the Commonwealth's own happy state is both a political and a moral fault—and that happy state is perhaps even as short-lived in England as it is in Eden.

Point of Departure

Eating the apple garners more attention than Eve's wandering toward the Tree of Knowledge, and it is easy to forget that Adam "forth to meet her went" (*PL,* 9.847), but the motions present within the poem are subtle and sound. The physicality of humankind's respective trespasses remains inherently connected to states of innocence and sin. By trespassing, Milton insists in *Second Defense*, Adam and Eve inflict "that first wound" (*CPEP*, 1103), and Restoration England will nearly succeed in replicating it. In book 3 of *Paradise Lost*, God anticipates humankind's propensity for transgression, yet he insists: "free they must remain, / Till they enthrall themselves" (*PL*, 3.124–25). Likewise, writing *The Ready and Easy Way* with something that resembles fore-knowledge, Milton bemoans England's "absolute determination . . . to enthrall" the country once again in kingship.

The epic's final scene offers a haunting description of Adam and Eve's last moments in Eden while also serving the last word on physical and ideological movement:

> The World was all before them, where to choose
> Thir place of rest, and Providence thir guide:
> They hand in hand with wandring steps and slow,
> Through Eden took thir solitarie way. (*PL*, 12.646–49)

Adam and Eve resign themselves, and their progeny, to a fate outside Eden, and the sentiment remains perched on a notion of uncertainty. Adam and Eve take their way "with wandring steps and slow" and no clear path. With wandering now an identity as well as a course of action, humankind must rely on divine direction. Indeed, without Providence, their "wandring steps" (*PL*, 12.648) would result in a circuitous, damaging path, like the "wandring mazes" found in Hell (*PL*, 2.561); yet, with "Providence thir guide" (*PL*, 12.647), humankind can maintain hope for the day they are brought back to Paradise, a state where they might then "[Remain] still happie" (*PL*, 9.1138). It is no longer a "strange / Desire" that propels Adam or Eve forward, but instead their destiny, and identity, as "long wanderd man." Yet, in Milton's England, the country has adopted their biblical ancestors' "strange / Desire," replete with "motionists" and "backsliders" embodying the country's regressive politics.

Taken as a whole, Milton's political prose remains sharp and devastating to Royalist opponents, but even taken in parts—at distinct word choices—it maintains the same level of acute critique. *Paradise Lost* shares this rebellious trait. Modern and early modern readers alike would not doubt the daring political nature of *The Ready and Easy Way* or *Second Defense*. Likewise, reading *Paradise Lost* closely and in proximity to Milton's earlier political pamphlets affirms that the poem is "a more daring political gesture than we often realize." *Paradise Lost* critiques humankind within the same linguistic and critical bounds that

Milton employs in his political writings. Milton began writing *Paradise Lost* at the Commonwealth's end, using the epic to detail humankind's "first wound" while witnessing England move toward one nearly as devastating. Hill proposes that all of Milton's late poems remain "deeply political, wrestling with the problem of the failed revolution, the millennium that did not come. They ask how good men should live in a world dominated by the powers of evil."[29] The poem ends while Adam and Eve continue to move toward a world riddled with opportunity for the sort of moral and political transgression that Milton witnessed in 1660, and when Milton publishes *Paradise Lost* in 1667, England continues under Charles II's rule. The English people crept away from their former happy state, separated from both Eden and the Commonwealth, and while Milton does not disqualify them from regaining a paradise of sorts, the way is hardly as ready or easy as it might have been within the garden—before humankind became "long wanderd."

Notes

1. I am sincerely grateful for the insight and support of Marissa Greenberg, Rachel Trubowitz, and John Rumrich throughout the composition of this chapter: thank you all for your generosity, curiosity, and steadfast encouragement.

2. While "wandring" and "happie State" appear multiple times within *Paradise Lost*, for the purposes of this chapter, the meaning of "wandring" and "happie State" are best distilled in the citations I use above in *PL*, 9.1136 and 8.331, respectively.

3. In *Second Defense* Milton hints at his poetic pursuits prior to his political involvement: "since I had asked myself whether I should be of any future use if I now failed my country . . . I decided, although at this time occupied with certain other matters, to devote to this conflict all my talents and all my active powers" (*CPEP*, 1093–94).

4. Merritt Y. Hughes provides a detailed example of comparisons between Satan and political figures in "Satan and the 'Myth' of the Tyrant," in *Ten Perspectives on Milton* (New Haven: Yale University Press, 1965), 165–95. For an example of the poem's larger implications in conversation with political context, consult Barbara Lewalski, *Life of John Milton: A Critical Biography*, rev. ed. (Oxford: Blackwell, 2003): "Into *Paradise Lost* Milton poured all that he had learned, experienced, desired, and imagined about life, love, artistic creativity, theology, work, history, and politics. His political disappointments did not lead him, as is sometimes supposed, to retreat to a spiritual realm, a 'paradise within'" (442).

5. Christopher Hill, *Milton and the English Revolution* (London: Faber and Faber, 1977), 356.

6. John Coffey affirms that the poet "escaped execution or incarceration partly because [he] had Anglican admirers who appreciated Milton's literary genius"; Coffey, "Pacifist Quietist, or Patient Militant? John Milton and the Restoration," *Milton Studies* 42 (2002): 151.

7. Robert Thomas Fallon, *Divided Empire: Milton's Political Imagery* (Pennsylvania: Penn State University Press, 1995).

8. David Loewenstein, "Writing Epic in the Aftermath of Civil War: *Paradise Lost*, the *Aeneid*, and the Politics of Contemporary History," *Milton Studies* 59 (2017): 165–98.

9. Cf. David Quint, *Epic and Empire: Politics and Generic Form from Virgil to Milton* (Princeton, NJ: Princeton University Press, 1993), for an extended discussion on *Paradise Lost* and *Paradise Regained* within the classical tradition.

10. Lewalski, *Life*, 443, 442.

11. Sharon Achinstein, *Milton and the Revolutionary Reader* (Princeton, NJ: Princeton University Press, 2014), 178.

12. Achinstein, *Milton and the Revolutionary Reader*, 181.

13. Nicholas Von Maltzahn, "The First Reception of *Paradise Lost* (1667)," *Review of English Studies* 47, no. 188 (1996): 494.

14. Von Maltzahn, "First Reception of Paradise Lost (1667)," 494.

15. Hill, *Milton and the English Revolution*, 365. Achinstein also argues that literature produced in the wake of the English Revolution was not intended to be devoid of politics (*Milton and the Revolutionary Reader*, 225).

16. Thomas H. Luxon, introduction to *The Tenure of Kings and Magistrates* (*JMRR*).

17. Ryan Hackenbracht expands on the demonic nature of creeping, showing the movement to be indicative of Satan's and the other fallen angels' self-deception, in "Milton on the Move: Walking and Self-Knowledge in *Paradise Lost*," in *Milton, Materialism, and Embodiment: "One First Matter All,"* ed. Kevin J. Donovan and Thomas Festa (Pittsburgh: Duquesne University Press, 2017), 59–80.

18. For example, "Errours den" in "the wandring wood," in Edmund Spenser, *The Faerie Queene*, ed. A.C. Hamilton (New York: Pearson Longman, 2007), 1.1.13.

19. While not a strictly political tract, Milton's *The Doctrine and Discipline of Divorce* (1643) includes another notable instance of wandering. An unhappy marriage, Milton warns, will predispose an individual to nefarious movement; indeed, "it drives many to transgresse the conjugall bed, while the soule wanders after that satisfaction which it had hope to find at home, but hath mis't."

20. As William Kerrigan, John Rumrich, and Stephen M. Fallon observe in their introduction to *The Ready and Easy Way*, "Milton was the last republican to put his name to a work opposing monarchy before the Restoration" (*CPEP,* 1112).

21. In chapter 5 of this volume, Achsah Guibbor investigates Milton's attitude toward Jewish readmission to England, further expanding on the idea of a fraught return for Milton.

22. Important to note in this case is the addition of the term "sway," which offers a few notable definitions: "To wield as an emblem of sovereignty or authority" or "to bend or move to one side, or downwards, as by excess of weight or pressure; to incline, lean, swerve" (s.v. "sway, v.8" and s.v. "sway, v.4"; *OED*). This vacillating motion, Milton makes clear, is both sanctioned

and controlled under a rational structure—an election decided by "reason only." Indeed, "no single person" in a functioning commonwealth ought to decide elections—or, simply, sway.

23. For a robust discussion of Milton's usage of "wandering" and its connection to the "fallen meaning," see Christopher Ricks, *Milton's Grand Style* (Oxford: Clarendon Press, 1963), 110.

24. "To traverse (a wide area), often in search or pursuit of something; to wander over or through (a place)" (s.v. "rove, v.2"; *OED*).

25. "Causing or involving trouble or mischief; objectionable, evil; naughty" (s.v. "unhappy, adj.5"; *OED*). In book 1 of *Paradise Lost*, Satan also employs the term "unhappy" to describe the demons' newfound home. Free from the burning lake, Satan considers his comrades who "Lye thus astonisht on th' oblivious Pool, / And call them not to share with us their part / In this unhappy Mansion" (*PL*, 1.266–68).

26. Adam refers to Eve's "wand'ring vanity" (*PL*, 10.875), a further indication of the adjectival nature of wandering after humankind's Fall.

27. On stillness in Milton, consult chapter 1 by John Rumrich in this volume.

28. "state (n.), sense I.i.2.b," and "state (n.), sense III.25," *OED*.

29. Hill, *English Revolution*, 362.

CHAPTER 3

~

Extraterrestrial Eden

The Migration of Paradise in the Early Modern European Imagination

Erin Webster

"Like those *Hesperian* Gardens fam'd of old"

This chapter explores the cultural consequences of the shifting location of Paradise in the European imagination between the time of Columbus's voyages (1492–1504) and the composition of Milton's *Paradise Lost* (1667) as one example of the political and theological dimensions of the seventeenth-century science of motion and the astronomical discoveries involved in and supported by it. More particularly, I argue that this science impacted early modern Europeans' understanding of the movement of various politically and theologically defined bodies through time and space, including that of the extraterrestrial realm. Parsing the logic behind the cartographical migration of Paradise from East to West and, from here, to the as yet undiscovered "new worlds" of outer space enables us to see how early modern Europeans mapped global cultural relations in both geographical and temporal terms, positioning themselves as the vanguard of a progressive, outward- and upward-oriented future. My argument thus extends Johannes Fabian's insightful work on the way in which Western science has historically used the connection between time and space to position non-Western societies as both geographically distant and historically antecedent to their own (whether they be "primitive," "traditional," or "developing").[1] My goal in this chapter is to determine what happens to Fabian's two-dimensional grid of global cultural relations when we add a third dimension by extending the map upward to include extraterrestrial locations, as happened in the seventeenth century with Galileo's (and others') contention that the heavens could be included in the realm of inhabitable space.

On the face of things, the question of the location of Paradise might not seem to be the most natural place to look when tracing the impact of Galileo's astronomical discoveries on global cultural relations. But Paradise and the heavens were connected in the minds of many seventeenth-century thinkers as places located outside the limits of human inhabitancy in both temporal and spatial terms, for both theological and physical reasons. At the same time, their inaccessible nature made them all the more enticing to many would-be explorers, imaginative and actual. Indeed, the question of Paradise's location was one involved in European exploration projects from at least the time of Columbus and on through the seventeenth century. Whereas medieval *mappae mundi* had conventionally located Paradise within the geographical and symbolic East, walled off from the inhabited/inhabitable world, Columbus's claim that he had seen "great indications of the earthly paradise" in the New World helped to bring the Americas and their inhabitants into a Christianized European worldview while also initiating a migration of Paradise from East to West, from Asia to the Americas, in Europeans' cartographic imaginations.[2] But by the time that Milton writes *Paradise Lost* in the mid-seventeenth century, Columbus's discovery had been superseded by further exploration projects, including Galileo's telescopic observations of what he described as an earthlike moon, complete with lakes and mountains.[3] Galileo's discoveries fueled considerable speculation as to the existence of other possible new worlds scattered throughout the heavens, while also offering up extraterrestrial space as a potential location for Paradise, or at least some version thereof. The writer Francis Godwin, for instance, imagines the Moon to be "another Paradise" inhabited by a sinless lunar race in his fictional story, *The Man in the Moone* (1638), while Cyrano de Bergerac makes it into the actual location of Eden in his *Comic History of the States and Empires of the Moon* (1657).[4] On the nonfiction side of things, Bishop John Wilkins includes a lengthy summary of classical and Christian scholarship on the possibility of a lunar Paradise in *The Discovery of a New World in the Moone* (1638), and while he himself refuses to stake a solid claim as to whether there are in fact other beings living there, he points us toward an affirmative answer when closing with the prediction that "our posterity, perhaps, may invent some meanes for our better acquaintance with these inhabitants."[5] It is this conversation—and others like it—that Milton alludes to when he describes Satan's interstellar flight among the "innumerable Starrs" that "nigh hand seemd other Worlds, / . . . or happy Iles, / Like those *Hesperian* Gardens fam'd of old" (*PL,* 3.565–68), as well as when he has Adam and Raphael discuss the possibility of "other Worlds" in space, "what Creatures there / Live, [and] in what state, condition or degree" they do so (*PL,* 8.175–76).[6]

While focused on outer space, conversations such as Adam and Raphael's tell us more about Milton's geocultural views than they do about his thoughts on extraterrestrial beings, particularly his views pertaining to the inhabitants of the previous paradisal New World of the Americas whose status has now been superseded by the promise of future, as yet to be discovered new worlds in space. In the following I will argue that Galileo's description of an earthlike Moon complicated early modern Europeans' imaginative constructions of the Americas as a kind of earthly Paradise by adding a new reference point against which to measure both their own civilization and those of the Americas, one that had not previously been visible on Europeans' mental maps of the universe. As we will see, one of the results of Galileo's discoveries was to introduce a vertical axis into what had previously been conceived—and still is in most scholarship on the subject—as a lateral, or East-West, relationship between the Old and the New World. The consequences of this introduction, I contend, can be seen in the more particular case of the shifting location of Paradise from a terrestrial to an extraterrestrial location over the course of the theological-historical narrative of human history related by *Paradise Lost*'s narrator and in the impact of this shift in location on Milton's depiction of global cultural relations. With significance to the concerns of this volume, I argue that the migration of Paradise from Asia to the Americas and, from there, to extraterrestrial space, can be read in relation to the changing perception of the status of its inhabitants—past, current, and future—within a Christianized understanding of the universe. At the same time, I posit that Paradise's cartographical migration takes place alongside and within related shifts in the science of motion that emphasize continuity and progression over discretion and stasis. Thus Galileo's astronomical discoveries do not simply change the content of early modern Europeans' mental maps but also alter their readers' understanding of how the bodies—and people—imagined to populate these maps relate to one another in space-time.[7]

Accounting for these differences from the perspective of a modern-day reader, David Woodward has argued that medieval *mappae mundi* are "the cartographical equivalent of narrative medieval pictures," in

74 Extraterrestrial Eden

which, rather than appearing "in sequence, as in a frieze or cartoon . . . the chief characters reappear in a static landscape to express the dimension of time."[8] By contrast, the equally narrative maps described in *Paradise Lost* are notable for their motion; the poem's "chief characters" move through them with ease, often altering them in the process, as when the "boiling Gulf" of Chaos "Tamely endur[es] a Bridge of wondrous length" to be built across it in the wake of Satan's passage so as to allow for smooth and continuous transit between Earth and Hell (*PL,* 2.1027–28). This latter, dynamic kind of map is in keeping with the principles of the new seventeenth-century science of motion and applies to the inhabitants of Milton's universe as much as it does to all other physical bodies within it, as Raphael explains to Adam in book 5's lecture on the ability of all matter to "ten[d]" either upward or downward in relation to the Almighty (*PL,* 5.476). It is for this reason that it is all the more significant that of Earth's inhabitants identified in *Paradise Lost,* there is one in particular—the figure of the American—who does remain static, presented to us in a frieze, as it were, rather than as part of the motion-driven cartography that comprises the majority of the poem's narrative.

Postcolonial readings of Milton's epic by John Martin Evans and others have considered the parallels between Eden and the Americas and between Adam and Eve and the figure of the American to whom Milton compares the couple immediately post-Fall.[9] But I posit that we can gain a fuller understanding of Milton's views on this subject by recognizing that Eden and the Americas (and, with this, post-Fall Eden as the Americas) are complemented within the universe of *Paradise Lost* by the other potentially unfallen Paradises of extraterrestrial space hinted at within the poem. Where Raphael suggests that Adam's progeny might one day migrate to one of these Paradises, Milton's decision to place the figure of the American in a decidedly earthly, postlapsarian, and temporally stagnant Eden excludes them (the American is significantly ungendered in the poem) from this narrative and, arguably, from the future of humankind as foretold by Milton. By understanding the logic behind the shifting location of Paradise in early modern thought, we gain insight into Milton's decision to place the American here, in the Paradise of the past rather than that of the future. In the process we also learn more about how the seventeenth-century science of motion combined with theology, geography, and politics to redraw the social boundary lines on early modern Europeans' imaginative maps by changing the narratives that gave direction to them.

"That spot to which I point is Paradise"

Alessandro Scafi's detailed history of the search for the earthly Paradise, *Mapping Paradise* (2006), charts the gradual displacement of Eden by actual geographical bodies on European world maps during the period of European exploration and colonization, positing that "as new regions were included on the maps, so some of the old places, such as the earthly paradise, disappeared entirely."[10] But if we expand our definition of maps to include those present in the literature of the period, thinking of them as narrative as well as visual constructions, the picture is somewhat different. Milton's *Paradise Lost* can be read as a kind of literary *mappa mundi* insofar as it relates both the history and the geography of the world as viewed from the perspective of a Christian narrator—in this case one who incorporates the astronomical discoveries of the seventeenth century into his representation of global geopolitical and theopolitical relations. Understood in this way, Milton's narrative placement of the classical Paradise of the Hesperides within the scope of worlds still to be discovered in space (*PL*, 3.568), coupled with Raphael's suggestion that there may be other planets whose inhabitants exist in a different "state, condition, or degree" (*PL*, 8.176) than does Adam—or, for that matter, than do we fallen humans—suggests that in fact Paradise might not have disappeared so much as moved upward and outward. As illustrated in Scafi's study, medieval *mappae mundi* tended to place the earthly Paradise in the extreme East, or top of the map, walled off by mountains, water, or flames so as to mark its status as both theologically and geographically inaccessible to fallen humans (see, e.g., figs 3.1, 3.2, and 3.3).[11] But this placement—and the symbolic inaccessibility it is designed to express—begins to give way during the age of European exploration, first to western locations in Africa and the Americas and, later, to extraterrestrial locations on the Moon and other planets that made up the next projected phase of discovery for many European thinkers.[12] Of significance to this shift is not only that Paradise migrates westward and outward along the same trajectory as Europe's geographical exploration and colonization projects but also that it shifts from being a land inhabited and inhabitable only in the past to a land both inhabited and inhabitable in the present and—in the case of the extraterrestrial Paradise—inhabited and inhabitable in the future as well.

Fig. 3.1. Psalter *Mappa Mundi*, or London Psalterkarte (ca. 1265), authorship unknown. Wikimedia Commons.

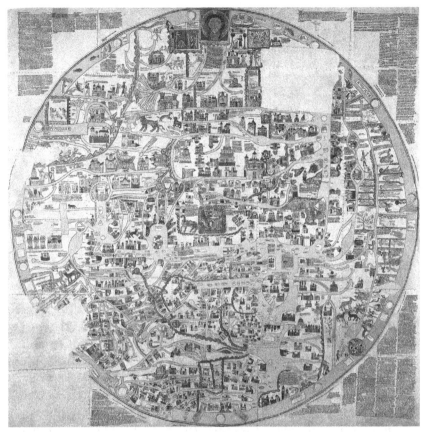

Fig. 3.2. *Mappa Mundi* (ca. 1235), attributed to Gervase of Ebstorf. Wikimedia Commons.

Fig. 3.3. Detail of Eden from the Ebstorf *Mappa Mundi* (ca. 1235).

The early stages of this geographical and temporal shift can be seen in Columbus's descriptions of the Americas from his initial voyages. Believing himself to have reached the easternmost edge of Asia, and responding to what he felt was a striking parallel between the geography at the mouth of the Orinoco River and the description of Eden in Genesis, Columbus speculated in his letters home that Earth was in fact shaped like a pear, and that the land he had discovered was the *pézon*, or stalk, in which Paradise was located.[13] On the one hand, we can see in this description an implicit reference to the structure of the medieval T and O maps that Scafi's study details, with their conventional placement of Eden in the extreme East, protruding from the pear-shaped body of the continents with Asia at the top and Europe and Africa rounding out the bottom. Yet at the same time, Columbus's description brings his newly discovered Eden out of an inaccessible biblical past and into the livable present. Even as he maintains that the site itself remains physically inaccessible except "by God's permission," located as he imagines it on the summit of a great mountain from which the waters of the Orinoco flow, the very fact that these waters do flow from it into the surrounding territory speaks to its connectedness to the present moment.[14]

We can see this temporal shift playing out more directly in Columbus's account of the Arawak peoples who live in the surrounding areas. Described as lacking in iron tools and going "naked as they came into the world," Columbus's Arawak resemble figures drawn from the classical golden age as well as Adam and Eve in their prelapsarian state.[15] And yet the fact that the Arawak continue to live this way well into the Iron Age and long after Adam and Eve's expulsion from the garden into the progressive history of human sin and salvation marks them out as distinct from their analogical counterparts, just as their geographically connected Eden differs from the walled garden of the medieval *mappae mundi*.[16]

Columbus's identification of the Americas with Eden spurred a westward geographical and temporal migration of Paradise within the early modern European imagination that had in fact already begun before his voyages. By the sixteenth century, references to the Americas as Eden or as another kind of earthly Paradise became a commonplace of European travel literature. In addition to promoting a view of the Americas as a virginal or innocent land, one of the effects of this migration was that it moved the ideological location of Paradise from the edge of what had once been known and lost to the edge of what might yet be known and discovered (or, potentially, recovered). Another was that it opened up the troubling possibility that, for some humans, Paradise had never been lost at all. For his part, Scafi cautions readers against taking literally the many references to the Americas as Eden with which Renaissance travel literature is "peppered," insisting that "it has to be asked whether Christopher Columbus or any other Renaissance explorer really intended to, or thought they could, discover the location of Eden and recapture for mankind the lost paradise of delights."[17] While Scafi answers this question in the negative and instead directs his study toward subsequent attempts to locate the geographical location of Eden in the Middle East, I read the figurative connection between the Americas and Eden as opening a whole new line of thought on the subject of the earthly Paradise that now had to confront the possibility that this Paradise was not only accessible to humans but also inhabited by some of them—a concern that becomes all the more acute when extended to include extraterrestrial Paradises as well.

Importantly, this concern was theological and cultural as well as economic and political. The realization that there existed on the other side of the Atlantic peoples unaccounted for in either classical or Christian texts challenged not only what Anthony Pagden refers to as the "Christian myth of a single progenitor of all [hu]mankind" in Adam but also "the singular narrative of Christian salvation."[18] For if these peoples did not derive genealogically from Adam, then it was possible that they did not fall with him either and thus (for better or for worse) had not been and indeed did not need to be redeemed through Christ. Identifying the Americas as another earthly Paradise—if not in fact the actual biblical Eden—offered Christian Europeans a means of addressing this concern. At the same time, it forced them to confront the issue of their own singularity as God's chosen people. As David Cressy notes, the questions that seventeenth-century Europeans were asking about the potential inhabitants of other planets—"whether they too were the seed of Adam, and whether they were covered by Christ's atonement"—were very much the same ones that sixteenth-century Europeans were asking about the actual inhabitants of the Americas.[19]

In the case of the Americas, the writers who grappled with these questions tended to rely on temporal and geographical manipulation to place the Indigenous inhabitants outside of the progression of Christian history. In *Milton's Imperial Epic* (1996) Evans outlines three major strands in the debate surrounding the genealogical origins and soteriological status of the Indigenous peoples of the Americas in early modern European discourse, all of which take their root in a Christianized reading of Genesis, adapted to account for the geographical and cultural distance between the American Eden and its biblical counterpart. Some, such as Paracelsus, felt that the inhabitants of the Americas were "descended from another Adam," raising the possibility that "in the newly discovered world across the Atlantic the forbidden fruit had remained untasted" and the peoples were thus left "living in a state of unfallen innocence."[20] Others countered this view by "denying the . . . humanity" of the Indigenous peoples altogether, a denial bolstered by the idea that neither Adam's descendants nor the first generations of the apostles could have traversed the world's oceans, leaving those who lived in the lands on the other side of them outside the fold of God's special care.[21] A third alternative was to view the Indigenous peoples of the Americas as one of the lost tribes of Israel or, alternatively, as genealogically descended from the line of Cain and thus the inheritors of a second "grevious and fearfull curse" laid upon them as a result of the "sinnes of their Ancestors."[22] In this view, as Evans explains, "the inhabitants of America were . . . doubly handicapped, . . . further corrupted by a second Fall which, together with their geographical isolation [from Christian Europe], cut them off completely from the knowledge of God."[23]

Galileo's observations of the Moon altered these readings by introducing an additional reference point to the relationship between Europe and the Americas, the Americas and Eden. Regularly hailed as the next Columbus, Galileo seemed to many to be ushering in a new stage in European exploration as well as in the progression of human history more generally by expanding the search for additional new worlds beyond Earth's sphere.[24] At the same time, his experiments with motion, coupled with his astronomical observations, argued in favor of a relationship of continuity between Earth and the heavens that would make such travel possible. In his early response to Galileo's findings, for instance, Johannes Kepler excitedly proclaims that "as soon as somebody demonstrates the art of flying, settlers from our species of man will not be lacking" and offers up his own services to "establish the astronomy" of the Moon in advance of its settlement.[25] Wilkins does much the same, closing out his proposition that it is likely that there is an inhabited world in the Moon with the prediction that while "wee have not now any *Drake* or *Columbus* to undertake [a] voyage [there], or any *Dædelas* to invent a conveyance through the aire . . . the industry of future times assisted with the labours of their forefathers, may reach unto that height which wee could not attain to."[26] John Donne too posits a connection between the Moon and the Americas, albeit an ironic one, when in his satirical anti-Jesuit tract *Ignatius His Conclave* (1611) a jealous Lucifer sends Ignatius off to establish a colony on the Moon from which the Jesuits can work to "reconcile the *Lunatique Church* to the *Romane Church*," given that they had such success doing the same in their missionary activities in the New World.[27] Thus what Evans says about the New World of the Americas—that its "discovery" was for early modern Europeans "tantamount to the discovery of another planet"—was also true on the inverse: if Galileo was correct and the wandering stars were earthlike in nature, then on each planet there lay a potential America.[28]

But these potential Americas differed from their terrestrial counterpart in important ways, many of which have to do with their spatiotemporal location within an early modern Christianized understanding of cultural relations. Significantly, the possibility that there existed other "Americas" in extraterrestrial space put pressure on all three of the arguments accounting for their inhabitants' soteriological status as either unfallen, inhuman, or geographically and morally lost. While these explanations served effectively to preserve both the doctrine of universal descent and the privileged position of Christian Europeans within redemptive history when applied to the peoples of the Americas, they did not translate easily into an account of the genealogical origins of the similarly extrabiblical inhabitants of the astronomical new worlds. After all, it was one thing to try to account for the migration of humans across an ocean but quite another to account for their migration through space. Moreover, while there existed in the cartographical model of the T and O maps a historical precedent for the idea that, like the sun, the course of history and of civilization "moves inexorably from East to West," so that America could be viewed as historically younger than Europe and Asia, no such precedent existed for the relationship between Earth and the wandering stars.[29] Indeed, quite the opposite was true; thought to be closer to God and the angels' heavenly habitation, these celestial new worlds provided their inhabitants a home that was at once spatially and morally more proximate to the Creator than that offered to Christian Europeans by the humble Earth. This proximate location presented real problems, as Kepler points out when he worries that "some might say, if there are globes in the heaven similar to our earth, do we vie with them over who occupies the better portion of the universe? For if their globes are nobler, we are not the noblest of rational creatures. Then how can all things be for man's sake? How can we be the masters of God's handiwork?"[30]

Attempts to address these concerns play out in both the literature and the cartography of the period as European thinkers attempted to expand and project their authority into extraterrestrial space. By the mid-seventeenth century, Kepler's excited request to Galileo that the two of them work side by side to "establish the astronomy" of the Moon "for the sake of those who, as it were, will presently be on hand to attempt this voyage" had eagerly been taken up by others.[31] Indeed, the process had begun even prior to Galileo's observations. Sometime in the mid-1590s, the English physician William Gilbert began work on a naked-eye lunar map in which he brought the Moon into the territory of earthly cartography by giving its various dark and light areas decidedly geographical names such as the Regio Magna Occidentalis (Great Western Continent), Cape Longum (Long Cape), and Mare Medilunarium (Middle Lunar Sea). As Scott Montgomery points out, these terms are borrowed from the Ptolemaic tradition of mapmaking and at the time "were still very much in use for various portions of the globe, especially those distant from Europe."[32] More telling with respect to the question of competition over relative position and status, however, is Gilbert's decision to label one of the Moon's "islands" after his own home nation of Britannia—an imperial term that, Montgomery notes, "planted a claim on the Moon and implied that England, the new naval power of Europe, might one day send ships of a different kind to these distant seas and lands."[33]

Subsequent selenographers followed suit. The Dutch cosmographer Michael Florent Van Langren labeled his seventeenth-century lunar map with the names of Catholic saints and Catholic royalty from whom he hoped to find favor.[34] His competitor Johannes Hevelius's scheme is even more direct, if less explicitly nationalistic. Having "found to [his] perfect delight that a certain part of the terrestrial globe"—that is, "that part of Europe, Asia, and Africa that surrounds the Mediterranean Sea, Black Sea, and Caspian Sea, and all the other regions including and adjacent to them"—is "very comparable with the visible face of the Moon and its regions," Hevelius simply elects to label his map so that "the lunar spaces agree with the terrestrial ones."[35] Thus we are given a lunar Mediterranean, Adriatic, Black, and Caspian sea; a lunar Malta, Sardinia, Sicily, and Crete; lunar Atlas, Taurus, and Caucasus mountains—even a lunar Athens and Byzantium.[36] The only thing missing, it would seem, is a lunar America, although perhaps we are to imagine that it occupies the Moon's antipodean dark side.

Read against the cartographical tradition we have been tracing above, the geographically inspired selenographies of the seventeenth century can give us a sense of how the East-West relationship between the Old and New World was changing so as to include an up-down orientation as well. I suggest that recognizing this additional, vertical axis can help us better to understand the complexity of the seventeenth-century European mindset toward exploration and colonization as one that involved more than a unilateral, westward-oriented drive toward political and economic conquest. By the mid-seventeenth century, Europeans' imaginative colonization plans had expanded to include any number of other new worlds in extraterrestrial space, and, with this, new concerns over their own relative status within a rapidly expanding universe in which they potentially stood to compete not only with each other but also with other, extraplanetary civilizations for theological and political precedence. I contend that one of the ways in which Europeans responded to these pressures was to project the location of Paradise into extraterrestrial space while simultaneously identifying it as a place that could be discovered and inhabited by subsequent generations, much as the Edenic Americas had been in the century before. If Columbus's description of the Americas as Eden had brought Paradise into the present, this next phase of migration would bring it into the future—a future that implicitly and significantly included only an exclusive subset of humanity as suitable for settlement.

As the above examples indicate, the central point from which this new axis between the Old and New Worlds extends continues to be Europe, mirrored back on itself from the heavens, rather than Earth as a whole. If both medieval T and O maps and early modern projection maps operate according to the logic of a spatiotemporal scheme in which Europe occupies the space of the present, seventeenth-century selenographies imagine a future in which Europe and its inhabitants have moved upward as well as outward, replicating its geographical colonization projects on the lands and waters of the Moon. The course of civilization, having reached its zenith in the once western, now central, European continent, is envisioned as breaking free from its Earth-bound progression and expanding into the heavens. But with what parts left behind? Hevelius's America-less Moon brings us back to the question with which I began about the relationship between the Moon and the Americas in the early modern European colonial imagination. If America is conspicuously absent from Hevelius's antichthon map, then where, we might ask, has it gone? What space does it occupy in the new three-dimensional space of Europeans' mental maps of the world? Equally important, what space do its inhabitants occupy, and how do thinkers such as Milton draw and redraw the boundaries between the world's various peoples in line with these future-oriented projections of the progression of human history?

These are of course big questions, and ones that I cannot hope fully to answer in the scope of the current chapter. As an entry point into that larger exploration, however, I want to turn now to Milton's treatment of the subject as worked out through the cosmology of *Paradise Lost*. Arguably the first post-Galilean epic in the European literary tradition, *Paradise Lost* provides us with an example of the Americas' displacement by the Moon as the newest of the New Worlds in the European imagination when Milton has Adam and Raphael actively engage in debate over the Moon's potential inhabitancy during book 8's astronomical dialogue. At the same time, the poem's purportedly universal spatial and temporal scope, coupled with the narrator's general investment in relating God's providential design to his audience, locates *Paradise Lost* within the cartographical tradition that I have been tracing above and makes it a logical place to begin this discussion.

"Such of late Columbus found th' American"

In a 2017 *Milton Studies* volume on Milton's relationship to the Americas, Elizabeth Sauer comments pointedly that "scholars venturing into the territory of Milton in the Americas readily discover that there is no conspicuous New World orientation in Milton, John Martin Evans's influential argument in *Milton's Imperial Epic* notwithstanding."[37] But this is only true if we understand the idea of the New World to be entirely synonymous with the Americas. As Evans's study shows, *Paradise Lost* is rife with references to the New World, it is just that these references tend more often to be oriented toward the various potential new worlds of extraterrestrial space rather than that which has already been discovered in the Americas. Indeed, as early as the poem's first book we are alerted to the fact that the question is no longer whether time will reveal further new worlds on the terrestrial Earth but, rather, whether "space may produce" (*PL*, 1.640) them (or, less heretically, whether God might produce them in space). This is not to say that one kind of new world has simply replaced the other. On the contrary, as Sauer herself notes, by Milton's time, the imaginative scope of Europe's Age of Exploration had expanded to include these extraterrestrial new worlds alongside the remaining earthly terra incognita in a more general picture of what remained to be discovered and, potentially, conquered or colonized, by the various European powers.[38] The incorporation of the extraterrestrial into Europe's imperial aspirations lends credence to Evans's argument that Milton has the European conquest of the Americas in mind when dramatizing Satan's attempted conquest of other potential new worlds in space, Eden most particular among them. Nevertheless, I contend that Evans makes the mistake—and it is not his alone—of conflating the new extraterrestrial new worlds of the seventeenth century with their imaginative precedent of the Americas. Tellingly, when listing off the "four figures from recent history named in the poem," Evans claims that, of these figures, "three were inseparably connected with the colonial enterprise—Columbus ([*PL*,] 9.116), Montezuma ([*PL*,] 11.407), and Atabalipa ([*PL*,] 11.409)."[39] The unnamed fourth figure here—and the only one who is Milton's actual contemporary—is presumably Galileo, the so-called new Columbus and the very same man who, if his apologists were to be believed, would eventually be credited with extending Europe's colonial enterprise to the Moon and beyond. By leaving Galileo and his discoveries out of the story of *Paradise Lost*'s imperial investments, Evans's reading both too readily and too neatly associates Eden directly with the New World of the Americas, at the expense of considering how both terms have migrated from a solely terrestrial present to a potentially extraterrestrial future location in the time between Columbus's voyages and Milton's poem. As a result, he also risks overlooking how the Americas themselves have been changed in the seventeenth-century colonial imagination by the possible existence of additional new worlds—and new Edens—in extraterrestrial space.

So what would it look like if we were to add Galileo and his new lunar world to the picture of *Paradise Lost*'s imperial investments? Sauer is quite right about the relative paucity of references to the Americas themselves in *Paradise Lost*. In fact, they occur in only a couple of places. The first comes at the moment of Adam and Eve's fall, when the pair are compared via simile to "th' American so girt / With feathered cincture, naked else and wild," that Columbus found "of late . . . / Among the trees on isles and woody shores" of South and Central America (*PL*, 9.1115–18). The second occurs during the cartographical catalog of the world's great empires revealed to Adam by Michael as he surveys Earth from the top of Eden's highest mountain on the brink of his own departure from the garden (*PL*, 11.406–11). Of these references, the first has received the most sustained critical analysis in terms of Milton's views toward the Americas and the peoples thereof. Evans, as I noted above, reads the simile as making explicit a connection between Adam and Eve and the inhabitants of the Americas that the poem has established from its very beginning: "As the first human occupants of the New World in *Paradise Lost*, Adam and Eve are the most obvious counterparts of the [American] Indians."[40] At the same time, however, he sees the instance of the Fall as marking a shift in terms of what kind of New World "Indians" Adam and Eve resemble. Prior to their lapse, Adam and Eve are for Evans reminiscent of the innocent, childlike, and fundamentally teachable Amerindians described by the Franciscan missionary Bartolomé de las Casas in his *A Short Account of the Destruction of the Indies* (1552); just as the Amerindians, through patient instruction, could "become fully developed members of the civilized Christian community," so too can "the natives of Eden . . . one day become indistinguishable from God's colonial emissary [Raphael] as the colony itself is absorbed into the homeland [of heaven]." After the Fall, however, Adam and Eve "degenerate" into the kind of Indians envisioned by de las Casas's adversary in the Valladoid debates, Juan Ginés de Sepúlveda, who portrayed the Amerindians as animalistic beings, lacking in rationality and unable to control their passions, along the lines of Aristotle's category of the natural slave.[41] By choosing to depict "th' American" as imperfectly clothed "With feathered cincture," Evan argues, Milton not only makes clear that he "did not subscribe to the theory that the recently discovered inhabitants of the New World were exempt from the effects of the Fall" but also implies that "the condition into which Adam and Eve fell through their disobedience is the condition in which the natives of [the Americas], untouched by European civilization, still exist."[42]

Or at least still exist*ed*, up to the point that the simile itself re-creates. In gazing on and identifying the figure of the American (itself a term derived from Columbus's contemporary, Amerigo Vespucci, and anachronistically applied here by Milton) with the figures of Adam and Eve, Milton's Columbus does not leave them "untouched" but, rather, incorporates them into European civilization on (and in) its own terms. Indeed, Milton is roughly echoing history here. As discussed above, Columbus was the first European to identify the Americas with Eden, and his description helped to bring the Americas into Christianized Europeans' worldview while also contributing to the migration of Eden from East to West, Asia to America, on early modern Europeans' imaginative maps. But by the time that Milton writes *Paradise Lost*, Columbus's discovery is already nearly two hundred years out of date—or "of late," as the narrator puts it (*PL*, 9.1115).

This temporal marking is important. In fact, I would go so far as to argue that the 150-year gap between Milton and Columbus is precisely why Milton finds it necessary to include Columbus in the simile in the first place, rather than simply stating that Adam and Eve are like the feather-cinctured American, regardless of by whom and in what moment the American is found. Sauer argues that, in stressing the "belatedness" of Columbus's discovery, Milton "locates the Spanish explorer and the Americans in a postlapsarian historical timeframe," while at the same time differentiating the Americas, found "of late"—or, recently—by Columbus, from the parts of the world known to the Ancients.[43] But I would also add to her assessment the related idea that, by including Columbus in the simile, Milton tags the figure of the American with a particular location in time and space that is not only postlapsarian and postclassical but also antecedent to the narrator's own. In other words, he tags the body of the American with a specific location in both theological and historical space and time that is separate from and relative to that of his own seventeenth-century readers as they themselves move through the poem's narrative. The American as found by Columbus in 1492 may very well have looked to Columbus like an immediately postlapsarian Adam and Eve, but this does not necessarily mean that they look this way to the narrator, or to the narrator's seventeenth-century European audience.

Locating Milton's treatment of the figure of the American alongside the other instances of contorted temporal distancing that she finds in early modern depictions of the Indigenous inhabitants of the Americas, Mary Nyquist has written perceptively about how the "perspectivally mobile temporalities" of this scene work to position the figure of the

American outside of the poem's "increasingly linear narratives" so as to create both temporal and theological distance between Milton's Protestant English readership and the inhabitants of the Americas. By juxtaposing Adam and Eve's inward-oriented "psycho-spiritual nakedness" with the American's "literal unclothedness," Milton's simile, in her view, ultimately serves to differentiate the two rather than to unite them, as is confirmed when the Son replaces Adam and Eve's "inept self-covering" with a more proper means of clothing themselves. The American, meanwhile, remains stuck in their description as "naked," despite their feathered cincture.[44] Thus, Adam and Eve, along with their Protestant European progeny, enter into a progressive, ultimately redemptive, view of history while the American, by contrast, fails to develop along these same lines even as time continues to pass for them. Put in the terms of the science I have been discussing, we might alternatively say that the body of the American in the poem is not in motion in the way characteristic of the poem's other characters, such as Adam and Eve or even the angels as they traverse God's universe for purposes ranging from protection and maintenance to curiosity. (Satan, as a special exception and test case of sorts, is perhaps the poem's most mobile character even as his spiritual and physical status tends continually toward Hell [PL, 4.75] regardless of his spatial and temporal orientation.) Reading the figure of the American with an awareness of their unique placement in the poem's narrative space-time adds important nuance to Evans's claim that Milton's Adam and Eve map neatly onto conventional sixteenth-century depictions of the Indigenous peoples of the Americas. Enough time has elapsed between Columbus's identification of the Americas with Eden and Milton's own period to challenge the claim that one might find an actual Eden there; indeed, the partially clothed and thus fully fallen figure of the American suggests quite the opposite. Nevertheless, I feel that we can productively extend Nyquist's analysis by considering where the additional coordinate points of the poem's other new worlds come into play when plotting the position of Milton's imagined audience in relation to their various cultural others. By associating the Americas with Eden, even if only to undercut its paradisal associations in favor of its postlapsarian ones, Milton brings them into a distinctly Eurocentric, Christianized conception of time and space. At the same time, as I have been arguing, this conception has itself been altered by Milton's time period to include the heavens as part of the inhabited (and inhabitable) world.

Understood in this context, Nyquist's cogent claim that, in Milton's view, "'right reason' is the privileged product of European

Christendom's civilizing process, . . . restoring [in some] to a degree the unblemished divinity their Fall has marred [while] leaving others, such as the American, only partly clad and fully precivil," invites the question of where this civilizing process is headed and whether there might in fact be *other* others elsewhere in God's created universe, inhabiting spatiotemporal positions more advanced than European Christendom. In fact, this is the very question that Raphael cautions Adam against asking merely one book earlier, at the end of their discussion over the possibility not only that the Moon might be inhabited but also that "other Suns perhaps / With thir attendant Moons" might likewise be engaged in an animating exchange of light for the benefit of the "some that live" on their soil (*PL*, 8.144–52). While Raphael acknowledges that the question of the other inhabited worlds is open to debate, he nevertheless counsels Adam to "Sollicit not thy thoughts with matters hid," leaving it up to God to place his other creations wherever—or whenever—he sees fit (*PL*, 8.166):

> Dream not of other Worlds, what Creatures there
> Live, in what state, condition or degree,
> Contented that thus farr hath been reveal'd,
> Not of Earth only but of highest Heav'n. (*PL*, 8.175–78)

Significantly, the questions that Raphael tells Adam not to ask of these otherworldly creatures are the very same questions that Evans and Nyquist see Milton himself answering with respect to the Indigenous inhabitants of the Americas. Their "state, condition [and] degree" in relation to Adam's European descendants has already been established, it would seem, by the point in time inhabited by the poem's narrator. By implicit contrast to the (fallen) American, the soteriological status of the potential inhabitants of Milton's extraterrestrial "other worlds"—and, with this, the question of what that status means for early modern Christian Europeans who might no longer be able to consider themselves unique among God's creation—remains unknown, at least for now.

I have written elsewhere about how Raphael's (lack of) concern over the relative "state, condition or degree" in which these imagined extraterrestrial beings live ties into contemporary anxieties over the plurality of worlds debate.[45] At the moment, however, I want to focus more closely on Raphael's suggestively temporal phrase "thus farr," which I feel balances out the American simile's "of late" with a potential future to match its completed past. Raphael's counsel that Adam ought to be "Contented that *thus farr* hath been reveal'd" carries with it the suggestion that, at some point in the future, either Adam or his descendants will go farther, both in time and in space, and, moreover, that the direction of their progress will be upward, toward the "highest Heav'n." Now, this predicted trajectory of progress may be intended to be understood primarily in a spiritual sense—certainly, it is in keeping with Raphael's earlier lecture on the innate tendency for all material things to "ten[d]" upward toward God as they become "more refin'd, more spiritous, and pure" (*PL*, 5.475–76). But given the immediate context, it would seem that Raphael also has in mind a potential future in which God will reveal more of the created universe to Adam or his progeny, including those parts of it located in extraterrestrial space.

Such a reading is bolstered by the fact that the poem is full of teasing references to just such a future. In addition to book 8's astronomical debate, which draws heavily on seventeenth-century astronomical science, allusions to Galileo and his "Optic Tube" (*PL*, 3.590) pop up repeatedly and are often accompanied by references to the Moon's earthlike qualities as described by Galileo in *Sidereus Nuncius* (1610) (*PL*, 1.290–91, 5.261–63, 8.145–49). Indeed, even the description of Satan choosing not to "sta[y . . .] to enquire" (*PL*, 3.571) whether the "innumerable Starrs" (*PL*, 3.565) he passes on his way to Eden might in fact be home to other beings invites the poem's seventeenth-century readers to reflect on their contemporaries who are at the time engaged in that very same act of enquiry:

> Down right into the Worlds first Region [he] throws
> His flight precipitant, and windes with ease
> Through the pure marble Air his oblique way
> Amongst innumerable Starrs, that shon
> Stars distant, but nigh hand seemd other Worlds,
> Or other Worlds they seemd, or happy Iles,
> Like those *Hesperian* Gardens fam'd of old,
> Fortunate Fields, and Groves and flourie Vales,
> Thrice happy Iles, but who dwelt happy there
> He stayd not to enquire . . . (*PL*, 3.562–71)

Anticipating Raphael's speculations about the possibility of other, extraterrestrial worlds, the narrator's suggestively declarative "but who dwelt happy there / He stayd not to enquire" offers readers a carefully couched answer to the questions about "state, condition

[and] degree" that Raphael cautions Adam against asking (and which Satan himself also avoids by skirting these stars altogether). While the status of the worlds themselves might be questionable—thus far, they only "seem" to be worlds—our narrator is at least willing to hedge his bets that, if they are worlds, their inhabitants "dwel[l] happy" within them, untouched by Satan and thus by sin.

I want to argue that this detail about the "happiness" of the imagined extraterrestrial beings is significant when thinking about the relative soteriological status of the figure of the American in the poem, as well as that of Milton's Christian European readership. Put to us in the form of a simile, Milton's comparison of these potential extraterrestrial worlds to the classical paradise of the Hesperian Gardens complements his later simile comparing the Americas to Eden. Deriving from classical mythology, the Hesperides, or "Fortunate Islands," had long been associated—and contrasted—with Eden as an earthly, pagan Paradise, not to be confused with the Christian one, which was no longer accessible to humans.[46] In geographical terms, they were sometimes loosely identified with the Canary Islands or with the British Isles, both thought to be located at the edge of the known world. In other instances, such as the case of the Hereford *Mappa Mundi*, they were located off the southwest coast of Africa, according to the same logic. In addition to marking their quasi-mythical status, placing the Hesperides at the extreme bottom, or western, edge of these maps had the additional advantage of preserving the term's etymological roots in the Greek word *hersperos* (evening), as well as its etymological connection with the English word "west" (*OED*), and thus served to position this earthly Paradise both visually and linguistically at the time-place where the sun sets and civilization reaches its terminal point.

A lover of both ancient Greek and puns, Milton was no doubt aware of the conventional association of the Hesperides with the westernmost edge of the world—an edge that by his time had shifted to the Americas, the very same place that Columbus had identified with Paradise and Milton with an immediately postlapsarian Eden. And yet Milton does not place the Hesperides in the Western Hemisphere, either off the coast of Europe or in the Americas. (In fact, due to the position of the sun, we are shown nothing of what lies on the other side of the "*Atlantic* Seas / Beyond th' *Horizon*"; *PL,* 3.559–60). Rather, having initially invoked the structure of a geometric projection map in the early lines of this description, Milton set this view aside in favor of a new kind of map, one which incorporates the vertical axis I have identified above as being of particular importance to seventeenth-century

European conceptions of the New World. Certainly, the passage begins with Satan assuming an aerial view of Earth and its associated heavenly spheres that spans the easternmost and westernmost points visible to him as well as the "breadth" between Earth's two poles, much as would a conventional geometrical projection map. But this quickly changes as Satan plunges downward through three-dimensional space on his way to Earth's surface, winding his way through the innumerable stars that themselves appear to be additional mappable worlds. In this new map of the universe we find the Hesperides-like islands, not in the West nor even on the edges of the known world, but scattered throughout the heavens, reflecting each other much as does Milton's neatly mirrored—indeed, almost antichthon—syntactical arrangement, "but nigh hand seemd other Worlds, / Or other Worlds they seemd" (*PL*, 3.566–67).

As Milton's map changes to include this third dimension, so too does its spatiotemporal logic. By translating the Hesperides-like "Iles" from the West to the heavens, Milton shifts them away from history's endpoint and toward its future. Their position in extraterrestrial space—a space just beginning to be explored in Milton's own seventeenth century—paradoxically locates them a time-place subsequent to the poem's narratorial present even as it associates them with a classical past. This positioning perhaps becomes more clear if we consider it in relation to the poem's second reference to the Americas, which likewise comes in the form of a map, this time one presented to Adam as he surveys the world outside Eden from the top of its highest peak. Readers of this section often note that Adam has to experience the Americas "in spirit" only, as the Western Hemisphere is physically too far away for him to see it in actuality.[47] The subsequent description makes apparent, however, that the Americas are also at a temporal remove from Adam and—all the more relevant to our current concerns—from the rest of the world. Michael's survey of the world's great empires—its cities "of old or modern Fame" (*PL*, 11.386)—follows the east to west progression of the T and O maps discussed above. The empires of the East head off the list and are described in the past tense:

> . . . from the destind Walls
> Of *Cambalu*, seat of *Cathaian Can*,
>
> . . .
>
> Down to the golden *Chersonese*, or where
> The *Persian* in *Ecbatan sate* . . . (*PL*, 11.387–93, emphasis on "sate" mine)

Erin Webster 93

As we move westward, closer to Europe, time also moves forward:

> . . . *or since*
> In *Hispahan*, or where the *Russian Ksar*
> In *Mosco*, or the Sultan in *Bizance*,
> *Turchestan*-born (*PL*, 11.393–96, emphasis on "or since" mine)

From here we are taken through the contemporary Ethiopian and Ottoman empires of Africa, parts of which are identified (as they were on medieval *mappae mundi*) with legendary sites, such as "*Sofala* thought *Ophir*" (*PL*, 11.400). Yet these empires also are set to give way, as we can see when from "thence" Adam's eye moves on to "*Europe* . . . where *Rome* was to sway / The World" (*PL*, 11.405–6). Straddling what is imagined to be future to Adam but recent past—perhaps even present?—to his seventeenth-century readers, Milton's temporally contorted "was to sway" locates Rome as the center of Christian culture and the terminus of the progress of civilization up to his own time, while also perhaps hinting that Rome as the center of Catholicism represents yet another empire that will one day be eclipsed by the true Christian church.

At this point in the survey, Adam's vision shifts into the hypothetical "in Spirit perhaps he also saw" and, with this, into a possible future that is at the same time suggestive of a more innocent past. The Americas are home to the empires of Montezuma and Atabalipa, both "rich" with gold, and, as such, sites of potential conquest for the European—in this case Spanish—empires of Milton's own day. But they are also home to "yet unspoil'd / *Guiana*, whose great Citie *Geryons* Sons / Call *El Dorado*" (*PL*, 11.407–11). Like "was to sway" before it, the temporally strained syntax of Milton's phrase "yet unspoiled" describes Guiana both as it exists currently and as it will exist at an indeterminate future date. To Adam, perhaps even to Milton, it remains untouched, unmapped—perhaps even precivil when read in contrast with Aztec and Incan empires. But the suggestive presence of "yet" alerts us that this state is temporary. At some point in the future, Guiana *will* be "spoiled," and the ahistorical quality that for the moment allows it to play host to the legendary paradise of El Dorado will give way to its inclusion in the world's temporal and geographical frame, much as the American's sighting by Columbus brings him into Christian history.

Coming back to the description of the Hesperides-like extraterrestrial worlds, we can now see that the narrator's speculations about

94   Extraterrestrial Eden

those who "dwelt happy there" thus locates them at a double remove
from the inhabitants of the Americas, who are both already fallen and
temporally and spiritually antecedent to European Christians. While
Milton does not provide us with much in the way of detail about day-
to-day life in these "fortunate isles," the fact that Satan chooses to
avoid them in favor of Eden hints at their placement in an alternative history in which their equivalent Adam and Eve figures were *not*
tempted and did *not* fall but, rather, continued to exist in a state of
blessedness similar to that which Raphael imagines for Adam in book
5, when he informs him that, eventually:

> Your bodies may at last turn all to Spirit,
> Improv'd by tract of time, and wingd ascend
> Ethereal, as wee, or may at choice
> Here or in Heav'nly Paradises dwell. (*PL*, 5.497–500)

With their "happy" inhabitants and heavenly positions, Milton's Hesperian stars bear a suggestive resemblance to the significantly plural
"Heav'nly Paradises" mentioned here. At the same time, they balance out the images of America as a lost or spoiled paradise, allowing
Milton to present us with a sort of paradisal triptych: America as the
spoiled Eden of the past, Europe as the internal Eden of the present
(whose Protestant inhabitants carry in themselves a "Paradise within
[. . .], happier far"; *PL*, 12.587), and the extraterrestrial new worlds as
the unspoiled Eden of the future to which Adam's (European) descendants might one day aspire.

Interestingly, Raphael's suggestive comments about the potential for
Adam's progeny eventually to expand to fill the many possible unfallen
Edens scattered throughout the heavens have an afterlife in twentieth-
century space exploration. Reporting on the launch on July 16, 1969,
of the Apollo 11 mission, which successfully placed humans on the
Moon for the first time, CBS commentator Heywood Broun commented philosophically:

> Some of us think that the tremendous interest in space travel is,
> in a sense, a search for another Eden—that man has a kind of
> guilt about the world in which he lives and that he has despoiled
> the place where he is, and that perhaps he ought now in his
> maturity to set out to find another place, a place which man
> could go to, leaving behind the rusty cage in which his own mis-
> takes have held him.[48]

Less optimistic than Milton's vision of the "happy Iles," Broun's reflection captures the spirit of a generation that felt their earthly Paradise long since lost, not by their biblical ancestors but by their own actions. Rather than earning their place in the heavens through obedience, they have been forced there as a result of their sins, which have "despoiled" both their own innocence and that of the world. Nevertheless, the temporal logic is eerily similar to that of Milton's poem; in Broun's view it is only "now," in the period of humankind's "maturity," that we have progressed to the spiritual and technological point at which we can leave the earthly Paradise behind in search of other Edens on other planets. As to the question of what creatures we might find there—as well as which ones might be "le[ft] behind" in the "rusty cage" of our lost innocence—Broun follows Raphael's advice in leaving the question unexplored. Yet the connections between his lunar Paradise and those of the seventeenth century give us an indication as to where we might begin to look for answers, as well as alerting us to the cultural and theological assumptions that continue to guide the search for an extraterrestrial Eden.

Notes

1. Johannes Fabian, *Time and the Other: How Anthropology Makes its Object* (New York: Columbia University Press, 1983; 2002), chap. 1, esp. 17–18.

2. Christopher Columbus, quoted in Alessandro Scafi, *Mapping Paradise: A History of Heaven on Earth* (Chicago: University of Chicago Press, 2006), 240–41.

3. References to an "earthlike" moon are numerous in Galileo's text; see Galileo Galilei, *Sidereus Nuncius*, ed. and trans. Albert Van Helden (Chicago: University of Chicago Press, 1989), 36, 40, 41, 42, 43, 47, 49, 53 and 55.

4. Francis Godwin, *The Man in the Moone*, ed. William Poole (Peterborough: Broadview Press, 2009), 114; and Cyrano de Bergerac, *Other Worlds: The Comical History of the States and Empires of the Moon and Sun*, trans. Geoffrey Strachan (London: Oxford University Press, 1965), 15. As Elijah explains to the narrator, Adam, upon eating the fruit and fearing God's wrath, "decided that the moon, your earth, was the only refuge where he might seek shelter from the sanctions of his Creator" (18). The identification of Earth as the Moon's moon sets up one of the *History*'s many ironic inversions of perspective.

5. John Wilkins, *The Discovery of a World in the Moon* (London, 1638), 207, *Early English Books Online*, https://eebo/docview/2248555190/29616684/E2B8A4EB3C24558PQ/3?accountid=15053.

6. Grant McColley identified Wilkins's *Discovery* as one of the principal sources for Milton's dialogue on astronomy in a series of articles on the subject published in the 1930s; see his "Milton's Dialogue on Astronomy: The Principal Immediate Sources," *PMLA* 52, no. 3 (1937): 728–62; "The Astronomy of *Paradise Lost*," *Studies in Philology* 34 (1937): 209–47; and "A Theory of a Plurality of Worlds as a Factor in Milton's Attitude Toward the Copernican Hypothesis," *Modern Language Notes* 47 (1932): 319–25.

7. For a related discussion of how Galileo's study of motion impacted Milton's understanding of borders—physical and sociocultural—see chapter 4 by Rachel Trubowitz in this volume.

8. David Woodward, "Reality, Symbolism, Time, and Space in Medieval World Maps," *Annals of the Association of American Geographers* 75, no. 4 (December 1985): 514.

9. John Martin Evans, *Milton's Imperial Epic: Paradise Lost and the Discourse of Colonialism* (Ithaca, NY: Cornell University Press, 1996).

10. Scafi, *Mapping Paradise*, 18.

11. As Scafi explains, the placement of Eden in the East comes about through a convenient conflation of geographical and temporal location: "The grounds for identifying the site of the earthly paradise rested on the *Vetus Latina* (the old Latin translation of the Hebrew text of Genesis), which had explained that paradise had been planted not 'from the beginning'—as Jerome rendered it in the Vulgate—but 'in the east' " (*Mapping Paradise*, 47).

12. Scafi, *Mapping Paradise*, 226–30, 261–64.

13. Phillip Usher, "Chopping up Columbus' Pear: World Roaming after 1492," in *Space: New Dimensions in French Studies*, ed. Emma Gilby and Katja Haustein (Oxford: Peter Lang, 2005), 84.

14. Christopher Columbus, *Select Letters of Christopher Columbus, with Other Original Documents, Relating to His Four Voyages to the New World*, ed. and trans. R. H. Major (Surrey, UK: Ashgate, 2010), 137.

15. Columbus, *Select Letters*, 65, 61.

16. Mary Nyquist cogently theorizes the theological and cultural significance of this kind of temporal distancing of the Indigenous peoples in her "Contemporary Ancestors of DeBry, Hobbes, and Milton," *University of Toronto Quarterly* 77, no. 3 (2008): 837–75. I am indebted to her work on this subject, which I discuss in further detail below.

17. Scafi, *Mapping Paradise*, 241.

18. Anthony Pagden, *The Fall of Natural Man: The American Indian and the Origins of Comparative Ethnology* (Cambridge: Cambridge University Press, 1982), 19.

19. David Cressy, "Early Modern Space Travel and the English Man in the Moon," *American Historical Review* 111, no. 4 (2006): 981.

20. Evans, *Milton's Imperial Epic*, 86–87.

21. Evans, *Milton's Imperial Epic*, 88.

22. Achsah Guibbory explores this view—and its consequences for the Jewish readmission debate—in more detail in chapter 5 of this volume; John Eliot, quoted in Evans, *Milton's Imperial Epic*, 94.

23. Evans, *Milton's Imperial Epic*, 94.

24. Comparisons of Galileo and Columbus were routine in the seventeenth century; see, e.g., Johannes Kepler, *Kepler's Conversation with Galileo's Sidereal Messenger*, ed. and trans. Edward Rosen (New York: Johnson Reprint Corporation, 1965), 17, 37; Thomas Campanella, *Defense of Galileo*, ed. and trans. Grant McColley (Northampton, MA: Smith College, 1937), 35, 47; and Godwin, *Man in the Moone*, 67.

25. Kepler, *Conversation*, 39.

26. Wilkins, *Discovery of a World in the Moon*, 207.

27. John Donne, *Ignatius His Conclave* (London, 1611), 118, *Early English Books Online*, http://quod.lib.umich.edu/e/eebo/A20624.0001.001.

28. Evans, *Milton's Imperial Epic*, 124.

29. Anthony Pagden, "Europe: Conceptualizing a Continent," in *The Idea of Europe from Antiquity to the European Union*, ed. Anthony Pagden (Cambridge: Cambridge University Press, 2002), 36; see also Seymour Philips, "The Outer World of the European Middle Ages," in *Implicit Understandings: Observing, Reporting and Reflecting on the Encounters between Europeans and Other Peoples in the Early Modern Era*, ed. Stuart B. Schwarz (Cambridge: Cambridge University Press, 1994), 44; and Evans, *Milton's Imperial Epic*, 24–25.

30. Kepler, *Conversation*, 43.

31. Kepler, *Conversation*, 39.

32. Scott Montgomery, *The Moon and the Western Imagination* (Tucson: University of Arizona Press, 1999), 101.

33. Montgomery, *Moon and the Western Imagination*, 103. Anna Marie E. Roos likewise posits that Gilbert's nomenclature "could be seen as a reflection of the flood of cartographic naming, classification, and subsequent territorial claims that occurred with the advent of the Age of Discovery," so that "Gilbert's naming of a lunar continent after the island of Britain may thus have paralleled the process of claiming lands a celestial New World." Roos, *Luminaries in the Natural World: The Sun and the Moon in England, 1400–1720*, WPI Studies Vol. 20, ed. Lance Schachterle (New York: Peter Lang, 2001), 89–90.

34. Montgomery, *Moon and the Western Imagination*, 157–68.

35. Hevelius, quoted in Montgomery, *Moon and the Western Imagination*, 186–87.

36. Montgomery, *Moon and the Western Imagination*, 187.

37. Elizabeth Sauer, "Milton and the 'Savage Deserts of America,'" *Milton Studies* 58 (2017): 5.

38. Sauer, "Milton and the 'Savage Deserts of America,'" 9.

39. Evans, *Milton's Imperial Epic*, 5.

40. Evans, *Milton's Imperial Epic*, 94.

41. Evans, *Milton's Imperial Epic*, 97–100.

42. Evans, *Milton's Imperial Epic*, 100–3.

43. Sauer, "Milton and the 'Savage Deserts of America,'" 20.

44. Nyquist, "Contemporary Ancestors," 251–53.

45. Erin Webster, "Starry Messengers: Galileo and the Role of the Observer in *Paradise Lost*," in *Milton and the New Scientific Age: Poetry, Science, Fiction*, ed. Catherine G. Martin (New York: Routledge, 2019), 133–34.

46. Scafi, *Mapping Paradise*, 145.

47. Sauer, "Milton and 'Savage Deserts of America,'" 21. See also Thomas Luxon's note on this line, in which he explains that Adam is unable to view the Western Hemisphere "physically, since these other places are half-way round the globe" (*JMRR*).

48. *Chasing the Moon*, dir. Robert Stone, Robert Stone Productions, 2019, PBS, https://www.pbs.org/wgbh/americanexperience/films/chasing-moon/#part01, 4:29–5:00.

CHAPTER 4

Milton's Moving Bodies at the Border

Kinopolitics in *Paradise Lost*
and *Samson Agonistes*

Rachel Trubowitz

In *Theory of the Border*, Thomas Nail argues that "the common mental image many people have of borders as static walls is neither conceptually nor practically accurate."[1] Nail chooses instead to look at borders as dynamic processes that not only control and redirect social motion but also are themselves in a state of perpetual flux: "The history of the border is the history of social motion" (*TB*, 21). Rather than analyze societies (and their internal and external borders) as primarily static and spatial, Nail proposes to review the nation, the state, and the nation-state "primarily as regimes of motion" (*TB*, 24). Social motion creates the dynamic borders that delimit states; states do not come into existence by imposing fixed borders. "Kinopolitics" is the broad term that Nail coins for his dynamic approach to borders and states: "Kinopolitics is the theory and analysis of social motion: the politics of movement" (*TB*, 24).

In making his case for a kinopolitical approach to understanding borders, Nail looks to the seventeenth century for one important point of origin:

> We find during the seventeenth century an explosion of scientific descriptions of flows of all kinds: flows of food, flows of money, flows of blood, and flows of air. In 1614 the Italian physiologist Sanctorius founded the study of metabolism, the science of transformative biological flows, recorded in *Ars de Statica Medicina*. In his 1628 book, *Exercitation Anatomica de Motu*

dordi et Sanguinis in Animalibus, William Harvey conducted the first controlled experiments on and popularized the idea of pulmonary circulation as originating in the heart, circulation previously thought to originate in the liver. In 1671, Isaac Newton invented a mathematics of flow in *Method of Fluxions*, now called differential calculus. . . . This legacy continues today. Borders still define the limits and transition points of human flows. If the border is the political ground of our time, the flow is our conceptual starting point. (*TB*, 25)

Nail's term "kinopolitics" also refers to kinematics: the science that describes the motion of particles from one place to another. Kinematics studies the trajectories of points, lines, and other geometric objects and their differential properties, such as velocity and acceleration. As with the study of metabolism, pulmonary circulation, and differential calculus, kinematics dates to the seventeenth century. Galileo formulated the foundations for his "geometry of motion" (now called kinematics) by 1609 in *De systemate mundi*.[2] In this essay I focus on how, anticipating Nail's kinopolitics, Milton applies Galileo's kinematics to his depiction of social flows across borders that are themselves in motion in *Paradise Lost*. In so doing, I offer a new explanation for why Galileo is the only contemporary thinker to whom Milton directly refers in his epic.

In reconsidering Milton's political views from a new kinopolitical perspective, my essay also supplements the emphasis on space and place that has dominated literary theory, philosophy, and geopolitics since the mid-1970s.[3] In early modern literary studies the turn to space and place put "the map" on the map, so to speak. More than anything else perhaps, as Richard Helgerson's pivotal *Forms of Nationhood* attests, literary scholarship on early modernity's chorographic imagination has revitalized our understanding of the rise of the nation-state.[4] The 1648 Treaty of Westphalia, which radically redrew the map of medieval Europe, offers one indisputably important early modern historical point of origin for the space and place narrative of the modern nation and nationalism. Yet, although incredibly fruitful, the space and place approach has blocked other paths to the rise of the modern nation. As Nail observes, "the border cannot be understood in terms of space alone" (*TB*, 9). Indeed, when we reconsider the border as a flow rather than a fixed abstract line on a map, we upend our customary assumptions about nation formation. As Nail observes, we customarily see the border as "a derivative social product" (*TB*, 10). Against the grain, kinopolitics shows us that the border is a "primarily productive process"

Rachel Trubowitz

(*TB*, 21)—one that is required for "'the state' to exist at all" (*TB*, 15). For the very first time, we recognize that "the border precedes the state historically . . . and logically" (*TB*, 14–15).

To understand how Milton anticipates these kinopolitical assumptions, I focus in the first half of my essay on the two expulsions that bookend his epic: Satan's expulsion from Heaven; and Adam's and Eve's expulsion from Eden. In the second half I focus on the horrific scene of the dead "*Samson* . . . immixt" (*SA*, 1657) with the bodies of the Philistines whom he has slaughtered.[5] I demonstrate that this scene newly illuminates Milton's bifurcated view of the temporal Judeo-Christian border as continuous for some and discontinuous for others. *Paradise Lost* concludes with Milton's depiction of Adam and Eve as deportees from Paradise who are about to enter the as yet undivided, but soon to be endlessly conflictual postlapsarian "World . . . all before them" (*PL*, 12.646). Through this restless "World," they will wander perpetually until they "choose / Thir place of rest" (*PL*, 12.646–47). By contrast, *Samson Agonistes* ends with the errant hero's double return "Home to his Father's house" (*SA*, 1733): backward to the house of his earthly Hebrew father, Manoa, and forward to the heavenly house of the Christian God, his divine father.[6]

Of particular relevance here is that, toward the end of book 12, Michael prepares Adam for his new life as a migrant by exhorting him to "add / Deeds to thy knowledge answerable, add Faith" (*PL*, 12.581–82), a reference to the Protestant doctrine of *sola fide*. It seems plausible that, when embarking on *Samson Agonistes*, Milton had these same "Deeds [of] Faith" (*PL*, 12.582) in mind. As has been much discussed in recent years, Milton had many reasons for choosing Samson as his hero. Most scholars agree, however, that Milton's Samson alludes to Hebrews 11:32, which supersessionally identifies Samson, along with Abraham, Moses, and other Hebrew Bible leaders, as a proto-Christian "hero of faith" (Hebrews 11:21).[7] In the final lines of the drama, the Chorus identifies Samson as God's "faithful Champion" (*SA*, 1751). Whether the Chorus's testimony is true or false remains a subject of considerable debate. But the horror that the Hebrew Messenger conveys when he reports on the scene of Samson's dead body "immixt" (*SA*, 1657) with the dead bodies of the Philistines cannot be disputed. I reread this scene of horrible "immix[ing]" in kinopolitical terms as a "human flow" (*TB*, 9) and thus as a brutal illustration of the dynamics of the border. Yet, for Milton, although horrible, this border scene is potentially also salvific. Only by confronting the most extraordinary horror can we gain the enhanced vision we need to look beyond the corrupt status quo of perpetual international and intranational conflict and toward the regenerate and peaceful one-world community of the Protestant faithful. Milton firmly believes that this new worldwide, godly community can, and will, redeem the corrupt and conflictual realm of the everyday, both within time and at the end-time.

This redemptive present and future vision of a godly international recurs throughout Milton's oeuvre. *The Tenure of Kings and Magistrates* contains an especially resonant depiction of the poet's ideal of a godly global "neighbour[hood]":

> He therfore that keeps peace with me, neer or remote, of whatsoever Nation, is to mee as farr as all civil and human offices an Englishman and a neighbour: but if an Englishman forgetting all Laws, human, civil and religious, offend against life and liberty, to him offended and to the Law in his behalf, though born in the same womb, he is no better then a Turk, a Sarasin, a Heathen. This is Gospel, and this was ever Law among equals. (*The Tenure*)

As this passage makes clear, neighborliness and nationality have nothing to do with "neer"-ness or "same"-ness, understood in terms of geographical proximity or the closeness of kinship bonds. Notably, Milton's ideal definition of what it means to be "an Englishman and a neighbour" (anyone "that keeps peace with me" whether "neer or remote") emphasizes the pacific in stark contrast to the bellicosity, which, as Michael teaches Adam in books 11 and 12 of *Paradise Lost*, governs all relations in the corrupt world of the everyday. Yet, although Milton expands what it means to be a "neighbour" beyond kinship bonds ("though born in the same womb") and across geographical and national borders, he nonetheless reinforces the divide between the godly Englishman ("of whatsoever Nation") and the ungodly one ("no better then a Turk, a Sarasin, a Heathen"). "This is Gospel, and this was ever Law among equals," Milton concludes.

The same English Protestant ideal of worldwide godly community animates *Samson Agonistes*. Milton invokes Galatians 3:28's negation of difference as a proof text for this ideal: "There is neither Jew nor Greek, there is neither bond nor free, there is neither male nor female: for ye are all one in Christ Jesus." The salvific influence of Galatians 3:28 finds especially acute expression in the profoundly disturbing scene of the dead Samson "immixt" (*SA*, 1657) with the dead bodies

Rachel Trubowitz

of the Philistines. Milton asks us to read this scene twice: the first time with horror; the second time with "calm of mind all passion spent" (*SA*, 1758). As the Hebrew Messenger reports, gazing on this scene is traumatizing:

> O whither shall I run, or which way flie
> The sight of this so horrid spectacle
> Which earst my eyes beheld and yet behold;
> For dire imagination still persues me. (*SA*, 1541–44)

Unlike the messenger, who is a Hebrew, Milton's "fit" (*PL*, 7.31) readers can redeem this scene by reviewing it a second time through the lens of Galatians 3:28. When newly seen from this Pauline perspective, the "horrid spectacle" of "immixt" dead bodies converts into a salvific scene that not only replicates and anticipates the erasure of ethnic, social, and gender borders celebrated in Galatians 3:28 but also defines what it means for "all" to be "one in Christ Jesus." In this scene of "immix[ing]," as in the passage on neighborliness from *The Tenure of King and Magistrates*, Milton new-models what it means for the truly faithful to belong to the same godly global community. Despite its egalitarian implications, however, the new-modeled godly global neighborliness celebrated in both *Tenure* and *Samson Agonistes* reasserts the exclusive inclusiveness in which St. Paul's Christian universalism in Galatians 3:28 is grounded.

Many modern theorists, most notably, Alain Badiou, have praised the revolutionary thrust of Galatians 3:28, which, by laudably obliterating enduring ethic, social, and gender boundaries, breaks down the seemingly indestructible frame of the us against them status quo.[8] Yet, while beatifically evoking a new, wholly transfigured, peaceful, and equalitarian community, Paul's leveling of difference simultaneously creates a new limiting transition point that bifurcates those who recognize Christ as their redeemer from those who do not. As Achsah Guibbory demonstrates in chapter 5 of this volume, Paul's bifurcation of Christians and Jews in Galatians and elsewhere in his Epistles animates Milton's depiction of Jesus's progressive separation of himself from the Jews and Judaism in *Paradise Regain'd*.

Nail's account of how "borders emerge where there is a continuous process that reaches a bifurcation point" can help us better to understand how Paul's border-breaking vision creates a new bifurcation in which "a qualitative divergence occurs, and two distinct pathways can be identified" (*TB*, 3). While some people experience Paul's border "as a continuity," others experience it "as a discontinuity" (*TB*, 3). Those who pass through this border into oneness in Christ will be swept up in the "allness" that Paul celebrates in Galatians 3:28. Those who are stopped at the border are deported, both in time and space. In time they are consigned to the outmoded pre-Christian/pre-Pauline past—a temporal detention camp, in which some are held indefinitely. Others are swept into the dustbin of history or, as "shadowy Types" (*PL*, 12.303), put to work in service of the elect, that is, those who choose the continuous pathway to oneness in Christ. In space those who experience the border as a discontinuity are doomed to migrate aimlessly forever, sometimes approaching but never crossing the threshold that divides the plenitudinous Christian universal from the empty non-Christian particular. Adam and Eve look forward to choosing "Thir place of rest" (*PL*, 12.647) at the end of *Paradise Lost*. As already noted, Samson, the double Hebrew and proto-Christian hero, returns home twice: backward to Manoa's house and forward to the house of the Christian God, his *real* father. Whereas ultimately Samson passes through the temporal threshold between the Hebraic and the Christian, as the Epistle to Hebrews attests, Manoa and the other unreconstructed Old Testament characters in *Samson Agonistes* will be stopped at the border between the two dispensations.[9] They will find "no direction home," as Bob Dylan so aptly puts it. How we read *Samson Agonistes* is contingent on our experience at the Judeo-Christian border: do we pass through or are we turned back?

Expulsion and the Galilean Science
of Motion in *Paradise Lost*

Paradise Lost contains many depictions of borders and border crossings, physical and metaphysical. Indeed, the border is a veritable motif (one albeit that is as yet largely unacknowledged) in Milton's epic. I focus on the two expulsions that bookend the epic: Satan's expulsion from Heaven; and Adam's and Eve's expulsion from the garden of Eden. For Milton, Satan's and the rebel angels' expulsion from Heaven forms the archetype of all expulsions to come. We do not hear the full story of this inaugural expulsion until book 6 when Raphael tells Adam and Eve how the Son pursued Satan and the rebel forces to Heaven's walled border, "the bounds / And Chrystal wall of Heav'n" (*PL*, 6.859–60). That Heaven's "wall" is made of "Chrystal" is a possible reference to the Aristotelian proposition that the heavens are literally composed of fifty-five solid, concentric, crystalline spheres, to which celestial objects are attached and through which they rotate at different velocities. Milton's heavenly "Chrystal wall," however, does not remain solid or static for very long. Instead, the wall's animist, self-moving matter organically generates a border crossing: "op'ning wide, / [It] Rowld inward, and a spacious Gap disclos'd / Into the wastful Deep" (*PL*, 6.860–62). Instead of facing the "far worse" behind them, Satan and the apostate angels opt for "the monstrous sight" of Chaos that they see through the "spacious Gap" in the wall (*PL*, 6.863, 862, 861). Freely choosing to escape from Heaven, "headlong themselves they threw / Down from the verge of Heav'n" (*PL*, 6.864–65). Evacuated of this horrid crew, Heaven's border repairs itself: "Disburdnd Heav'n rejoic'd, and soon repaird / Her mural breach returning whence it rowld" (*PL*, 6.878–79). Just as Heaven's wall opens up its own "breach," so it closes it as well.

The opening and closing up of the "breach" in the border are equally dynamic. In each case the dynamic is "Rowl[ing]" (*PL*, 6.861). "Rowl[ing]" could mean "churning, or agitation of the stomach" (*OED*). This connotation gains strength through Milton's scatological depiction of Heaven as "Disburdened" (*PL*, 6.878), as of waste, after its discharging of Satan and his followers. Milton makes similar references to Heaven's discharging of excrement elsewhere in the epic as when at the Creation the Spirit of God "downward purg'd / The black tartareous cold Infernal dregs / Adverse to life" (*PL*, 7.237–39). The biological implications of "Rowl[ing]" in *Paradise Lost* are beyond the purview of my argument in this chapter.[10] My interest is in a different kind of rolling: "The action of turning over and over, rotating about an axis; the action or act of travelling or covering distance in this manner" (*OED*).

This kind of rolling prompts us to think of Galileo, since rolling of this sort was the key to his experiments on moving bodies. Galileo (speaking through his character, Salviati) formulates his law of falling bodies on day three in *Dialogues Concerning Two New Sciences*. After describing his inclined plane experiments, Salviati concludes: "we always found that the spaces traversed were to each other as the squares of the times, and this was true for all inclinations of the plane" (or, in modern notation, $d = 16t^2$ where "d" is the number of feet the body falls in "t" seconds).[11] Galileo's discovery that the distance that any falling object travels is directly proportional to the square of the time it takes to fall invalidated two of Aristotle's most influential premises: (1) that heavier bodies fall faster than lighter ones and (2) that only earthly bodies fall—not celestial ones. Because early modern technology was unable to record such high speeds, Galileo could not directly observe the object's free-falling motion. Instead, he tried to decelerate motion by replacing the falling object with a ball rolling down an inclined plane. Since free falling is essentially equivalent to rolling down a completely vertical ramp, he assumed that a ball rolling down such a ramp would speed up in the exact same way as a free-falling object would. In the brief span (five lines) between the "Chrystal wall of Heav'n . . . op'ning wide," to the animist wall's rolling inward, to Satan's and the rebel angels' free fall from Heaven to Hell, Milton compresses the entire history of scientific theories about motion, from Aristotle's physics in classical antiquity to Galileo's physics in the present day of Milton's poem.

Although we must wait until book 6 to get the full story about Satan's and the fallen angels' expulsion from Heaven, we first hear of the event, albeit with some small but crucial differences, from the narrator in book 1:

> Him the Almighty Power
> Hurld headlong flaming from th' Ethereal Sky
> With hideous ruine and combustion down
> To bottomless perdition. (*PL*, 1.44–47)

The narrator relates that "the Almighty Power" forcibly "Hurld" Satan "headlong." Possibly Milton is setting us up in book 1 to sympathize with Satan's view of the Father as a tyrant in that same book, only to correct us in book 6 when we learn the Son, not the Father, pursues Satan to the brink of Hell and that Satan is not hurled but that he hurls himself headlong into Chaos down to "bottomless perdition." "Gotcha," as Stanley Fish might say. But Milton also asks us to attend to congruencies as well as discrepancies between the narrator's and Raphael's accounts. The most important of these congruencies, for my purposes here, is that both accounts feature the action of rolling. Although the wall of Heaven ceases to roll after it rolls up its breach, rolling, having been set into motion in Heaven, nonetheless continues in Hell, where Satan and his horrid crew end up "lay[ing] vanquished, rowling in the fiery Gulfe" (*PL*, 1.53). Yet, even as we identify the rolling wall in book 6 with the "rowling" of Satan and his crew in book 1, we once again seemingly encounter a discrepancy between the narrator's and Raphael's accounts. Raphael reports of Satan and the fallen angels: "Nine days they fell" (*PL*, 6.870); by contrast, the narrator states that for "Nine times the space that measures day and night / To mortal men" they "Lay vanquisht" (*PL,* 1.50–52). So, who is right? Did Satan and his crew "[fall]" for nine days? Or did they "Lay vanquisht" for nine days?

Milton does not help us much here, but what he does do, by focusing our attention on rolling in both Raphael's and the narrator's accounts, is to teach us that, in the new world of Galilean physics, motion and stasis are the same, despite appearances to the contrary. Stasis ("Lay[ing] vanquisht"; *PL,* 1.52) is a kind of motion (acceleration equals zero), which is no different from rolling and falling. Galileo's view that stasis is an instantiation of a universal law of motion represents one definitive way that modern Galilean science differs from the ancient Aristotelian model. Aristotle divides the cosmos between the superlunary and the sublunary. Based on commonplace observation, he asserts that sublunary objects stay in motion only if they are pushed, but if left to themselves, they will stand still. For Aristotle, the state of rest is the natural state to which all sublunary things aspire. The fundamental assumption in Aristotelian physics is that the natural state of sublunary matter is rest.[12] By contrast, based on his experiments and mathematical models, Galileo eradicates the Aristotelian divide between the super- and sublunary. The same laws of motion apply to any object anywhere in the universe. All objects moving at a constant speed in a straight line will continue to move along at the same constant speed in the same straight line forever. As Galileo puts it, "all external impediments removed, a heavy body on a spherical surface concentric with the earth will maintain itself in that state in which it has been; if placed in movement towards the west (for example), it will maintain itself in that movement."[13] Also, any object that stands still will, if left to itself, maintain its stillness. This is Galileo's law of inertia, which he first formulated in 1612. Whereas Aristotle treats rest as the natural state to which all sublunary things aspire, Galileo treats rest as a special case of universal motion. A resting object moves at a constant velocity of zero miles per hour. Taken together, Raphael's and the narrator's identical focus on rolling reflects Galileo's anti-Aristotelian view of rest as uniform motion where acceleration equals zero. Milton applies Galileo's laws to both falling and resting bodies alike.

As John Rumrich observes in chapter 1 of this volume, Galileo's observations and thought experiments focus exclusively on falling inanimate bodies, such as the balls he rolled down inclined planes and the spheres of different masses that he supposedly dropped from the top of the Tower of Pisa.[14] Taking one step further than Galileo, Milton applies the great scientist's universal law of free fall to self-aware, animate beings (humans and angels), specifically to their inward states of mind and feeling. In book 4 rolling moves inward as Satan

> Begins his dire attempt, which nigh the birth
> Now rolling, boils in his tumultuous breast,
> And like a devilish Engine back recoils
> Upon himself. (*PL*, 4.15–18)

As this passage makes clear, in Milton's monist universe, physical, intellectual, and affective activities are one and the same. Just as he will roll out his military advance on Adam and Eve and Paradise, Satan's inward "rolling," "boil[ing]," and "back recoil[ing]" commence in "his tumultuous breast." A thought or emotion is continuous with a bodily or mechanical ("a devilish Engine") action. As Marissa Greenberg astutely observes, Milton's phrase "much revolving" (*PL*, 4.31) (a cognate of "rolling") "is not simply a figure of speech for abstractions of the mind. It also denotes visible, outward transformations":

> while he spake, each passion dimm'd his face,
> Thrice chang'd with pale, ire, envy and despair,
> Which marr'd his borrow'd visage. (*PL*, 4.114–16)

Greenberg points out that, "as Satan's face changes with his emotions, it turns between the objects of his gaze":

> Sometimes towards Eden which now in his view
> Lay pleasant, his griev'd look he fixes sad,
> Sometimes towards Heav'n and the full-blazing Sun,
> Which now sat high in his Meridian Tow'r. ([*PL*,] 4.27–30)

As Greenberg concludes, "Satan's much revolving thus includes not only 'perturbation' but also 'gestures fierce / . . . and mad demeanor' ([*PL*,] 4.120, 128–29)."[15] Whether inward or outward, cognitive or physical, everything is in motion, even rest. Whereas for Aristotle rest is both the negation of motion and the ultimate state toward which all things tend, for Galileo uniform motion (moving at a constant velocity, including motion at zero miles per hour) is the baseline dynamic state for all objects, even those that seem to be standing still. After the Copernican Revolution, Galileo, and Milton after him, recognized that everything on Earth and in the heavens is in flux. Motion, not stasis,

Rachel Trubowitz

has to be the starting point for coming to terms even with seemingly static phenomena, including geographically fixed boundaries and border walls such as the "Chyrstal wall of Heav'n."

This is the same kind of kinopolitical philosophy that Nail exhorts us to apply to borders today. Rather than see the US-Mexico border wall as reinforcing a fixed line of demarcation, we should recognize instead that this wall is in a state of flux. Time and again, the wall's more than three thousand documented holes are plugged up only to reopen somewhere else in the wall (or very beautiful slat fence). Because borders and border walls are not static, they cannot be reduced to a stable, fixed idea, even or especially to a failed idée fixe like Donald Trump's wall at the US-Mexico border.[16]

Returning to Milton after this short excursion into twenty-first-century American politics, I focus now on Adam and Eve's expulsion from Eden. As John Rogers cogently observes in *The Matter of Revolution*, the Father proposes two very different methods for this expulsion. The first follows justly from the law God gives to Nature. Adam's and Eve's now-sinful bodies cannot remain in Eden because Eden's "pure immortal Elements" will "eject" them and "purge [them] off / As a distemper" (*PL*, 11.53–54). As Rogers observes, "the theodicial project behind *Paradise Lost* requires at least an attempt to absolve God of direct responsibility for its loss. Although the Father would like to pardon fully the sinful pair, he cannot abolish the laws of nature he established at the Creation; these laws prohibit man's further habitation in the garden."[17] Within a short span of lines, however, this charitable deity is superseded by an authoritarian one when God not only issues a harsh inquisitional edict but also commands Michael to implement it "Without remorse":

> from the Paradise of God
> Without remorse drive out the sinful Pair,
> From hallowd ground th' unholie, and denounce
> To them and to thir Progenie from thence
> Perpetual banishment. (*PL*, 11.104–8)

For Rogers the irreconcilability of God's charitable and authoritarian approach to expulsion "might suggest that the poem ends in a state of radical undecidability." As Rogers argues, Milton instead asks us to imagine these political antimonies "as elements in a historical transformation," specifically, the paradigmatic historical shift from types to truth.[18]

Rogers's interpretation is illuminating. Nonetheless, I would like to supplement his powerful reading by proposing that Milton also asks us to identify God's dynamic depiction of the expulsion with the deity's assertion that it results from his unwavering decree. We are to consider the dynamic account alongside the static one so that we might learn from God himself that the divide between motion and stasis in the post-Galilean universe no longer exists. Expulsion is dynamic and static, since, after Galileo, stasis becomes a special instantiation of moving.

Not unlike the "Chrystal wall of Heav'n," which seems to be a static, inert structure, but which in fact turns out to be a dynamic and organic one, the eastern border of Eden, through which Adam and Eve are expelled, also is simultaneously solid and fluid, fixed and moving. The narrator describes this border as the "fixt Station" (*PL,* 12.627) for the cherubim who serve as God's border patrol. With the cherubim standing on watch, the border appears as a "Gate / With dreadful Faces throng'd and fierie Armes" (*PL,* 12.643–44). But, while the cherubim stand "fixt" in "bright array" (*PL,* 12.627), brandishing the "Sword of God before them" (*PL,* 12.633), they simultaneously flow, or, more precisely, "glid[e] meteorous" (*PL,* 12.629). Just as when a meteor hits the earth's atmosphere, it melts or vaporizes due to air friction, so the cherubim, when they descend to earth, "glid[e]" like "Ev'ning Mist / Ris'n from a River o're the marsh" (*PL,* 12.629–30). The repetition of "gliding" and "glides" at the beginning of book 12, line 629 and at the end of book 12, line 630 seems at odds with the fearful depiction of the cherubim as steadfast and dreadful sentinels. Nonetheless, Milton wants us to see this angelic border patrol both ways, "fixt" and "gliding," all at the same time.

At the end of book 12, the cherubim brandish the Sword of God. Their waving of the sword generates "torrid heat / And vapour as the *Libyan* Air adust," which begins "to parch" Eden (*PL,* 12.634–35, 637). Ultimately, however, as Michael teaches Adam in book 11, Paradise moves fluidly to its demise at the Flood:

> then shall this Mount
> Of Paradise by might of Waves be moovd
> Out of his place, pushd by the horned floud,
> With all his verdure spoil'd, and Trees adrift
> Down the great River to the op'ning Gulf,
> And there take root an Iland salt and bare,
> The haunt of Seales and Orcs and Sea-mews clang. (*PL,* 11.829–35)

Rachel Trubowitz

The series of verbs in this passage ("moovd," "pushed" "spoil'd," "[set] adrift") underscores the kinetic nature of Paradise's approaching endpoint. And the end is not really an end but a new (albeit much diminished but still vital) beginning. In the ruins of Paradise, referenced by the unspecific indicative "there," an "Iland salt and bare" takes "root" (*PL*, 11.834). As Michael teaches Adam, the purpose of Eden's double dynamic of destruction, first by "torrid heat" (*PL*, 12.634) and then by "might of Waves" (*PL*, 11.831), is "To teach thee that God attributes to place / No sanctitie" (*PL*, 11.836–37). Michael also insists that Adam and Eve must see the "World . . . all before them" (*PL*, 12.646) as devoid of borders, or in other words, as a globe with "a purely pre-social, undivided surface" (*TB*, 4), to borrow Nail's phrase. Notably, we see our "pendant world" (*PL*, 2.1052) in its prelapsarian form for the first time from this same undivided global perspective, albeit through Satan's divisive eyes. For Nail, this presocial perception of Earth as a globe or planet permits us to recognize (1) that borders give birth to social formations (rather than the other way around) and (2) that border walls are dynamic and fluid rather than static and solid structures. Society, argues Nail,

> is first and foremost a product of the borders that define it and the material conditions under which it is divisible. Only afterward are borders (re)produced by society. This is another important consequence for the theory of the border as a continuous division. If we want to understand the border, we should start with the border and not with societies or states, which presuppose its existence. The border has become the social condition necessary for the emergence of certain dominant social formations, not the other way around. (*TB*, 4)

By depicting "the World . . . all before them" as "a purely pre-social, undivided surface" at the end of the poem, Milton provides his readers with an opportunity to recognize that borders introduce the divisions and bifurcations that make nations, states, and nation-states possible and not the other way around. Borders are not reducible to governing definitions of the limits of a sovereign state. The kinopolitics of *Paradise Lost* depend on our seeing our world through a Galilean lens, not only that of the "*Tuscan* artist['s] . . . Optic Glass" (*PL*, 1.288) but also from the vantage point of the great scientist's new science of kinematics, which radically revises the traditional Aristotelian model of motion and stasis and teaches us that nothing stands still and that

112   Milton's Moving Bodies at the Border

standing still is a kind of motion. Anticipating Nail's kinopolitics, Milton goes beyond Galileo by recognizing that continuous motion is not only a physical or organic phenomenon but also a social and psychic one. Time and again, Milton invites us to revolutionize the ways that we see ourselves and others, as well as our planet and our place in the universe.

Samson "immixt": (Re)moving Borders in *Samson Agonistes*

Just as *Paradise Lost* concludes by reminding us that, as Nail so aptly puts it, the motion of the border is "a primary process" (*TB*, 4), so too does *Samson Agonistes*. At the end of Milton's epic, Adam and Eve look back at the heavily guarded eastern border of Paradise. This border will disappear into the foreboding distance behind them, ultimately to be obliterated. As already noted, Milton kinematically narrates the demise of Paradise: "by might of Wave," it will "be moovd," "pushd," "spoil'd," and sent "adrift / Down the great River to the op'ning Gulf" (*PL*, 11.830–35). But even as Adam and Eve look back and lament their loss of Eden, they also look forward to the beginning of human history in the solid, as yet undivided "World . . . all before them" into which they will "make their solitary way" (*PL*, 12.646, 649).

The end of *Samson Agonistes* provides us with a similarly dynamic backward-forward vision of the border. The backward glance in Milton's dramatic tragedy is to the old sacred border between the circumcised and the uncircumcised—a border marked repeatedly in *Samson Agonistes*. Toward the beginning of the drama, the Chorus recounts how Samson, with the jawbone of a dead ass, "A thousand fore-skins fell" (*SA*, 145). Samson refers contemptuously to "the uncircumcis'd, our enemies" (*SA*, 640) when he laments that, whereas once God "led me on to mightiest deeds" (*SA*, 638), he "now hath cast me off as never known" (*SA*, 641). Dalila derisively identifies her enemies, Samson and the Hebrews, as "the Circumcised" (*SA*, 975), when she argues that "Fame if not double-fac't is double-mouth'd" (*SA*, 971) and therefore, although she may "In *Dan*, in *Judah*, and the bordering Tribes, / To all posterity may stand defam'd" (*SA*, 976–77), she will "in my countrey where I most desire" (*SA*, 980) be "nam'd among the famousest / Of Women" (*SA*, 982–83). Harapha boasts that, had he been on the field when Samson "wrought such wonders with an Asses

Jaw" (*SA*, 1095), he would have "left thy carkass where the Ass lay thrown" (*SA*, 1097), winning "the glory of Prowess" (*SA*, 1098) back to the Philistines "From the unforeskinn'd race" (*SA*, 1100).

I have spent time detailing these references because they help to support my claim that Paul's epistle to the Galatians profoundly informs Milton's drama. The issue of circumcision looms large in Galatians. Paul assumes that the churches he addresses consist primarily of Hellenized Gentile converts to Christ. His purpose is to persuade them, against the claims of rival missionaries, that they do not need to complete their conversion with circumcision. As Gerald Hammond and Austin Busch maintain in their introduction to "the Epistle of Paul, the Apostle to the Galatians," Paul's argument against Gentile circumcision "is heated, and at times, even ugly." The apostle is convinced that Gentile circumcision "represents a dangerous denial of the radically new thing God is now doing through Christ: 'neither is circumcision anything, nor uncircumcision.'" Only through what Paul terms "faith of Christ"—and decidedly not through circumcision or adherence to Mosaic law—can anyone, Jew or Gentile (Hebrew or Greek, bond or free, male or female) receive God's blessing and be reborn as "a new creature" (Galatians 6:15).[19] Paul's preoccupation with desacralizing circumcision finds particularly clear expression in *Samson Agonistes* when Samson's dead body lies "immixt" (*SA*, 1657) with those of the Philistines. Because Paul believes that the end-time will begin when the distinction between circumcision and uncircumcision is annulled (Galatians 1:4), the scene of the dead Samson "immixt" with the dead Philistines prepares us to look forward to "the close" (*SA*, 1748), not only the end of Milton's drama but also the unveiling of the universal salvation that is prophesied in Revelation. At the end of *Paradise Lost*, Adam and Eve look forward to our own "fenceless" (*PL*, 10.303) world in which they, moving "with wandring steps and slow" (*PL*, 12.648), will inaugurate what David Loewenstein describes as the "tragedy" of postlapsarian human history.[20] At the end of *Samson Agonistes*, we look forward in epic fashion to the same "New Heav'ns, new Earth" (*PL*, 12.549) to be founded in the end-time that Michael celebrates, not uncoincidentally, toward the end of his tutorial with Adam in the last book of *Paradise Lost*. If in the final books of Milton's epic, the poet must "change / Those notes to tragic" (*PL*, 10.5–6), in his tragedy he ends in an epic key.

Not unlike Michael, but much more elliptically, the Chorus celebrates the eventual advent of the "ever best" of the end-time by emphasizing the extraordinary importance of "the close" (*SA*, 1748):

> All is best, though we oft doubt,
> What th' unsearchable dispose
> Of highest wisdom brings about,
> And ever best found in the close. (*SA*, 1745–48)[21]

The double temporal scheme of time and eternity are conjoined by the "And" that connects "All is best" with "ever best"; both are "found in the close." The "close" reveals that the "All" that "is best" *now*, at the end of *Samson Agonistes*'s plotline, which readers experience in the present tense, is simultaneously "ever best" from the vantage point of eternity. At the "close" we arrive at the very last syllable and event in Milton's drama, but we also look forward to the end of human history. What Macbeth calls "the last syllable of recorded time" (*Macbeth*, 5.5.21) also is, for Milton, the precise moment when the new apocalyptic world order will begin as proclaimed in the Book of Revelation. In this simultaneously sorrowful end and joyous end, Samson becomes the compound double Hebrew and proto-Christian "faithful Champion" (*SA*, 1751) who is celebrated in the Epistle to Hebrews. The Epistle to Hebrews' more general purpose is to announce that Jewish law, the cornerstone of the beliefs and traditions of the Hebrews, is now superseded by a new covenant that applies to Gentiles. God's "faithful servants" (*SA*, 1755), that is, Milton's "fit" readers (*PL*, 7.31), mark this occasion by exiting the drama with "peace and consolation" (*SA*, 1767) and "calm of mind, all passion spent" (*SA*, 1758). Despite— and because of—the horror they've witnessed, the truly faithful at "the close" will happily recall the inaugural moment of the new covenant announced in Hebrews. Even more happily, they will foresee the postapocalyptic era hailed at the end of *Paradise Lost*: "ages of endless date / Founded in righteousness and peace and love" (*PL*, 12.549–50).

The "endless" (*PL*, 12.549) and borderless postapocalyptic universe (to which the Chorus alludes through its reference to the "ever best") first kairotically crashes into *Samson Agonistes* in the climactic scene of mass destruction. We gain access to this horrific scene only secondhand through the traumatized Hebrew Messenger. Paradoxically, the peaceful confluence between divine providence and human history on which the Chorus remarks in its closing sonnet finds its most specific antecedent in the brutal scene in which Samson's dead body is "immixt, inevitably" (*SA*, 1657) with the dead bodies of the Philistines he has slaughtered. Even secondhand, it is horrible to gaze on the entwisted arms, legs, heads, and torsos of Samson and his enemies. But, as Milton suggests, by gazing on this carnage, we gain the enhanced

Rachel Trubowitz

visual-conceptual acuity to see across the temporal border that divides the chronological from the eternal. With this higher vision and understanding, we also can foresee the salvific, borderless new world of the postapocalypse, in which God's "faithful servants" (*SA*, 1755) will be reborn. The shock and horror of witnessing the "heap of the dead," to borrow Gordon Teskey's evocative phrase, empower us to see through the confining frame of the everyday and gaze on the emancipatory realm of the real world that transcends our quotidian one.[22] Put another way, in the terrible mixing of Samson's dead body with those of the Philistine overseers whom he has assassinated, Milton allows his readers to foresee Apocalypse *now* in the quotidian present moment.[23]

How does the plotline of *Samson Agonistes* (such as it is) lead to this transformative, in and out of time vision of horror and redemption? Most scholars agree that Milton organizes his dramatic poem as a series of dialogues. Samson first converses with the Danite Chorus and Manoa, then Dalila, next Harapha, and finally, the Philistine Officer. After Samson's peripatetic reversal of his refusal, three times, into his acquiescence, three times, to perform at the Philistines' festival for Dagon, the hero follows the Philistine Officer and exits from the stage. From here on we learn only secondhand from the Hebrew Messenger about Samson's actions: his performance at the Dagonalia, his seeming prayer, and his destruction of Dagon's temple, whereby he slaughters his Philistine enemies and "inevitably" (*SA*, 1657) kills himself.

That Milton organizes *Samson Agonistes* in this fashion is undeniable. I nonetheless would like to propose an alternative organizational framework, one that is centered on Samson's dynamic series of sacred border crossings.[24] Although a Nazarite, "a person separate to God" (*SA*, 31), Samson is a heroic character defined by his crossing of sacred borders. Samson's most egregious transgression, or so it would seem, is against Yahweh, when he breaks his sacred Nazarite vow of silence about the secret source of his strength. Yet, at the same time, we learn that God sanctions Samson's lawbreaking. The hero's divinely appointed exemption from the Mosaic law is established early on in the tragedy, when, in response to the Chorus's bewilderment, Samson justifies his exogamous marriages first to the Philistine woman from Timna, "the daughter of an infidel" (*SA*, 221), and second to Dalila, both of whom Samson chooses to wed "before all the daughters of my tribe / And of my nation" (*SA*, 876–77) as "motioned . . . of God" (*SA*, 222). Both marriages break the Deuteronic law against intermarriage: "You shall not give your daughter to their son, nor take their daughter for your son" (Deut. 7:3). Nonetheless, Samson claims that he "knew / From intimate impulse" (*SA*, 222–23) that his illicit marriage to the woman of Timna was divinely sanctioned: it provides the "occasion" to "begin Israel's deliverance / The work to which I was divinely called" (*SA*, 224–26).[25] Samson uses a similar justification for his illicit marriage to Dalila, but with a difference. Instead of acting on "intimate impulse" (*SA*, 223), he argues from the precedent established by his first marriage that his second marriage is legal: "I thought it lawful from my former act, / And the same end; still watching to oppress / *Israel's* oppressours" (*SA*, 231–33). For many readers, this difference makes all the difference.[26]

Notably, the Danite Chorus does not agree. They argue that God "hath full right to exempt / Whom so it pleases him by choice / From National obstriction without taint / Of sin, or legal debt" (*SA*, 310–13). To assist Samson's delivery of Israel from its oppressors, the deity

> prompted this Heroic *Nazarite*,
> Against his vow of strictest purity,
> To seek in marriage that fallacious Bride [Dalila]
> Unclean, unchaste. (*SA*, 318–21)

Many scholars warn us not to trust the Chorus.[27] Still, as already noted, we cannot ignore that, in a passage adjacent to one just cited above, the Chorus claims that "Just are the ways of God, / And justifiable to Men" (*SA*, 293–94), echoing the reliable narrator of *Paradise Lost*, whose sacred aim is "to justify the ways of God to men" (*PL*, 1.26).

And then, yet once more, Samson breaks the Law when he chooses to perform at the Dagonalia. That the Philistines have ordered Samson to participate in their celebration of Dagon is "a worse thing" (*SA*, 433), as Manoa maintains, even than the hero's illicit marriages. As Manoa tells his beloved son: "of all thy sufferings think [this] the heaviest, / Of all reproach the most with shame that ever / Could have befall'n thee and thy Fathers house" (*SA*, 445–47). To Manoa, by performing at the Dagonalia, Samson, not unlike Satan after his expulsion from Heaven, falls farthest away from God. But if this is the nadir of Samson's career as a traditional hero, it is the apex of his redemptive career as a transgressor. Manoa's superlatives—"the heaviest / Of all" (*SA*, 445–46); "the most . . . ever" (*SA*, 446)—underscore that Samson's heroic narrative will reach his absolute lowest point when he performs at Dagon's temple. Unlike his father, however, Samson recognizes this border-crossing moment as the ultimate occasion, prompted by God, to fulfill his elevated role as Israel's "great Deliverer" (*SA*, 40).

Rachel Trubowitz

This highest-lowest threshold moment, as already mentioned, coincides with Samson's exit from the stage. Freud ascribes the "special tendency to reduce two opposites to a unity" to the dream-world, a realm that breaks the frame of everyday time, place, and logic.[28] Not dissimilarly, Milton associates this "special tendency" with the sacred or, more specifically, with the Latin term *sacer*, which means accursed and consecrated, horrible and holy, all at the same time.[29] When Samson exits from our direct view, he no longer exists for us in the everyday. His actions transpire not only offstage but also in sacred time.

Because it does not conform to sequence or chronology, sacred time is incompatible with the Aristotelian notion of plot in tragedy. For Aristotle, "The plot, then, is the first principle, and, as it were, the soul of a tragedy." It contains a beginning, a middle, and an end, where the beginning is what is "not posterior to another thing," while the middle needs to have something happen before and something to happen after it, but, after the end, "there is nothing else."[30] Even events that transpire offstage must fit into this chronological time scheme and be described narratively. In *Oedipus Rex*, for example, the messenger from Corinth recounts the events that have happened before the play begins: the messenger tells Oedipus that King Polybus and Queen Merope of Corinth are not his actual parents; he himself gave Oedipus as a baby to the Corinthian king and queen; he got the baby from a Theban shepherd whom he met in the woods; and so forth.

Like Sophocles, Milton uses a messenger to narrate offstage events: Samson's performance at the Dagonalia; his toppling of the walls of Dagon's temple; and his slaughter both of himself and the Philistines. Unlike the messenger from Corinth in *Oedipus Rex*, however, the Hebrew Messenger fails as a narrator. He "know[s] not how" to tell his story (*SA*, 1547). As he reports, "earst my eyes beheld" (*SA*, 1543) was a "so horrid [a] spectacle" (*SA*, 1542) that he "yet behold[s]" (*SA*, 1543) time and again with dread: "For dire imagination still persues me" (*SA*, 1544). The Hebrew Messenger cannot determine whether "providence," natural "instinct," or "reason though disturb'd" (*SA*, 1546) safely directed his course back to his countrymen. Breaking with the Aristotelian stipulation that plot (both onstage and offstage) must be chronological, the Hebrew Messenger's terrified and incoherent account reflects the jumbled holy and horrible temporal domain of *sacer*.

Most holy and horrible of all is the narrator's account of "the heap of the dead," to once again borrow Teskey's phrase.[31] For Teskey this scene is one "of defilement." As the Hebrew Messenger shows us, it is "a traumatic event from which the mind cannot gain relief." But, as

Teskey also maintains, if this event evokes shock and horror, it simultaneously generates catharsis and "spiritual transcendence." Although Teskey focuses exclusively on "the horror of defilement," he nonetheless asserts: "There is no vision of God without a vision of a heap of the dead."[32] *Samson Agonistes*'s "heap of the dead" generates the state of "delirium" that, for Teskey, makes Milton a great poet.[33]

This same scene also illustrates what Dayton Haskin magisterially describes as Milton's distinctive view of the scriptures and of the Protestant doctrine of *sola scriptura*: "Far from a commitment to 'the Bible only' as implicating readers in a fixed system," Milton views scripture as "a copious storehouse of places the very nature of which required that they be drawn out and put to new uses."[34] Building on Haskin, I maintain that Milton puts Galatians 3:28 to new use by making it the proof text for his depiction of "the heap of the dead" in his retelling of the Judges narrative in *Samson Agonistes*. By placing the immixing of Samson's dead body with the dead bodies of the Philistines as recounted in Judges 16:30–32 next to Paul's vision of "allness" in Christ in Galatians 3:28, Milton conjoins both old and new scriptural "places" to generate a reformed "both/and" Judeo-Christian scriptural view of his new-modeled Old Testament hero. "[T]angl'd in the fold" (*SA*, 1665), "immixt, inevitably" (*SA*, 1667) in death with his enemies, Samson *both* profanely obliterates the old sacred border that divides the circumcised from the uncircumcised *and* regeneratively ushers in Paul's universal Christian community, all at the same time.

We must not forget, however, that Milton's affiliation of these two scriptural "places" depends on his positing a conceptual a priori border wall separating those whom Paul describes as "one in Christ Jesus" (Galatians 3:28) from those who are not. In chapter 5 of this volume, Achsah Guibbory demonstrates that Paul's verses inform Milton's depiction of Jesus's progressive separation from the Jews and Judaism in *Paradise Regain'd*. Nail's definition of the motion of the border as a "primary process" (*TB*, 4) can help us to see how the border dynamic of bifurcation is required to inaugurate not only Paul's boundary-bursting vision of universal Christianity but also Milton's Radical-Reformational ideal of a godly international. From a kinopolitical vantage point, Paul's and Milton's bifurcations open two pathways. One pathway leads continuously to the apocalyptic close of Christian history, alluded to in the regenerative "close" (*SA*, 1748) of *Samson Agonistes*. The other loops backward to the outmoded past of the *Old* Testament.

In Manoa's response to Samson's death, we can detect the backward looping pathway to historical oblivion. It has become something of

Rachel Trubowitz   *119*

a scholarly commonplace to identify Manoa's vantage point as limited. In a landmark essay, John Guillory, to take one notable example, associates Manoa, Samson's earthly father, with the constraints of the normative, the narratable, and the calculable as proscribed by the law. By contrast, Samson's heavenly father, the Christian "Father-God" (whose salvific demands, as Guillory maintains, are "quite beyond Manoa's comprehension") wants his son to break through the frame of the normative and narratable—to transgress, interrupt, and act on "intimate impulse" (*SA*, 223) and "rousing motions" (*SA*, 1382). Guillory argues that Samson is able to fulfill the contradictory demands of both fathers by "a single, fantasmatic 'great work of destruction.'"[35]

Pointing Guillory's elegant argument in a somewhat different direction, I contend that, for Manoa, Samson's violent death proves that his son "heroicly hath finish'd / A life Heroic" (*SA*, 1710–11). As the repetition of "heroic" ("heroicly," "Heroic") underscores, Manoa evaluates Samson's violent death in terms of the same, soon to be outmoded, Hellenic-Hebraic ideal of heroism that Milton repudiates time and again in *Paradise Lost* and *Paradise Regain'd*. By contrast, Samson's Christian "Father-God," in his "highest wisdom," recognizes that Samson's violent but sacred (horrible and holy) death interrupts, transgresses, and overturns the very same outmoded Hellenic-Hebraic norms that, for Manoa, his son preserves "heroicly."[36] Put another way, if Manoa celebrates Samson as a Hellenic-Hebrew hero, Milton's God reveals that Samson, "his faithful Champion" (*SA*, 1751), is neither Hebrew nor Greek but the Christian "new creature" heralded by Paul in Galatians. A New Testament hero of faith, as acknowledged in Hebrews 11, the regenerate Samson looks forward to both the new universal Christian world order and the "new heavens and new earth" (Isaiah 66:22) of the world to come. By contrast, the outmoded Manoa, Samson's Old Testament father, loops backward into historical oblivion.

To make matters worse, Manoa unknowingly tries to prevent the providential progression of Christian history "From shadowie Types to Truth" (*PL*, 12.303) when he asks his fellow Hebrews from the tribe of Dan to help him separate Samson's dead body from those he has slaughtered and cleanse it of Philistine blood:

> Let us go find the body where it lies
> Sok't in his enemies blood, and from the stream
> With lavers pure and cleansing herbs wash off
> The clotted gore. (*SA*, 1725–28)

That Manoa wishes to "wash off / The clotted gore" underscores his shortsightedness (at least from Milton's point of view). Manoa fails to recognize that, although horrible and repellent, "The clotted gore" that unites the dead Samson with his enemies inversely (and perversely) foreshadows Paul's universal definition of new Christian personhood ("neither Jew nor Greek"), to which, through his sacrificial death, Jesus gives spiritual birth. Manoa clearly is on the wrong side of providential Christian history.[37]

As Jason P. Rosenblatt argues, however, Manoa deserves to be understood from a more charitable perspective:

> Instead of merely disparaging Manoa for his parental inadequacies and for crude ethnocentrism associated with Judaism, a monistic reading would understand even from a Christian perspective the love expressed by laying out money for one's child instead of laying it up for oneself and by preparing to spend the rest of one's life nursing that child ([*SA*,] ll. 1485–9).[38]

Reviewing Rosenblatt's reassessment of Manoa as a loving father from a kinopolitical vantage point, we recognize that what Guillory argues is Samson's regenerative return to his Christian Father-God's house at the end of the drama is contingent on a cruel immigration policy of family separation at the Judeo-Christian border. To be reunited with the Christian God (his *real* father), Samson must be separated from Manoa, his Hebrew father. This family separation policy finds clear expression in the Gospel of Luke, when Jesus defines what it means to be his follower:

> If any man come to me, and hate not his father, and mother, and wife, and children, and brethren, and sisters, yea, and his own life also, he cannot be my disciple. And whosoever doth not bear his cross, and come after me, cannot be my disciple. (Luke 14:26–27)

Luke equates love of family with love of material goods: both are equally carnal. To follow the continuous pathway to Christian redemption, one must hate one's father, mother, wife, husband, children, sisters, and brothers in the same way—and to the same degree—that one must despise all material possessions. Consciously or not, Luke's views animate the contempt that many scholars feel for Manoa. For most readers, Manoa's money, as Rosenblatt remarks, "is merely an index of

Rachel Trubowitz

his carnality" as is his love for his son.[39] Haskin epitomizes this governing view when he deprecates Manoa's love for his son: "[Manoa's] very willingness to lay out his treasure to buy his son's release from prison suggests that he would be unlikely to appreciate the more inward conception of the locus of value that Mary has [in *Paradise Regain'd*]."[40] If, however, with Nail, we make the border "our conceptual starting point" (*TB*, 25), we freshly can appreciate not only why Rosenblatt's charitable interpretation of Manoa is warranted but also why *Samson Agonistes* is "Of that sort of Dramatic Poem which is call'd Tragedy."

As I have argued, reading *Paradise Lost* and *Samson Agonistes* through the lens of what Nail terms "kinopolitics" opens a new window on both texts. We learn that Galileo's radical revision of Aristotelian principles of motion is crucial to understanding Milton's depictions of border walls and border crossings in *Paradise Lost*, especially the expulsions that bookend his epic. Kinopolitics also gives us a new vantage point on the political theology that shapes *Samson Agonistes*. How we experience Milton's drama depends largely on how we interpret the border dynamics that organize the "immix[ing]" of Samson's dead body with those of his Philistine enemies and overlords.

Notes

1. Thomas Nail, *Theory of the Border* (Oxford: Oxford University Press, 2016), 7. All references will be to this edition and noted in the text as *TB*.

2. Winifred Lovell Wisan argues that *De systemate mundi* provides evidence that "the new science of motion originated in Galileo's cosmology during the last decade of the sixteenth century," in "Galileo and the Process of Scientific Creation," *Isis* 75, no. 2 (June 1984): 270.

3. Henri Lefebvre's 1974 *The Production of Space*, which delineates the physical, mental, and social spaces of everyday life, helps to inaugurate the turn to space and place. Henri Lefebvre, *La production de l'espace* (Paris: Éditions Anthropos, 1974); first English translation, Henri Lefebvre, *The Production of Space*, trans. David Nicolson-Smith (Oxford: Blackwell, 1991).

4. Richard Helgerson, *Forms of Nationhood: The Elizabethan Writing of England* (Chicago: University of Chicago Press, 1992).

5. *OED* cites this line in Milton's *Samson Agonistes*, to illustrate the meaning of "immix" as a transitive verb: "To mix in (*with* something else); to mix intimately, mix up, commingle."

6. My claim that *Samson Agonistes* dramatizes the ultimate triumph of exclusive Christian universalism over Hebraic/Judaic particularity differs from three influential arguments concerning the relationship between the Hebraic/Judaic and the Christian in the poet's tragedy: first, that Milton denigrates the Hebraic as barbaric (Joseph Wittreich identifies Samson's fault as "that primitive Hebraic element which persists in Renaissance Christianity," in *Interpreting* Samson Agonistes [Princeton, NJ: Princeton University Press, 1986], 231); second, that Milton resists Christianizing Samson (Balachandra

Rajan argues that "the decorum of *Samson* excludes mention of grace in the theological sense, and though the restoration of the hero is compatible with and may even seem to invite a Christian reading, it must avoid announcing itself in those terms" in "to which is added *Samson Agonistes*," in *The Prison and the Pinnacle*, ed. Balachandra Rajan [Toronto: University of Toronto Press, 1973], 106–7); and third, that Milton provides a charitable and inclusive (or monistic) view of Mosaic law and of Samson as "an *Ebrew*" (*SA*, 1319) in his tragedy; see Jason Rosenblatt, "Samson's Sacrifice," in *Renaissance England's Chief Rabbi: John Selden* (Oxford: Oxford University Press, 2006), 93–111.

7. "And what shall I more say? for the time would fail me to tell of Gedeon, and of Barak, and of *Samson*, and of Jephthae; of David also, and Samuel, and *of* the prophets" (Hebrews 11:28, emphasis added).

8. Alain Badiou, *Saint Paul: The Foundation of Universalism*, trans. Ray Brassier (Stanford: Stanford University Press, 2003), 40–41.

9. Whereas the Danites are "pious followers of the Lord, but incapable of faith," Samson eventually "reaches the limits of the old law and hence is able to transcend and fulfill it"; see Joan S. Bennett, *Reviving Liberty: Radical Christian Humanism in Milton's Great Poems* (Cambridge, MA: Harvard University Press, 1989), 120, 124.

10. Should you wish to pursue this topic, I refer you to David Goldstein's award-winning essay, "Manuring Eden: Biological Conversions in *Paradise Lost*," in *Ground-Work: English Renaissance Literature and Soil Science*, ed. Hillary Eklund (Pittsburgh: Duquesne University Press, 2017), 171–93.

11. *Dialogues Concerning Two New Sciences*, trans. Henry Crew and Alfonso de Salvio (New York: Macmillan 1914), 150, http://files.libertyfund .org/files/753/0416_Bk.pdf

12. All references to Aristotle's *Physics* are to R. P. Hardie and R. K. Gaye's translation, available on the *Internet Classics Archive* by Daniel C. Stevenson, Web Atomics (1994–2009), http://classics.mit.edu/Aristotle/physics.html.

13. Stillman Drake, ed., *Discoveries and Opinions of Galileo* (New York: Doubleday Anchor, 1957), 113–14.

14. According to a biography by Galileo's pupil, Vincenzo Viviani, in 1589, Galileo dropped two balls of different masses from the Leaning Tower of Pisa to demonstrate that their time of descent was independent of their mass; Viviani, *On the Life of Galileo: Viviani's Historical Account and Other Early Biographies*, ed., trans., and annotated by Stefano Gattei (Princeton, NJ: Princeton University Press, 2019). While this story has been retold in popular accounts, Galileo himself provided no written record of such an experiment. Most historians contend that this event was a thought experiment, which did not actually take place.

15. Marissa Greenberg, "Milton Much Revolving," in "Milton and the Politics of Periodization," ed. Rachel Trubowitz, special issue, *Modern Language Quarterly* 78, no. 3 (September 2017): 379.

16. For a stimulating comparison of border walls in *Paradise Lost* and at the US-Mexico border, see Sydney Bartlett, "'Facile Gates': Walls and Identity across *Paradise Lost* and Along the US-Mexico Border," in "Milton Today, Part I," ed. Stephen B. Dobranski, special issue, *Milton Studies Milton Studies* 62, no. 2 (2020): 294–305.

17. John Rogers, *The Matter of Revolution: Science, Poetry, and Politics in the Age of Milton* (Ithaca, NY: Cornell University Press, 1998), 148.

18. Rogers, *Matter of Revolution*, 170.

19. Gerald Hammond and Austin Busch, eds, *The English Bible, King James Version: The New Testament and The Apocrypha*, vol. 2 (New York: Norton Critical Editions, 2012), 391–93.

20. David Loewenstein, *Milton and the Drama of History: Historical Vision, Iconoclasm, and the Literary Imagination* (Cambridge: Cambridge University Press, 1990), 94.

21. Jeffrey Shoulson describes the Chorus's concluding sonnet as an "infuriatingly facile summation of Samson's story"; nonetheless he also confirms that this passage "acknowledges the convergence of divine justice and mutability"; Shoulson, *Milton and the Rabbis: Hebraism, Hellenism, and Christianity* (New York: Columbia University Press, 2001), 247.

22. Gordon Teskey, "Samson and the Heap of the Dead," in *Delirious Milton: The Fate of the Poet in Modernity* (Cambridge, MA: Harvard University Press, 2006).

23. Milton makes a point of emphasizing that Samson's destruction of Dagon's temple kills only the Philistines' ruling elite: "Lords, Ladies, Captains, Councellors, or Priests, / Thir choice nobility and flower, not only / Of this but each *Philistian* City round" (*SA*, 1653–55).

24. My alternative framework takes its cue from John Guillory's assessment of "Samson's vocation" as "a compulsion to transgress the Law" in "The Father's House: *Samson Agonistes* in Its Historical Moment," in *Remembering Milton: Essays on the Texts and Traditions*, ed. Mary Nyquist and Margaret W. Ferguson (New York: Methuen, 1987), 160.

25. Samson's marriages to Philistine women are not as transgressive as they might at appear at first glance. The Hebrew Bible contains many examples of Israelite men marrying foreign women. Judah marries Shu'a the Canaanite; Joseph marries Asenath, daughter of the Egyptian priest Potiphera; Moses marries Zipporah, daughter of the Midian priest Jethro; and the list goes on and on. Indeed, the Book of Ruth strongly supports intermarriage. Samson is the fifteenth judge of Israel. Biblical scholars have determined that he reigned as a judge for up to twenty years, sometime between 1154 BCE and 1124 BCE. The Deuteronomic Code was probably introduced in the late seventh century BCE. Moreover, the Deuteronomic law against intermarriage does not forbid all marriages to non-Israelites. Rather, it limits the marriage ban to seven Canaanite nations (the Hittites, Girgashites, Amorites, Canaanites, Perizzites, Hivites, and Jebusites). The Philistines are not among these seven nations. During the Babylonian Exile in the sixth century BCE, the issue of intermarriage seems to have become a more acute problem. The prophet Malachi decries intermarriage as a profanity. Ezra the Scribe (whom the Persians appointed to lead the Hebrew exiles back to Judea) expanded the Deuteronomic prohibition against intermarriage to encompass not only the seven banned nations but also all foreign nations. Rabbinical Judaism continued this stricter line of judicial reasoning, banning marriage with all Gentiles, citing the passage from Deuteronomy. (See Avodah Zarah 36b; Avodah Zarah is included in *Nashim* [*Women*], the order of the Talmud that deals with issues

between the sexes, including laws of marriage [*kiddushin*] and of divorce [*gittin*].) Milton (and most Milton scholars) appears to be reading the account of Samson's intermarriages in the Book of Judges (the seventh book of the Hebrew Bible) through the lens of the Talmud's comprehensive ban against intermarriage. For Milton's indebtedness to Talmudic commentary, see Jeffrey Shoulson, *Milton and the Rabbis: Hebraism, Hellenism, and Christianity* (New York: Columbia University Press, 2001).

26. For example, Tobias Gregory emphasizes the difference between the divine inspiration that leads Samson to marry the woman of Timna and the "mere inference" through which he justifies his marriage to Dalila: "Samson himself distinguishes between 'the intimate impulse' that led him to marry his first Philistine wife, and his mere inference about the second marriage: 'I thought it lawful from my former act' (*SA*, line 231)"; Gregory, "The Political Messages of *Samson Agonistes*," *Studies in English Literature, 1500–1900* 50, no. 1 (Winter 2010): 179.

27. David Gay writes of the Chorus, for example: "Invariably, they endorse a restrictive and submissive posture"; Gay, "The Circumscription of Time in *Samson Agonistes*," *Christianity and Literature* 42, no. 2 (Winter 1993): 273.

28. Sigmund Freud, "The Antithetical Sense of Primal Words," in *The Standard Edition of the Complete Psychological Works of Sigmund Freud*, trans. and ed. James Strachey, vol. 11 (London: Hogarth Press, 1957), 155. Freud here quotes a passage from his own *The Interpretation of Dreams* (1900). https://www.sas.upenn.edu/~cavitch/pdf-library/Freud_Antithetical.pdf.

29. My use of the term *sacer* differs from Giorgio Agamben's in *Homo Sacer: Sovereign Power and Bare Life*, the first book of his multivolume Homo Sacer project. Nonetheless, Agamben's notion of *homo sacer* is relevant to the concerns of my chapter, albeit in ways that are beyond the scope of my argument here. Agamben's *homo sacer* (Latin for "the sacred man" or "the accursed man") refers to a figure of ancient Roman law: a person who is banned from society and may be killed by anybody, but who cannot be sacrificed in a religious ritual. *Homo sacer*, writes Agamben, "has been excluded from the religious community and from all political life: he cannot participate in the rites of his gens, nor . . . can he perform any juridically valid act. What is more, his entire existence is reduced to a bare life stripped of every right by virtue of the fact that anyone can kill him without committing homicide; he can save himself only in perpetual flight or a foreign land"; Agamben, *Homo Sacer: Sovereign Power and Bare Life*, trans. Daniel Heller-Roazen (Palo Alto, CA: Stanford University Press, 1998), 28. For Agamben, the position of the refugee coincides with that of *homo sacer*.

30. Aristotle, *Poetics*, trans. S. H. Butcher, *The Internet Classics Archive*, by Daniel C. Stevenson, Web Atomics (1994–2009), http://classics.mit.edu /Aristotle/poetics.1.1.html.

31. My contention that Milton associates the Hebrew Messenger with the sacred gains support from Jason P. Rosenblatt's observation: "The Bible uses the same word to designate 'angel' and 'messenger' both in the Hebrew and the Greek (*mal'akh, angelos*). Milton assumed everyone's familiarity with this identity"; Rosenblatt, *Renaissance England's Chief Rabbi*, 97.

32. Teskey, *Delirious Milton*, 190, 188, 189.

Rachel Trubowitz

33. For Teskey, artistic "delirium works by a kind of oscillation, a flickering on and off of hallucinatory moments in rapid succession driven by some underlying contradiction." Milton's delirium springs from "his oscillation between two incompatible perspectives, at once affirming and denying of the presence of spirit in which he creates"; Teskey *Delirious Milton*, 4–5.

34. Dayton Haskin, *Milton's Burden of Interpretation* (Philadelphia: University of Pennsylvania Press, 1994), 146.

35. Guillory, "Father's House," 160, 152.

36. Guillory, "Father's House," 160.

37. That, for Milton, Manoa stands on the wrong side of providential history finds further expression in his proposed monument to his son. Although Manoa hopes that the monument will keep Samson's Hebraic-Hellenic heroic legacy alive, he fails to recognize that this shrine will showcase the obsolescence of such heroism. As Ernest B. Gilman remarks, the proposed monument "will be a stony thing that only petrifies the outward features of Samson's 'adventures'"; Gilman, *Iconoclasm and Poetry in the English Reformation* (Chicago: University of Chicago Press, 1989), 175.

38. Rosenblatt, *Renaissance England's Chief Rabbi*, 106.

39. Rosenblatt, *Renaissance England's Chief Rabbi*, 106n32.

40. Haskin, *Milton's Burden of Interpretation*, 143.

CHAPTER 5

Moving Jewish Bodies, Moving Jewish Souls

Milton's *Paradise Regain'd*, the Jewish (Readmission) Question, and John Toland

Achsah Guibbory

Five years after Menasseh ben Israel's *The Hope of Israel* (1650) was published in England, the Amsterdam rabbi petitioned Oliver Cromwell to readmit Jews, banished from England since 1290 by edict of Edward II. The ensuing controversy raised the intersecting issues of moving Jewish bodies and souls. Should England allow the Jews, lacking a land or home of their own and always in exile, to immigrate and live in England? What would be the effect on England and her Protestant identity? Could Jews be persuaded to convert, or would they move the English from their true Protestant faith? These questions, raised in the middle of the seventeenth century, have not disappeared.

The controversy surrounding Jewish readmission has been explored but not exhausted, and the topic remains important, indeed timely. A version of "The Jewish Question"—what to do with the Jews? —has been asked ever since early Christianity, even before, and it persists. Antisemitism is on the rise globally. Hate crimes in America targeting Jews have increased every year in the past decade, with 2021 recording the highest number of incidents since the American Defense League began keeping records in 1979.[1] Hatred seems endemic in America, with violent crimes against Black, Brown, and Asian people, Muslims, immigrants, transgender people, women, and children, with Jews one of the most frequent targets. White supremacists are driven by fear that Jews, people of color, and immigrants will "replace" them. My chapter demonstrates that "replacement theory" (a conspiracy theory) is twenty-first-century America's version of early modern England's controversy over Jewish readmission, expanded. I turn to *Paradise Regain'd* to illustrate how replacement theory sheds fresh light on Milton's characterization of Jesus and the question of Jewish resettlement in England. Milton never officially weighed in on the readmission of the Jews—a silence uncharacteristic of the very opinionated poet. I argue that in *Paradise Regain'd* Milton obliquely but pointedly makes clear why England (and any Christian nation?) cannot allow the emigration of Jews to their homeland. He articulates his opposition to Jewish readmission through his Pauline representation of Jesus's progressive separation from the Jews and Judaism over the course of the brief epic.

The armed demonstration at Charlottesville, Virginia, in August 2017, featured the slogan "Jews will not replace us." Since then, we have heard that phrase frequently. The man who killed eleven Jews worshipping in the Pittsburgh Tree of Life Synagogue on Saturday, October 27, 2018, invoked the great replacement theory. So did the eighteen-year-old white shooter charged with killing ten older Black men and women in a Buffalo supermarket on a Saturday morning, May 14, 2022. The replacement theory is no longer a fringe phenomenon in America but has metastasized, entering the mainstream, voiced even by some people in Congress or running for election.[2]

The question "do Jews belong in our nation?" persists. Howard Jacobson brilliantly satirized the British anxiety in his novel, *The Finkler Question* (2010), which won the Man Booker prize.[3] Now in America, the issue of who "belongs," who is a real "American," focuses more sharply on racial difference. But race and religion are inextricably intertwined as white (predominantly evangelical Christian) supremacists have made clear.

In the January 6, 2021, violent insurrection at the Capitol, we watched white "patriots" armed with a variety of weapons, determined to take back "their country" supposedly run by a Jewish cabal of pedophiles. One leader wore a Viking helmet (signifying Nordic/Anglo-Saxon racial supremacy). We saw Nazi paraphernalia, swastikas, and confederate flags waiving. As this linking of Jews with Blacks, common among hard-right white supremacists, shows, Jews are not always considered really "white," even while enjoying "white privilege."[4] The status of Jews has remained ambiguous and slippery.

Early modern scholarship on "race before race" has been exploring the construction of Blackness, continuing the work begun with Kim F. Hall's groundbreaking *Things of Darkness* (1995). Kimberly Anne Coles's *Bad Humor: Race and Religious Essentialism* (2022) shows how the Protestant Reformation (with its new distinctions between true and false religion) linked religion to race. English Protestants imagined Catholics and Moors as dark or black—darkness as the sign of irreligion literally embodied in Africans, their supposed spiritual darkness reflected in their skin color. Coles describes an emerging "taxonomy" of Christians that divided them into Black and white. Before the Reformation, however, Jews were already identified as racially different from Christians. Geraldine Heng's meticulous research in *The Invention of Race in the European Middle Ages* (2018) shows that the racializing of Jews began in the medieval period, making them the first people that European and English people considered racially distinct.[5]

Racializing of Jewish difference did not disappear with the Reformation. Rather, it remained part of English culture, Protestant as well as Catholic. As James Shapiro's *Shakespeare and the Jews* (1996) shows, Jews were understood to be "racially different," and "notions of race, nation, and alien began to emerge in relation to confused and often contradictory ideas about the Jew."[6] Jewish religious difference was supposedly carried in the blood, but was also marked in the flesh, if not by obvious skin color, certainly by circumcision, making conversion of Jewish males especially difficult to imagine.

We have no record of Milton's opinion about Jewish readmission, although it was the subject of intense debate in the 1650s while Milton was Secretary of Foreign Tongues to Cromwell's Council of State. Milton's circle included philosemites who supported Jewish readmission, like the Baptist millenarian Henry Jessey, who chaired Cromwell's Whitehall Conference to consider "resettlement of the Jews," which lasted from December 4 to 18, 1655. Milton's friend, Moses Wall, had translated Menasseh's *Hope of Israel* (1652). The other side was represented by the Presbyterian William Prynne's *Short Demurrer To the Jewes Long discontinued barred Remitter into England* (1656) and William Hughes's *Anglo-Judaeus, or The History of the Jews, Whilst here in England* (1656). Both tracts invoked Christian antisemitic tropes and libels, representing the Jews as hateful enemies but also fearing that Jews, if they were allowed to live in England, would pollute English soil and English souls.[7] Prynne's and Hughes's pamphlets forced Cromwell abruptly to end the conference without a ruling on Jewish readmission.

Though Milton apparently never weighed in on the question, his final poem *Paradise Regain'd* most directly concerns the relation between Christianity and Judaism, the Son and Jews. In an earlier essay I argued that Milton's poem shows that by 1671 he had moved away from his earlier millenarianism and that of his radical contemporaries.[8] I have never attempted a full reading of this brief epic, perhaps avoiding a poem that is so exclusively Christian. But Milton is one of my most beloved authors, and I believe he always has something to tell us. In his imaginative retelling of the Son's temptation in the wilderness (the same one the Israelites walked through), Milton invokes verses of the apostle Paul that defined an anti-Judaism that could easily slide into antisemitism. Milton illuminates the uncomfortable truth—necessary to acknowledge as we try to move toward a more just, inclusive society—that the Bible can be and has been used in ways that encourage either tolerance and acceptance or intolerance and rejection of those who are not like us.

All Satan's temptations of Jesus involve the issue of the Son's relation to Jews and Judaism, but this feature of *Paradise Regain'd* has been not properly examined, in part, perhaps, because it is such an uncomfortable issue, but also because religious studies have recovered the "Jewish Paul" and a Jewish Jesus, recognizing that conversion does not necessarily mean one has severed their Jewish roots.[9] Eric Song sees Milton's Jesus as "a Jewish prophet living under Roman rule" and embracing his "pure Hebraic heritage." Song finds a "cleavage between the Jewish Jesus and the Christian Milton."[10] But, I would argue that Milton's *Paradise Regain'd* creates a Son in his image, and "pure Hebraic" is the catch. There is an anti-Jewish strain in Milton, even as he is England's most Hebraic poet. Offering a new reading, I show how *Paradise Regain'd*, in its use of the Pauline epistles as they marked the difference between Christian and Jew, gospel and law, foregrounds the Son's progressive detachment from the Jews and Judaism in ways suggesting Milton's likely attitude toward Jewish conversion and readmission to England. The final section of this chapter considers the controversial 1753 bill that would have allowed the naturalization of Jews living in England, and John Toland's *Reasons for Naturalizing the Jews in Great Britain* (1714). Toland's pamphlet appeared forty years after Milton's death, and almost forty before the so-called Jew Bill triggered anti-Jewish Protestant outrage. A devoted admirer of Milton who was responsible for promoting Milton's prose, a deist who considered himself a Christian, Toland presented an eloquent case for welcoming Jews into England, expressing an unusual and radically tolerant point of view.

Milton, Jews, and Liberty

No major English poet immersed himself so deeply in the Hebrew Bible and Jewish learning as Milton, much of his knowledge filtered through John Selden.[11] Milton imagined in his hopeful period that the English were God's chosen people like ancient Israel. Yet Protestants could embrace the Hebrew Bible, and not be philosemitic or embrace Jews.[12] Milton's prose describes the Jews as inclined to slavery, unworthy of freedom, and thus unlikely candidates for being admitted to an England that he had hoped would be a beacon of liberty and the Reformation but seemed too often inclined to backslide from the true religion, unwilling to do the hard work for liberty.

The Old Testament history of "Jewish" Israel could be positively appropriated by Protestants as their story—the story of the chosen, of Israel—and for precedent. It could also be used to condemn Jews, thought to be descendants of biblical Israelites but not "spiritual" (Christian) Israel since they had rejected Christ. *The Tenure of Kings and Magistrates* invokes God's words to the Israelites in Deuteronomy 17:14 ("When thou art come into the land which the Lord thy God giveth thee, and shalt say, I will set a king over me, like as all the nations about me") to defend the English people's right to get rid of Charles I. But even that mention of the ancient Israelites was double-edged. As Milton observes, "their changing displeased him." Earlier in *Tenure*, Milton had spoken of freedom as the "natural birthright" of all people, only to add that "generally the people of Asia, and with them the Jews also, especially since the time they chose a King against the advice and counsel of God, are noted by wise Authors much inclinable to slavery."[13] Is it monarchy that makes a people incapable of freedom? Or is it a people's incapacity for freedom that leads them to want a king? Is the inclination to servitude natural in some people, or learned? And even if learned, does it then become imprinted in their nature? These are the questions Milton also considered in relation to the English after they welcomed the return of the king in 1660.

While admiring the republicanism of the ancient Greeks and Romans, Milton tied liberty to Christianity, specifically reformed Christianity. His theology was complex, at once radical and conservative, but as Warren Chernaik observes, Milton always defined "Christian liberty in terms of freedom from slavery."[14] Toward the end of his *Second Defense of the English People* (1654), Milton warned the English that their liberty will "prove the worst of slavery. Unless by means of piety . . . you clear the horizon of the mind from those mists of superstition which arise from the ignorance of true religion"—that is, true Protestant religion.

And then, of course, there is Milton's fear in *The readie and easie way to establish a free Commonwealth* (1660) that the English people, desiring the return of Charles II, have proved that they are indeed like biblical (Jewish) Israel, about to lose their chosen status, choosing slavery over liberty, preferring to worship an "idol" rather than God. The English "seem now chusing them a captain back for Egypt," impetuously running to "a precipice of destruction" in their "epidemic madness." *Paradise Lost* does not treat Jewish Israel kindlier. Though the Israelites are given "Lawes" and "Rites" at Sinai that instruct by signs about Christ ("informing them, by types / And shadowes, of that destin'd Seed"; *PL*, 12.230–33), they are incapable of reading them. Solomon indulges his wives' idol worship even as he builds the temple. The Israelite nation is characterized by sin. When the Son is born, he is "naild to the Cross / By his own Nation" and "The Law" is "there crucifi'd" (*PL*, 12.413–17), a violent image for the death of Mosaic law, even though Milton at the beginning of the poem invoked as his muse the spirit that inspired Moses. Adam becomes a Christian, accepting the Son as his savior in this final book of Milton's epic, having learned the inadequacy of Judaism even before such a thing exists. Milton's negative remarks about the Jews, Judaism, and Jewish Israel consistently echo verses in the New Testament and especially Galatians that identify Jews, in their devotion to "the law" and refusal to embrace Jesus, as unfree, in bondage, incapable of "Christian liberty."

Rabbi Menasseh ben Israel and the Readmission Issue

Menasseh's petition to have the Jews once again allowed to reside in England—even if it had an economic and commercial aspect—was driven by his messianic expectation of the gathering of all the Jews including the Ten Tribes back to their "promised land," to Jerusalem, as Isaiah had prophesied. According to Jewish tradition, God will only gather the Jews when they have been scattered throughout all corners of the world. Menasseh thought that once the Jews lived in England and the British Isles, the ingathering and redemption would start, and God would bring them back to the land of Israel. England, that is, would only be a waystation. That their stay would be temporary did not assuage the anxiety of the English. Menasseh also was concerned with the souls of Jews; thus, his petition to Oliver Cromwell and his

Council of State asked that the Jews be able to worship openly in England, not just to dwell there. He asked that Jews be allowed to "have our Synagogues, and keep our own publick worship," to have a cemetery outside town, where they could bury their dead according to Jewish traditions, and even their own courts of law for their own matters.[15] Such requests frightened those English Christians who, rather than expecting the Jews' conversion, thought they were inconvertible, or even would actively seduce the English to Judaism.

Prynne feared that the English people would lose their English and Christian liberty. Throughout his *Short Demurrer*, he labels the Jews as "alien" as well as "anti-Christian." He was distressed at the thought that Jews would be buried in "English soyl."[16] William Hughes charged in *Anglo-Judaeus* that the Jews are "National enemies" of England as well as of Christians.[17] Why would you let an enemy invade your land?

Those few English people, such as Henry Jessey and John Dury, who supported readmission, did so on millenarian expectations that the Jews might be converted, whether coinciding with or ushering in the Second Coming of Jesus, with his thousand-year reign with the saints. Christian millenarian expectations in the mid-seventeenth century intersected with Jewish messianic hopes raised by pogroms in Eastern Europe since catastrophe was for Jews a sign that their Messiah was soon to come. For all three groups—Jews seeking asylum, English millenarians hoping for Jewish conversion, and English Protestants thinking Jews were not convertible—the movements of Jewish bodies and souls, resettlement and redemption, were interconnected.

England was anti-Catholic, but hostility toward Jews was different. The ancestors of English Protestants had been Catholic. Jews were "alien" in a way that Catholics were not. William Hughes insisted there is a natural "antipathy betwixt the English Nation" and the Jews that can never "admit of an reconciliation."[18] Then there was their supposed stubbornness, which meant they would never convert, could never be moved to become reformed Christians. If their suffering was, for Christians, the "witness" of their error (see the essay by Rachel Trubowitz in this volume), the Jews' very faithfulness to their religion, throughout millennia of persecution, was evidence of the Jews' stubborn resistance to Jesus and the truth of the gospel. So how could they find a home in a Christian nation? Indeed, Prynne wrote, Jews "always have been and still are professed Enemies in arms against the Person, Kingdom, and Gospel of our Lord Jesus Christ."[19] Rather than being converted, they were likely to convert (if not kill) the English. Prynne recounted meeting a group of English "soldiers" who worried, "We must now all turn

Jews."[20] Jessey, in his *Narrative* of the Whitehall Conference on the readmission of the Jews, noted that "some . . . though desiring heartily the Jews conversion, yet feared greatly, it would prove the subversion of many here, if Jews were suffered to return hither, because so many here are soon carried aside to new Opinions."[21]

There was a paradox: Jews were spiritually unmovable, and yet always moving, with no place of rest. In chapter 1 of this volume, John Rumrich speaks of "their migratory impulse," and cites Jack Goldman, who pointed out that the word "Hebrew" "first occurs in the Bible as 'an epithet for Abraham,' deriving from a Hebrew root meaning 'crossing over or passing through.' "[22] But migration is often punishment in the Hebrew Bible, or a consequence of persecution, not something considered positive but exile for biblical Israelites and for later Jews.

Milton's *Paradise Regain'd*

Milton was someone with "new Opinions" (disliked by Prynne), but his Protestant faith was firm, unlikely to be "subverted" by the presence of Jews. Only once before had Milton raised the issue of the conversion of the Jews, in his *Observations upon the Articles of Peace with the Irish Rebels* (1649) at the height of millenarian fervor. But the issue assumes prominence in *Paradise Regain'd* (1671), to which he added *Samson Agonistes*.

Kathy Lavezzo has a compelling reading of *Samson Agonistes* as a closet drama that presents "an indirect yet important Miltonic statement on readmission."[23] Samson's lack of interest in the deliverance of the Jews, she argues, reflects Milton's disinterest in their restoration. *Paradise Regain'd*, however, directly brings up the question about whether at least some of the Jews will in the future be "grafted in," as Paul said in Romans 11:19, whether they will accept Jesus and be redeemed. This issue weaves throughout the fabric of this poem in ways that suggest Milton was not simply disinterested but opposed to bringing in Jews to an England inhabited by people who were behaving like those biblical Israelites who longed to return to Egypt.

Milton's poem is, of course, about Satan's Temptation of the Son, taken from the brief account in Luke, but he fleshes it out, much as he did the biblical account of Adam and Eve in Genesis. Milton's interpretation of Luke is shaped by Paul's epistles, which defined an opposition between Jew/Judaism and Christian/gospel that became part of mainstream Christianity, and the opposition to Jewish readmission.

Achsah Guibbory 135

The Jews' conversion explicitly comes up at the end of book 3 of *Paradise Regain'd*, where the Son's words dash millenarian hopes that the Jews would soon convert, inaugurating the reign of Jesus. But before turning to that passage, we must look at the complex relation of "Jesus Messiah Son of God" (*PR*, 2.4) to the Jews as it unfolds up to that point in the poem.

The three temptations of the Son in *Paradise Regain'd* are based on the account in the Gospel of Luke: to make bread out of stone, to accept the kingdoms of the world and all their glory from Satan, and to cast himself from the pinnacle of the Temple at Jerusalem. Milton adds two more temptations to this trinity: the temptation to rescue/save the Jews, who are supposedly his people, and the temptation of classical (secular) wisdom. We watch the Son progressively, decisively separating himself from his fellow Jews and Israelites, even though he is going to be the fulfillment of their history and story, conquering sin and death, recovering Paradise by redeeming "mankind, whose sins / Full weight must be transferr'd upon my head" (*PR*, 1.266–67). Are the Jews part of "mankind"? It is not clear that the Jews will enter that paradise; maybe some of the Ten Tribes, but not the Jews—a distinction we will return to.

Since Milton offers a new, updated gospel, he begins the poem, as he did *Paradise Lost*, by invoking the spirit of God, here described as the "Spirit" who led the Son into the "Desert," to "inspire, / As thou art wont, my prompted Song . . . to tell of deeds / Above Heroic, though in secret done, / And unrecorded left through many an Age" (*PR*, 1.8, 9, 11, 14–16). Milton's brief epic is itself a hidden, secret "deed" (or written document), now published, the mirror of the secret "deeds" of the Son. Invoking this divine muse, Milton gives himself poetic liberties and liberty of imagination but also liberty to add things to the Bible as he did in *Paradise Lost*. What he inserts into Luke's gospel is the contemporary question of what will happen to the Jews, what to do with them.

In book 1 we learn that the problem of the Jews has been on the Son's mind ever since he was twelve and went into the Temple during the feast of Passover to talk with "The Teachers of our Law" (*PR*, 1.212). It was a significant moment, as Passover marks deliverance of the Israelites from the bondage of Egypt, a feast that Jews celebrate as anticipating their redemption in a messianic time when Jerusalem and the Temple will be restored (however they might interpret that symbolically). Christians, of course, see Jesus as fulfilling it with his Last Supper and his Crucifixion redeeming Adam and Eve's sin. As the Son describes his experience as a twelve-year-old child whose "mind was set / Serious to learn and know" (*PR*, 1.202–3), he says that even at that time he was inflamed with the idea of "heroic acts," one of which would be "To rescue *Israel* from the *Roman* yoke" (*PR*, 1.216–17). That is, to rescue her from bondage. But Milton always thought of bondage in spiritual as well as political and material terms; for him the "yoke" of bondage was never just political. At twelve, apparently, the Son thought of Israel's bondage in this material way. At that point, he had "read" "The Law of God . . . and found it sweet" (*PR*, 1.207). We will soon see he is different now. He has matured.

Milton divides the first temptation the Son faces in the desert between the challenge to make bread out of stones and the temptation to eat the food of the banquet Satan provides. These two challenges occur in the first two books of the poem, and both reveal a Son separating himself from "the Law," from Judaism as described by Paul in the New Testament.

The first temptation seems simple enough, but Milton's phrasing differs from Luke's in a significant way. Luke 4:3 reads: "The devil said to him, 'If you are the Son of God, tell this stone to become bread.' " But Milton's version is as follows: "if thou be the Son of God, Command / That out of these hard stones be made thee bread" (*PR*, 1.342–43). Why "hard stones"? I suggest Milton saw in the Son's first temptation an echo of the stony heart that is the biblical trope for sin. It appears first in Exodus where Pharaoh's heart is "hardened" (Ex. 9:12) and then in Ezekiel 11:19: "And I will give them singleness of heart and put a new spirit within them; I will remove their heart of stone and give them a heart of flesh." Ezekiel warns Israel, "Cast away from yourselves all the transgressions you have committed, and fashion for yourselves a new heart and a new spirit. Why should you die, O house of Israel?" (Ezekiel 18:31). What was in the Hebrew Bible a criticism of Israel for having strayed from the path and disobeyed God, became a way for Christians to define themselves against the Jews. Paul in Romans 11:25 said "a partial hardening has come upon Israel," but the "stony heart" became a trope that Christians regularly applied to the Jews, considered not only guilty of deicide (as Milton says in *PL*, 12) but hardened in their stubborn devotion to their religion, their refusal to accept Jesus as Messiah. The Jews reside, quietly, in Milton's changes to Luke's language.

In refusing to perform Satan's first temptation, the Son performs the patience that will characterize him throughout, patience that makes some readers (like Satan) complain that he does not actually do anything. Patience is what the Son commends in Job, "righteous *Job*" whose "patience won" (*PR*, 1.425–26). As we know, Milton looked to the Book of Job in writing this poem, but it is important to note

Achsah Guibbory   137

that while it is part of the Hebrew Bible, Job is a righteous Gentile, not a Jewish Israelite.[24] In book 3 of *Paradise Regain'd*, the Son will again turn to Job, God's "servant," as the example of true "fame" and "glory"; "Patient *Job*" (*PR*, 3.67, 65, 69, 95).

This patience is not exactly the standing and waiting that Milton proposed to himself in his early sonnet, but a vigorous, active refusal to perform "works" or visible, corporeal "deeds"—the terms that Paul uses to describe Jews who are under the Law, who live according to the Mosaic law. Only God's grace will save. "A man is justified by faith" not by "the works" of "the law" (Rom. 3:27–28; Rom. 5:1). For Paul, faith and belief are opposed to "works" and "deeds," terms he associates with Judaism, the "law" that is being superseded. "By the deeds of the law there shall no flesh be justified in his [God's] sight" (Rom. 3:20). Milton's Son's refusal to act echoes these verses in Romans. The Son performs the contrast between Christian faith and Jewish law, between faith and deeds. When Satan urges deeds that would show the Son's lack of faith in God, the Son's very refusals to act demonstrate his faith. Milton's Jesus, that is, embodies the righteousness of a Christian long before the Crucifixion. Grace has already replaced the law. Because faith properly precedes works, the poem can conclude with the Angelic Choir telling Jesus, "thy glorious work / Now enter, and begin to save mankind" (*PR*, 4.634–35).

Even in the first book Milton's Son shows he has moved from outward "deeds" to "inward" things, but the Son also moves beyond the Hebrew Bible's distinction between Israel and "the Nations" (the "Gentiles") who are idolaters, worshipping false gods and idols (*PR*, 1.215, 463, 432, 456). After refusing Satan's command to create bread out of stones, he denounces Satan's lying "Oracles," declaring they are now "ceast" (*PR*, 1.456), an echo of Milton's *Nativity Ode* where the Son's birth silences the Delphic oracles. But here the Son speaks, and "Oracles" is a complicated word. In Romans 3:2 Paul remarks that "the oracles of God" were committed to the Jews, only a few verses later to contrast the Jewish "law of works" with the Christian "law of faith." Perhaps Milton, like Paul, is indirectly linking Jewish "law" with the pagan oracles, both of which have been silenced now that (as the Son says) "God hath now sent his living Oracle / Into the World, to teach his final will" (*PR*, 1.460–61).

Maybe the Jews are no better than the idolatrous nations that have not yet embraced the Son: "God hath justly giv'n the Nations up / To thy Delusions; justly, since they fell / Idolatrous; but when his purpose is / Among them to declare his Providence / To thee not known"

(*PR*, 1.442–46). Within five lines, the Son moves from condemning the nations' idolatry to suggesting that the Gentiles will in time be the people God has chosen, those to whom Jesus's apostles will spread the word. Though many of Jesus's apostles were Jews by birth, it is "the Nations" who will become Christians, not the Jewish nation. This is of course the story of Christianity. But in Milton's poem, the Son seems to be already in the first book leaving most of the Jews behind.

Historically, Christianity emerged as a sect of Judaism, and only gradually did it separate, increasingly defining itself against Judaism and Jews. But in *Paradise Regain'd* in the Son's resistance to Satan's temptations, he performs that separation from Jews, Judaism, and things Jewish.

The second book begins with Andrew and Simon who "With others though in Holy Writ not nam'd" had been baptized and remained at the Jordan (*PR*, 2.8). These are Jews who have accepted the Son: "our eyes beheld / Messiah certainly now come, so long / Expected of our Fathers" (*PR*, 2.31–33). Expecting that "deliverance is at hand, / The Kingdom shall to *Israel* be restor'd" (*PR*, 2.35–36), Simon and Andrew still think as Jews. They are disappointed, "fall'n" from "high hope" that deliverance would happen quickly, and that it would involve God "free[ing] thy people from thir yoke" (*PR*, 2.31, 30, 48)—their bondage under Roman rule. Simon and Andrew still understand things materially and literally, much like Satan, who interprets prophecies literally, and who thinks physical might and power and earthly wisdom are what will enable the Son to rule. Maybe these baptized Jews are not yet fully Christian; they still think of the Jews as the Son's "people." At this point, Simon and Andrew are like Paul's Jews who, not having fully achieved Christian liberty, not having fully evolved, do not recognize that restoration of Israel is not material, a matter of moving bodies.

This raises the troubling question: are baptized and converted Jews ever considered truly Christian? Maybe a select few are for Milton, because we soon see Andrew and Simon achieve the Christian patience the Son will show and that the Son's mother achieves (*PR*, 2.102), for they say, "let us wait; thus far He hath perform'd, . . . Let us be glad of this, and all our fears / Lay on his Providence; he will not fail" (*PR*, 2.49, 53–54).

The second book features the banquet scene, where Satan tempts the Son with food as well as young boys. The Son had slept, dreaming of "meats and drinks" (*PR*, 2.265). Satan now prompts him with the offer of food, saying that he does not "mention . . . Meats by the Law unclean" (*PR*, 2.327–28), offering the Son "A Table richly spred" with "meats of noblest sort / And savour, Beasts of chase, or Fowl of game" (*PR*, 2.340–42). Also "all Fish from Sea or Shore, / Freshet, or purling Brook, of shell or fin" (*PR*, 2.344–45).[25] Satan tells the Son, "These are not Fruits forbidden, no interdict / Defends the touching of these viands pure" (*PR*, 2.369–70). He is lying, of course, because shellfish are "unclean" as are at least some "beasts of chase" and "Fowl" (rabbit, ostrich, foxes, boars, to name a few). The Son has a dilemma: if he tells Satan that these are forbidden, he shows he is still tied to the Law; if he eats these foods, he has obeyed Satan. But Satan is challenging the Son not just to *eat* but also to *say* that these foods are forbidden to Jews. The Son's solution is brilliant. In not addressing the obvious fact of "unclean meats," the Son shows he has already moved beyond being concerned with Jewish dietary law; it is not worth talking about. This silence actually speaks, as the Son distinguishes between "giver[s]" (*PR*, 2.322; like the Lady in Milton's *Mask*, line 775) and not between "clean" and "unclean" foods. Though the Son asserts his power to "command" his own food "When and where likes me best" (*PR*, 2.382), for now he shows his power through refusal, restraint, withholding, patience.

Book 2 ends with the Son emphasizing "the inner man, the nobler part" (*PR*, 2.477), contrasting the spiritual with the corporeal, rejecting Satan's offers of wealth as well as food as irrelevant. The opposition between the spirit and bodily desires expresses a Pauline dualism at odds with the Hebraic monism of the middle, Edenic books of *Paradise Lost*. The consensus that Milton was a monist derives from the excellent work of Stephen Fallon and Jason Rosenblatt. But Milton was, as Rachel Trubowitz argues in her *PMLA* article, "a dualist as well as a monist." Rosenblatt also sees Pauline dualism both in Milton's earlier writing and in his later *De Doctrina Christiana*, observing that the Pauline epistles are "among the most dualistic of Western texts."[26]

Has *Paradise Regain'd* moved beyond Milton's earlier monism? Maybe not entirely. Philippa Earle finds Hebraic monism in Milton's representation of the Son's progress in "divine understanding," a progress "based on Maimonides' teaching" about prophecy.[27] Yet it should not surprise us that this poem about the Temptation of Jesus recounted in the New Testament is essentially Pauline, and Pauline dualism has implications for how Milton's Son treats the question of the Jews and their redemption that the Son will face in book 3.

In book 3 of *Paradise Regain'd* the Son rejects the appeal of earthly glory, the offer of earthly kingdoms, in favor of a heavenly glory or spiritual kingdom, again enacting the Pauline opposition between the

140   Moving Jewish Bodies, Moving Jewish Souls

corporeal or "fleshly" and the spiritual or inward (*PR*, 3.387). In this context the Jewish Israel comes up as Satan urges the Son to rescue the Jews who are living under Roman rule:

> Zeal of thy Fathers house, Duty to free
> Thy Country from her Heathen servitude;
> So shalt thou best fullfil, best verifie
> The Prophets old, who sung thy endless raign. (*PR*, 3.175–78)

Satan pretends to accept that the Son is the Messiah who will fulfill the prophets' words, but the Son again refuses the call to act. "All things are best fulfill'd in their due time" (*PR*, 3.182). Satan has just appealed to the Son's ties to his people by describing their suffering. "*Judaea* now and all the promis'd land / Reduc't a Province under Roman yoke" (*PR*, 3.157–58); "The Temple" and "the Law" desecrated by the Romans (*PR*, 3.161–62)—the things sacred to the Jews. What is striking is the Son's silence about these things and the suffering of the Jews under Rome. Are they not his people anymore? Is the Temple he visited when he was twelve, debating with the rabbis, no longer important to him? Or Jerusalem? The Son's detachment is part of the pattern in the poem whereby the Jews become not his concern. The "Saviour of mankind" (*PR*, 1.187) is no longer eager as he was as a youth "To rescue *Israel* from the *Roman* yoke" (*PR*, 1.217).[28]

The Tempter then brings the Son to a high mountain to show him the empires he is offering and brings up Judah's time in Babylon, a "long captivity" that "*Israel* . . . still mourns" (*PR*, 3.279). It is only Judah that the Son is here asked to rescue, Judah conquered by Babylon in 587 BCE and now in bondage under Rome. But soon Satan turns to the Ten Tribes of the Northern Kingdom of Israel, who were conquered by the Assyrians in 722 BCE, taken into captivity and scattered. Satan tells the Son he needs the power of Parthia to regain the "royal seat" of his "Father *David*" (*PR*, 3.373, 353) and to effect "Deliverance of thy brethren, those ten Tribes / Whose off-spring in his Territory yet serve" (*PR*, 3.374–75). As usual Satan imagines the throne will be material and that military weapons will be necessary, but also important is Satan's reference to "David" four times in thirty-one lines, echoing Satan's earlier insistence on Jesus's Jewish father.

> . . . to a Kingdom thou art born, ordain'd
> To sit upon thy Father *David*'s Throne;
> By Mother's side thy Father. (*PR*, 3.152–54)

Satan is obsessed with Jewish genealogy, although the poem repeatedly calls Jesus "the Son of God," an identity Satan cannot comprehend. The Son's "answer" refers to God as "The Father" who has "decreed" his "raign" (*PR,* 3.181, 184–86).

What about those dispersed Israelites from the Ten Tribes? Satan insists that only if the Son will "deliver" them "from servitude" will he "reign" on the "Throne of *David* in full glory" (*PR,* 3.380–85). To Jesus, however, genealogy matters no more than a material, earthly throne. Both are a matter of bodies and blood, the fleshly and corporeal, rather than the spiritual.

> My brethren, as thou call'st them, those Ten Tribes
> I must deliver, if I mean to raign
> *David*'s true heir, and his full Scepter sway
> To just extent over all *Israel*'s Sons. (*PR,* 3.403–6)

Does the Son consider them his "brethren?" With his mocking phrase "as thou call'st them," he distances himself from those Northern Tribes. The biblical David united the Twelve Tribes of Israel. In the tenth century BCE, after Solomon's death, the kingdom of Israel split into the Northern Kingdom of the Ten Tribes and the Southern Kingdom of Judah and Benjamin, always referred to as Judah. The Hebrew prophets prophesied that in the future God would gather them and unite all twelve tribes. That was the hope that inspired Menasseh ben Israel when he published *The Hope of Israel* and petitioned Cromwell. The Son's response to Satan implicitly but strongly dismisses this Jewish belief. There will be no united Jewish nation under a Davidic king. The Son's kingdom will include the Gentiles and will not be tied to genealogy. But will it include Jews beyond those who have already embraced Jesus?

The Son has already shown indifference to the plight of Judaea. Perhaps only Jews like Simon and Andrew who have been baptized are the "remnant of [Jewish] Israel" that Paul, reinterpreting Isaiah, said would be saved (Rom. 9:27). "As for those captive Tribes [the Northern Kingdom], themselves were they / Who wrought their own captivity, fell off / From God to worship Calves, the Deities / Of *Egypt, Baal* next and *Ashtaroth*" (*PR,* 3.414–17). The Northern Tribes embraced "the Idolatries" of the heathen, committed "other worse then heathenish crimes" (*PR,* 3.418–19), never were penitent, and "left a race behind / Like to themselves, distinguishable scarce / From Gentils but by Circumcision vain" (*PR,* 3.423–25). Milton's Jesus rejects them abruptly: "No, let them serve / Thir enemies, who serve Idols with God" (*PR,* 3.431–32).

Yet the Son holds out the possibility of redemption for the Ten Tribes through a miracle not of his doing. God

> at length, time to himself best known,
> Remembring *Abraham*, by some wond'rous call
> May bring them back repentant and sincere . . .
> To his due time and providence I leave them. (*PR*, 3.433–35, 440)

In 1987 N. I. Matar published an essay in which he read the Son's words about the Ten Tribes as suggesting that Milton was a "Restorationist" who believed the Jews would be "restored," in the sense of embracing Christ as their savior.[29] Northrup Frye heard in these lines "a gentle tone" and suggested that "Milton cannot allow Christ to dismiss the unfaithful tribes without adding a few wistful cadences in another key."[30] I do not read these lines or their tone in the same way, but rather as part of Milton's Son detaching himself from all Jewish Israel, the Ten Tribes as well as Jews of Judaea. Still the Ten Tribes get the Son's attention, for he says that at some indefinite (unpredictable) time, God "May bring them back." Are they potentially more redeemable than Judah? Or potentially unredeemable, like Judah?

Many Christians distinguished between the Ten Tribes of the northern kingdom of Israel and the Jews from the southern kingdom of Israel. No one knew where the Ten Tribes, dispersed and scattered after Assyria's conquest of the Northern Kingdom, were now. But in seventeenth-century England there was considerable interest and some theories. Menasseh's *Hope of Israel* opens with an account of Antonio Montezino's testimony in front of the Torah in an Amsterdam synagogue about a group of "Indians" he encountered in Quito Province in South America. He was convinced they were Jews. Montezino's "discovery" seemed to confirm a theory that already had currency in the seventeenth century—that the Indians in the New World were descendants of the "Lost" Ten Tribes. The same year that Menasseh published *Hope of Israel*, Thomas Thorowgood published *Jewes in America* (1650). In 1631 the Cambridge-educated minister John Eliot had immigrated to New England as the missionary or "Apostle" to the Indians, convinced they were descendants of the lost tribes.

The distinction between the Ten Tribes and the Jews gained traction in seventeenth-century England as Protestants pondered the possible conversion of the Jews as well as of the Indians in America. The theory that the American Indians were descendants of the Ten Tribes persisted in America well into the nineteenth century, repeated by Ezra Stiles, president of Yale in the late eighteenth century, and featured in Joseph Smith's *The Book of Mormon* (1830). In nineteenth-century Britain, the notion of the "Two Houses" of Israel (one Judah and the other "Israel," or Ephraim, the "lost" tribes) became the basis of British-Israel ideology promoted by John Wilson's *Our Israelitish Origin: Lectures on Ancient Israel, and the Israelitish Origin of the Modern Nations of Europe* (1840). Wilson claimed that the British, Anglo-Saxon, Celtic, Germanic, and Nordic people were genealogical descendants of the Ten Tribes, but definitely not Jews, that is, of the House of Judah. We still find traces of this ideology today.

Perhaps the Ten Tribes are redeemable in a future the Son cannot imagine, but it would take an act of God, since all Jewish Israel is in a state of bondage, both physical and spiritual. Behind Milton's expansion of Luke to highlight the Son's changing relation to Jewish Israel lies Paul, as we have seen. But it is chapter 4 of the Epistle to Galatians that provides the critical subtext of Milton's entire poem, for there Paul, the converted Jew, defined "Christian liberty" against Jewish bondage, rewriting the Old Testament narrative of the promise, transferring it to Christians.

> [22] For it is written, that Abraham had two sons, the one by a bondmaid, the other by a freewoman.
> [23] But he who was of the bondwoman was born after the flesh; but he of the freewoman was by promise.
> [24] Which things are an allegory: for these are the two covenants; the one from the mount Sinai, which gendereth to bondage, which is Agar.
> [25] For this Agar is mount Sinai in Arabia, and answereth to Jerusalem which now is, and is in bondage with her children.
> [26] But Jerusalem which is above is free, which is the mother of us all.
> [27] For it is written, Rejoice, thou barren that bearest not; break forth and cry, thou that travailest not: for the desolate hath many more children than she which hath an husband.
> [28] Now we, brethren, as Isaac was, are the children of promise.
> [29] But as then he that was born after the flesh persecuted him that was born after the Spirit, even so it is now.
> [30] Nevertheless what saith the scripture? Cast out the bondwoman and her son: for the son of the bondwoman shall not be heir with the son of the freewoman.
> [31] So then, brethren, we are not children of the bondwoman, but of the free. (Gal. 4:22–31)

Addressing the Galatian Christians who thought they needed to follow Jewish law and undergo circumcision, Paul defines the difference between Jew and Christian as the contrast between those in bondage and those who are free. How different this passage is from Paul's universalist claim in Galatians 3:28, "There is neither Jew nor Greek, slave nor free, male nor female for you are all one in Jesus Christ," though actually only if you accept Jesus and his gospel. In her essay in this volume, Rachel Trubowitz finds that this verse figured in "the profoundly disturbing" yet potentially redemptive scene of the dead Samson in *Samson Agonistes*, "immixt" with the dead bodies of the Philistines, with Samson at the end as both the dead Jew, memorialized by his earthly father, and the one who returns to his divine father's house, joining the lineup of proto-Christian heroes in Hebrews 11.

In contrast to Galatians 3:28, Galatians 4 is thoroughly supersessionist in its revision (or rather, inversion) of the story of Sarah and Hagar in Genesis 16 and 21. Christians become the children of Sarah, while the Jews are children of the "bondwoman" Hagar. Christians are the "heir" of God's promises, the Jews are now Ishmael cast out into the desert. This passage held antisemitic potential, as we see in Pauline Hopkins's early twentieth-century serial novel *Hagar's Daughter*, which is discussed in this volume by Reginald A. Wilburn, to whom I am indebted for his innovative work on Milton and Black writers in America.

Wilburn shows how Hopkins's *Hagar's Daughter* deftly uses Milton's "Satanic epic" *Paradise Lost* to indict "slavery's white supremacist ideology," "preaching a gospel of Black revolt." That gospel also includes a poem "Hagar" by Eliza Poitevent Nicholson, the final stanza of which Hopkins uses toward the end of the first part of her novel. Explaining both the poem and the title of Hopkins's book, Wilburn underscores the tradition in African American culture of identifying with the Egyptian slave Hagar. But there is more to say, for in addition to identifying the Egyptian Hagar with the Black experience of enslavement in the United States, Nicholson reads the Genesis story of Hagar through Galatians 4:22–31, transforming it in troubling, if fascinating, ways.

That Hagar (servant/slave of Sarai/Sarah) is an "Egyptian slave" allows two different biblical narratives to be combined: the story of Hagar in Genesis and the later story of the Israelites in Egypt. As a shared narrative important to both Jewish and Black identity, the Exodus story of liberation could provide an opportunity for alliance, as it did in the civil rights movement, when in 1965 Rabbi Abraham Joshua Heschel marched alongside Martin Luther King Jr. from Selma

Achsah Guibbory 145

to Montgomery. But not always, especially when the Exodus story and the story of Hagar are read through Galatians, as both Nicholson and Hopkins do. In Nicholson's poem—and thus Hopkins's novel—Hagar takes the place of the ancient Israelites in bondage, while Sarah and Abraham take the place of the hated Pharoah. The Hebraicized Pharoah is cursed, whereas the Egyptian Hagar belongs to the "nations" that inherit God's earlier promises to Jewish Israel. In the genealogy of the novel, Nicholson and Hopkins, descendants of enslaved Black women, Hagar's daughters, are God's beloved. Sarah (and Abraham) and Jewish Israel are not just disinherited and replaced, as in Galatians, but now identified as white enslavers. The poem's final stanza, which addresses Abraham in outrage, declares that "Egypt's Gods" (having replaced Old Testament Israel's God) now accompany the modern Hagar and will be her "avengers" in the future.

> . . . in whatever distant land your god,
> Your cruel god of Israel, is known,
> There, too, the wrongs that you have done this day
> To Hagar and your first-born,
> Shall waken and uncoil themselves, and hiss
> Like adders at the name of Abraham.[31]

Bearing the guilt of all white enslavers, Jews are doomed to be the objects of divine vengeance.

The Jews are not doomed in Milton's *Paradise Regain'd*, but, except for the earliest disciples, they are stuck under the covenant from Sinai, "which gendereth to bondage" (Gal. 4:24). The formerly chosen are now unchosen. Whether they are Judaea under Roman yoke or the Ten Tribes in captivity, Jewish Israel is marked as unfree, their future uncertain, inscrutable even to the Son of God. In his early divorce tracts Milton suggested a harmony between Mosaic law and the gospel, but not in book 12 of *Paradise Lost* or in his late *Paradise Regain'd*.[32]

Galatians informs Milton's poem, not the verses in Romans 11, in which Paul envisions a remnant of his brethren in "the flesh" being redeemed by God's "election of grace" (Rom. 11:14, 5). Millenarians cited the verses from Romans 11 when they supported Jewish readmission, expecting that the Jews would convert and there would be "one fold" (John 10:16). But they have no place in *Paradise Regain'd*. Long experience, and probably disillusion with the English, whom he had identified with biblical Israel, have dashed the hopes for peace and reconciliation that Milton may have had in 1649.

146   Moving Jewish Bodies, Moving Jewish Souls

Not only does Milton's poem identify Jewish Israel with bondage; there is an unsettling association between the Jews and Satan. Satan's "carnal" and "literal" understanding of the prophecies and of Israel, represents what Christians insisted was a Jewish incapacity to understand the spiritual meaning of scripture. He embodies both "materiality" and the spiritual blindness that Paul decried in Romans 8, with its contrast between flesh and spirit, between those "carnally minded" (Jews bound to the "law") and those "spiritually minded" (having faith in Christ). It is Satan, not the Son, who reads scripture Jewishly, blind to its spiritual meaning, and whose offers are always material, the Son having long ago left that perspective behind.[33]

The final temptation occurs in book 4, introduced by Milton's long addition to Luke in which Satan offers the Son classical learning, wisdom, and poetry, saying the Son will need this learning to "converse" with the "*Gentiles*" (*PR*, 4.229), who will be his people. But the Son declares he has already received "Light . . . from the fountain of light" (*PR*, 4.289) and exalts the "inspir'd" songs (*PR*, 4.350) of the Bible, its hymns and psalms, above Gentile wisdom gained "by light of Nature" (*PR*, 4.352). Those poetic songs and hymns are the part of the Jewish Bible that the Son continues to embrace; they will endure beyond "the Law." An angry Satan leaves the Son in the wilderness to endure a dark night, full of storms, then the next day transports him to the Temple in Jerusalem, the place where he debated the rabbis when he was twelve. Milton again elaborates Luke's plain verse, "And he brought him to Jerusalem, and set him on a pinnacle of the temple" (Luke 4:9), and draws on Matthew's account chapter 4, making it even more emphatically the final instance where the Son defines himself in relation to the Jews.

The Jewish Temple is beautiful, but its beauty is tainted. The "glorious Temple" which "rear'd / Her pile" "higher" than the "Towers" of Jerusalem, "far off appearing like a Mount / Of Alabaster, top't with golden Spires" (*PR*, 4.545–48) is suggestive of pride. It also echoes the description of Pandemonium in *Paradise Lost*, "Built like a Temple" (*PL*, 1.713) on a hill, and the opening scene of book 2, with Satan sitting "High on a Throne of Royal State, which, far / Outshone the wealth of *Ormus* and of *Ind*" (*PL*, 2.1–2), imitating and rivaling the "high mount of God" (*PL*, 5.643). The visual image of the Son, his feet on the Temple's "highest Pinacle" (*PR*, 4.549), contrasts with the picture of Satan in the opening of book 2 of *Paradise Lost*, and places Jesus above the Temple that will be destroyed by the Romans in 70 CE.

Achsah Guibbory

The scene is complicated. As in Luke and Matthew, first Satan and then the Son quote Jewish scripture:

> Now shew thy Progeny; if not to stand,
> Cast thyself down; safely if Son of God:
> For it is written, He will give command
> Concerning thee to his Angels, in thir hands
> They shall up lift thee, lest at any time
> Thou chance to dash thy foot against a stone.
> To whom thus Jesus: also it is written,
> Tempt not the Lord thy God; he said and stood.
> But Satan smitten with amazement fell. (*PR*, 4.554–62)

Dueling with scriptural quotations, Satan quotes Psalm 91 where David says God is his "refuge" and "fortress" against the wicked and declares his faith: "For he shall give his angels charge over thee, to keep thee in all thy ways. They shall bear thee up in their hands, lest thou dash thy foot against a stone" (Ps. 91:2, 11–12). Satan's appropriation of the psalm is doubly ironic because *Satan* is the Hebrew word meaning "adversary" (the enemy that the psalmist says God will protect him from) but also because Satan's words are sarcastic, mocking both God's power to save and the Son's being special. The Son responds with a verse from Deuteronomy: "also it is written, / Tempt not the Lord thy God" (*PR*, 4.560–61; cf. Deut. 6:16). What is the Son doing quoting from a book of Jewish law that he had supposedly moved beyond?

Deuteronomy is the last book of the "Five Books of Moses," a retelling of the Laws given at Sinai, and it ends with Moses's death and the Israelites about to enter Canaan. Moses repeatedly admonishes the Israelites to obey "the commandments, the statutes, and the judgments, which the Lord your God commanded to teach you, that ye might do them" (Deut. 6:1). But the later chapters (27–32) turn dark as they say that the Israelites will not obey these laws once in Canaan. These chapters, that is, concern Israel's apostasy. Prophesying at God's command the future for the people of Israel, Moses describes the blessings they will enjoy if they keep God's laws, and the curses that will afflict them if they are unfaithful. The curses receive far more space, and are detailed, horrific. Of the sixty-nine verses in chapter 28 (one of the longest chapters in the entire Bible), the curses comprise verses 15–68. In chapter 31 God again says that his people will "forsake" him, and God in turn will "forsake them" (Deut. 31:16–18). God tells Moses to write a song for the Israelites and "to put it in their mouths" (Deut. 31:19) so it may, like "the book of law" (Deut. 31:26), serve as "a witness" against them in the future (Deut. 31:19, 21, 26). Moses's poem takes up the first forty-three of chapter 32's fifty-two verses, and although it ends with a promise of God's deliverance, unlike Miriam's joyous song after the crossing of the Red Sea that delivers the Israelites from Egypt, Moses's song is a grim catalog of the curses that will descend on the Israelites. Deuteronomy becomes the proof text for the Augustinian idea of "Jewish witness"—the notion that Jews in their suffering (punished for not accepting Jesus) exist as the "witness" to the truth of Christianity, their continued suffering proving that the curses have been fulfilled in them, proving the truth of Christianity.[34]

Deuteronomy was a Protestant favorite. Calvin preached more than 160 sermons on the entire book of the Bible, and an English translation of them by Arthur Golding was published in London in 1583. Calvin's first sermon, on the opening verses of chapter 1, begins by indicting the Israelites, showing how Christians might read and appropriate that book of the Law:

> Seeing then that the Lawe was given to the people, to make them perceive why they had been delivered from the bondage of Egypt; it was good reason that they should yeelde themselves to the obeying of God . . . Nevertheless the people were untowards . . . Had the people had one drop of wisdom, they should have yielded themselves with all humilitie, to receive the doctrine that was preached to them by Moses.[35]

Calvin defines Jewish Israel as incapable of obedience and undeserving of redemption.

But Calvin does not reject Deuteronomy. Instead, he insists, it speaks to "us," to Christians, which is the emphasis of Calvin's sermons. Paradoxically, the Law is dead but we must "obey" "God's Lawe," there being a Christian and a Jewish way of understanding it.[36] He rejects the idea of the Jews as a separate, specially loved people, only to rescue it for Christians. Verses in Deuteronomy warning the Israelites to keep separate from the other nations in Canaan are actually about the "election" or separateness of Christians. "It is a worde well worth the marking, where Moses sayeth that GOD had separated us from all other nations of the world . . . chosen us of the brood of all Adams children . . . chosen us to himself for his heritage."[37]

Calvin appropriated Deuteronomy for Christians, and this is what Milton and his Son are doing. When the Son, standing on the Temple,

Achsah Guibbory   149

quotes Deuteronomy 6:16 to answer Satan, he is not returning to Jewish law. Milton's Jews in *Paradise Regain'd* are the witness that the prophecies of Deuteronomy have been fulfilled. They are thus "proof" of Christian truth. Moses told the Israelites, "Your sons and daughters shall be delivered to another people" (Deut. 28:32) and "Because you would not serve the Lord your God . . . you shall have to serve . . . the enemies whom the Lord will let loose against you. He will put an iron yoke upon your neck" (Deut. 28:47–48). Now Judaea is suffering in bondage to Rome. The Ten Tribes have been scattered and "serve / Thir enemies" as their punishment for idolatry (*PR*, 3.431–32). The present condition of Jewish Israel is what Moses, speaking for God, prophesied. But God also promised to raise a prophet like Moses in Deuteronomy 18: "And the Lord said unto me . . . I will raise then up a Prophet from among their brethren, like unto thee, and will put my words in his mouth; and he shall speak unto them all that I shall command him" (Deut. 18:17–18). Christians believed Jesus filled that position (Acts 3:22).

Speaking Moses's words to Satan ("Tempt not the Lord thy God"; *PR*, 4.561; cf. Deut. 6:16), the Son shows he is that second Moses. As readers have long recognized, the Son's words are equivocal. He does not necessarily declare his divinity but neither does he deny it, an equivocation frustrating Satan but allowing Milton's Arian heresy to be hidden from suspicious readers.[38] But what happens next is not equivocal.

Satan falls, and for a moment the Son, standing top of the Temple, rises above the symbol of Judaism, only to be dramatically rescued by a "fiery Globe / Of Angels" who gently carry the Son through the air (*PR*, 4.581–82). The words of David's Psalm 91 that Satan mocked with its promise that God will reward faith—"angels . . . shall bear thee up in their hands" (Ps. 91:11–12)—have come true. The typology of David's psalm has been fulfilled. "In a flow'ry valley," the angels "set him down / On a green bank" (*PR*, 4.581–86)—not in the desert, nor within the earthly city that Paul in Galatians said is not the true Jerusalem, but in a paradisal setting, with a table of celestial, Edenic foods from the tree of life, even if only temporarily. Rescued and fed, the Son "unobserv'd / Home to his Mother's house private returned" (*PR*, 4.638–39), leaving the Temple, which will not be physically destroyed by the Romans for forty years, for the private space of his mother's house, Mary whose womb even earlier had been the holy temple housing the incarnate Son of God.[39]

What might all this mean for whether the Jews should be readmitted to England? The Son's progressive detachment from Jewish Israel,

150   Moving Jewish Bodies, Moving Jewish Souls

his refusal to accept them as his people, the identification of the Jews with bondage and idolatry, and his skepticism about whether even the lost Ten Tribes will be "delivered"—all suggest how unlikely it is that Milton would have welcomed Jews claiming to be from the tribe of Judah into an England, which itself had reverted to idolatry and bondage with the reestablishment of monarchy and the national Church of England. Petitions to enforce laws against the Jews or enact new ones for their expulsion were presented to Charles II and the Privy Council, suggesting the persistence of anti-Jewish sentiment and the fears that the king would bring the Jews in. In 1664 Charles II, responding to a Jewish petition, granted Jews permission to dwell in England so long as they remained peaceable and obedient. In 1671 when Milton published *Paradise Regain'd*, Jews were openly living in England, even if they were not welcomed.

There were limits to what was tolerable for Milton. Defender of liberty and freedom of conscience and religion, he drew the line against Catholicism in *Areopagitica* and his treatise *Of True Religion*, published in 1673, after Charles II's Declaration of Indulgence. But he also drew the line against Jews. Milton's idea of true religion was also grounded in an anti-Judaism reaching back to the New Testament, which made toleration of Jews, known for their stubborn loyalty to their religion, impossible.[40] Milton's treatment of the conversion of the Jews in *Paradise Regain'd* separates him from the millenarians who had hoped for readmission and conversion of Jews. It also stakes out an anti-Jewish position through the Son, who identifies the Jews as unfree in every sense (politically, materially, spiritually) and has cast them off. It is understandable that we want to redeem Milton from positions that seem intolerant, but Don M. Wolfe was right, many years ago, when he wrote in "The Limits of Milton's Toleration" that Milton did not tolerate unconverted Jews.[41] I would add that *Paradise Regain'd* makes clear that Milton, like his Son, also was deeply skeptical that they could be converted.

John Toland, Jewish Readmission, and the Jew Bill

By the end of the seventeenth century, the Spanish and Portuguese Jewish community in London had been granted permission to build a synagogue that would become Bevis Marks Synagogue. Built by Quakers, finished in 1701, it has conducted services for over three hundred years. By the early eighteenth century, Jews were not only living

Achsah Guibbory 151

in England but also had a place to worship, openly practicing their religion.

Controversy over Jews being readmitted had quieted down and did not revive until Parliament passed (and then was forced to repeal) the Jewish Naturalization Act, the so-called Jew Bill of 1753. But in 1714 John Toland published the treatise *Reasons for Naturalizing the Jews in Great Britain*. As far as I know, there was no bill under consideration, but Toland is worth looking at both because of his connection with Milton and because he took a stand on the Jewish question.

Toland wrote "The Life of John Milton" as a preface to *A Compete Collection of the Historical, Political, and Miscellaneous Works of John Milton*, published in Amsterdam in 1698. He was only twenty-eight years old at the time, and two years earlier had published *Christianity Not Mysterious*, a major statement of deism but also an argument that Christianity is rational, a reasonable religion. Like Milton he was intellectually precocious. Toland's book was burned in Ireland, as an embodiment of its author, in an ugly version of the censorship *Areopagitica* had decried, and Toland was charged with being a dangerous heretic. In his short life, born in 1670 and dying in 1722, he defended liberty of conscience and reason; he was fearless in pursuit of truth. He and Milton shared so much, yet their attitudes toward Jews and Judaism differed profoundly.

In 1753 Parliament passed the Jewish Naturalization Act (which came to be known as the Jew Bill), introduced by the Whigs, and supported by King George II and the bishops of the Church of England. The bill would allow foreign Jews living in England to apply to Parliament for naturalization without having to receive the sacrament in the Church of England. Immediately it raised angry opposition in newspapers, pamphlets, ballads, and prints, and the bill was repealed in 1754.[42] Among the antisemitic charges circulated were the ideas that the Jews would turn St. Paul's Cathedral into a synagogue and force all English males to be circumcised, charges that suggest the fear of danger to both bodies and souls of English Christians.

The most vigorous pamphlet against the Jew Bill was William Romaine's *An Answer To a pamphlet, entitled, Considerations on the Bill to permit Persons professing the Jewish Religion to be naturalized* (London, 1753). Romaine predicted that masses of Jews would flock to England once they were given the right to become naturalized Englishmen. They would take over the country. He also imagined them as revolutionaries, with military weapons, intent on killing English Protestants. Repeatedly, Romaine insisted Jews must "be separated and cast out of our Christian Society" because they "are Anathema."[43] They will "set up a false Messiah" and "take up Arms"; they will buy up our "Landed Estates."[44] Toland, however, was not worried about Jews polluting England's purity, robbing them of their land, harming or killing Christian bodies, or damaging their souls.

Though Toland was a deist, he considered himself Christian. He believed in a reasonable, natural religion, and he thought Christianity reasonable. Still, he was concerned with the universal, what is shared among people, rather than what divides humanity. So, though he believed Christianity was universal because reasonable, he rejected the position of people like William Prynne who had vigorously opposed Jews moving to England and had expressed in their antisemitism a fierce hatred of both Jewish bodies and souls—the same hatred that would appear in the diatribes against naturalizing the Jews in 1753. Where William Prynne's lengthy "history" of the Jews in England demonized them, recounting the various accusations of child murder and well poisoning, John Toland presented a very different history that taught that Jews had long been part of England and belonged there, despite the persecutions that he noted began in Henry III's time.

Jews had been living in England ever since William of Normandy had brought them over. Opponents of the Jews also pointed this out to argue that Jews were alien, did not belong in England. But Toland stresses that Jews had become part of England, even had synagogues in "towns of note."[45] They built a sumptuous synagogue, though rapacious monks took it over during the reign of Henry III and consecrated it to the Virgin Mary. These were, for Toland, marks of the Jews' contribution to England's richness, rather than evidence of a danger they posed. History shows, he argues, it was the English Christians, not Jews, who were dangerous, the source of problems, robbing and murdering Jews, and spreading libels.

Toland explains that England never became free of Jews with their expulsion in 1290. When Edward II expelled the Jews, forcing them to leave on ships, some Jews went to Scotland. Others converted to Christianity "at the Rolls in Chancery-Lane."[46] Moreover, Toland points out that Jewish children younger than six were separated from their parents and remained in England, raised by English Christians as Christians. Jews thus had long been intermixed with the English, not just in towns (with no danger to Christians, only to themselves) but in families and in marriage. They likely became part of English nobility, even though that Jewish ancestry had long been forgotten, perhaps erased but certainly not known or acknowledged. So Jewish blood is

Achsah Guibbory

in fact mixed into English blood, and who could separate them? What an amazing argument against those who insist on keeping England and the English pure.

Toland does not fear the Jewish religion, or that the Jews will corrupt the souls of English Christians, making them convert to Judaism. Of course, he insists on the economic advantages that they will bring to England. And here he borrowed from Rabbi Simone Luzzatto's 1638 *Discourse on the state of the Jews . . . in . . . Venice.*[47] But Toland's other arguments are much more interesting and take an unusual turn that puts him at odds with attitudes toward Jews and Judaism that Milton and others had expressed.

Jews do not seek to convert others where they live, so they would pose no danger to corrupting the souls of English Christians. Toland points out that their Hebrew Bible makes clear that, though the Jews had their revelation at Sinai, "the rest of the world was not left without Revelation, Miracles, and Prophets, as may be seen by the instances of Melchesedik, Balaam, Jethro, and Job." Indeed Naomi (in the Book of Ruth) would never have tried to "persuade her daughter in law Ruth, to go back again to her own People and Gods, had she been persuaded there was no Salvation out of the Pale of the Jewish Church."[48] It is not Jews but Christians who are uncharitable, intolerant. And here is Toland's most shocking attack on Christianity, at least as its theology had been developed, a theology of salvation and damnation that found its perfect expression in Calvinist predestination theology. "Some Christians only of all mankind, have established the Damning Theology . . . part of 'em expressly damning all other Christians . . . restraining salvation in effect though not in words, to the few elect of their own cant and livery."[49] He raises a question: does not Calvinism, with its distinction between the elect and the reprobate, encourage the kind of anti-Jewish position we find so often, particularly in the Presbyterian Prynne, but even in Milton?

We might think of Milton's movement away from Calvinist theology, particularly in *Paradise Lost*, where God says he will offer grace to all and only turn away those who reject it. But where are the Jews in this picture? Does Milton consider Jews irredeemable as they are the stubborn race, continuing to reject God's grace in rejecting Jesus Christ? Moreover, Milton rejects rigid predestinarianism, yet holds that God chooses some "Elect above the rest" (*PL*, 3.184).[50] Milton is no deist, and there is a limit to his universalism and emphasis on the sameness of humanity (all being born naturally free). He opposed religious toleration for Catholics, and we cannot imagine Milton voicing

Toland's words about Jews. For all his Hebraism, his emphasis on free-dom of conscience, on liberty and toleration, on reason that (as in the Enlightenment) he ties to toleration, Milton still conceives of liberty as "Christian liberty," as in Paul's Epistle to Galatians. This liberty seems impossible for Jews who remain under bondage as Jews (bound to the "law"), "inclinable to slavery," especially after they chose a king. We should remember that it was Charles II whose action actually let Jews back in.

Toland's final arguments for naturalizing the Jews (accepting them as "natural" citizens of England) are the most radical. Toland has already suggested that their bodies, their appearance, do not differ from oth-ers where they live. They are not "distinguished by a peculiar sort of smell."[51] They are not a peculiar (in the sense of strange) people but part of a general, universal "humanity." But even their religion turns out to be, at least in large part, universal, and rational. Anticipating the position that Moses Mendelssohn would take in *Jerusalem* (1783), a landmark in Jewish Enlightenment, Toland seems to have changed his opinion since writing his preface to *Christianity not Mysterious* eighteen years earlier. There he attacked the "Jewish Rabbis" who "set the Law of God at naught by their traditions" and "nonsensical Super-stitions."[52] Now he insists that, even if the Jews have a religion that is particular to them, having particular feasts and worship that come from and are part of their history, their religion actually is universal. Even if the Jews were to have their own country and government, they "would not endeavor to convert all the world to their theocracy." They would only want people to "acknowledge and honor one supreme Being, or First Cause, and to obey the Law of Nature, as the adequate rule of their lives and manners."[53] In other words, much of the Jews' religion—perhaps its core—is universal, natural, reasonable religion. That is, Judaism is a relative of deism! Toland remarkably envisions Jews as sharing in a common and universal humanity. So, neither their bodies nor their souls pose any danger to the English. As Isaac E. Bar-zilay has observed, Toland seems to be "the first European Christian who attempted to teach his coreligionists . . . that the Jew constitutes no exception to nature and human behavior."[54]

In 1753 the virulent antisemitic pamphlets and outcry imagined Jews naturalized in England as waging war on the Protestant English. Killing their bodies, not just trying to convert their souls. The imagina-tion of these hysterical diatribes, revealing fear as well as hatred, was a kind of Protestant zeal, the zeal that Toland said was the enemy of rea-son, humanity, and peace. Milton, prophet of reason, did not express this kind of zeal, and yet "zeal" was never far from his religion.[55] Zeal (with its offspring intolerance) is possible in virtually any religion, even the religion of secularism. We see it in Israel, in Muslim countries in the Middle East, and in the Hindu government's attitude in India toward Muslims in their nation. Zeal stands in the way of acceptance, the embrace of humankind. We see it now in the United States when antisemitism can erupt from the progressive "left" as well as from an authoritarian, white supremacist Christian right. As usual, thinking about Milton leads us to large issues that are still of urgent concern. But reading John Toland shows how someone, like myself, inspired by Milton's writing, and particularly his writing about political liberty and freedom of conscience, could hope to walk a very different, more tolerant path.

Notes

1. "ADL Audit Finds Antisemitic Incidents in United States Reached All-Time High in 2021," *ADL*, April 25, 2022, https://www.adl.org/resources /press-release/adl-audit-finds-antisemitic-incidents-united-states-reached-all -time-high.

2. Southern Poverty Law Center, *The Year in Hate and Extremism Report in 2021*, https://www.splcenter.org/20220309/year-hate-extremism-report-2021.

3. Howard Jacobson, *The Finkler Question* (New York: Bloomsbury, 2010).

4. Isabel Wilkerson's *Caste: The Origins of Our Discontents* (New York: Random House, 2020), in its excellent discussion of race as actually a caste system in America in which Jews eventually moved into the category of white privilege, does not address the fact Jews are still not always considered white.

5. Kim F. Hall, *Things of Darkness: Economies of Race and Gender in Early Modern England* (Ithaca, NY: Cornell University Press,1995); Kimberly Anne Coles, *Bad Humor: Race and Religious Essentialism in Early Modern England* (Philadelphia: University of Pennsylvania Press, 2022); and Geraldine Heng, *The Invention of Race in the European Middle Ages* (Cambridge: Cambridge University Press, 2018).

6. James Shapiro, "Race, Nation, or Alien," in *Shakespeare and the Jews* (New York: Columbia University Press, 1996), 169, 170. The book has been reissued in 2016 in a twentieth-anniversary edition by Columbia University Press.

7. On the readmission and the controversy, see David Katz, *Philosemitism and the Readmission of the Jews to England*; Achsah Guibbory, "Revisiting the Question of Jewish Readmission," in *Christian Identity, Jews, and Israel in Seventeenth-Century England* (Oxford: Oxford University Press, 2010), 220–50; and Kathy Lavezzo, "Readmission and Displacement: Menasseh ben Israel, William Prynne, John Milton," in *The Accommodated Jew: English Antisemitism from Bede to Milton* (Ithaca, NY: Cornell University Press, 2016), 211–47.

8. Achsah Guibbory, "Rethinking Millenarianism, Messianism, and Deliverance in *Paradise Regained*," *Milton Studies* 48 (2008): 135–59.

9. Alan F. Segal, *Paul the Convert* (New Haven, CT: Yale University Press, 1992); and Daniel Boyarin, *A Radical Jew: Paul and the Politics of Identity* (Berkeley: University of California Press, 1994). See also Susannah Heschel, *The Aryan Jesus: Christian Theologians and the Bible in Nazi Germany* (Princeton, NJ: Princeton University Press, 2008), on how German Protestant theologians transformed Jesus into an Aryan.

10. Eric B. Song, "'Unspeakable desire to see and know': *Paradise Regained* and the Political Theology of Privacy," *Huntington Library Quarterly* 76, no. 1 (2013): 138, 153. In chapter 1 of this volume, John Rumrich finds Milton adopting "a Hebrew identity" in his paraphrase of Psalm 114.

11. Jason P. Rosenblatt, *Renaissance England's Chief Rabbi: John Selden* (Oxford: Oxford University Press, 2006).

12. Achsah Guibbory, "England, Israel, and the Jews in Milton's Prose, 1649–1660," in *Milton and the Jews*, ed. Douglas A. Brooks (Cambridge: Cambridge University Press, 2008), 13–34. On the important distinction Christians made between the Hebraic and Judaic, consult Samuel S. Stollman, "Milton's Dichotomy of 'Judaism' and 'Hebraism,'" *PMLA* 89, no. 1 (January 1974): 105–12.

13. See also Rachel Trubowitz's brilliant "'The People of Asia and with Them the Jews': Israel, Asia, and England in Milton's Writings," in Brooks, *Milton and the Jews*, 151–77.

14. For that complexity in relation to freedom, and the mixture of radicalism and conservatism, consult Warren Chernaik, *Milton and the Burden of Freedom* (Cambridge: Cambridge University Press, 2017), esp. 3.

15. Menasseh ben Israel, *To His Highnesse the Lord Protector of the Common-wealth . . . The Humble Addresses . . . in behalf of the Jewish Nation* ([London?], 1655), A2v–A3r.

16. William Prynne, *A Short Demurrer To the Jewes Long discontinued barred Remitter into England*, 2nd ed. Enlarged (London, 1656), 7, 105.

17. William Hughes, *Anglo-Judaeus, or the History of the Jews, Whilst here in England* (London, 1656), 46, 14.

18. Hughes, *Anglo-Judaeus*, 46.

19. Prynne, *Short Demurrer*, 105.

20. Prynne, *Short Demurrer*, A2v.

21. Henry Jessey, *A Narrative Of the late Proceeds at White-Hall, concerning the Jews* (London, 1656), 8.

22. Jack Goldman, "Milton's Intrusion of Abraham and Isaac upon Psalm 114," *Philological Quarterly* 55 (1975): 119–21.

23. Lavezzo, "Readmission and Displacement," 213.

24. See Barbara K. Lewalski, *Milton's Brief Epic* (Providence, RI: Brown University Press, 1966), on the importance of the Book of Job to Milton's brief epic. Victoria Kahn shows that Job is a model for Milton's Son's distinctive rhetoric in "Job's Complaint in *Paradise Regained*," *ELH* 76, no. 3 (2009): 625–60. Cf. Marshall Grossman, "Poetry and Belief in '*Paradise Regained, to which is added Samson Agonistes*,'" *Studies in Philology* 110, no. 2 (2013): 382–401, which argues that the Epistle to Hebrews in the New Testament is the "proof text" for the two poems, which he reads together as one.

Achsah Guibbory

25. A useful note in Merritt Hughes's edition cites Michael Fixler's "The Unclean Meats of the Mosaic Law and the Banquet Scene in *Paradise Regained*," *Modern Language Notes* 70, no. 8 (1955): 573–77, which pointed out that shellfish and other animals Satan offers in his banquet are unclean. As Hughes rightly observes, the offer puts the Son in a dilemma "since Christ has come to supersede the Mosaic dietary laws . . . if he refuses the unclean meats, he seems to confirm the law; if he accepts then, he seems to accept the giver with them." Merritt Y. Hughes, ed., *John Milton: Complete Poems and Major Prose* (Indianapolis: Hackett Publishing, 1957), 501n328–47.

26. Stephen Fallon, *Milton among the Philosophers: Poetry and Materialism in Seventeenth-Century England* (Ithaca, NY: Cornell University Press, 1991); Rachel Trubowitz, "Body Politics in *Paradise Lost*," *PMLA* 121, no. 2 (2006): 389; and Jason P. Rosenblatt, *Torah and Law in "Paradise Lost"* (Princeton, NJ: Princeton University Press, 1994), 72–73, on *De Doctrina Christiana*.

27. Philippa Earle, "'Til Body Up to Spirit Work': Maimonidean Prophecy and Monistic Sublimation in *Paradise Regained*," *Milton Studies* 62, no. 1 (2020): 159–89.

28. The title for Jesus "King of the Jews," which appears in all four gospels, never appears in Milton. It was featured in Aemilia Lanyer's *Salve Deus Rex Judaeorum* (1611), and Thomas Hobbes made it central to what Mary Nyquist describes as his novel political Hebraism; see Nyquist, "Hobbes Reenvisions Hebraic and Christian History," *Hobbes Studies* (2022), 1–23. Its absence in Milton may be yet another instance of his erasure of Jews, and particularly from his polity.

29. N. I. Matar, "Milton and the Idea of the Restoration of the Jews," *Studies in English Literature* 27, no. 1 (Winter 1987): 110.

30. Northrop Frye, *Return to Eden: Five Essays on Milton's Epics* (Toronto: University of Toronto Press, 1965), 132.

31. The entirety of Eliza Poitevent Nicholson, "Hagar," *The Cosmopolitan* (November 1893), is reproduced in appendix D: The Figure of Hagar in Pauline Elizabeth Hopkins, *Hagar's Daughter: A Story of Southern Caste Prejudice*, ed. John Cullen Gruesser and Alisha R. Knight (Petersborough, Ontario: Broadview Press, 2021), 295–99.

32. Chernaik, *Milton and the Burden of Freedom*, 160–61, points out that Milton is not consistent in his writings about the relation between gospel and Mosaic law.

33. The late Marshall Grossman and I shared a conversation years ago, at a Milton seminar, about the Jewishness of Satan in Milton's poem. I acknowledge my debt to him in this essay.

34. Jeremy Cohen, *Living Letters of the Law: Ideas of the Jew in Medieval Christianity* (Berkeley: University of California Press, 1999); and Paula Fredricksen, *Augustine and the Jews: A Christian Defense of Jews and Judaism* (New York: Doubleday, 2008).

35. John Calvin, *The Sermons of M. John Calvin upon the fifth booke of Moses called Deuteronomie . . . Translated out of the French by Arthur Golding* (London, 1583), 1.

36. Calvin, *Sermons*, 2, 9.

37. Calvin, *Sermons*, 955.

38. On Milton's anti-Trinitarian heresy, see John P. Rumrich, "Milton's Arianism: Why it Matters," in Dobranski and Rumrich, *Milton and Heresy*, 75–92.

39. This is clear in Augustine's writings but explicit in Masses of the BVM: 23 The Blessed Virgin Mary, Temple of the Lord: "Lord God, / with artistry beyond all telling / you fashioned a holy temple for your Son / in the virginal womb of Blessed Mary" ("Prayers," BreviaryWeb, http://www.ibreviary.com /m2/preghiere.php?tipo=Preghiera&id=728).

40. See David Nirenberg, *Anti-Judaism: The Western Tradition* (New York: W. W. Norton, 2013), on "how, across several thousand years, myriad lands, and many spheres of human activity, people have used ideas about Jews and Judaism to fashion the tools with which they construct the reality of their world" (468).

41. Don M. Wolfe, "The Limits of Milton's Toleration," *Journal of English and German Philology* 60 (1961): 834–46.

42. Albert M. Hyamson, "The Jew Bill of 1753," *Transactions (Jewish Historical Society of England)* 6 (1908–10): 156–88, remains an excellent detailed account. See also Thomas W. Perry, *Public Opinion, Propaganda, and Politics in Eighteenth-Century England: A Study of the Jew Bill of 1753* (Cambridge, MA: Harvard University Press, 1962); and Avinoam Yuval-Naeh, "The 1753 Jewish Naturalization Bill and the Polemic over Credit," *Journal of British Studies* 57, no. 3 (2018): 467–92.

43. Romaine, *Answer To a Pamphlet*, 14.

44. Romaine, *Answer To a Pamphlet*, 35, 40.

45. John Toland, *Reasons for Naturalizing the Jews in Great Britain and Ireland* (London, 1714), 28.

46. Toland, *Reasons for Naturalizing the Jews*, 31.

47. Isaac E. Barzilay, "John Toland's Borrowing from Simone Luzzato," *Jewish Social Studies*, 31, no. 2 (1969): 75–81.

48. Toland, *Reasons for Naturalizing the Jews*, 53.

49. Toland, *Reasons for Naturalizing the Jews*, 52–53.

50. Stephen M. Fallon, *Milton's Peculiar Grace: Self-Representation and Authority* (Ithaca, NY: Cornell University Press, 2007).

51. Toland, *Reasons for Naturalizing the Jews*, 18–19.

52. John Toland, *Christianity not Mysterious: Or, a Treatise Shewing That there is nothing in the Gospel Contrary to Reason, Nor Above it* (London, 1696), xx.

53. Toland, *Reasons for Naturalizing the Jews*, 54–55.

54. Barzilay, "John Toland's Borrowing from Simone Luzzato," 76.

55. See Michael Lieb, "'Hate in Heav'n': Milton and the Odium Dei," *ELH* 53, no. 3 (1986): 519–39; Thomas Kranidas, *Milton and the Rhetoric of Zeal* (Pittsburgh: Duquesne University Press, 2006); and Feisal G. Mohamed, "Confronting Religious Violence: Milton's *Samson Agonistes*," *PMLA* 120, no. 2 (2005): 327–40.

CHAPTER 6

Decomposing Milton

Romantic Reading and Demotic Dispersal

Jennifer Wallace

On a warm summer morning in London in the year 1790, the body of John Milton was secretly disinterred. He had been dead for more than a century. The initial discovery of his coffin, beneath the flagstones in the church of St. Giles Cripplegate, close by the old Roman wall and a stone's throw from Bunhill Fields, had been conducted legitimately the previous afternoon, authorized by the "principal parishioners" of Cripplegate and undertaken carefully and with restraint.[1] There was a widely held desire to erect a memorial to Milton, for which substantial funds had been raised, and so the authorities wanted confirmation of the exact location of the poet's final resting place. Workmen, having dug a whole area of the church, found two coffins, one lead and one wooden, which seemed to match the description of Milton's burial beside his father, and one of the principal parishioners diligently measured the lead coffin and noted its dimensions. What happened next, however, was not in the official parish plans. According to literary scholar Philip Neve, who published an account of the event in a pamphlet just over a week later, word of Milton's coffin spread in the nearby pub that evening and, amid the merriment, the drinkers decided that they should "satisfy their curiosity" (15) and take a look the following morning. Accordingly, between 8 A.M. and 9 A.M. on August 4, the local pawnbroker Mr. Laming, the publican Mr. Fountain, a surgeon Mr. Taylor, coffin-maker Ascough, and his apprentice pulled the coffin out of its hole in the church floor, wrenched it open, and exposed the body for the first time since its funeral in 1674.

Philip Neve is reticent in the matter of the feelings of the group when they first saw Milton, preferring to follow his own agenda of

159

outraged condemnation, but I like to think they were moved by a mixture of wonder and excitement. The corpse, like that of a saint, had allegedly been miraculously preserved, a fact that the staunchly anti–Roman Catholic Milton would have hated. Filled with idolatrous fervor, the group's natural instinct was to reach out and touch it. Within minutes, the ribs had crumbled, the teeth and upper jawbone were somehow in the pocket of Mr. Fountain, and men were grabbing chunks of the poet's hair. After this initial ransacking of the corpse for relics, the group left the security and protection of the excavation site to the gravedigger and servant, one Elizabeth Grant, who, not to be undone by the men, turned the discovery of Milton into a business opportunity of her own:

> She kept a tinderbox in the excavation and, when any persons came, struck a light, and conducted them under the pew; where, by reversing the part of the lid that had been cut, she exhibited the body, at first for 6d. and afterwards for 3d. and 2d. each person. The workmen in the church kept the doors locked to all those who would not pay the price of a pot of beer for entrance, and many, to avoid that payment, got in at a window at the west end of the church. (20–21)

Philip Neve's account of the "disinterment of Milton's coffin and of the treatment of the corpse, during that, and the following day" is a tale partly about readership and class. Despite the fact that both he and the Cripplegate parishioners approach Milton's body equally as saintly relics and as the objects of economic transaction, he emphasizes the distinction between them. He represents the poet's remains as no more than loot for the likes of Mr. Fountain, Elizabeth Grant, and the others, while portraying them as almost holy for him. He acknowledges that he purchased a number of Milton's body parts but explains that he did this by way of research and to restore the body to the grave:

> In recording a transaction, which will strike every liberal mind with horror and disgust, I cannot omit to declare, that I have procured those relics, which I possess, only in hope of bearing part in a pious and honorable restitution of all that has been taken. (32)

In this way Neve portrays himself as the ideal appreciator of the bard, the owner of Milton's fragmented body temporarily only to restore it,

Jennifer Wallace   *161*

literally and metaphorically, to the wholeness of the grave. Readers of Milton like himself, whom he describes as "liberal," view the violation of the body with "horror and disgust" but later will revere the poet's lock of hair with appropriate respect, while not questioning its provenance. The other group of Cripplegate devotees, whom he casts as sacrilegious looters, cannot, according to his account, be true readers.

But who were these people? What did Milton mean to them in 1790? Questions like these intrigued me when I first came across Philip Neve's account and made a fictional exploration seem the most appropriate response. Many of what one might call the more discerning violators had taken clumps of the poet's hair, perhaps aware of the significance that hair held for Milton. Known according to John Aubrey as the "Lady of Christ's College" when he was a student on account partly of his flowing locks, the poet had used "the potency of hair" as a crucial element of his "depiction of prelapsarian desire" in *Paradise Lost*.[2] To take possession of Milton's locks was maybe an attempt to share in that precarious, utopian privilege. Strikingly, too, the group had reached for Milton's jawbone. Were they trying to grab their portion of the bard's "adventurous song" (*PL*, 1.13), seeking their own powers of expression? In historical fiction I could give voice to the voiceless, telling the story from the perspective of Lizzie Grant, illiterate gravedigger and servant but feisty businesswoman, unable to read *Paradise Lost* herself but not immune to the ideas it conveys about desire and temptation, free will and damnation. Moreover, Philip Neve's pamphlet is very brief, no more than thirty-four pages in its first edition, and the tale is unfinished. He calls for the "pious and honorable restitution" of the body parts, with the understanding that both soul and body should sleep in the grave until Judgment Day, but with no assurance that this will take place. In the second edition, published September 8, Neve describes various subsequent events as a result of the publicity surrounding his publication: doubts were cast on the authenticity of the body, a second disinterment was conducted, and expert inspections were carried out. But again, there is no indication that the "restitution" was happening. The liberal readers were losing control of the narrative, as current parlance might put it, even as they were strenuously trying to centralize authority. What happened, ultimately, to the pieces of Milton: the teeth, the hair, the jawbone? This was the third question behind my novel *Digging Up Milton*. Structuring my fictional treatment into twelve chapters, the novel mirrored the twelve books of Milton's epic. The epigraph to each chapter was taken from the corresponding book in Milton's poem, framing Lizzie Grant's supposed

162 Decomposing Milton

retrospective confession within a classical arc that might have been recognizable to Philip Neve's readers. My story thus filled in the gaps in Neve's pamphlet and traced Lizzie Grant's own fall from innocence into experience, a deconstructed reading of her own paradise lost.[3]

The Bard in the 1790s

Milton in the 1790s was once more associated with republicanism. Some of the characters in *Digging Up Milton* co-opt the poet's remains to galvanize support for the revolutionary cause, producing a piece of Milton's jaw with dramatic flourish during a seditious meeting.[4] If they are violating and misusing the body for their own ends, they are arguably in good company. The revolutionaries mobilized him for their cause too. Back in 1649 Milton had advocated beheading Charles I; the French revolutionaries had stormed the Bastille in 1789 and were preparing to send their monarch to the guillotine in January 1793. The Comte de Mirabeau adapted, and quoted sections of, *Areopagitica* in his *Sur la liberté de la presse* (1788), demonstrating "his conviction that Milton's voice was the most fitted to liberate his countrymen from a tyrannical censorship."[5] A year later he published anonymously a translation of Milton's *Defensio pro Populo Anglicano* as *Théorie de la royauté, d'après la doctrine de Milton*. Mirabeau's pamphlet was republished by the revolutionaries after his death under the title *Défense du peuple anglais sur le jugement et la condamnation de Charles Ier, roi d'Angleterre, par Milton: Ouvrage propre à éclairer sur la circonstance actuelle où se trouve la France* (1792) to strengthen the campaign to execute Louis XVI and, as Christophe Tournu puts it, add to the "radicalization of anti-tyrant rhetoric leading to regicide."[6]

Milton's ideas and that of other leaders of the British Interregnum were circulated among the Jacobins, just as French ideas in the 1790s were shared in radical underground circles back in England. Milton's was the voice against tyranny, the cry of liberty and rebellion, for both revolutionary constituencies. His Satan scorned flattering obedience of totalitarian rulers, the cowardly inclination "To bow and sue for grace / With suppliant knee," valuing instead the "courage never to submit or yield" (*PL*, 1.111–12, 108). No wonder William Blake famously wrote in *The Marriage of Heaven and Hell* in the early 1790s that "the reason Milton wrote in fetters when he wrote of Angels & God, and at liberty when he wrote of Devils & Hell, is because he was a true Poet and of the Devil's party without knowing it."[7] Blake read *Paradise*

Lost against the grain, releasing what he considered Milton's fettered meaning and revising the triangular relationship between God, Satan, and Adam, so that God becomes the source of restriction and placidity, while Satan promises energy, creativity, and revolutionary liberty: "Good is the passive that obeys Reason: Evil is the active springing from energy. Good is Heaven; Evil is Hell."[8] Rewriting the Bible and Milton, Blake offers his own version of the Creation as simultaneously also the Fall in *The First Book of Urizen* (1794). According to Blake's mythology, Urizen is both a divisive, repressive, creative God and an expelled, pride-filled, and rebellious Satan.[9]

But while Milton was once again becoming associated with political liberty and rebellion in the 1790s, he had also been acquiring a reputation through the course of the eighteenth century as a poet of the sublime. This was not so much a matter of ethics or politics but more to do with the development of the concept of aesthetics, allowing the "splendour of the poet [to] eclipse the merit of the man," glossing over the polemical politics by focusing on the poetic "genius."[10] He might have been the blind poet for whom the sensory experience of touch was so important although "never secure," as Joe Moshenska has shown, but for readers in the 1790s he was the primary model for the imaginary conjuring of what cannot be touched, what can only be sublimely apprehended rather than comprehended.[11] Philip Neve himself noted that Milton

> inhabits . . . the court of the Deity: and leaves on your mind a stability and a permanent character of divine inhabitation and divine presence of which no other poets give you a thought. Others rise to sublimity, when they exceed; Milton's institution, his quality, his element is sublimity: from his height he descends to meet the greatness of others.[12]

The paradoxes peppering Milton's descriptions of Hell or Chaos or the whole cosmos became recognized as key features in the sublimity of his verse: "darkness visible," the "dark unbottomed infinite abyss," the "palpable obscure" (*PL*, 1.63, 2.405, 2.406). These striking oxymorons created ironic tensions that lent themselves to the awe-inspiring uncertainty associated with the sublime, the "difficulties [that] were temptations," as Philip Neve put it.[13] John Boydell, engraver and publisher, helped to cement this notion of Milton with his illustrated edition that censored the political material included in William Hayley's biography and focused instead, through Richard Westall's plates, on him as the sublime poet of "darkness visible."[14] Henry Fuseli and Blake also painted and engraved scenes from *Paradise Lost* in the 1790s, responding to the "immortal symmetry" of his visionary imagination, while the full sublime effects of the "dark unbottomed infinite abyss" were given visual treatment in the mezzotints of John Martin a couple of decades later.[15]

Above all Milton was considered the prime example of poetic genius, at a time when writers and readers were trying to pinpoint the source of that talent. Genius allowed the poet to soar above the material world and yet there was an ongoing search for a possible identifiable cause for such a transcendent imagination. The late eighteenth-century interest in physiognomy played its part in these types of investigations. Genius could supposedly be identified in the very head or skull of the artist. A phrenologist could feel, from the shape of the cranium, the basis for the poet's immortal visions. The Cripplegate parishioners could have been, consciously or unconsciously, undertaking a tactile investigation of their own, running their hands over the head of the poet before the construction of a memorial to him in their church. After all, the remains of Robert Burns were to be subjected to a similar treatment, again prompted by a desire to erect a memorial to the poet.[16] Burns's coffin was dug up from its resting place in St. Michael's Churchyard, Dumfries, in 1817, in a poor state, disintegrating upon touch. The brow and the enormity of the head impressed those crowding in to look. John MacDiarmid of Dumfries recalled "the lordly forehead, arched and high—the scalp still covered with hair, and the teeth perfectly firm and white."[17] Some of the men endeavored to examine its proportions, feeling the lumps and bumps of the cranium in their search for the source of genius. Not content, in 1834, the grave was opened a second time and the skull studied again in the presence of a professional phrenologist, tasked with the assessment of its "size and character." It was prodigiously large, according to James Hogg, an indication of the miraculous imagination of the "Heaven-taught ploughman," who despite his humble origins revealed in his physiognomy his natural authority.[18] "The largest hat . . . was found too narrow to receive the skull—a sufficient proof of its extraordinary size," Hogg commented.[19] One imagines a semireligious frenzy of moonlit hat swapping, each man devotedly hoping his hat would fit the remarkable skull.

The fate of both Milton's and Burns's bodies raises the ambiguous issue of the transformation of human remains into relics. According to Lorna Clymer's "corpse theory," a corpse "exists simultaneously and uncannily as both human and as gross matter," unsettling our capacity to interpret its "nexus of meanings" and making us rethink the imposition of meaning at all onto a lifeless object. As such, she argues, a dead body takes on the charm of a "fetish," "an apparently lifeless object that carries mystical power."[20] What, then, of hair? Clymer's simultaneous and uncanny "fetish" is certainly evident in John Keats's poem, "Lines On Seeing a Lock of Milton's Hair":

> When I do speak, I'll think upon this hour,
> Because I feel my forehead hot and flush'd,
> Even at the simplest vassal of thy Power,—
> A lock of thy bright hair![21]

The "Power" of this moment derives from the fetishistic juxtaposition of the prosaic object with its mystical associations. The ordinary lock of hair is imbued with the extraordinary aura connected to Milton. "I was startled, when I caught thy name / Coupled so unaware," Keats continues.[22] Keats apparently was shown Milton's hair when he visited Leigh Hunt in 1818, Hunt himself having acquired it from a physician, Robert Batty.[23] Keats's poem attempts to do justice to the sublime, religious or prophetic qualities associated with the poet as well as thinking about what, for Keats, is a bewildering disparity between that and the mundane curl he has seen: "For many years my offerings must be hushed."[24] Neither Keats nor Hunt has anything to say about where Robert Batty acquired the lock or how it reached him. Was this one of the Cripplegate 1790 relics? Could the sordid events, which had so shocked Philip Neve, have ultimately led to the source of Keats's poem? His poem combines hyperbole and bathetic reduction to ambiguous effect, as does Leigh Hunt's own sonnet on the occasion:

> There seems a love in hair, though it be dead.
> It is the gentlest, yet the strongest thread.[25]

Such verses playfully tease out Clymer's "nexus of meanings," finding in the lock of hair a source for both Romantic creativity and reductive humor.

But what is absent is an acknowledgment of class-based hypocrisy. Rather, as surgeons in respectable Edinburgh dissected the bodies brought to them by the criminals Burke and Hare, while not asking questions about their origins, Keats and Hunt ponder the miraculous powers of the lock lying before them, and even imagine themselves "beside / The living head," while not thinking about the gritty provenance of such a relic.[26] Just as with the oxymoronic paradox of the sublime, I was intrigued by the bathetic conflation or "coupling" of genius and the grotesque in these types of encounter.[27] And so in my fictionalized account, the silenced worship or appreciation of Milton's relics is demonstrated in an alternative but equally ambivalent way by those first excavators in Cripplegate. In the words of Lizzie Grant:

> I slipped the jaw into my bosom, and says—"This is our secret, Mr Fountain. Never breathe a word to any man!" And all morning, when I felt the awkward corners of the jaw press painfully upon my chest, I thought with pleasure of Mr Fountain and the private transaction between us.[28]

Despite her working-class status scorned by Philip Neve, Lizzie reveals here an advanced sense of metonymy. The jaw serves as a symbol of the contract between her lover Fountain and herself, a precious souvenir of this private moment, but it is also a fetishistic substitute for her lover's sexual intimacy, the phallic jaw "slipped . . . into [her] bosom" and "pressing" furtively "upon [her] chest." Mingling the erotic and the macabre, Lizzie's engagement with Milton's remains is just as sophisticated as Keats's grotesque "coupling" in his poem "On Seeing a Lock of Milton's Hair."

Grounding Milton in London

The events of August 4, 1790, grounded Milton in the city, both literally and more metaphorically. As a writer, he had not been known for his London roots. International in appeal and in subject matter, he had composed some of his poems in Latin and the rest in classical cadences, his epic modeled on Homer and Virgil and his tragedy *Samson Agonistes* a strenuous effort to rescue the genre from its recent corruption by avoiding "the poet's error of intermixing Comic stuff with Tragic sadness and gravity; or introducing trivial and vulgar persons, which by all judicious hath been counted absurd; and brought in without discretion, corruptly to gratify the people" ("Of that sort of Dramatic Poem which is call'd Tragedy"). Writing about the discovery of Milton's copy of Shakespeare's plays, John Rumrich points out that Milton "did not lack comic sensibility"; nevertheless, Milton's "moral fastidiousness" and "priggish" tendencies prevented him from responding enthusiastically to Shakespeare's vernacular traditions of humor, which depended on a diversity of class and relished "sexual innuendo and bawdiness."[29] Instead, in *Samson Agonistes* Milton would supposedly elevate Shakespeare's tone ("the poet's error") by returning his readers to the ancient Greeks: "they only will best judge who are not unacquainted with Aeschylus, Sophocles and Euripides." Appointed the Secretary for Foreign Tongues for the Commonwealth in 1649, he translated Cromwell's republican policy into Latin for communication with foreign governments. And with the restoration of the monarchy in 1660, he retreated into the mode of biblical prophet, not supposedly situated in Artillery Walk (as he really was) but rather in the celestial realms of his imagination, partly soaring "above th' *Olympian* hill" and partly on earth but "in darkness, and with dangers compast round, / And solitude; yet not alone," visited nightly by the Muse (*PL,* 7.3, 27–28). It is striking that there is no museum to Milton in London but rather one in Chalfont St. Giles, Buckinghamshire, where he only spent eighteen months of his life. "Why is it that Bread Street has not become Stratford?," Aaron Santesso has rightly asked.[30] In fact, early literary tourists in the seventeenth century do seem to have paid visits to "see the house and chamber where [Milton] was born," and William Hayley declared in 1796 that the house where *Paradise Lost* was composed was "consecrated by his genius."[31] Nevertheless, the fact that the urban bustle of the streets where the poet was born and lived did not conform with readers' prior expectations of a poet who in *Eikonoklastes* set himself apart from the "boisterous folly" of the "vulgar sort" in the city impeded the development of a tradition of Milton as a London poet. Santesso concludes: "Bread Street frustrated expectations of environmental consistency with a monolithic Milton, and therefore prevented a gaze that sought to eliminate surprise and imagination in order to recognise what was already known about the subject."[32] By the eighteenth century, literary tourists wanted to see the supposedly authentic dwelling place, surrounding landscape, and personal possessions that inspired any writer, as John Keats confirmed in his "Sonnet Written in the Cottage Where Burns Was Born."[33] Bread Street, obliterated by the Great Fire and not fitting the developing contemporary image of Milton, could be no Stratford nor indeed the humble two-roomed thatched cottage in Alloway, Ayrshire. In this way the heritage industry has further cut off the deracinated Milton from his roots.

For Milton was truly a London man. Born in Bread Street, he was educated at St. Paul's, and apart from a few years in Cambridge and traveling in Italy, lived all his days in the labyrinth of streets that circled around Cripplegate: Aldersgate Street, Barbican, York Street, Artillery Walk, Bunhill Fields. Since this was the area heavily bombed in the Blitz and largely obliterated in the postwar reconstruction and later development of the modern Barbican Centre, my research for *Digging Up Milton* compelled me to pour over old eighteenth-century street atlases and walk the missing routes of my characters.[34] The current rather soulless concrete blocks, underground car parks, and elevated walkways of the Barbican covered what were once the bustling narrow throughfares of Fore Street, Grub Street, Beech Street, and Red Cross Street. Bread Street is now a steel and glass road of offices and sandwich outlets. But in my imaginary mapping, I was repeopling the place with erased figures and buildings in ways that felt analogous to the "violation" of August 4, 1790. For what Fountain, Laming, Lizzie Grant, and others were doing was to reclaim Milton as one of them, a Cockney poet. They pinpointed his burial place in their church, in the heart of what is now known as the East End. They distributed the body parts to people living in streets that Milton would once have known well, even if he repressed the fact: Mr. Ellis of Lamb's Chapel and Mr. Poole, the watch-spring maker, from Jacob's Passage. When Philip Neve came to investigate the story, I realized, he had been forced to travel from the newer, more respectable neighborhood of Holborn in the West, where the air was cleaner, down the hill, across Smithfield, to Cripplegate. He would have acquired physical bits of Milton, scattered around the streets the poet once frequented, compelled to negotiate and trade with their now proud owners, the publicans, pawnbrokers, and gravediggers of my novel.

In placing Milton geographically in London, the Cripplegate parishioners were, in many ways, contributing to the zeitgeist. Blake imagined the spirit of the bard "descending down the Nerves of my right arm" as he sat composing and etching his prints.[35] His redemptive visionary book *Milton* (1804–10) begins with an image of mythical invocation heard across the London region, mingling mystical prophecy, literary necromancy, and specific geography:

> Loud sounds the Hammer of Los: & loud his Bellows is heard
> Before London to Hampsteads breadths & Highgates heights
> To Stratford and old Bow; & across to the Gardens of Kensington
> On Tyburns Brook; loud groans Thames beneath the iron Forge.[36]

Prior to this invocation, of course, Blake had given us the apocalyptic vision of "those feet in ancient time" walking on English soil, with the

Jennifer Wallace

vow to renew that paradise and build "Jerusalem in Englands green & pleasant Land."[37] Meanwhile, Wordsworth was co-opting Milton as a patriotic British voice, a bulwark against foreign corruption and internal degeneracy, vanity, and loss of nerve:

> Milton! thou should'st be living at this hour:
> England hath need of thee: she is a fen
> Of stagnant waters: altar, sword and pen,
> Fireside, the heroic wealth of hall and bower,
> Have forfeited their ancient English dower
> Of inward happiness. We are selfish men;
> Oh! Raise us up, return to us again;
> And give us manners, virtue, freedom, power.
> Thy soul was like a Star and dwelt apart:
> Thou hadst a voice whose sound was like the sea;
> Pure as the naked heavens, majestic, free,
> So didst thou travel on life's common way,
> In cheerful godliness; and yet thy heart
> The lowliest duties on itself did lay.[38]

This sonnet, significantly titled "London. 1802," claims Milton as the guardian of the English spirit, the model writer of what Wordsworth had described in a letter as "manly and dignified compositions, distinguished by simplicity and unity of object and aim."[39]

But while Wordsworth's claiming of Milton in aid of the British patriotic effort during the ongoing war with France portrayed him as a "Star . . . dwel[ling] apart," "pure as the naked heavens, majestic, free," in a way that Milton would have appreciated, the Cripplegate parishioners' much more hands-on appropriation (literally) was very different. It is hard for a corpse to remain "manly and dignified" while it is being ransacked for souvenirs. In fact, it is tempting to see Fountain, Laming, and the others as just the kind of "trivial and vulgar persons" that Milton condemned in the preface to *Samson Agonistes*, those who supposedly read in the wrong way, who "corrupt" and "intermix" and are motivated by the popular desire to "gratify" themselves. In this case Milton's dismemberment becomes a subversive misreading of him, part of the tradition of ambiguously disruptive gender- and class-based responses anatomized by Sandra Gilbert and Susan Gubar and many other critics.[40] It is also ironically an act of just the kind of comic-tragic hybrid associated with the Shakespearean vernacular that Milton condemned, my Lizzie Grant following in the footsteps of the gravedigger

170   Decomposing Milton

in *Hamlet* or—her closest precursor—Mistress Quickly. It is in this
spirit that she speaks, mingling local pride and fateful naivety: " 'It'll be
sixpence or nothing,' says I, standing my ground. 'It's the greatest bard
of England in there, not the poor hole of St Giles.' "[41]

"The mind is its own place"

While the Cripplegate disinterment could be considered a "vulgar"
misreading with "comic" intermixture, it also contained a tragic arc
of its own worthy of *Paradise Lost*. Milton's structure of innocence
and knowledge, temptation and fall, underpinned much of the literature of the late eighteenth century. The interdependence of guilt and
innocence, articulated by Adam, came to permeate Romantic ideas of
knowledge and experience:

> since our eyes
> Op'nd we find indeed, and find we know
> Both Good and Evil, Good lost, and Evil got,
> Bad Fruit of Knowledge, if this be to know
> Which leaves us naked thus[.] (*PL*, 9.1070–74)

So in William Godwin's *Caleb Williams* (1794), for example, we see
Falkland, who plays "both God and Satan to Caleb's Adam," pointing
out to Caleb Williams that he has now condemned himself to sharing his guilty secret: " 'Do you know what it is you have done? To
gratify a foolishly inquisitive humour you have sold yourself . . . It is a
dear bargain you have made.' "[42] The Wedding Guest in Samuel Taylor
Coleridge's "Rime of the Ancyent Marinere" (1798), after hearing the
story of the albatross's killing and the mariner's damnation, arises "a
sadder and a wiser man.[43] Wordsworth himself undergoes a second fall
through the French Revolution, from a youthful, paradisiacal sense
of the earth as "an inheritance new-fallen" to a mature, awkwardly
phrased recognition that

> Then was the truth received into my heart,
> That under heaviest sorrow earth can bring,
> Griefs bitterest of ourselves or of our Kind,
> If from the affliction somewhere do not grow
> Honour which could not else have been . . .
> . . . The blame is ours, not Nature's.[44]

These accounts of naive innocence and guilt-laden experience must necessarily be written retrospectively. Only with the benefit of hindsight can one recognize a state of innocent bliss now lost, since such self-consciousness requires the requisite degree of knowledge and sophistication. Writing innocence and experience in the 1790s necessitates this kind of irony. And in this spirit my Lizzie Grant retrospectively registers the last moments of her innocence in the first chapter, before participating in the ransacking of Milton's remains and her tragic fall:

> We all stood silent for a few minutes, staring down at the box. I have thought since that, had we but realised, we had the chance then to leave the dead in peace and continue to live a blessed life, but at the time we thought only that we were standing as if upon the brink of a vast and thrilling chasm, which we could choose to enter or ignore.[45]

By the following chapter, with its prefatory quotation of Sin unlocking the gates of Hell, she is charging visitors to view Milton's body and advertising the opportunity for relics: "'There's hair and legs and more than a few teeth remaining and I daresay you could even find a finger.' I dropt a curtsey, as low and polite and ladylike as I knew how."[46]

The Miltonic fall in the Romantic period interrogated the relationship between innocence and guilt. In part this was to continue Milton's own investigation of God's purpose. Divine creation, after all, was able "Good out of evil to create" or to transform the darkest moments (*PL,* 7.187). And by extension, writing and reading could have a similar transformative effect, acknowledging the worst experiences for educational or moral purpose. So Wordsworth repeatedly identifies the imaginative gain amid the visionary loss ("We will grieve not, rather find / Strength in what remains behind") and indeed my Lizzie Grant's memoir is framed by its Miltonic structure as "evil turn[ed] to good" (*PL,* 12.471).[47] But the relationship between innocence and guilt was also internalized to ambiguous and subversive effect. The difference between blessing and damnation, or between innocence and experience, became relative, no more than a matter of individual judgment. Taking as their cue Satan's lines that "The mind is its own place, and in itself / Can make a Heav'n of Hell, a Hell of Heav'n" (*PL,* 1.254–55), writers in the late eighteenth and early nineteenth centuries could reverse the Fall, imagining the "blessing" in the expulsion from Eden and the gain of wisdom from the eating of the apple.[48]

Milton's Adam and Eve were sent from Paradise with the promise that they would find "A Paradise within thee, happier farr" (*PL*, 12.587), creating their own tribunal of judgment within themselves. The finale of *Paradise Lost*—

> Som natural tears they drop'd, but wip'd them soon;
> The World was all before them, where to choose
> Thir place of rest, and Providence thir guide:
> They hand in hand with wandring steps and slow,
> Through *Eden* took their solitary way (*PL*, 12.645–49)

—becomes the opening image of Wordsworth's *Prelude*, as he leaves the city of London:

> Now I am free, enfranchised and at large,
> May fix my habitation where I will.
> What dwelling shall receive me? In what Vale
> Shall be my harbour? . . .
> . . . The earth is all before me: with a heart
> Joyous, nor scared at its own liberty,
> I look about, and should the guide I chuse
> Be nothing better than a wandering cloud,
> I cannot miss my way.[49]

While Adam and Eve's expulsion is from daily intimacy with God in Paradise, their need to "choose" a resting place is "solitary" and their "guide" a reliance on Providence, Wordsworth reverses this. For him expulsion means freedom and his choice is guided by a "wandering cloud," the "corresponding mild creative" spirit of nature, which means that he is never alone and solitary.[50] Life outside Milton's paradise becomes heavenly.

On the other hand, such internalization of the Fall could mean that individuals were able to turn their heaven into hell as easily as creating their "Paradise within" themselves. Lord Byron, in particular, conjured up isolated figures, tormented by their own guilt and sense of self-damnation. Both Manfred and the Giaour, driven to undisclosed terrible and desperate deeds because of their doomed love for another woman, brood obsessively over their guilt, refusing any form of consolation or even the chance of confession or forgiveness offered to them. They condemn themselves to their own internal hell, long before their deaths and a supposedly divine judgment. Damnation becomes a form

Jennifer Wallace

of self-hatred; blessing takes the characteristic of a dimly remembered perfect love for another:

> Despair is stronger than my will.
> Waste not thine orison, despair
> Is mightier than thy pious prayer:
> I would not, if I might, be blest;
> I want no paradise, but rest.[51]

The Giaour wants "rest" because his hellish despair has taken horrifyingly active form; he is condemned to prey on his descendants with the appetite of a self-disgusted vampire:

> But first, on earth as Vampire sent,
> Thy corse shall from its tomb be rent:
> Then ghastly haunt thy native place,
> And suck the blood of all thy race.[52]

My Lizzie Grant's husband, Nathaniel, who participated in the rending of Milton's corpse from its tomb, in subsequent weeks takes on the manner of a Giaour-like self-condemnation, walking the London streets as if damned: "now he stooped with bended head and slow, melancholy gait, broken in spirit and without fixed purpose, shuffling in a futile circle—Beech Street, Red Cross Street, Fore Street, Grub Street—like a ring of Hell."[53] Another character, Mr. Laming, concludes his days in Bedlam, convinced that "the *cold hand of Milton has me in its grasp!*"[54] In his mania, he repeats Satan's words: "Which way I flie is Hell; my self am Hell."[55] His deteriorating mind, like the collapsed corpse, cannot be reconstituted any more than Satan's heavenly place and perhaps for the same reason—despair.

If the notion that the "mind is its own place," first coined by Milton's Satan, is taken much further, then subjective feeling becomes the benchmark of truth. For this reason the Romantic reading of Milton produced a new challenge to objectivity, an era of relativity and competing evaluations. As Lucy Newlyn has noted, this gave rise to "an explosion of juxtaposed perspectives, fictional editors, unreliable narrators, and tales within tales."[56] In many texts we see the unaccountability of truth and yet, at the same time, the frenzied search for its basis in evidence. James Hogg's *Private Memoirs and Confessions of a Justified Sinner* (1824), for example, connects the questioning of narrative veracity, which Milton's *Paradise Lost* had raised, with the theology of antinomianism. In the novel the state of guilt or exoneration through God's grace becomes based on individual faith, dependent on believing that one is among God's elect. The doubts of Robert Wringham, the "justified sinner," are based on the uncertainty of reassurance that his private faith would be corroborated by the unknowable justice of God: "chosen as he knew he was from all eternity, still it might be possible for him to commit acts that would exclude him from the limits of the covenant."[57] But these anxieties are answered by the Satan-like persuasions of the doppelgänger Gilmartin, who of course might be the solipsistic alter ego of Wringham himself: "The other argued, with mighty fluency, that the thing was utterly impossible, and altogether inconsistent with eternal predestination."[58] The novel begins with the narrative of the "Editor," followed by Wringham's confessions, facilitating the sense that truth is prismatic, dependent on multiple perspectives. And this relativity gives extra succor to the warped theology, namely Wringham's belief that he is "justified," thus allowing him paradoxically to sin with impunity. The conclusion of the novel, however, returns us to the Editor's narrative, which includes an extract from an actual published letter by James Hogg, printed in *Blackwood's Magazine*, August 1823. The letter, which according to the Editor "bears the stamp of authenticity in every line," narrates the account of digging up the body of the "sinner," Wringham, whose corpse (following his suicide, possibly at the hands of the devil) has been miraculously preserved.[59] The Editor decides to investigate, and although the fictionalized Hogg refuses to help him, he is assisted in a second excavation by another "shepherd" during which not only the body and artefact are unearthed but also a "printed pamphlet" that, once treated to a "thorough drying" and "unrolled," turns out to be "The Private Memoirs and Confessions of a Justified Sinner."[60] Hogg's playful mise-en-abyme text, which allows its own material tale to be excavated with the body, toys with our credulity, the blurring of fact and fiction, the pleasure and fear of "being well deceived."[61]

So, Lizzie Grant's tale of excavating Milton seemed to me to offer a Hogg-like hybrid of fact and fiction that tests the limits of credulity. Like Hogg, I mingled extracts from newspaper accounts and Philip Neve's pamphlets with fictional speculations and unreliable narrators. Like Hogg, I thought about the evidentiary basis of relics and material texts and their potential for alternative facts and forgeries. In my research I found what I became certain was a spoof in the *Public Advertiser*, testifying to the explosion of interest in the event and the opportunities it offered for commercialization:

Jennifer Wallace

> A correspondent, passing along Barbican about a week ago, picked up the following curious bill of parcels ...
> Ebenezer Ashmole, Esq. F. S. A.
> Bought of Timothy Strip-dead, Gravedigger to the parish of St Giles's, Cripplegate:

Aug, 3, 1790.	l.	s.	d.
To two eye-teeth of one Mr. Milton	0	4	0
...			
To finger-bone of ditto	0	5	0
To jaw-bone of ditto, with one broken tooth in it	0	7	0

> ...
> N. B. All the above goods are warranted, there being counterfeits abroad.[62]

My characters read this report and are briefly extremely worried, fearing they have competition for their trade in relics, only for the possibility that this might be a mock bill of sale to dawn on them: "Suddenly it hit me like the thousand lanterns being lit all at once in Vauxhall. Mr Timothy Strip-dead did not exist!"[63]

The multiplicity of perspectives and sources and the questioning of truth, based partly on "the mind [as] its own place" and partly on the implications of satiric irony, start to put pressure on the reliability of Philip Neve's account, the reliability of my Lizzie Grant's account, and the question of credibility across different classes. Whom do we believe? What are the class-based politics behind the composition and editing of texts? I do not want to reveal the ending of *Digging Up Milton* here, but suffice it to say that the novel explores the political gatekeeping of literary heritage and what is at stake in the silencing and recovery of different voices along with the pieces of Milton.

Those few academic studies of the Cripplegate disinterment and the Philip Neve pamphlet that have been published have strikingly echoed Neve in condemning the Cripplegate parishioners. Jared Richman argued that the "violation of ... [the] body becomes a form of censorship" and that a "kind of castration of Milton's literary body" metaphorically occurs during the "dissection of the corpse at St Giles in 1790."[64] Lorna Clymer maintained that the dissection and dispersal of Milton's body parts produced "a late eighteenth-century homeopathic remedy for any political threat posed by a reminder of the Interregnum."[65] She added that William Cowper's subsequent poem on the event, "On the Late Indecent Liberties Taken With the Remains of the Great Milton, Anno 1790," further ensured that the relics became "the property of hands that write" so that Milton could become "the right sort of literary saint."[66] But I prefer to see the event as an alternative demotic "reading" of Milton. A reassessment of the class-based prejudices of Philip Neve reveals fault lines of hypocrisy, deflection, and repression concerning the poet's relics, secularized notions of Miltonic innocence and guilt, and the reception of Milton's radical politics in 1790.

The 1790 disinterment could be considered a new form of Romantic tragedy. Milton had lamented "the poet's error of intermixing comic stuff with tragic sadness and gravity; or introducing trivial and vulgar persons, which by all judicious hath been counted absurd" (*SA*, "Of That Sort of Dramatic Poem Which is Called Tragedy"). But *Digging Up Milton*, which deconstructs Milton literally and metaphorically, corrupts Milton's desired purity of genre into the intermixture of comedy and tragedy that he condemned. These three moments in literary history (early modern, Romantic, twenty-first century), which come together through the bodies of writers, readers, and texts, open the possibility for a new hybrid notion of genre: a black comedy that contains within it a forgotten tragic fall.

Notes

1. Philip Neve, *A Narrative of the Disinterment of Milton's Coffin in the Parish-Church of St. Giles, Cripplegate, on Wednesday, 4th of August, 1790, and of the Treatment of the Corpse, during that, and the following day*, 2nd ed., with additions (London: T and J Egerton, 1790), 7. Subsequent references cited in text.

2. John Aubrey, *Brief Lives*, ed. Kate Bennett, 2 vols. (Oxford: Oxford University Press, 2015), 1:662. Stephen B. Dobranski, "Clustering and Curling Locks," in *Milton's Visual Imagination: Imagery in* Paradise Lost (Cambridge: Cambridge University Press, 2015), 156. Hair features prominently in artistic portraits of Milton; see, for example, Angelica Duran's chapter in this collection.

3. Jennifer Wallace, *Digging Up Milton* (Manchester, UK: Cillian Press, 2015).

4. Wallace, *Digging Up Milton*, 161–62.

5. Don M. Wolfe, "Milton and Mirabeau," *PMLA* 49, no. 4 (1934): 1120.

6. Christophe Tournu, "John Milton, the English Revolution (1640–60), and the Dynamics of the French Revolution (1789)," *Prose Studies* 24, no. 3 (2001): 35.

7. William Blake, *The Marriage of Heaven and Hell* (1790), in *The Illuminated Blake: William Blake's Complete Illuminated Works with a Plate-By-Plate Commentary*, ed. David Erdman (1974; New York: Dover, 1992), 103 (plate 6, lines 10–13).

8. Blake, *Marriage of Heaven and Hell*, 100 (plate 3, lines 11–13).

9. William Blake, *The First Book of Urizen* (1794), in *Illuminated Blake*, 182–210, esp. 188 (plate 6).

10. William Hayley, *The Life of Milton, in three parts. To which are added, Conjectures on the Origin of Paradise Lost* (London: T. Cadell and W. Davies, 1796), 51.

11. Joe Moshenska, *Feeling Pleasures: The Sense of Touch in Renaissance England* (Oxford: Oxford University Press, 2014), 283.

12. Philip Neve, *Cursory Remarks on Some Ancient English Poets, Particularly Milton* (London: [Priv. printed], 1789), 142.

13. Neve, *Cursory Remarks*, 144.

14. William Hayley, *The Poetical Works of John Milton. With a life of the Author by William Hayley* (London: W. Bulmer, for John and Josiah Boydell, and George Nicol, 1794–7).

15. *The Paradise Lost of Milton. with illustrations designed and engraved by John Martin* (London: Septimus Prowett, 1827). Fuseli painted forty-seven paintings for his "Milton gallery," modeled on Boydell's example, and exhibited in 1799. Most of the paintings are lost. See David Irwin, "Fuseli's Milton Gallery: Unpublished Letters," *Burlington Magazine* 101, no. 69 (1959): 436–40.

16. For this episode, see Jennifer Wallace, *Digging the Dirt: The Archaeological Imagination* (London: Duckworth, 2004), 63–65, 67.

17. John MacDiarmid, "St Michael's Churchyard—Disinterment of Burns," in *Sketches from Nature* (Edinburgh: Oliver and Boyd, 1830), 377.

18. Henry Mackenzie, *The Lounger*, no. XCVII (December 9, 1786), 387. It is tempting to draw a comparison between the "extraordinary size" of Burns's skull and the "fair large Front" of Milton's Adam that "declar'd / Absolute rule" (*PL*, 4.300–1).

19. James Hogg and William Motherwell, eds, *The Works of Robert Burns*, vol. 5 (Glasgow: A. Fullarton and Co., 1839–41), 258.

20. Lorna Clymer, "Cromwell's Head and Milton's Hair: Corpse Theory in Spectacular Bodies of the Interregnum," *Eighteenth Century* 40, no. 2 (1999): 92.

21. John Keats, "Lines on Seeing a Lock of Milton's Hair," in *Keats: Poetical Works*, ed. H. W. Garrod (Oxford: Oxford University Press, 1956), 378, lines 34–37.

22. Keats, "Lines," in *Keats*, 378, lines 39–40.

23. Leigh Hunt, "To Robert Batty, M.D., On His Giving Me a Lock of Milton's Hair," in *Foliage; or Poems Original and Translated* (London: C. and J. Ollier, 1818), cxxxi.

24. Keats, "Lines," in *Keats*, 378, line 33.

25. Leigh Hunt, "To the Same, On the Same Subject," in *Foliage*, cxxxii, lines 9–10.

26. Hunt, "To the Same, On the Same Subject," in *Foliage*, cxxxii, lines 2–3.

27. Keats, "I was startled, when I caught thy name / Coupled so unaware," in Keats, "Lines," in *Keats*, 378, lines 39–40.

28. Wallace, *Digging Up Milton*, 19.

29. John Rumrich, communications to volume contributors, November 4, 2021.

178 Decomposing Milton

30. Aaron Santesso, "The Birth of the Birthplace: Bread Street and Literary Tourism before Stratford," *ELH* 71, no. 2 (2004): 390.

31. Helen Darbishire, *The Early Lives of Milton* (London: Constable and Co., 1932), 48; Hayley, *Life of Milton*, 191.

32. Santesso, "Birth of the Birthplace," 394.

33. In "Sonnet Written in the Cottage Where Burns Was Born" (in *Keats*, 385), Keats is both awed and numbed while metaphorically (and literally?) "pledging [Burns's] great soul" (line 6) in his cottage with his own "Barley-bree" (line 5):

> Yet can I stamp my foot upon thy floor,
> Yet can I ope thy window-sash to find
> The meadow thou hast tramped o'er and o'er,—
> Yet an I think of thee till thought is blind, —
> Yet can I drink a bumper to thy name,—
> O smile among the shades, for this is fame! (lines 9–16)

34. John Roque, *A Plan of the Cities of London and Westminster, and Borough of Southwark* (1746), available on *Locating London's Past* (December 2011), https://www.locatinglondon.org/.

35. William Blake, *Milton* (1804–11), in *Illuminated Blake*, 218 (plate 2, line 6).

36. Blake, *Milton* (1804–11), in *Illuminated Blake*, 222 (plate 6, lines 10–13).

37. Blake, preface to *Milton* (1804–11), in *Illuminated Blake*, 216 (lines 29, 43–44). The only other fictional treatment of the disinterment of Milton—Michael Hughes, *The Countenance Divine* (London: John Murray, 2016)—connects the event with London-based William Blake who acquires one of the poet's ribs and is led further along his journey of idiosyncratic religious fanaticism.

38. William Wordsworth, "London 1802," in *William Wordsworth*, ed. Stephen Gill (Oxford: Oxford University Press, 1984), 286.

39. Letter possibly to Charles Lamb, November 1802, in *The Early Letters of William and Dorothy Wordsworth*, ed. Ernest de Selincourt (Oxford: Oxford University Press, 1935), 312.

40. Sandra M. Gilbert and Susan Gubar, "Milton's Bogey: Patriarchal Poetry and Women Readers," in *The Madwoman in the Attic: The Woman Writer and the Nineteenth-Century Literary Imagination* (New Haven, CT: Yale University Press, 1980), 187–212. See also Paul Stevens, "Robert Graves Misreading Milton," *Milton Studies* 57 (2016): 3–30.

41. Wallace, *Digging Up Milton*, 26.

42. Lucy Newlyn, Paradise Lost *and the Romantic Reader* (Oxford: Oxford University Press, 1993), 130; William Godwin, *Caleb Williams*, ed. David McCracken (Oxford: Oxford University Press, 1970), 136.

43. Samuel Taylor Coleridge, "The Rime of the Ancyent Marinere," in *Lyrical Ballads*, ed. R. L. Brett and A. R. Jones, 2nd ed. (London: Routledge, 1991), 35, l. 657.

44. *The Prelude* (1805), in *William Wordsworth*, book 10, 550, line 729; 543, lines 422–26, 429.

45. Wallace, *Digging Up Milton*, 16.

46. Wallace, *Digging Up Milton*, 28.

47. William Wordsworth, "Ode: Intimations of Immortality From Recollections of Early Childhood," in *William Wordsworth*, 302, lines 182–83.

48. William Wordsworth, "O there is blessing in this gentle breeze," *The Prelude*, in *William Wordsworth*, book 1, 375, lines 1.

49. William Wordsworth, *Prelude*, in *William Wordsworth*, book 1, 375, lines 9–12, 15–19.

50. Wordsworth, *Prelude*, in *William Wordsworth*, book 1, 375, line 18; 376, line 43.

51. *The Giaour*, in *Byron: Poetical Works*, ed. Frederick Page, 3rd ed., corrected by John Jump (Oxford: Oxford University Press, 1970), 263, lines 1266–70.

52. *The Giaour*, in *Byron: Poetical Works*, 259, lines 755–58. This is the first reference to the vampire tradition in English literature, besides a brief mention in Robert Southey's oriental epic *Thalaba* (1801), which Byron acknowledges in his footnote to his poem (*Byron: Poetical Works*, 894).

53. Wallace, *Digging Up Milton*, 137.

54. Wallace, *Digging Up Milton*, 182, original emphasis.

55. Wallace, *Digging Up Milton*, 182; *PL*, 4.75. A local newspaper, the *St. James Chronicle*, reported that one of the men involved in the disinterment "was haunted for months afterwards by the feeling of being clutched by an icy hand": see Joseph Crawford, *Raising Milton's Ghost: John Milton and the Sublime of Terror in the Early Romantic Period* (London: Bloomsbury, 2011), 27.

56. Newlyn, *Paradise Lost and the Romantic Reader*, 133.

57. James Hogg, *The Private Memoirs and Confessions of a Justified Sinner* (1824), ed. John Carey (Oxford: Oxford University Press, 1969), 86. Hogg's "justified" ironizes Milton's declared intent to "justifie the wayes of God to men" (*PL*, 1.26).

58. Hogg, *Private Memoirs*, 86.

59. Hogg, *Private Memoirs*, 245.

60. Hogg, *Private Memoirs*, 247, 252, 253.

61. Jonathan Swift, *A Tale of a Tub* (1710), in *Jonathan Swift*, ed. Angus Ross and David Woolley (Oxford: Oxford University Press, 1984), 145.

62. "News," *Public Advertiser* (London, England), September 3, 1790.

63. Wallace, *Digging Up Milton*, 140.

64. Jared Richman, "Milton Re-membered, Graved and Press'd: William Blake and the Fate of Textual Bodies," *European Romantic Review* 19, no. 4 (2008): 396.

65. Clymer, "Cromwell's Head and Milton's Hair," 105.

66. Clymer, "Cromwell's Head and Milton's Hair," 106. Cowper's poem imagines "the hands that heaved the stones / Where Milton's ashes lay"; William Cowper, "On the Late Indecent Liberties Taken With the Remains of Milton," in *The Poems of William Cowper*, ed. John D. Baird and Charles Ryskamp, vol. 3 (Oxford: Oxford University Press, 1980–1995), 65, lines 17–18.

CHAPTER 7

❧

Shapes of Things to Come

Milton, Evolution, and the Afterlife of Species in Tennyson's *In Memoriam, A. H. H.*

Ryan Hackenbracht

Affectionately referring to Milton as "grand old fellow" and "sublimest of all poets," Alfred, Lord Tennyson admired his predecessor's skill in painting majestic panoramas of celestial and terrestrial scenes.[1] Often reading Milton's works aloud to friends and family (including his aging mother), he could quote *Paradise Lost* at length, and so far as "the 'grand style' of poetic diction," considered Milton superior to Virgil (*Mem.*, 2:284). "What an imagination the old man had[!]" Hallam Tennyson recalls his father exclaiming; "Milton beats everyone in the material sublime" (*Mem.*, 2:521). Tennyson would not have understood T. S. Eliot's complaint about Milton's "weakness of visual observation"; admittedly, few have.[2] Tennyson's paean to the poet, written in an undulating Greek meter that would have made Milton giddy, praises him for the spectacular views *Paradise Lost* offers the mind's eye:

> O mighty mouth'd inventor of harmonies,
> O skill'd to sing of Time or Eternity,
> God-gifted organ-voice of England,
> Milton, a name to resound for ages;
> Whose Titan angels, Gabriel, Abdiel,
> Starred from Jehovah's gorgeous armouries,
> Tower, as the deep-domed empyrëan
> Rings to the roar of an angel onset!
> Me rather all that bowery loneliness,

181

182   Shapes of Things to Come

> The brooks of Eden mazily murmuring,
> And bloom profuse and cedar arches
> Charm, as a wanderer out in ocean,
> Where some refulgent sunset of India
> Streams o'er a rich ambrosian ocean isle,
> And crimson-hued the stately palm-wood
> Whisper in odorous heights of even. ("Milton: Alcaics")[3]

Tennyson's praise of Milton registers, among other places, in his delayed verbs ("Tower" and "Charm"), which recall the Latinate syntax of Miltonic verse, and in the simile of a wanderer on the ocean, reminiscent of the many delightful similes worming their way through *Paradise Lost*. Tennyson divides Milton's crowning achievements between, on the one hand, his cosmic themes of God and the angels in Heaven, and on the other, the natural wonders of Eden. In these instances Milton demonstrates sublimity by both Burkean and Kantean definitions popular in Victorian England: Milton's "Titan angels" and "deep-domed empyrëan" inspire feelings of terror while simultaneously impressing on the mind its inadequacy in grasping their magnitude (*Größe*).[4] Milton's value lies in his ability to show readers things no one has ever seen. In antiquity Virgil sang of "arma virumque" (arms and the man) and Ovid of "mutates . . . formas" (shapes transformed).[5] Milton, however, sings the more challenging themes of "Time or Eternity," divinity, and celestial hosts. It is thus as a blind *vates* who "see[s] and tell[s] / Of things invisible to mortal sight" that Milton wins Tennyson's admiration (*PL*, 3.54–55). Milton would prove indispensable, in this regard, when Tennyson sought to capture the metaphysical wonders of the afterlife in his own epic-elegy *In Memoriam, A. H. H.* (1850).

It is unsurprising that Tennyson would turn to Milton, for no other poet was held in higher esteem by the Victorians than that "mighty mouth'd inventor of harmonies" ("Milton: Alcaics," 1).[6] Nineteenth-century Britain was an exciting period in Milton studies, academically and culturally. It witnessed the discovery of the manuscript of *De Doctrina Christiana*, the publication of David Masson's voluminous biography, and the hunt for relics of the poet—with one Victorian boasting that he "handled one of Milton's ribs" when the poet's grave at St. Giles, Cripplegate, was disturbed, an event discussed by Jennifer Wallace in this current collection.[7] Charles Darwin, setting out in the *Beagle*, always brought along a copy of *Paradise Lost*, which was his "chief favourite" for leisure reading.[8] Leigh Hunt owned a lock of Milton's hair, taken from the grave site, which he displayed on occasion to friends, including John Keats.[9] In 1839 Thomas de Quincey wrote, "Milton is not an author amongst authors, not a poet amongst poets, but a power amongst powers; and *Paradise Lost* is not a book amongst books, not a poem amongst poems, but a central force amongst forces."[10] Assessments of Milton's presence in *In Memoriam* often operate within a Bloomian model of influence, in which the relationship between poets is defined through antagonism.[11] On the contrary, *In Memoriam*, "Milton: Alcaics," and the testimony of Tennyson's son all indicate that Tennyson cherished Milton as a kindred spirit and found his poetry helpful, not harmful, to his own endeavors. Throughout *In Memoriam*, in particular, Tennyson treasures Milton as a farsighted guide to metaphysical realms beyond this life, much as Dante revered Virgil for showing him the anterooms of eternity.

In particular, *Paradise Lost* supplied Tennyson with the imagery and language he needed to envision death and resurrection as stages of human evolution. Fascinated by modern theories on the transmutation of species, which he studied in detail, Tennyson used *In Memoriam* as an opportunity to go where men of science could not: into the afterlife. The poem reflects a broader cultural obsession in the period with burial rites, relics of the dead, bodily decay, and metaphysical reunion.[12] As Deborah Lutz observes, "the dead body's materiality held a certain enchantment for Victorians, a charmed ability to originate narrative" to the extent that the body of the deceased becomes a "special type of information"—a text, that is, which may be read.[13] Similarly, Ashley Miller notes an increase in the Victorian era of a poetics that "draws attention to, rather than effaces, the mediacy of the body" as a conduit for knowledge about the self and the world.[14] Reflecting on Arthur Henry Hallam's body in *In Memoriam*, Tennyson embarks on a scientific thought experiment that ushers evolutionary doctrines into the period after death where, the poet postulates, the self continues to undergo radical changes in being. For his knowledge of evolutionary change, Tennyson turned to the works of Goethe, Jean-Baptiste Lamarck, Robert Chambers, Charles Lyell, and later in life to Darwin—but their treatises contain no mention of changes after death. For that Tennyson turned to Milton. Trying to imagine the shapes of things to come, Tennyson sees but through a glass darkly, and so he turns to *Paradise Lost* for its vivid scenes of afterlife existence and its firm confidence in salvation. "I can hardly understand," Tennyson once declared, "how any great, imaginative man, who has deeply lived, suffered, thought and wrought, can doubt of the Soul's continuous progress in the after-life" (*Mem.*, 1:321)—yet doubt Tennyson did. His great elegy for Hallam "displays, at key points, a fully internalised skepticism about the possibility of maintaining a spiritual vision," as Aidan Day points out.[15] Originally intended for personal use, not for publication, *In Memoriam* registers both Tennyson's private doubts and the creative ways he used Milton's heavenly scenes to overcome them.[16]

Herein lies a great irony. Milton's materialism was unknown to Tennyson, as it was to most mid-nineteenth-century Milton critics. It would take another three-quarters of a century before Denis Saurat, in *Milton: Man and Thinker* (1925), would recognize Milton's rejection of Cartesian dualism in *De Doctrina Christiana* for what it was—the outline of a materialist ontology—and apply that information to a reading of *Paradise Lost*.[17] To this day Saurat's brilliant contributions to Milton studies remain underappreciated, but as Jeffrey Shoulson reminds us, "Saurat was the first scholar to make extensive use of the *de Doctrina* in a systematic reading of Milton's poetry and prose."[18] In the pre-Saurat world of the mid-nineteenth century, Tennyson was ignorant of Milton's materialist philosophy. To peer into the spiritual world beyond this world, Tennyson borrows Milton's sight. But what Tennyson takes for Milton's depictions of a spiritual afterlife—the Heaven and Hell of *Paradise Lost*—are, for Milton, not a spiritual afterlife at all but very much a part of *this* material life. Drawn to the otherworldliness of Milton's Heaven and Hell, Tennyson does not know that within Milton's materialist philosophy, such places are not in fact otherworldly; rather, they are extensions of *this* world (for more on this idea, see Erin Webster's essay in this volume). Tennyson mines *Paradise Lost* for its religious confidence in the resurrection and an unseen afterlife. But unbeknownst to Tennyson, Milton's animistic materialism, with its doctrine of biological change, anticipated the evolutionary discoveries that Tennyson believes he is capturing, for the first time, in scientific verse.

"Thou wilt not leave us in the dust": Tennyson and the Transmutation of Species

In the estimation of Thomas Huxley, "Darwin's bulldog," Tennyson was "the only poet since the time of Lucretius, who has taken the trouble to understand the work and tendency of the men of science."[19] Tennyson earned the praise. His extensive knowledge of modern scientific theories greatly influenced his literary style, such that "the material basis of aestheticism, not in the Marxist but the Lucretian sense, could be said to start with Tennyson," as Angela Leighton notes.[20] The poet's interest in the emerging fields of geology and biology coincided with a monumental shift in how species were perceived. The teleological model, in which God created living things perfect "after their kind," was being abandoned (Gen. 1:21). Increasingly, animals and plants were seen as mutable and able (over eons) to assume different shapes. Metamorphosis was the rule of life, not the exception. As Darwin put it, "not one living species will transmit its unaltered likeness to a distant futurity."[21] Termed "the transmutation of species" (i.e., evolution), the theory of mutable bodies was as ancient as Anaximander of Miletus (ca. 610 to ca. 546 BCE), who believed humans evolved from fish, and his disciple Xenophanes of Colophon (ca. 560 to ca. 478 BCE).[22] But it was also a modern doctrine associated with the French naturalist Jean-Baptiste Lamarck.[23] Unlike Darwin, who argued for transmutation *via* natural selection, Lamarck maintained that environments were the agents provoking adaptation and thus biological transformation. One example, Lamarck attested in *Philosophie zoologique* (1809), was man, who evolved from orangutans that long ago forsook trees and learned to walk upright.

The concept was taken up by Robert Chambers, fellow of the Geological Society, who published *Vestiges of the Natural History of Creation* (1844).[24] For some readers, the book was "revelatory," while for many, it was offensive or "incoherent," but it was nevertheless a tome Tennyson owned and read.[25] The objective of Chambers's treatise was to consider man "zoologically, and without regard to the distinct character assigned to him by theology"—that is, to consider man as an animal among animals.[26] Chambers, who would later become acquaintances with Huxley, was interested in race as an evolutionary index for gauging the progressiveness or primitiveness of a human. "Why are the Mongolians generally yellow, the Americans red, the Caucasians white?" he wondered; "all of these phenomena appear, in a word, to be explicable on the ground of *development*."[27] His work shows that questions of evolution had been applied to humanity long before Darwin's *On the Origin of Species* (1859), which makes no mention of human morphology, and before Darwin's *The Descent of Man* (1871), which built its thesis on human evolution on ideas already in circulation.[28]

Those ideas were available to Tennyson, who would enrich them with Miltonic images of bodies changing in eternity.[29] In autumn 1833 Tennyson received a letter notifying him that Hallam "[was] no more"—he had died in Vienna of a brain hemorrhage.[30] Tennyson and his sister Emily, who was engaged to Hallam, were devastated. But it also provided Tennyson with an opportunity to do something that

186   Shapes of Things to Come

had not been done since Lucretius, Virgil, and Ovid: construct an epic
that engaged modern scientific doctrines, thereby merging natural philosophy with literary aesthetics. First published in 1850 by Edward
Moxon, *In Memoriam*'s alternate title, "The Way of the Soul," hints
at Tennyson's scientific ambitions in tracing the transmutation of the
human species into the afterlife through poetic fictions.[31] Invoking
Christ as muse in the prologue, Tennyson signals the heroic intent of
his work, which like Miltonic epic takes as its conflict an inner struggle
of the will, rather than a physical contest of force. For Milton that
conflict is choosing to be good when it is more fun to be bad, and for
Tennyson it is the difficulty of choosing to believe in an afterlife no one
has ever seen.

Throughout *In Memoriam* the poet struggles to resolve this crisis
and believe there is something after the darkness. The hymns, prayers,
aubades, symbols of light and sight, references to resurrection, and references to Lazarus are all different manifestations of the poet's attempt
to generate, within himself, the faith he needs to believe that Hallam
still exists. Evoking Herbert's "Love (1)," which begins, "immortal
Love, author of this great frame" (a reference to "God is love"; 1 John
4:8), Tennyson lays out the poem's agon, which is the challenge of trying to visualize the invisible:[32]

> Strong Son of God, immortal Love,
> Whom we, that have not seen thy face,
> By faith, and faith alone, embrace,
> Believing where we cannot prove;
>
> Thine are these orbs of light and shade;
> Thou madest Life in man and brute;
> Thou madest Death; and lo, thy foot
> Is on the skull which thou hast made.
>
> Thou wilt not leave us in the dust:
> Thou madest man, he knows not why,
> He thinks he was not made to die;
> And thou hast made him: thou art just. (*In Memoriam*, prologue, 1–12)

Delineating both the difficulty and necessity of having faith, the
opening lines allude to scripture: "faith is the substance of things hoped
for, the evidence of things not seen" (Heb. 11:1). Tennyson's play on
"orbs" as eyes and suns locates this spiritual quest within a cosmic

and physical scope. Tracing the soul's progress through the afterlife becomes an astronautical mission, like soaring between planets and stars. And while the anguished Herbert is a fitting companion for the poem's embarkation, it is to Milton and *Paradise Lost* that Tennyson turns for a resolution to that crisis. The third stanza opens with a reference to the Son's heroic offer to the Father to "account mee man" and to "on me let Death wreak all his rage" (*PL,* 3.238, 241). In Milton's epic the Son is confident that, upon death, the Father will not forget him:

> Thou wilt not leave me in the loathsome grave
> His prey, nor suffer my unspotted soul
> For ever with corruption there to dwell;
> But I shall rise victorious, and subdue
> My vanquisher, spoiled of his vaunted spoil;
> Death his death's wound shall then receive, and stoop
> Inglorious, of his mortal sting disarmed.
> I through the ample air in triumph high
> Shall lead hell captive maugre hell, and show
> The powers of darkness bound. (*PL,* 3.247–56)

The Son anticipates the confidence of King David, who prays to God, "thou wilt not leave my soul in hell" (Ps. 16:10). In Tennyson's poem the confidence of Milton's Son becomes the speaker's confidence, who now knows that a further transmutation of the body will occur after death. This is the doctrine of the resurrection of the dead and of glorified bodies, when Christ would "raise [the faithful] up at the last day" (John 6:44) and "descend from heaven with a shout, with the voice of the archangel, and with the trump of God: and the dead in Christ shall rise first" (1 Thess. 4:16). For Tennyson, scripture provided the promise of life after death, and *Paradise Lost* supplied the optics. In the Son's confident account of his resurrection from the grave, Tennyson found the personal assurance he was looking for that God was good, Hallam was alive, and Tennyson would one day see his friend again.

But resurrection did not mean for Tennyson what it did for Milton. For Tennyson, who chose instead to emphasize the disembodied existence of the soul, resurrection was a mystery—its design and purpose known only to God. *In Memoriam* gestures toward the resurrection of the dead as that "one far-off divine event" (*In Memoriam,* 131.155), but it declines to provide any details, or articulate how (or why) the soul becomes incarnate again. Rather, the poem ends abruptly as soon as the resurrection is sighted—as if to say, the poet's scientific thought experiment has reached the limits of what it can reasonably assess. This is convenient for Tennyson, since it allows him to avoid any sort of scientific explanation for how this might occur and retreat from fact into the vagaries of affect—joy, notably, at the wonder of this future event. In this way Tennyson is at odds with Milton, who as a monist materialist stressed the fabulously physical nature of the resurrection throughout *Paradise Lost*. Neither flesh nor motion disappear in Milton's universe but are transmuted into different forms, different vehicles for vitality—until the resurrection at Christ's Second Coming, at which time matter would reconstitute itself into a prior configuration. Milton understood well the prophet's joy that those who "dwell in dust" would one day "awake and sing" (Isa. 26:19), for unlike Tennyson, he rejected the notion of disembodied existence, maintaining instead that death was death—until the miraculous act of revitalization through resurrection. For a materialist such as Milton the resurrection of the dead is a theological necessity, since without it, one could not confirm that God is good. Whether resurrecting Jesus on the third day or humanity at the Second Coming, it is this ultimate expression of divine grace that proves (in Milton's mind) that God is indeed a merciful, loving God.

This desperate struggle to prove God's goodness imbues Miltonic theodicy with its characteristic complexity. Milton is "struggling to make his God appear less wicked," William Empson writes, but the poet's inability to exonerate God is nonetheless "the chief source of [*Paradise Lost*'s] fascination and poignancy."[33] Agreeing with Empson on the failure of that endeavor, Richard Strier has a different take on the outcome: "[Milton's] attempt at theodicy—whether one regards it as successful or not—produces most of the aesthetic and religious failures of the poem."[34] If Milton's epic is galvanized by its theodicy, failed or otherwise, we might equally say that Tennyson's religious verse is energized by the tension between a lack of scientific evidence for resurrection and the stubborn will to believe it will happen, and thus God is good, regardless. Ironically, in a poem that purports to be a scientific thought experiment, Tennyson quite often believes in something—like the disembodied survival of the soul—simply because he wants to. His God is not proved good; rather, goodness is an underlying precondition of Tennyson's God being God. Like Augustine, who saw faith as prerequisite to understanding and only then came to the knowledge that "*semper vivis et nihil moritur in te*" (nothing dies if it is in the ever-living God), Tennyson begins from a point of belief in metaphysical existence and from there ventures out into the

Ryan Hackenbracht   *189*

vast expanse of the afterlife to chart the soul's progress.[35] "We have but faith: we cannot know," the poet reasons, "for knowledge is of things we see" (*In Memoriam*, prologue, 21–22). As a scientific poem, *In Memoriam* takes as its laboratory the poet's mind and investigates therein the certitude of metaphysical existence after death. But there, the poem is on shaky ground, since the very evidentiary preconditions for that investigation into the soul's afterlife draw their data from religious belief—not empirical fact. The truth is that *In Memoriam* is, quite often, a great deal less scientific than Tennyson would care to admit. On that point, Tennyson's comments on the science of Milton and Goethe offer insight into his own endeavor, for both poets left an indelible mark on the allegedly scientific method of *In Memoriam*'s metaphysical thought experiment.

"On stepping-stones / Of their dead selves": Miltonic Materialism and Goethean Science

If the Miltonic afterlife has such a presence in *In Memoriam*, what are we to make of Tennyson's criticism that "Milton's physics and metaphysics are not strong" (*Mem.*, 2:521)? According to Tennyson's son, Hallam, Tennyson was referring to book 5 of *Paradise Lost*, in which Raphael informs Adam of the further bodily changes available to him and Eve, "if [they] be found obedient" (*PL*, 5.501). Even with the aid of the recently discovered *De Doctrina Christiana* manuscript, the passage caused confusion before Saurat recognized it as a profession of materialism. But to Tennyson and the Victorians, those passages made little scientific sense:

> time may come when men
> With angels may participate, and find
> No inconvenient diet, nor too light fare:
> And from these corporal nutriments perhaps
> Your bodies may at last turn all to spirit,
> Improved by tract of time, and winged ascend
> Ethereal, as we, or may at choice
> Here or in heavenly paradises dwell. (*PL*, 5.493–500)

Tennyson can hardly be blamed for thinking, upon reading this passage, that Milton was "not strong" in his physics or metaphysics. Earlier commentators—some careful readers of Milton's text, some not—failed to see what Saurat would. In *Explanatory Notes and Remarks on Milton's "Paradise Lost"* (1734), the Jonathan Richardsons (father and son) addressed Raphael's claim that "body [may] up to spirit work" (*PL,* 5.478) and his metaphor of the tree of creation (*PL,* 5.479–84). "'[T]is a fine Paradisaical Notion," they wrote, "and (by the way) a Comment on the Doctrine of a Natural Body Chang'd into a Spiritual one; or of the Resurrection, as I *Cor.* XV."[36] The Richardsons were dismissive of the possibility that there was any serious metaphysical speculation taking place; for them, this was poetical fancy—not science or philosophy. Victorian critics also struggled to make sense of Milton's materialism.[37] In his 1825 translation of *De Doctrina Christiana*, Charles Sumner, chaplain in ordinary to King George IV, admitted Milton was an Arian (a claim circulating since the early eighteenth century) but insisted Milton's theology was Christocentric and therefore largely orthodox.[38] On Milton's rejection of Cartesian dualism, Sumner bristled that Milton was simply being biblical.[39] In August of the same year, an essay by Thomas Macaulay appeared in the *Edinburgh Review*, in which Macaulay positioned himself against the accusations of modern Johnsonites that, in *Mask* and *Paradise Lost*, Milton "[ascribed] to spirits many functions [e.g., eating] of which spirits must be incapable."[40] By asserting that Milton's "angels are good men with wings," Macaulay claimed angelic anthropomorphism and posited a narratological solution to what was in fact an ontological quandary.[41]

The keenest critic was David Masson, who identified Milton's materialism for what it was but rejected the results of his own discovery. His six-volume *The Life of John Milton* (1859–80) was known to Tennyson through their mutual friend, Thomas Carlyle, historian of the French Revolution.[42] Masson, who had connections to the Free Church of Scotland movement, saw Milton as a fellow independent who, barring a few heresies, was largely orthodox. Milton wrote *Paradise Lost* "with the Bible for his main authority and the Spirit of God for his guide," according to Masson.[43] Regarding *De Doctrina Christiana*, Masson makes note of Milton's monism and materialism:

> Milton's cosmological conception, his conception of the processes of the visible world, those of mind included, is undoubtedly materialistic. All cosmic life, he holds, is but a diversified organization of that common matter which was originally an efflux or production out of the substance of God . . . [Milton allows for] the possibility of such a gradual evolution of the common matter of all things from lower to higher.[44]

Despite this acknowledgment, Masson concludes that "these propositions are sufficiently in accord with the most evangelical Christian orthodoxy, save in so far as the form of statement here and there may betray a tinge of Milton's Arminianism or of his Arianism."[45] Masson is quick to draw the poet back within the fold of "safe" Christianity. As this sampling of critics suggests, at the time Tennyson was writing *In Memoriam* in the 1830s–40s, he did not have sufficient critical tools at his disposal to identify Milton's materialism as such. What Tennyson found instead—insofar as "one first matter all" and "bodies . . . turn[ing] all to spirit"—was poetic fancy, or heresy, but not hard science. Hence his observation that "certainly Milton's physics and metaphysics are not strong." In this pre-Saurat period, Tennyson had little reason to think they would be.

If, for Tennyson, Milton was not a scientific poet, then who was? There is a clear answer: Johann Wolfgang von Goethe.[46] Reading his works in German and able to recite poems from memory, Tennyson admired Goethe as an intimidating model of the poet-scientist he himself aspired to be. "Goethe lacked the divine intensity of Dante," Hallam Tennyson recalls his father saying, "but he was among the wisest of mankind as well as a great artist" (*Mem.*, 2:287–88). On a trip to Germany Tennyson visited Goethe's house in Weimar and marveled at pairs of the man's boots left untouched by the door. In Goethe's study Tennyson was filled with "awe and sadness" (*Mem.*, 2:26) at seeing the cramped quarters, replete with empty wine bottles and a partially boarded up window, in which the poet composed his masterpieces.[47] It follows, then, that we might interpret Tennyson's remark as such: "Milton's physics and metaphysics are not strong *in comparison to those of a writer like Goethe.*" Tennyson even attributed the theme of mutability coursing throughout *In Memoriam* to Goethe's influence. In response once to a fan from South Carolina on that subject, Tennyson replied, "I believe I alluded to Goethe[.] Among his last words were these, 'Von Aenderungen zu hoheren Aenderungen' [or] 'from changes to higher changes'" (*Mem.*, 2:391). The stanza in question was this:

> I held it truth, with him who sings
> To one clear harp in divers tones,
> That men may rise on stepping-stones
> Of their dead selves to higher things. (*In Memoriam*, 1.1–4)

Given Tennyson's familiarity with Goethean science, the passage certainly resonates of Goethean principles regarding metamorphosis.

The problem, however, as pointed out by Christopher Ricks, Susan Shatto, and Marion Shaw (all editors of Tennyson's works), is that the phrase "von Aenderungen zu hoheren Aenderungen" does not appear anywhere in Goethe's corpus.[48] While Goethe did not write the words Tennyson ascribes to him, several poems do have themes of ascension. In "Talismane" ("Talismans"), Goethe writes, "mit dem Staube nicht der Geist zerstoben, / Dringet, in sich selbst gedrängt, nach oben" (spirit is not scattered with the dust, but grows denser in its ever-upward thrust).[49] In "Höheres und Höchstes" ("Higher and Highest Matters"), Goethe professes "entschiedener empfindet / Der Verklärte sich unendlich" (transfiguration gives us surer hope of life unending), and he imagines his ascension into the empyreum:[50]

> Und nun dring ich aller Orten
> Leichter durch die ewgen Kreise,
> Die durchdrungen sind vom Worte
> Gottes rein-lebendger Weise.[51]

> (Lightlier now I pass through all the
> Timeless cycles God created
> Which by his pure word and living
> Motion all are penetrated.)

Similar as these passages are to the opening of *In Memoriam*, they are not a clear point of origin for Tennyson's imagery. Assuredly, Tennyson's verse is influenced by Goethean themes. But influence is a far cry from allusion. If the stanza's imagery is not Goethean, then was Tennyson subconsciously channeling Milton, when he spoke of "changes to higher changes"? Perhaps. Critics have teased other contenders, but all the same, a different alternative presents itself.

Like the poem's broader theme of transmutation, the image of souls rising "on stepping-stones / Of their dead selves" up into eternity is polygenetic rather than monogenetic. It is an image cobbled together from bits and pieces of Milton, Goethe, Ovid, and Dante, among others, and inspired by Tennyson's scientific readings on evolution. The stanza expresses a sentiment similar to Raphael's claim that "body [can] up to spirit work"; it also echoes Adam's declarations that "by steps we may ascend to God" (*PL*, 5.512) and that God can "raise [his] creature to what height [he] wilt" (*PL*, 8.430). These are Milton's contributions, but they are small, and the image is still Tennyson's. We would be mistaken in assuming that Tennyson, alone in his generation of Milton admirers, correctly discerned the animistic materialism at play in *Paradise Lost*, which the Richardsons, Sumner, and others all missed. Tennyson did not, but neither did his poetry suffer for it.

On the subject of influence, Tennyson once complained about literary critics and their methods. "The critics won't allow me any imagination," he wrote; "they take a line like 'Moanings of the homeless sea' [*In Memoriam*, 35.9] and say: "'Moanings,' Horace; 'homeless,' Shelley, and so on . . . As if no one else had heard the sea moan except Horace."[52] When it comes to Tennyson's arresting image of souls leaping from form to form in the afterlife, as a child skips across stones, I propose we let the poet have his imagination.

Revitalizing Matter: Tennyson's Orphic Descent to the Underworld

If modern discoveries in the transmutation of species offered new ways of thinking about life, they also introduced new ways of thinking about death. In *In Memoriam* the poet's descent into the underworld (katabasis) reflects Tennyson's awareness of major scientific shifts in the perception of mortality. One shift was the news that the world was far older than presumed. Darwin, quoting Gottfried Wilhelm Leibniz, explained, "*Natura non facit saltum*" (Nature does not rush things), that is, evolutionary processes occur over a massive time span.[53] The second revelation was that many species had lived and died before recorded history, a fact prompting awareness of a new kind of death: extinction, or the annihilation of a species. This was not an entirely foreign concept. Europeans had heard of the extinction of a flightless bird in Madagascar called the dodo; they also knew of the disappearance of the aurochs, which had been spotted in the forests of Poland in the 1620s but then seen no more. But extinction as a common and large-scale phenomenon, occurring with mechanistic cyclicality for eons before human existence, was unknown. This was in part because such an idea did not accord with popular opinions of Earth's age. In *Annales Veteris Testamenti* (*Records of the Old Testament*; 1650), James Ussher, archbishop of Armagh and Milton's opponent in the prelacy debates, deduced that the world was created on October 23, 4004 BCE, by the Julian calendar, based on tallies of records from the Old Testament.[54] While chronologies like Ussher's persisted for centuries, in Tennyson's day, mounting pressure from scientific communities was discrediting Ussherian chronology.

194 Shapes of Things to Come

In Tennyson's lifetime an apocalyptic scenario heretofore inconceivable suddenly became conceivable: mankind, the flower of creation, might be erased from the face of the earth. Humanity might exist only in the fossil record like so many other animals. One of Tennyson's favorite books, *Principles of Geology* (1830–33) by Charles Lyell, claimed that, based on the fossil record, "the language of nature signified millions [of years]" as far as the age of the earth.[55] Earlier naturalists were "under a delusion as to the age of the world," Lyell asserts, but "however fantastical some theories of the sixteenth century may now appear to us," the truth is at last coming to light.[56] The Earth was not simply older than six thousand years—it was *far* older. During the vast desert of time before humans came onto the scene, Lyell explains, many species blinked in and out of being. As Darwin (who consulted Lyell on a draft of *On the Origin of Species*) would later remark, "the number of specimens in all our museums is absolutely as nothing compared with the countless generations of countless species which certainly have existed."[57] What this amounted to was a decentering of man from his ontological throne atop the hierarchy of living beings. All species wage war against death, and all share the common fear, hardwired into their biology, of failing in that endeavor. And with the knowledge that multitudes of species once ceased to exist came the revelation that humanity might do so as well.

Accordingly, Tennyson expands his concern for death in *In Memoriam* to encompass the entire human species. His descent into the underworld is modeled on Orpheus, the legendary musician who used his gift of song to bargain for the life of his dead wife. In Orphic katabasis, the life-death boundary is permeable (hence the necromantic rituals of ancient Orphic cults), and the tale supplied the poets of antiquity with an allegory for their own labors of preservation and immortalization. Such is the case in the *Metamorphoses*, when Ovid imparts to Orpheus a plaintive speech to melt even the heart of hell:

> Per ego haec loca plena timoris,
> per Chaos hoc ingens vastique silentia regni,
> Eurydices, oro, properata retexite fata.
> Omnia debemur vobis, paulumque morati
> serius aut citius sedem properamus ad unam;
> tendimus huc omnes, haec est domus ultima, vosque
> humani generis longissima regna tenetis.
> Haec quoque, cum iustos matura peregerit annos,
> iuris erit vestri; pro munere poscimus usum.[58]

(By this place full of dread, by the huge underworld and these vast and silent realms, I beg you, unroll Eurydice's fate, so quickly wound up. All things are promised to you, and despite the small delay of living, we all make our way to this one home sooner or later. We all wind our way down here, to this final abode, and you hold the longest rule over humanity. This woman, too, will be yours by right, when at a ripe age she reaches a fair number of years. I ask her company in the meanwhile, as a gift.)

Persephone, moved to tears by the plea and the music, grants Orpheus permission to lead Eurydice back to the realms of the living. But with a backward glance, Orpheus undoes everything, and his wife's shade is lost to him forever. If, as a type of the poet's labors, Orpheus's song suggests the animating and salvific capacities of verse, it also suggests the ultimate futility of that endeavor, since all things are, in the end, "promised to death."

In the katabasis sections of *In Memoriam*, Nature replaces Persephone, and Tennyson bargains with her for the life of Hallam and all living things. Hallam becomes emblematic of all life, and accordingly, his death becomes a metonym for extinction, the death of species. As Jesse Oak Taylor points out, the poem asks a question never before asked in the elegiac tradition: "how do we mourn species?"[59] Mindful of Orpheus's failure, and mindful of humanity's ultimate fate in one day joining Hallam, Tennyson reasons that if poetry cannot bring the dead back to life, it can at least thrust the poet forward into an encounter with the natural forces that took the departed away. From these forces, as gods of the underworld, the poet can demand an explanation for his friend's death. Tennyson wonders whether:

> The wish, that of the living whole
> No life may fail beyond the grave,
> Derives it not from what we have
> The likest God within the soul?
>
> Are God and Nature then at strife,
> That Nature lends such evil dreams?
> So careful of the type she seems,
> So careless of the single life, (*In Memoriam*, 55.1–8)

To which Nature, indifferent to the poet's pleas, responds,

196   Shapes of Things to Come

"So careful of the type?" but no.
From scarpèd cliff and quarried stone
She cries, "A thousand types are gone;
I care for nothing, all shall go.

Thou makest thine appeal to me:
I bring to life, I bring to death:
The spirit does but mean the breath:
I know no more." (*In Memoriam*, 56.1–8)[60]

The poet's plea of ransom for the dead is met with cold ambivalence not
only to the single life extinguished but also to the species—the "type"—
from whence it came. These are not the gods of Ovid or Virgil, who
might pity mortals and extend a boon. These are the natural gods (if
so they can be called) of Lucretius, those physical agents at work in
the cosmos, shaping matter and dissolving the same without the least
regard for vitality. These godlike forces count lives by millions of years,
during which time "a thousand types are gone," and more shall go just
as easily. "Thou makest thine appeal to me," Nature scoffs, and her
response is not sympathy or cruelty but sheer indifference to the plight
of this species or that. The mechanical nature of her processes is captured in the teeter-totter line, "I bring to life, I bring to death." Anaphora
and antithesis establish a rhythmic nonchalance with regard to birth or
death, which to Nature are all the same. Were Tennyson's theodicy to
end there, it would seem that indeed "God and Nature [are] at strife."
The divinely ordained purposes to which life was created, as described
in scripture, do not accord with Nature's recklessness in throwing those
lives away. But while Nature claims her knowledge stops at the grave
("I know no more"), when biological processes cease, Tennyson knows
(or believes) something more: there is life beyond death.

To counter the apocalyptic scenarios that Nature presents, Tennyson
turns again to the divine perspective of the Son in *Paradise Lost*. In the
face of a world-ending catastrophe, the Son offers a reminder to Tennyson
that all things operate within God's plan. Even death submits to the workings of providence. Wrestling with Nature's indifference to his Orphic
pleas, Tennyson reinforces his faith in the afterlife by returning to the
Miltonic scene that brought him comfort, when the Son's confidence in
his resurrection emboldened Tennyson's hopes for an afterlife existence:

Nor blame I Death, because he bare
The use of virtue out of earth;

Ryan Hackenbracht

I know transplanted human worth
Will bloom to profit, otherwhere.

For this alone on Death I wreak
The wrath that garners in my heart:
He put our lives so far apart
We cannot hear each other speak. (*In Memoriam*, 82.9–16)

The passage recapitulates the scientific aims of *In Memoriam*, which are to trace, by faith, the progress of the soul through the "otherwhere" of a foreign and invisible afterlife. As before, Milton's Son is the source of Tennyson's confidence in the immortality of the soul. The Son is a visualization of the biblical promise that, through Christ's sacrifice, the human species will exist in perpetuity. Offering to bear man's punishment for sin, the Son says to the Father,

on me let Death wreck all his rage;
Under his gloomy power I shall not long
Lie vanquished; thou hast given me to possess
Life in myself for ever, by thee I live,
Though now to Death I yield, and am his due (*PL*, 3.241–45)

As Tennyson reverses agencies in the Miltonic line, the speaker of *In Memoriam* steals authority away from Death and becomes the one to "wreak" (from the Old English *wrecan*, meaning both "to give expression to anger" and "to avenge") his rage on a helpless victim.[61] Faith in the afterlife of species is thus for Tennyson a source of empowerment, much as confidence in the resurrection of humanity prompted Paul to taunt, "O death, where is thy sting? O grave, where is thy victory?" (1 Cor. 15:55). By revising the Miltonic line, Tennyson becomes Milton's Son, becomes the bold conqueror of doubts whom Tennyson wishes he could be. All humanity is subsequently invited to share in his victory and thus bear witness to God's goodness, which Tennyson is able to verify with help from Milton.

The resolution to Tennysonian katabasis is an ingenious revision of classical epic tropes. The logic by which Tennyson "wreak[s] / [his] wrath" upon Death is Orphic and Ovidian: just as Eurydice's return to life would constitute a small delay (*paulum morati*) to her eventual death, so for Tennyson is death a small delay (albeit a frustrating one) to the life he and Hallam would enjoy together for eternity. Hallam is not dead; he is simply too far removed to be heard by the living or

198   Shapes of Things to Come

to hear their own doleful cries. But Tennyson's self-identification with
Milton's Son is also a revision of epic wrath. In *Paradise Lost* Death
is the culmination of his ill-tempered epic predecessors, from Achil-
les with his *mēnis* (wrath) to Aeneas with his final *ira* (anger). In his
Protestant poem Milton revises the epic formula by allocating the better virtues "of patience and heroic martyrdom" (*PL,* 9.32) to his new
Protestant heroes, Adam and Eve. But in *In Memoriam* Tennyson recu-
perates rage as the virtue of the godly. No longer a vice, heroic wrath
merges with elegiac mourning, as the speaker vents his frustrations at
the enemy of humanity, Death, who has set his friendship with Hallam
on a long pause. Thus, while Orpheus leads Tennyson into the underworld, Milton's Son leads him out of it, but not without an impressive
feat on Tennyson's part in reshaping the epic materials he has inherited.

An Epic for All Species: Tennyson and Cosmic Salvation

Tennysonian katabasis is evidence toward C. S. Lewis's point that epic,
by means of its unique formal coding, seeks the "enlargement" of its
subject in successive generations.[62] Virgil wrote of a man and Milton
of humanity, yet Tennyson surpasses both by writing an epic celebrat-
ing all living things. The epic hero of *In Memoriam* is life in all its
wondrous and variegated forms. The enemy, as we have seen, is annihilation, whether of an individual or a species. The battlefield on which
they duel is the mind, wherein the poet's challenge (and the readers'
as well) is to find the faith to believe that the former lives on after
the latter. This is the nucleus of Tennysonian theodicy: for God to be
"just," as the prologue proclaims him, life *must* live on after death—
but such a thing can only be believed, not proved. We have seen two of
Tennyson's strategies for believing this: one which centers on visualizing humanity's transmutation through the Son's resurrection; and one
that addresses the phobia of extinction through the Orpheus narrative, when the Son again comes to the poet's rescue. A third technique
involves the doctrine of cosmic salvation, which Tennyson visualizes
with aid from Milton. Toward the middle of *In Memoriam* Tennyson
resolves the epic conflict between life and death by committing himself
to what he calls "the larger hope" (*In Memoriam,* 55.20) of salvation
for all things. In these sections, unbeknownst to Tennyson, Milton's
monist materialism is used to reinforce the belief in some Victorian
circles that eternal torment, as described in the Bible, was not an actual
place of suffering but only a metaphor for spiritual immaturity.[63]

Cosmic salvation goes a step further. It teaches the redemption of all living things, human and nonhuman, zoological and botanical alike. In Christianity this heterodoxy originated with the Greek patristic Origen of Alexandria (ca. 184–ca. 254 CE), who preached apocatastasis.[64] According to this doctrine, at the end of the world, all things would return to their original condition at the world's beginning (though animals, Origen noted, would not participate in beatific union, since they lacked the *imago Dei*). In *De principiis* Origen wrote, "sane finem putamus quod bonitas Dei per Christuum suum universam revocet creaturam" (we believe, without question, that the goodness of God through his Christ will revive all creation).[65] By a long process of spiritual amendment and correction, God would restore creation to its primal state of original goodness before the Fall of Man. Such a model of history was cyclical and Greek rather than Hebraic and linear (for this reason, among others, Western fathers were skeptical of Origen's views). In seventeenth-century Britain apocatastasis made a resurgence, among other places, in the poetry of Henry Vaughan, who prayed for the day when God "shalt restore trees, beasts, and men, / And Thou make all new again."[66] It also surfaced in the eclectic theology of Milton who, as a monist, believed that all creation would eventually be reconciled to God (else God would be eternally divided against himself).[67] Milton interpreted literally the Pauline omen that, at the world's end, God will be *panta en pasin* (all in all; 1 Cor. 15:28). In book 3 of *Paradise Lost* the Father tells the Son of the future beatific union of all things into himself:

> Meanwhile
> The world shall burn, and from her ashes spring
> New heaven and earth, wherein the just shall dwell
> And after all their tribulations long
> See golden days, fruitful of golden deeds,
> With Joy and Love triúmphing, and fair truth.
> Then thou thy regal sceptre shalt lay by,
> For regal sceptre then no more shall need,
> God shall be all in all. (*PL*, 3.333–41)

Later, Raphael relates to Adam what he heard in Heaven. Only now, it is the Son who "make[s] all things new" (Rev. 21:5). On the Last Day the Son would

> be revealed
> In glory of the Father, to dissolve

Satan with his perverted world, then raise
From the conflagrant mass, purged and refined,
New heavens, new earth, ages of endless date
Founded in righteousness and peace and love,
To bring forth fruits, joy and eternal bliss. (*PL*, 12.545–51)

In both instances the material of the old world (i.e., this world) is not
discarded but reshaped into the "new heaven and a new earth" (Rev.
21:1) of biblical prophecy. In the first instance the new world arises
"from the ashes" of the old, and in the second the existing world is
alchemized ("purged and refined") into a more perfect version of itself.
In monistic ontology God does not (or cannot) annihilate matter, since
to do so would be to annihilate part of himself. Nor are the new heaven
and new earth a spiritual realm; rather, they are every bit as physical as
the old heaven and old earth, from which they would spring.

Hardly the polemicist Milton was, and distrustful of creeds, Tennyson embraced a large-tent picture of Christian salvation. In Tennyson's
opinion all humanity would be granted eternal life. The wicked would
cease to be wicked and, joining the ranks of the faithful, they too
would attain salvation. "He never would believe that Christ could
preach 'everlasting punishment,'" according to Hallam Tennyson, who
reports his father once said, "[I] would rather know that [I] was to be
lost eternally than not know that the whole human race was to live
eternally" (*Mem.*, 1:322, 321). As far as Tennyson's "larger hope" for
humanity, Hallam Tennyson explains: "he means . . . that the whole
human race would through, perhaps, ages of suffering, be at length
purified and saved" (*Mem.*, 1:321–22). Similarities to the thought of
Milton and Origen—the eschatological optimism, alchemical metaphors, and cyclical notion of time—are striking. The salvific vision
painted in *In Memoriam* is quite expansive, and extending throughout
the cosmos, it encompasses every living thing:

Oh yet we trust that somehow good
Will be the final goal of ill,
To pangs of nature, sins of will,
Defects of doubt, and taints of blood;

That nothing walks with aimless feet;
That not one life shall be destroyed,
Or cast as rubbish to the void,
When God hath made the pile complete;

That not a worm is cloven in vain;
That not a moth with vain desire
Is shrivelled in a fruitless fire,
Or but subserves another's gain.

Behold, we know not anything;
I can but trust that good shall fall
At last—far off—at last, to all,
And every winter change to spring. (*In Memoriam*, 54.1–16)

At the theological apex of *In Memoriam* Tennyson articulates his vision of cosmic salvation through Miltonic language. The antithesis of moral opposites in the first stanza recalls memorable lines from *Paradise Lost* on the subject of God's goodness: Satan's recognition that God's "providence / Out of our evil seek[s] to bring forth good" (*PL*, 1.162–63) and his lament that "all [God's] good proved ill in me" (*PL*, 4.48); the narrator's observation that "all [Satan's] malice served but to bring forth / Infinite goodness" (*PL*, 1.217–18); and Adam's joyful exclamation at the poem's end: "Oh goodness infinite, goodness immense! / That all this good of evil shall produce, / And evil turn to good" (*PL*, 12.469–71). The difference between Milton and Tennyson, however, is that Tennyson has "defects of doubt" about God and the afterlife—and Milton does not. Tennyson's humble lack of confidence is evident in the first line and in the fourth stanza: we can only trust—not *know*—that good comes after the bleakness of death, as spring follows winter. Tennyson's perspective is noticeably fallen and more akin, in this instance, to those of Adam or Satan rather than to the Son. Whether in *Paradise Lost* or *In Memoriam*, the sight of the fallen is always blindered by sin. In this respect, the scientific knowledge that defines Tennyson's identity as a poet-scientist becomes, ironically, an impediment to his ability to write about things he cannot see. For this, he needs Milton and the faith of an earlier age, both of which were unencumbered (as Tennyson saw it) by modern discoveries about the mortality of species and the material basis of human existence. To move forward in time and imagine eternity, Tennyson is compelled to go back two centuries to Milton, who though blind saw the shape of things to come with greater clarity than Tennyson can.

In the universe of *In Memoriam* morphology is evident not only in physical matter and its many incarnations but also in Tennyson's sense of the moral code separating right from wrong. The poet's Origenic hope in the salvation of all living things—whereby "not one life shall be destroyed, / Or cast as rubbish to the void"—depends on the transmutation of "ill" into "good." Like the furtive biological processes shaping evolution, this transmutation is hidden from view. The poet can only trust, rather than know, that it will occur (or perhaps is already occurring). His hope that God's concern extends even to the worms and moths is based on biblical truths to that effect—for instance, when Christ tells the multitudes, "are not five sparrows sold for two farthings, and not one of them is forgotten before God?" (Luke 12:6) and "consider the lilies of the field . . . even Solomon in all his glory was not arrayed like one of these" (Matt. 6:28–29). In Tennyson's epic, as in the Bible, divine regard for animals is a reminder of providence. There is soteriological assurance in thinking that, if God preserves worms and moths, surely he will also preserve humankind?

On the one hand, such logic is taxonomically leveling, since it locates man within the animal kingdom (rather than above it) and renders elegiac mourning—for the first time in British poetry—a transpecial activity. But on the other hand, such logic retains the anthropocentrism it pretends to eschew, since it makes use of animals to justify or explain a human ontological telos. For Tennyson, living in a time of exciting discoveries about humanity's animal origins, the doctrine of cosmic salvation was a theological safeguard against the fear that God had no plan and there was no afterlife. In response to the scientific revelation that man was just another animal, Tennyson broadens his net of salvation, so that now it holds even animals and plants securely within its grasp. In this regard *In Memoriam* is a testament not only to the morphology of man and of species but also to the ingeniously dynamic nature of Christianity, which contains within its history a host of doctrines, some recessive and others dominant, which can be called up from reserve when the cultural environment changes and faith is forced to either adapt or die.

Conclusion: Tennyson's Doubts and Milton's Literary Afterlife

Tennyson's vision of cosmic salvation entered an intellectual marketplace already cluttered with competing ideas of afterlife existence. *In Memoriam* pitted itself against three camps: hardline Calvinists, advocates of conditional immortality, and agnostics. Of the first, Tennyson had little patience for double predestination, whereby some were chosen for election and some for damnation (a doctrine Calvin himself did not teach). As a child Tennyson had a "rigid Calvinist" of an aunt, who would wail for hours and cry out, "has [God] not damned most of my friends? But *me, me* He has picked out for eternal salvation." One day, she turned to the boy and said, "Alfred, Alfred, when I look at you, I think of the words of Holy Scripture—'Depart from me, ye cursed, into everlasting fire [Matt. 25:41]'" (*Mem.*, 1:15). This had a lasting impression on Tennyson, as it would on anyone. Decades later the cosmic salvation of *In Memoriam* was an inclusive response to the exclusive eschatology of Calvinists of this ilk.

Tennyson was equally opposed to the doctrine of conditional immortality (mortalism or soul sleep), whereby eternal life occurs only through God's gift of resurrection. This is the gist of John Donne's confidence that "one short sleep past, we wake eternally."[68] In the Victorian period, under the influence of the Higher Criticism, conditional immortality gained traction among theologians and divines as the original, Hebraic doctrine of the soul, before the faith became polluted by Hellenic philosophy. Among the doctrine's advocates was William Gladstone, who argued that innate immortality was unscriptural and "crept into the church, by a back door as it were" through the teachings of Origen of Alexandria, a city long associated with Platonic metaphysics.[69] For Tennyson the idea that the soul was dissoluble was barbaric. "The cardinal point of Christianity is the Life after Death [2 Tim. 1:10]" (*Mem.*, 1:321), he once professed to J. B. Lightfoot, bishop of Durham. Tennyson's "larger hope" is thus best understood not only as a holistic soteriology of creation but also as a negation of those doctrines—soul sleep, damnation, and annihilation—that questioned, or denied, either the soul's innate immortality or the final bliss of humanity.

Tennyson's relationship to agnosticism was more complex. This was a relatively new theological stance that grew in popularity among Victorian readers following the publication of Darwin's *On the Origin of Species* and *The Descent of Man*. In an essay titled "Agnosticism" Thomas Huxley gave an account of how he arrived at this position:

> I took thought, and invented what I conceived to be the appropriate title of "agnostic." It came into my head as suggestively antithetic to the "gnostic" of Church history, who professed to know so much about the very things of which I was ignorant; and I took the earliest opportunity of parading it at our [Metaphysical] Society . . . To my great satisfaction, the term took.[70]

As Huxley explains, agnosticism is not at all a denial of the afterlife but a humble recognition that metaphysical doctrines can only be arrived at through belief in divine revelation (i.e., scripture) and not through the scientific method. Of the three papers Huxley delivered to the Metaphysical Society, all three focused on this tension between revealed and empirical knowledge. The second paper, titled "Has a Frog a Soul?," argued that if a frog does indeed have a soul, such a fact cannot be ascertained through scientific means.[71] So too with humans. Because things invisible to mortal sight exist outside the realm of the observable universe, they require something other than empirical evidence to be believed—namely, they require faith.

On the necessity of faith, Huxley and Tennyson were in agreement. Publicly, Tennyson projected an image of unflinching confidence in the world to come. When one fan wrote to him asking his opinion of man's descent from lower animals, Tennyson replied, "that makes no difference to me, even if the Darwinians did not, as they do, exaggerate Darwinism. To God all is present. He sees present, past, and future as one" (*Mem.*, 1:322). Tennyson's sagacious tone suggests an awareness of being in the national spotlight. While there, he felt compelled to make a public profession of faith—one that would bolster the faith of others. Privately, however, Tennyson had doubts. When Darwin called on the Tennysons at their house on August 17, 1868, the poet sought confirmation from the scientist that "your theory of Evolution does not make against Christianity," to which Darwin (a lifelong churchgoer) replied, "no, certainly not" (*Mem.*, 2:57). And as we have seen, *In Memoriam*, which was not originally intended for publication, is riddled with doubts that plague the speaker like locusts. "Doubt is Devil-born" (*In Memoriam*, 96.4), the speaker says. But all the same, he has moments "when [his] faith is dry" (*In Memoriam*, 50.9), and at times, he cannot help but "wrong the grave with fears untrue" (*In Memoriam*, 51.9)—presumably, by believing that there is nothing after death and Hallam is gone forever. We might even read the triumphant marriage concluding *In Memoriam*, which Tennyson modeled after Dante's *Commedia*, as somewhat "forced," as Day proposes.[72] While Tennyson presented himself publicly as a man of solid faith, he nonetheless harbored in secret some of the same doubts agnostics like Huxley dared to share openly.

Tennyson's metaphysical doubts surfaced in a poem written four years before his death, in which he imagined a final transmutation—his own. In February 1888 he fell ill and was confined to his house. He was already, by then, an "old man," as he wrote to Walt Whitman (*Mem.*, 2:343). By day, lying on a sofa and looking outside, he had "wonderful thoughts about God and the Universe, and felt as if looking into the other world." But by night, he had fevered dreams, including one where he was "Pope of the world, and weighted down by all its sins and all its miseries" (*Mem.*, 2:348). "At the crisis of his illness" (*Mem.*, 2:348), Hallam Tennyson recounts, the poet penned epigrams that became the poem "By an Evolutionist," which reads,

> The Lord let the house of a brute to the soul of a man,
> And the man said "Am I your debtor?"
> And the Lord—"Not yet: but make it as clean as you can,
> And then I will let you a better."
> I. [*Man*]
> If my body comes from brutes, my soul uncertain, or a fable,
> Why not bask amid the senses while the sun of morning shines,
> I, the finer brute rejoicing in my hounds, and in my stable,
> Youth and Health, and birth and wealth, and choice of women
>   and wines?
> II. [*Man*]
> What hast thou done for me, grim Old Age, save breaking my bones
>   on the rack?
> Would I had past in the morning that looks so bright from afar!
> OLD AGE
> Done for thee? starved the wild beast that was linkt with thee eighty
>   years back.
> Less weight now for the ladder-of-heaven that hangs on a star.
> I. [*Man*]
> If my body comes from brutes, though somewhat finer than
>   their own,
> I am heir, and this my kingdom. Shall the royal voice be mute?
> No, but if the rebel subject seek to drag me from the throne,
> Hold the sceptre, Human Soul, and rule thy Province of the brute.
> II. [*Man's Soul*]
> I have climbed to the snows of Age, and I gaze at a field in the Past,
> Where I sank with the body at times in the sloughs of a low desire,
> But I hear no yelp of the beast, and the Man is quiet at last
> As he stands on the heights of his life with a glimpse of a height that
>   is higher.

In the poem Darwinian evolution meets Pythagorean metempsychosis meets epic *fama*, as Tennyson retrofits an Ovidian episode for the modern scientific age. The theme of ascension derives from the ending of the *Metamorphoses*, when Ovid reflects on his death and envisions "parte tamen meliore mei super alta perennis / astra ferar" (the greater part of me will be born above the heights and everlasting stars).[73] But while Ovid is confident, even gleeful, about transforming into his literary legacy, Tennyson is noticeably less certain about his afterlife existence. The Man can see and touch his brutish body, but his immaterial soul is "uncertain, or a fable." Amid the fragmentation of poetic voices, the Man can only speculate on what may happen to him in the future. Only the immortal part of him, his Soul, which the Man fears might be a daydream, can see the changes yet to come.

But if Tennyson did not have doubts, he would not have needed Milton. While the poem's Ovidian content is a conduit for despair, its Miltonic structure opens up a route into hope. The appearance of Old Age and the Soul, who offer consolation to the Man, recalls the many theophanies littering Milton's poetry in which a god or godlike figure brings illumination to a mortal. Among them are Lancelot Andrewes in Elegy III, Sabrina in *A Mask*, Fame in *In Quintum Novembris*, Patience in Sonnet 19 ("When I Consider How My Light Is Spent"), and of course, Raphael and Michael in *Paradise Lost*. But perhaps the most memorable, certainly the most relevant, is Apollo's appearance in "Lycidas," when the Swain is tempted to indulge in sensual pleasures and abandon his poetry. "What boots it with uncessant care / To tend the homely slighted Shepherds trade[?]," the Swain complains. "Were it not better done as others use, / To sport with *Amaryllis* in the shade, / Or with the tangles of *Neaera*'s hair?" ("Lycidas," 64–65, 67–69). The Swain's logic makes a resurgence in Tennyson's poem, as the Man asks himself, "why not bask amid the senses while the sun of morning shines," enjoying his women and wine? Like Apollo revealing a heavenly world beyond the Swain's view, where "all judging *Jove* . . . pronounces lastly on each deed" ("Lycidas," 82–83), so do Old Age and the Soul instruct the Man on the glorious afterlife to come, to which sensual pleasures cannot compare. The Man cannot see this world; he can only trust it exists. In this respect he emblematizes Tennyson's own skepticism and doubt about the afterlife. Like the Man, Tennyson struggles to believe transformation is possible; he wants to know, for a certainty, that he will enter a "second state sublime" (*In Memoriam*, 61.1), as he hopes Hallam has. For that, he needs *Paradise Lost*. Only then, by seeing what Milton sees, can Tennyson catch a glimpse of the celestial afterlife he hopes is there.

Notes

My thanks to Chloe Brooke and Paul Zajac for their helpful comments on an earlier draft of this essay. Translations of German are from Peter Luke's edition of Goethe's poetry; translations of all other languages are my own.

1. Hallam Tennyson, *Alfred, Lord Tennyson: A Memoir by His Son*, 2 vols. (London: Macmillan, 1897), 2:236; 1:36. *A Memoir* is hereafter cited in the text as *Mem.*, followed by volume and page number.

2. T. S. Eliot, *Selected Prose*, ed. Frank Kermode (New York: Harcourt Brace Jovanovich, 1975), 269.

3. Tennyson, "Milton: Alcaics," lines 1–16, in *The Poems of Tennyson*, 3 vols., ed. Christopher Ricks (Berkeley: University of California Press, 1987). This poem, *In Memoriam, A. H. H.*, and "Lucretius" all appear in volume 2 of *Poems*; "By an Evolutionist" appears in volume 3. References to Tennyson's poetry are hereafter given in the text by line number, or, for *In Memoriam*, section and line number.

4. See Edmund Burke, *A Philosophical Enquiry into the Origin of Our Ideas of the Sublime and Beautiful* (London, 1757), 13; and Immanuel Kant, *Critique of Judgment*, trans. Werner S. Pluhar (Indianapolis, IN: Hackett Publishing, 1987), 114–15.

5. Virgil, *Aeneid* (1.1), in *Opera*, ed. R. A. B. Mynors (Oxford: Oxford University Press, 1969); and Ovid, *Metamorphoses* (1.1), ed. R. J. Tarrant (Oxford: Oxford University Press, 2004).

6. On Milton's legacy in the nineteenth century, see Erik Gray, *Milton and the Victorians* (Ithaca, NY: Cornell University Press, 2009); and James Nelson, *The Sublime Puritan: Milton and the Victorians* (Madison: University of Wisconsin Press, 1963).

7. *The Eclectic Magazine*, May to August 1853 edition, ed. W. H. Bidwell (New York, 1853), 499.

8. Charles Darwin, *The Life and Letters of Charles Darwin*, 2 vols., ed. Francis Darwin (New York: D. Appleton and Co., 1891), 1:57.

9. Browning Society, meeting minutes for April 25, 1884, in *The Browning Society Papers, 1881–84, Parts IV and V* (London: N. Trübner and Co., 1883–84), 124.

10. Thomas de Quincey, "Milton," in *De Quincey as Critic*, ed. John E. Jordan (London: Routledge and Kegan Paul, 1973), 253–54.

11. See N. K. Sugimura, "Epic Sensibilities: 'Old Man' Milton and the Making of Tennyson's *Idylls of the King*," in *Tennyson among the Poets: Bicentenary Essays*, ed. Robert Douglas-Fairhurst and Seamus Perry (Oxford: Oxford University Press, 2009), 160–80; and Buck McMullen and James R. Kincaid, "Tennyson, Hallam's Corpse, Milton's Murder, and Poetic Exhibitionism," *Nineteenth-Century Literature* 45, no. 2 (1990): 176–205.

12. On death and the Victorians, see Deborah Lutz, *Relics of Death in Victorian Literature and Culture* (Cambridge: Cambridge University Press, 2015); Mary Elizabeth Hotz, *Literary Remains: Representations of Death and Burial in Victorian England* (Albany: State University of New York Press, 2009); Pat Jalland, *Death in the Victorian Family* (Oxford: Oxford University Press, 1996); and James Stevens Curl, *The Victorian Celebration of Death* (Detroit: Partridge Press, 1972).

208 Shapes of Things to Come

13. Lutz, *Relics of Death*, 1, 2.

14. Ashley Miller, *Poetry, Media, and the Material Body: Autopoetics in Nineteenth-Century Britain* (Cambridge: Cambridge University Press, 2018), 2.

15. Aidan Day, *Tennyson's Skepticism* (New York: Palgrave Macmillan, 2005), 4.

16. Tennyson expressed "utter astonishment" when Edward Moxon offered to publish his elegies; see note on "the wedding of Alfred Tennyson and Emily Sellwood," in *The Letters of Alfred Lord Tennyson*, 2 vols., ed. Cecil Y. Lang and Edgar F. Shannon Jr. (Cambridge, MA: Harvard University Press, 1981), 1:327.

17. Denis Saurat, *Milton: Man and Thinker* (New York: Dial Press, 1925). The passage in question appears in *The Complete Poetry and Essential Prose of John Milton*, ed. William Kerrigan, John Rumrich, and Stephen M. Fallon (New York: Modern Library, 2007), 1202–9.

18. Jeffrey Shoulson, "Man and Thinker: Denis Saurat, and the Old New Milton Criticism," in *The New Milton Criticism*, ed. Peter C. Herman and Elizabeth Sauer (Cambridge: Cambridge University Press, 2012), 197.

19. Thomas Huxley, *Life and Letters of Thomas Henry Huxley*, 3 vols., ed. Leonard Huxley (London: Macmillan, 1908), 3:269.

20. Angela Leighton, "Touching Forms: Tennyson and Aestheticism," *Essays in Criticism* 52, no. 1 (2002): 67. Recent studies on Tennyson and science include Michelle Geric, *Tennyson and Geology: Poetry and Poetics* (Cham, Switzerland: Palgrave Macmillan, 2017); Stefan Waldschmit, "The Consolation of Physiology: *In Memoriam* and G. H. Lewes's *The Physiology of Common Life*," *Victorian Studies* 56, no. 3 (2014): 490–97; Valerie Purton, ed., *Darwin, Tennyson and Their Readers: Explorations in Victorian Literature and Science* (New York: Anthem, 2013); and Barri J. Gold, "The Consolation of Physics: Tennyson's Thermodynamic Solution," *PMLA* 117, no. 3 (2002): 449–64.

21. Charles Darwin, *On the Origin of Species* (London: John Murray, 1859), 489.

22. On the pre-Socratic evolutionists, see Radim Kočandrle and Karel Kleisner, "Evolution Born of Moisture: Analogies and Parallels between Anaximander's Ideas on Origin of Life and Man and Later Pre-Darwinian Evolutionary Concepts," *Journal of the History of Biology* 46, no. 1 (2013): 103–24.

23. On Lamarck's theory of evolution, see Richard W. Burkhardt Jr., *The Spirit of System: Lamarck and Evolutionary Biology* (Cambridge, MA: Harvard University Press, 1995), 115–85.

24. A helpful biography of Chambers is Milton Millhauser, *Just before Darwin: Robert Chambers and "Vestiges"* (Middletown, CT: Wesleyan University Press, 1959).

25. Millhauser, *Just before Darwin*, 116–17. On Tennyson's copy, see his letter to Edward Moxon, dated November 15, 1844, in *Letters*, ed. Lang and Shannon, 1:230.

26. Robert Chambers, *Vestiges of the Natural History of Creation* (London: John Churchill, 1844), 272.

27. Chambers, *Vestiges*, 306 (emphasis in the original).

28. The background to Darwin's theories is given in Michael Ruse, *The Darwinian Revolution: Science Red in Tooth and Claw* (Chicago: University of Chicago Press, 1999); and Peter J. Bowler, *Evolution: The History of an Idea* (Berkeley: University of California Press, 1983).

29. Tennyson's knowledge of these theories is documented in Lionel Stevenson, *Darwin among the Poets* (New York: Russell and Russell, 1963), 55–116; Graham Hough, "The Natural Theology of *In Memoriam*," *Review of English Studies* 23, no. 91 (1947): 244–56; and George R. Potter, "Tennyson and the Biological Theory of Mutability in Species," *Philological Quarterly* 16 (1937): 321–43.

30. Letter from Henry Elton to Alfred Tennyson, dated October 1, 1833, in *Letters*, ed. Lang and Shannon, I:93.

31. Cf. Hallam Tennyson: "My father sometimes called 'In Memoriam,' 'The Way of the Soul,' " in *A Memoir*, 1:393 n. 2.

32. George Herbert, "Love (1)," line 1, in *The Works of George Herbert*, ed. F. E. Hutchinson (Oxford: Oxford University Press, 1945). Tennyson later denied the Herbert allusion; see the commentary to *In Memoriam*, ed. Susan Shatto and Marion Shaw (Oxford: Oxford University Press, 1982), 160n on "introductory stanzas," lines 1–12.

33. William Empson, *Milton's God* (London: Chatto and Windus, 1961), 11.

34. Richard Strier, "Milton's Fetters, or, Why Eden Is Better than Heaven," in Herman and Sauer, *New Milton Criticism*, 25.

35. Augustine, *Confessions*, book 1, chap. 6, 2 vols., ed. William Watts (Cambridge, MA: Harvard University Press, 2002), 1:16.

36. Jonathan Richardson (Sr. and Jr.), *Explanatory Notes and Remarks on Milton's Paradise Lost* (London, 1734), 228.

37. John Leonard discusses the following critics at length in *Faithful Labourers: A Reception History of Paradise Lost, 1667–1970*, 2 vols. (Oxford: Oxford University Press, 2013).

38. See John Shawcross, ed., *Milton: The Critical Heritage, vol. 2: 1732–1801* (London: Routledge and K. Paul, 1972), 19; and Charles R. Sumner, "Preliminary Observations," in Milton, *A Treatise on Christian Doctrine*, trans. Charles R. Sumner (Cambridge: Cambridge University Press, 1825), xxxvi.

39. See Milton, *A Treatise on Christian Doctrine*, 190n.

40. James Macaulay, "Milton," in *Reviews and Essays from "The Edinburgh"* (London: Ward, Lock, and Co., 1859), 13.

41. Macaulay, "Milton," in *Reviews and Essays*, 16.

42. See H. Tennyson, *Mem.*, 2:236.

43. David Masson, *The Life of John Milton*, 6 vols. (Cambridge, UK: Macmillan, 1859–80), 6:521.

44. Masson, *Life of John Milton*, 6:828.

45. Masson, *Life of John Milton*, 6:831.

46. On Goethe's scientific studies, see David Seamon and Arthur Zajonc, eds, *Goethe's Way of Science: A Phenomenology of Nature* (Albany: State University of New York Press, 1998); Rudolf Steiner, *Goethean Science* (Spring

210   Shapes of Things to Come

Valley: Mercury Press, 1988); and Rudolf Magnus, *Goethe as a Scientist* (New York: Henry Schuman, 1949).

47. Taking an interest in German writers of Goethe's generation was fashionable in Victorian England, according to Richard Cronin, "Goethe, the Apostles, and Tennyson's *Supposed Confessions*," *Philological Quarterly* 72, no. 3 (1993): 337–56; see also Lore Metzger, "The Eternal Process: Some Parallels between Goethe's *Faust* and Tennyson's *In Memoriam*," *Victorian Poetry* 1, no. 3 (1963): 189–96.

48. See *The Poems of Tennyson*, ed. Ricks, 2:318n on section 1, lines 1–4; and *In Memoriam*, ed. Shatto and Shaw, 162n1, lines 1–4.

49. Goethe, "Talismane," lines 19–20, in *Selected Poetry*, trans. David Luke (London: Penguin, 2005).

50. Goethe, "Höheres und Höchstes," lines 30–31, in *Selected Poetry*.

51. Goethe, "Höheres und Höchstes," lines 37–40, in *Selected Poetry*.

52. Tennyson, quoted in *In Memoriam*, ed. Shatto and Shaw, 157.

53. Darwin, *Origin of Species*, 194.

54. James Ussher, *Annales Veteris Testamenti* (London, 1650), sig. A5ʳ.

55. Charles Lyell, *Principles of Geology*, 3 vols. (London: John Murray, 1830–33), 1:90. On Lyell's research and its significance, see Leonard G. Wilson, *Charles Lyell: The Years to 1841: The Revolution in Geology* (New Haven, CT: Yale University Press, 1972).

56. Lyell, *Principles*, 1:87.

57. Darwin, *Origin of Species*, 464.

58. Ovid, *Metamorphoses* (10.29–37).

59. Jesse Oak Taylor, "Tennyson's Elegy for the Anthropocene: Genre, Form, and Species Being," *Victorian Studies* 58, no. 2 (2016): 222.

60. These so-called evolution sections bear similarities to Chambers's *Vestiges of the Natural History of Creation*, but, according to Hallam Tennyson, the poet wrote them before Chambers's book had appeared in print; see *In Memoriam*, ed. Shatto and Shaw, 216n55 and 56; and 281n123.

61. *OED*; see also *An Anglo-Saxon Dictionary*, ed. Joseph Bosworth and T. Northcote Toller, s.v. "wrecan (II and IV)" (Oxford: Oxford University Press, 1898).

62. C. S. Lewis, *A Preface to Paradise Lost* (Oxford: Oxford University Press, 1942), 35; see also David Quint, *Epic and Empire: Politics and Generic form from Virgil to Milton* (Princeton, NJ: Princeton University Press, 1993), 3–18.

63. See Geoffrey Rowell, *Hell and the Victorians: A Study of the Nineteenth-Century Theological Controversies Concerning Eternal Punishment and the Future Life* (Oxford: Oxford University Press, 1974), as well as D. P. Walker, *The Decline of Hell: Seventeenth-Century Discussions of Eternal Torment* (Chicago: University of Chicago Press, 1964), who traces the origins of these debates back to the early modern period.

64. On Origen's doctrine, see Ilaria Ramelli, *The Christian Doctrine of Apokatastasis: A Critical Assessment from the New Testament to Eriugena* (Leiden, Netherlands: Brill, 2013).

65. Origen, *De principiis* (bk. 1, chap. 6), trans. Rufinus, in *Origenis opera omnia*, 7 vols., ed. J. P. Migne (Paris: J. P. Migne, 1857), 1:165.

66. Henry Vaughan, "The Book," lines 26–27, in *Works*, ed. by L. C. Martin (Oxford: Oxford University Press, 1957). On Vaughan and cosmic salvation, see Alan Rudrum, "For Then the Earth Shall Be All Paradise: Milton, Vaughan and the Neo-Calvinists on the Ecology of the Hereafter," *Scintilla* 4 (2000): 39–52, and "Henry Vaughan, the Liberation of the Creatures, and Seventeenth-Century English Calvinism," *Seventeenth Century* 4, no. 1 (1989): 33–54.

67. On Milton and cosmic salvation, see Neil Forsyth, *The Satanic Epic* (Princeton, NJ: Princeton University Press, 2003), 156, 285–86; C. A. Patrides, "The Salvation of Satan," *Journal of the History of Ideas* 28, no. 4 (1967): 467–78; and Harry F. Robins, *If This Be Heresy: A Study of Milton and Origen* (Urbana: University of Illinois Press, 1963).

68. John Donne, Holy Sonnet 10, line 13, in *The Complete English Poems*, ed. A. J. Smith (London: Penguin, 1996).

69. William Gladstone, *Studies Subsidiary to the Works of Bishop Butler* (Oxford: Oxford University Press, 1896), 195.

70. Huxley, *Life and Letters*, 1:461.

71. Huxley, *Life and Letters*, 1:458.

72. Day, *Tennyson's Skepticism*, 131.

73. Ovid, *Metamorphoses* (15.875–76).

CHAPTER 8

◥

Anon They Move

Two Hispanoamerican Translations of *Paradise Lost*, Book 3

Mario Murgia

Translation as Movement

The notions on which any act of translation is based are essentially of the kinetic order. Etymologically speaking, a translation entails a transference, or a carrying over, not only of meaning but also of linguistic-literary form and, frequently, of ideology. Both in English and Spanish, as in a number of other European languages, the verbs that denote the act of translation are followed by prepositions indicating direction and therefore movement—one "translates into," or *traduce a*. These prepositions, in turn, further echo both the constant journeying and the directionality implied in these terms' etymological ancestors in Latin: the past participle *translatus*, or "carried over"; and also the present active infinitive *traducere*, meaning something along the lines of "to direct from side to side."[1] Thus, and at least in the realm of historical semantics, a translation is always a transformative migration, one that implies not only the lexical transference between languages but also the creative scouting for aesthetic and cultural directionalities in the vast territories of verbality. In the special case of poetical translation (or, to be more descriptive, the translation of poetry and verse), such transportations, or "carryings over," strive to find their most demanding lanes and trails in the figurational, and not exclusively verbal, territories of allusion and implication. Susan Bassnett has stated that

213

Whether a text is *brought, placed or guided* across a linguistic boundary, the idea remains the same: something written in one language is *moved* into another, words and sentences are reshaped and remade, although the assumption is that the original will somehow still be present in the reformulated version. This means that there is always both a spatial and a temporal dimension in translation, for every translation *carries* within it the trace of the original from which it derived.[2]

This vivid description of the act of translation is parallel to the basic and widespread definition of motion and movement, which contemplates the change in orientation or position of a body within a certain period of time.[3] If we were to interpolate these notions to the translation of poetry in particular, we would need to take into account that the meanings of most kinds of verse, as "free" as it may be considered or labeled, are dependent on form and shape on the printed page, that is, the visual spatiality that is associated with the needs of prosody, rhetoric, and syntax. In this sense, poetical translation might well be said to conform to Bassnett's metaphor of translation as verbal kinesis: the transference of meaning is often realized through form. In this context it would not be completely outlandish to affirm that Milton himself, as a student of biblical languages, a polyglot, and a poet-translator, was well aware of the ideological relevance of such migratory practices between tongues and poetic modes.[4]

But speaking specifically of the translational transportation of *Paradise Lost*, Milton's magnum opus has been transferred, to a great degree of efficiency, into the Spanish language, both in Spain and the Hispanophone Americas. Starting in the late eighteenth century, these undertakings have been carried out on a number of occasions, in different formats and with distinct purposes.[5] Contrary to what their considerable number might suggest, however, the linguistic and poetic transpositions of Milton's poetical register and, more notably, his imagery and ideological stances, have proved to be quite challenging for Spanish-speaking adapters, artists, readers, and translators over the course of at least two centuries and across (cultural) borders, as the groundbreaking intercontextual study of Hispanic scholar Angelica Duran further evidences in ensuing pages. With regard to this challenge, one of *Paradise Lost*'s most celebrious adapters, the Ibero-Spanish Juan Escóiquiz, opines, in the "Prologue" to the 1886 edition of his prosified rendering, that the insertion in his volume of Joseph Addison's notes as clarifying aids is essential because "the matter of the poem is one of the most mysterious, delicate, and important in our Christian religion, and therefore it lends itself to more equivocations and errors."[6] On a similarly apologetic note, albeit in more recent times and with regard to the difficulties of maintaining a balance between form and content in poetical translation, Spain's Enrique López Castellón expresses his translational concerns in an introductory note to his 2005 versified transposition of Milton's epic: "Facing the sadistic task of becoming a mythical Procustes . . . , I decided to abide by the metrical rules and meaning, and to keep . . . a precarious balance that sometimes tilts towards the former, and some other times towards the latter."[7] López Castellón then calls his own task a "betrayal" for having exceeded the length of the original English epic by over three thousand lines.

As becomes clear from these assertions, vacillations with regard to transporting a canonical poem of the caliber of *Paradise Lost* from (Miltonic) English to Spanish are neither new nor trivial. As we shall see, this literary and often political enterprise would develop increased complications as the epic made its way into a few of Latin America's variants of Spanish. Such issues are mostly related to a number of the books or passages in *Paradise Lost* where religious controversies converge with, or correspond to, action-laden accounts of the physicality, directionality, and actions of spiritual entities rather than created beings. Specifically, the English poet and polemicist's notions of motion and movement, within the epic's postlapsarian presentation of prelapsarian events, and peculiarly those narrated in book 3, are no strangers to constant—frequently radical—shifts in terms of adaptation, reconfiguration, rewriting, or even unabashed censorship. More often than not, these textual transformations occur when the lines and syntactical structures of the poem are transported into specific regional or temporal dialects of Spanish and the prosodic forms accommodating their literary expressions in verse. In this chapter I will probe the manners in which two Spanish-speaking poet-translators, Mexico's Francisco Granados Maldonado and the Colombian Enrique Álvarez Bonilla, have tackled the "carrying over" into their target language of passages dealing with the perceivable mobility of nonphysical (or spiritual) figures in *Paradise Lost*, mostly those in book 3. Their translations are of enhanced interest because they remain the only complete, versified Spanish-language renditions of the poem to have been produced in Latin America by Hispanoamerican poet-translators. On the basis of these two verse translations of the epic—and by developing analogies between translational and poetical depictions of motion and movement—I will analyze how these translators have managed to transpose Milton's poetic (and essentially Protestant) depictions of out-of-time and out-of-place physicality to meet the ideological, poetical, and translational requirements imposed by their cultural and literary circumstances.

World of Words: "Motion" and "Movement"

Writing on Milton's Ludlow *Mask* of 1634, the principles of physics at play in it, and their possible relationship with Cartesian thought, Margaret Hoffman Kale states the following:

> In the seventeenth century, there were raging debates between philosophers on the nature of movement. There was a revival of Epicurean atomism, which explained the doctrine of the origin of the universe in the chance collision of atoms. Although Descartes maintained the existence and mental activity of incorporeal substance, he elaborated a mechanical model of causation in corporeal substance. In his writings, Descartes makes clear that the material world is governed by mechanical laws and not by final or formal causes.[8]

As becomes evident from Hoffman Kale's text, and since she writes on the Ludlow *Mask*, Milton's poetical ruminations on the relationship between the corporeal and the incorporeal, as well as their links with motion and moving matter, began to take shape much before the composition of his great epic. In this chapter, however, I show that the more mature Milton characterizes motion and movement, as well as the directionality that these imply, in *Paradise Lost* through a pairing of mind and body that acquires perceivable poetical substance. In the epic Milton's poetic persona suggests, almost from the first, that the "pushing" indicated in the action of moving signifies the presence not only of physical life in the pre- and postlapsarian universe but also of an ontological pulsion, or drive, that leads into quintessentially human failure—even if it is precisely in that drive that the possibility of salvation also exists in immanence. So, in book 1, the poetic voice rhetorically asks the Spirit-Muse to name "what cause / *Mov'd* our Grand Parents . . . to *fall off* / From thir Creator, and *transgress* his Will . . ." (*PL,* 1.28–31; my emphasis). In doing this, Milton's speaker provokes, through the naming of contiguous actions, a tension between an implied stasis equaling virtue and a kinesis suggesting potential (self) corruptibility. In the lines cited above, the implication of Adam and Eve's having been pushed (or inspired, which is also a semantic possibility of "moved") "to fall off" contributes to the picturing of the first couple directing themselves, both physically and spiritually, toward a metaphorical abyss that extends beyond the presence of God's grace. The verb "transgress," similarly, betrays a temerarious intentionality that necessarily will cause "our Grand Parents" to proceed to the commission of the first, and arguably the greatest, of human trespasses.[9]

The tension that such density of verbal allusion provokes might well explain why, despite constructing a narrative poem where action generally takes precedence over description, Milton is surprisingly frugal in his use of the noun "motion" and the verb "to move," also denoting directionality.[10] The former appears only twenty-three times in *Paradise Lost*, with notable absences in books 1 and 4. The latter, in various conjugations and morphological variants, turns up over sixty times in all the epic's books, its appearances being more numerous in book 6 (eight) and book 8 (eleven). For a poem that is over ten thousand lines long, this is certainly not a great number of repetitions. And yet, Milton seems to handle both terms in such a way that their comparatively few insertions provide their specific contexts with what can only be called effectual momentum. In this sense, it is allusively and symbolically suggestive that, also in book 1, and apart from its being associated with the first couple's fall from divine grace and their capital transgression, the verbally referred "moving," in a continuous tense, should first occur in "the deep Tract of Hell" (*PL*, 1.28). So, after hearing the enflaming words of the violence-inspiring Beelzebub, "the superiour Fiend [Satan] / Was moving towards the shoar" carrying his "ponderous shield" on his massive back (*PL*, 1.283–84). Satan's colossal body, weighed down by the impressive weapons he lugs along, appears heavy and slow—he even uses his spear "to support uneasie steps" (*PL*, 1.295). As the narrative unfolds, this heaviness will be in direct contrast with the alacrity of the angelic "pursuers from Heav'n Gates" (*PL*, 1.326) and even with Satan's own swift-winged flight out of the infernal pit in book 2 (see *PL*, 2.631–32). Kinetic details like these have characterizing effects not only on Satan as a fallen entity but also on the quality of motion and movement in the whole poem: by associating mass and slowness with the regions of Hell and their inhabitants, Milton's speaker will only accentuate, in ensuing books of the epic, the agility and swiftness of the spiritual beings that move outside that particular location in the created universe.

The gradual change of pace from the first two books of *Paradise Lost* picks up speed in book 3, as the viewpoint of Milton's speaker turns from the nether zones of his version of Tartarus to the heights of the created universe. This rhythmic shift affects not only the poem's characters and the manners in which they move but also the very syntax and prosodic style of the epic, which for the most part mirrors their actions. It is there, in book 3, that even incorporeal, yet personified, entities acquire the capability of moving and thus of manifesting their existence and even of creating. Light here is personally addressed as an "effluence," that is, an issuing forth, and not exclusively an "essence" (*PL*, 3.6). The effect of the double *f* and the double *s* in the euphonic "effluence-essence" pairing evokes the image of light pouring forward as a kind of stream of divine energy. Similarly, but in the context of artistic and intellectual invention, great thoughts "voluntarie move / Harmonious numbers" (*PL*, 3.37–38), thus producing both music and poetry. Here the spatial position of "move" at the end of the line of verse provides the verb with the possibility of being transitive and intransitive at the same time. The potentially double function of "move" implies not only an emphasis on the creative aspects of the meditations of Milton's speaker but also a brisk "wander[ing]" (*PL*, 3.27) of the poet's persona out of intellectual contemplation and toward a specific direction, that is, into the creative action inherent in the composition of verse.[11]

At this point, the speaker of *Paradise Lost* has already determined that his poetical passage from the "darkness visible" of Hell to the illumination of Light—and therefore into divine presence, because "God is light" (*PL*, 3.3)—has been made possible only through inspiration from the Holy Spirit, also identified with the muse Urania. This is a poetical revelation that, in the virtual, illuminated space evoked in the opening invocation of book 3, often referred to as the Prayer to Light, translates into a metaphorical voyage implying a clear vertical directionality and therefore an upward-downward transportation in space. The fact that Milton's narrator has been "Taught by the heav'nly Muse to venture down / The dark descent, and up to reascend, / Though hard and rare" (*PL*, 3.19–21) indicates that Milton's creative journey through this extraphysical atmosphere should be reminiscent of the portentous flights of other incorporeal yet humanized characters, like Satan himself, or indeed the angels. This "hard and rare" phenomenon suggests that the sense of motion and movement that readers see, and ultimately experience, in *Paradise Lost* results from a directionality and

Mario Murgia 219

spatiality imposed on the narrative by the creative drive and will of Milton's speaker. In other words, movement in the epic is the metaphorical realization of the power of the poet's mind over evoked, or purely poetical, matter. If, quite early in his literary career, "Milton states in *Comus* that actions can be determined by reason, that reason is a property of the soul, and that reason stems directly from the grace of God," then it is later in the development of his oeuvre, and especially in book 3 of *Paradise Lost*, that he internalizes the poetic possibilities of metaphoric motion and provides them with vigorous intellectual and narrative actionality.[12]

The fact that action, directionality, and movement in book 3 are not only described and experienced, but also witnessed within the diegesis (mainly by God himself), betrays Milton's apparent tendency to relate perceptible motion and movement with the state of fallenness.[13] The poetic voice of Milton thus confirms that passivity and stillness, though not absolute motionlessness, itself a spatiotemporal impossibility, are mental and physical states consistent with innocence and intrinsic virtue: readers are made aware that both God the Father and the Son are in a sitting position, and that the heavenly beings that surround them "Stood thick as Starrs" (*PL*, 3.61).[14] Similarly, the first couple are "in the happie Garden plac't" (*PL*, 3.66), and even if they are busy "Reaping immortal fruits of joy and love" (*PL*, 3.67), a few lines ahead the voice of God himself reassures us of the fact that "Man" has been "there plac't" (*PL*, 3.90), quite passively and in a state of yet-incognizant bliss.

The apparent stasis of either divine or unfallen beings at this point contrasts greatly with the manner in which Satan conducts himself. Having broken out of Hell, and "ready now," even if "To stoop with wearied wings" (*PL*, 3.72–73), the demon develops "willing feet" (*PL*, 3.73) and, moreover, "wings his way / . . . / Directly towards the new created World" (*PL*, 3.87–89) in his eagerness to take revenge against God through the recently created humans. It is important to underscore that guile and spite push Satan to break loose and, as it were, move at will in a universe outside Hell. God the Father himself points out that "rage / Transports our adversarie, whom no bounds / Prescrib'd, no barrs of Hell, nor all the chains / Heapt on him there, nor yet the main Abyss / Wide interrupt can hold" (*PL*, 3.80–84), thus evidencing that the archfiend's lowly motives, which originate in his fallenness, constitute his drive to substitute a place of suffering for a place of vengeance. As Maura Brady has pointed out,

220   Anon They Move

> In Satan [Milton] explores the psychology of space and place, and finds that, although space may represent a dream of free, unimpeded motion, it does not satisfy the desire for shelter and respite in the way that place does. Indeed, as some critics have argued, to be without a place and its boundaries is, in effect, Satan's punishment.[15]

This psychological amalgamation of displacement and punishment is surely what has compelled Satan, before breaking out of Hell, to utter his famous apothegm "The mind is its own place, and in it self / Can make a Heav'n of Hell, a Hell of Heav'n" (*PL,* 1.254–55), which in context is self-serving, self-delusional, and ultimately false. "Me miserable! Which way shall I flie / Infinite wrauth, and infinite despaire? / Which way I flie is Hell; my self am Hell" (*PL,* 4.73–75) acknowledges the devil later on in a desperate cry of torturing spatial and individual relativity. In stark contrast, for Adam and Eve, as yet unfallen, the garden of Eden—that is, the earthly antipode of Hell—is a place of the kind of sedentariness that is apparently granted by innocence. There is no need to move away from there simply because sin is still impending and thus nonexistent on their plane of being, the original *locus amoenus.* Meanwhile, God, who exists in "the pure Empyrean" (*PL,* 3.57), in his divinity occupies all places, times, and spaces; therefore, he is everywhere and nowhere at the same time. This is a metaphorical and metaphysical state where, for him, all motion or movement renders itself completely immaterial, except perhaps for the work that creation implied: very humanly, Adam characterizes this as a "holy Rest / Through all Eternitie" in book 7 (*PL,* 7.91–92). This divine immateriality of motion entails, on the other hand, that God's absolute viewpoint, as accounted for by the poem's speaker (see *PL,* 3.77–78), exerts a determining influence on the rest of the characters' mobility, position, placement, and temporality in Milton's epic. Whatever (or whoever) has been created asserts and manifests its existence either by moving or by being moved; but their manners of motion and movement depend, in the narrative of the poem, on how those created beings, or moving objects, are regarded within God's all-encompassing gaze.

In the closing lines of the famous Prayer to Light, Milton's speaker asks the divine emanation to "Shine inward, and the mind through all her powers / Irradiate . . . that [he] may see and tell / Of things invisible to mortal sight" (*PL,* 3.52–55). Having thus requested the gift of metaphysical vision, the poetic voice immediately presents his audience with a barely descriptive image of God viewing his own creation.

The actual position of the Father is established as being superior, since he "bent down his eye, / His own works and their works at once to view" (*PL*, 3.58–59). Soon are we also informed that the Son is sat to his right, which suggests that the two persons are restive spectators of God's own creational acts, which seem to belong in a past that can only be sensed as being recent. From the poem's narrative, however, readers can elicit no certitude as to the "physical" location of the divine characters, nor as to the time that has elapsed from the instant of creation, because there is simply no temporal or spatial reference against which the duration of an action, or the position of a body (even if spiritual), can be contrasted and thus determined. It should be borne in mind that, as regards the relation between the creation and the advent of time, Milton rejects the commonplace that the world was created in time (*in tempore*) or, in the Augustinian formulation, with time (*cum tempore*). Milton instead argues that the advent of time is signaled by the gap between the divine decree whereby God begot the Son and the act of begetting. The creation of the world, in his view, took place after the generation of the Son (and probably after the fall of the angels), and so was an event embedded in time rather than the mark of its inception.[16]

It seems that, since both the universe and time have emanated from God through the Son, his being remains, for all ontological purposes of the poem's diegesis, in an extraphysical and extrachronological domain where he is all- and self-referential. In the created, time-depending universe created by God, however, any kind of motion or state of rest is necessarily relative to some frame of reference. Because the Father and the Son exist in an poetical ambit where both space and time are necessarily metaphorical, that frame of reference can only be provided by the Creator's point of view as expressed, in turn, through the narration of Milton's speaker.[17] The language of this poetical speaker, like that of Milton himself, is nevertheless a product of the Fall (as would be every other aspect of postlapsarian existence), which makes chronological and spatial referentiality indispensable for any kind of human communication or manifestation. This is why God the Father is presented as being sat "High Thron'd above all highth" (*PL*, 3.58), in a seemingly redundant hyperbole that is intended to rhetorically make up for God's lack of physical dimensionality. Since there is actually no height available to human comprehension with which to compare God's stance, the only way for him—and for readers—to look, obvious though it may appear, is down, where the universe and the world are located.

222   Anon They Move

The difference and distance between the loftiness of the divine realm and the lower position where Satan moves is emphasized after the well-known passage of book 3 where the Father and the Son discuss the central matters of free will, redemption, and salvation. It is then and there that we see Satan taking action in the fully physical context of Creation:

> Thus they in Heav'n, above the starry Sphear,
> Thir happie hours in joy and hymning spent.
> Mean while upon the firm opacous Globe
> Of this round World, whose first convex divides
> The luminous inferior Orbs, enclos'd
> From *Chaos* and th' inroad of Darkness old,
> *Satan* alighted walks: a Globe farr off
> It seem'd, now seems a boundless Continent
> Dark, waste, and wild, under the frown of Night
> Starless expos'd, and ever-threatning storms
> Of *Chaos* blustring round, inclement skie;
> Save on that side which from the wall of Heav'n
> Though distant farr some small reflection gaines
> Of glimmering air less vext with tempest loud:
> Here walk'd the Fiend at large in spacious field. (*PL*, 3.416–30)

The speaker's emphasis on the circularity of these spaces and heavenly bodies corresponds with the pre-Copernican outlook of the universe that Milton's cosmic descriptions favor in the poem. Words like "convex," "globe," "round," and "sphere" convey a geocentricity that, in terms of the epic's narrative, makes of the natural/human realm—as opposed to the context of divinity—a focalized center of attention on the part of the poem's reading audience. Also significant is the fact that in these lower spheres lies the "spacious field" where Satan sets foot on flat surfaces rather than flies through the air—a type of action and motion that, in context, begins to humanize him. Now manlike from walking, his current bearing not only reminds of the downwardness of humankind's position (which will only deepen after the Fall) but also foreshadows the mundanity that, in the near future, the trespass against God will instill in the human race and many of its acts on Earth.[18] The ensuing digression, generally known as the Paradise of Fools passage, grossly illustrates the corruption of a yet to be encountered postlapsarian world, where, naturally, the directionality of all motion and movement will be chiefly horizontal, at least until Satan beholds "Ascending by degrees magnificent / Up to the wall of Heaven

Mario Murgia

a Structure high" (*PL*, 3.502–3). In time, this vision will turn the sense of orientation in book 3 back to the transitions between high and low characterizing Milton's cosmic spaces.

Miltonic Motioning in Nineteenth-Century Spanish

Miltonic representations of motion and movement in space, also contextualized in discussions about free will and its implications of humankind's reality and its relationship to God, have proved to be quite challenging to interpret and translate over the course of more than three centuries since *Paradise Lost* first appeared. Transmutations of book 3 of the epic have been especially strenuous in this regard, not only because of the complexities inherent in its rhetorical and ideological structures but also because of its tantalizing imagistic qualities. These images, for the most part, owe their amplitude to the vigorous presentation of the figure of Satan as one of the book's axes of action, poetic evocation, and narrative focalization. "Satan's wanderings," as Walter Curry has classically put it, "cover amazing stretches of hyperbolical infinitudes—infinitudes which may be said to represent the expanded universe of Milton's mind."[19]

The complications escalate when this already "expanded universe" overflows into the frames of mind of translators for whom Milton is ideologically foreign and poetically exemplary at once. This is the case with most Hispanophone translators of Milton, who have traditionally struggled with the idiomatic and ideological transposition of the poet's essentially Protestant epic to the Catholic persuasions of their cultural contexts, mostly prior to the twentieth century.[20] The intricate cosmogony and theodicy condensed in *Paradise Lost*, and especially the manner in which spiritual beings are presented, have been a matter of much concern among Spanish-speaking translators for two centuries now. Juan Escóiquiz, for example, comments the following in the "Prologue" to his 1886 prosified translation:

> Apart from allegorically providing the Angels with bodies, he [Milton] presumes these effective, albeit ethereal and subtle, which contradicts the Catholic doctrine, where they are believed to be absolutely incorporeal. Such a fiction, however, has proved indispensable to Milton for, without it, the composition of his work would have been impossible; or, in a poem's stead, he would have birthed a cold and exact treaty of metaphysics.[21]

Clearly, for the Ibero-Spanish translator, the physical portrayal of metaphysical entities and, by extension, of their mobility and countenance, was a matter of (re)creative speculation and justification, of Milton's possible motives as well as his own. Escóiquiz's colleagues in the Hispanophone Americas were not far removed from such poetical-translational apprehensions. The Mexican poet and Miltonic enthusiast Francisco Granados Maldonado, in a justificatory headnote to his 1858 hendecasyllabic rendition of *Paradise Lost* (*El Paraíso perdido*) echoes his Ibero-Spanish counterpart's thematic-translational angst and states that "readers will note the difficulties that the translator has had to overcome in order to ensure that, by my utilizing a few paraphrases which, at some points, have been necessary, a few episodes would not appear strange which, deprived from these requisites, may have seemed inappropriate."[22] Quite a few of such episodes, by which Granados means "passages," he seems to have encountered in book 3 of the epic, and they coincide with Milton's depiction of motion and movement.

Granados is intent on enhancing the sense of bodily physicality in action that Milton originally presents as being lofty or even ethereal. For example, in the Prayer to Light, where Milton's speaker claims "in my flight / . . . I sung of *Chaos* and *Eternal Night*" (*PL*, 3.15, 18), Granados's version avers: "He caminado con errantes pasos," or "I have *walked* with wandering steps" (emphasis mine). Similarly, the rage that, according to God the Father, "transports" Satan in line 81 is translated as a "rabia que alimenta al enemigo"; that is, a rage that "*feeds* the enemy" (emphasis mine). Satan's fury is, in the translation, the nourishing fuel that propels him forward, both physically and (im)morally. Also, where we see Satan winging his way "Directly towards the new created World, / And Man there plac't" (*PL*, 3.89–90), Granados offers "Marcha al cielo buscando nuevas víctimas, / Y á ese naciente mundo se dirije, / Donde al hombre, mis manos colocaron" ([Satan] *marches* to the skies searching for new victims, / And directs himself to that newborn world, / Where man my hands have placed). For Granados, the devil is a fierce predator on foot who is driven forth by malicious motivation. God, in turn, possesses physical limbs with which he performs his creative wonders, while, by contrast, humanity is presented as lacking direction or motivation to move: they "have [been] placed" rather than progress toward "that newborn world."

In exercising these verbal and imagistic transmutations, the Mexican translator not only ensures an appropriate fitting of Milton's blank verse and its contents into the traditional hendecasyllabic lines of Spanish cultured poetry but also transforms the active quality of the types of motions that Milton's characters display. This is very much an example of what the British translatologist Jeremy Munday has called "translatorial action," where both form and content are at the service of intercultural transfer.[23] Granados, as a seasoned poet-translator, is thus potentiating, for the likely Catholic readership of nineteenth-century Mexico, the bodily fictions that Escóiquiz, in his own interpretation of Milton's verse, had considered so necessary for the development of the Protestant epic. This becomes evident when Granados changes the directionality of movement to ensure that the Catholic doctrine is not contested or contradicted by Milton's Protestant views on specific topics. Take the following lines spoken by God the Father to the Son:

> . . . thy merit
> Imputed shall absolve them who renounce
> Thir own both righteous and unrighteous deeds,
> And live in thee transplanted, and from thee
> Receive new life. So man, as is most just,
> Shall satisfie for man, be judg'd and die,
> And dying rise, and rising with him raise
> His Brethren, ransomd with his own dear life. (*PL*, 3.290–97)

Two details in this passage deserve consideration. Here Milton gives precedence to the Calvinist notion that both righteous and unrighteous deeds must be renounced as essential steps to be taken toward salvation. Also, but now in terms of motion and movement, salvation itself, through Christ's incarnation and subsequent sacrifice, symbolically implies upward directionality, as the rhythmic and quite alliterative sequence "rise-rising-raise" suggests. Granados's translation provides a very different perspective on these aspects:

> . . . por tí solo
> Vá el hombre à renacer; marchito el àrbol
> Que ya inclinaba su follage triste,
> Ya vuelve á florecer, y de la vida
> El manantial sus aguas purifica;
> Por tí và á ser el hombre ennoblecido
> Del mismo vencedor dando cabida
> A la virtud en su ardoroso pecho.
> Tú à quien el cielo adora, vé á la tierra
> A ser proscrito por el bien del hombre,

Al infierno tu muerte harà la guerra,
Redentor generoso del humano.

(Only through thee / will man be reborn; the withered tree, / whose sad foliage drooped already, / blossoms once again, and again the spring of life / purifies its water. / By thee will man be ennobled, / and then he shall receive / the victor's virtue in his noble bosom. / Thou, whom Heaven adores, shalt go to Earth / to be vilified for man's own good. / Thy death will wage war on hell, / Generous redeemer of humankind.)

Granados has substituted Milton's Calvinist perspective of (un)righteousness for the notion of human rebirth, which is illustrated with the allegory of a withering tree being revivified by a spring of crystalline water. More notable in terms of motion and movement is the fact that Granados has dropped Milton's upward directionality to place emphasis on the Savior's descent to the world in human form: "vé á la tierra" ("go to Earth"), and then "Al infierno tu muerte hará la guerra" ("on hell your death will wage war"). Where Milton's verse imagistically goes up, Granados's translation—or rather, his transformative version—travels down, and with a type of Catholic visual quality that verges on the baroquely iconographic.

The translational approaches to *Paradise Lost* by the Colombian Enrique Álvarez Bonilla often prove even more baffling than Granados's in terms of being transpositions of Milton's verse, particularly those passages that present a kinetic quality in their imagery. This is partly due, no doubt, to Álvarez's formal choice for his 1896 translation of the poem—where Granados has opted for unrhymed hendecasyllables, the Colombian poet-translator has decided to use ottava rima, a stanzaic form to which Milton himself resorted for the closing lines of "Lycidas."[24] The strict rhyme scheme of the form, plus the hendecasyllabic measure of its lines, require from the poet a considerable amount of what the Czech translatologist Jiří Levý calls "linguistic stylisation" for the migration of English into Spanish verse.[25] Indicative of this requirement is, for example, his version of the Prayer to Light. Here is Milton's original English:

Thee I re-visit now with bolder wing,
Escap't the *Stygian* Pool, though long detain'd
In that obscure sojourn, while in my flight
Through utter and through middle darkness borne

Mario Murgia

> With other notes then to th' *Orphean* Lyre
> I sung of *Chaos* and *Eternal Night*,
> Taught by the heav'nly Muse to venture down
> The dark descent, and up to reascend,
> Though hard and rare . . . (*PL*, 3.13–21)

The vigor of Milton's speaker is dizzying here. He flies and revisits God's "holy Light" in search for inspiration and poetical vision. The voice literally hurtles up and down with regained strength so that he can fulfill his obligation as a poet of spiritual adventure and epic aspiration. Álvarez's translated journey, however, is more dramatically vivid in terms of action:

> II
>
> . . .
> Al presente retorno á tus riberas
> Inflamado en más férvida osadía,
> Del tenebroso Báratro salido,
> Do largo espacio vime retenido.
> III
> Cuando mi pobre Musa era llevada
> Al través de la noche pavorosa,
> Con voz canté por otros no inspirada
> Lo que apenas nombrar el mortal osa.
> Aventúreme en la infernal bajada,
> Y después la ascendí, más ardua cosa:
> Hoy, salvo yá, de nuevo te visito,
> Y siento en mí tu resplandor bendito.

(Presently do I return to thy shores, / Inflamed by a most fervent daring, / And coming out of dismal hell / Where I was long retained. / While my poor Muse was being dragged / Through the dreadful night / I did sing with voice uninspired by others / What mortals barely dare to speak. / I ventured down to hell, / And then did I ascend, most precariously. / Today, redeemed already, again I visit thee, / and I feel within me thy blessed radiance.)

An image that harkens back to Milton's use of the myth of the River Styx ("tus riberas" or, curiously, the Light's "shores") initiates the spiritual plunge into darkness for Álvarez's speaker. Then, stretched over two stanzas, hellish images—for the most part absent in Milton's lines—are hyperpoetized in Spanish. Álvarez thus uses the rare and highly poetic name "Báratro" to refer to Hell, and also characterizes Milton's "heav'nly Muse" as being "pobre," or "poor," no doubt because she is literally dragged through "la noche pavorosa," or "dreadful night," where Milton's voice offers instead an "eternal night." The "dark descent" in the original English Álvarez translates as "infernal," while rendering "descent" and "reascend" more literally as "bajada" and "ascendí" ("I ascended"), respectively. In this way the Colombian's additions, substitutions, and reconfigurations of Milton's imagistic and rhetorical structures—which inevitably result in rhetorical and syntactic asymmetry between the English and the Spanish poems—provide Álvarez's version with a heightened sense of agitation and despair. While these conversions somewhat deflect the readers' attention from the fact that Milton's speaker "flies" in this metaphorical journey, the licenses of Álvarez are justifiable in terms of the equivalence that, as a poet-translator, he is obviously seeking—the sense of movement and directionality is not so much respected here as it is amplified as Álvarez attempts to echo the English poet's lofty ambitions by means of evocative magnification.

It would be unforgivable not to comment, if briefly, on some of Álvarez's and Granados's translational approaches to the Paradise of Fools in book 3 of *Paradise Lost*. In the original English the characterization of Satan as a menacing vulture, as a lurking figure who "Walk'd up and down alone bent on his prey" (*PL*, 3.441), soon gives way to a fiercely satirical tirade targeting future fools (Empedocles and Cleombrotus among them) as well as Catholicism and its prelacy. In terms of motion and movement in the epic, this section, also as an ideologically laden digression, bears diegetic relevance because, as Frank L. Huntley stated more than half a century ago: "In a cosmic geography this strange passage carries us forward imaginatively to those who, like Satan, also pause on a journey."[26] And not only that: the objects of Milton's fierce mockery "stray'd so farr" (*PL*, 3.476) and are "upwhirld aloft" (*PL*, 3.494) in their vain wanderings. In a few words these lines are rich in kinetic energy. And yet, despite its vividness in English, the treatment that our two Hispanoamerican translators give to the passage is that of near-absolute silence—both Álvarez and Granados simply skip it or substitute less thorny observations on malice or sin. For the Mexican translator, Satan is not like "a Vultur on *Imaus* bred" (*PL*, 3.431) but simply, and rather oddly, an "hombre audaz," or "audacious man." And even though Granados tries to enhance the foolishness of all the figures appearing in the passage by repeating the adjective "loco" ("fool") and the noun "locura" ("madness," or "folly") as well as its derivatives over five times, the lines lack the condemnatory acridness of the Miltonic source. Neither the three orders of Catholic friars ridiculed by Milton nor the ludicrous images of Saint Peter at the gates of Heaven are to be found here. Very soon, the English poet's caustic imagery becomes, in Granados's translation, a conventional and self-serving condemnation of avarice and greed.

As for Álvarez, his translation of the Paradise of Fools simply stops in its tracks after he presents "Empédocles que, henchido de quimera / Tan hueca é inesperada como impía, / En el Etna saltó con alegría . . ." (Empedocles who, swollen like a chimera / As hollow and unexpected as it is impious, / Into the Aetna gladly jumped). After this, readers can only see Satan regarding the world's sphere and the famous "Structure high" leading to Heaven (*PL,* 3.503). Just as in Granados's version, the clerical institutions of Catholicism have disappeared in what cannot be considered but a clear act of self-censorship. Unfortunately, the volume containing Álvarez's *Paraíso perdido* does not include a prologue expressing his stances and viewpoints as a translator. Yet, and given both translators' social and religious contexts, we can infer that Álvarez, just like Granados, uses ellipsis not only as a manner of self-protection but also as a way to make up for what they might have considered the poem's "defects," those relating to what the Mexican translator calls "the episodes that critics have deemed as foreign to the poem."[27] Undoubtedly, and while Álvarez and Granados efficiently accompany Milton on his journey toward poetical grandeur and spiritual uplifting, they occasionally move away from him when some cultural and linguistic decorum is required from them.

The translations of *Paradise Lost* that Enrique Álvarez Bonilla and Francisco Granados Maldonado undertook over 120 years ago are now practically forgotten. Neither one has been reissued ever since they were first published, and their initial status as considerable works of aesthetic and linguistic exchange between cultures has been overshadowed by other translational efforts often coming from Spain, the nation that for centuries was considered the hub of Hispanophone art and literature. Notwithstanding this neglect, a contemporary approach to the Miltonic incursions of Álvarez and Granados reveals a localized transcultural interest in disseminating the English poet and polemicist's masterpiece in a region of the world that, in the late nineteenth century, was still vying to shake off the remnants of a colonial past and to build its own plural, multifarious identity. The ideological, poetical, religious, and even political exploration that Milton proposes in his work was not only appealing to these Hispanoamerican poet-translators as a foreign piece of poetry that presented an opportunity to exercise their interlinguistic talents. For them, it was also to determine their own development as creatively sophisticated men of letters: Álvarez authored *Santafé redimida* (1885) and Granados composed *La Zaragozaida* (posthumously published in 1904), both epic poems where the diction, register, and rhetorical nuances of Milton can easily be identified, recognized, and traced. In their respective renditions of *Paradise Lost*, and through the ingenuity that they display in carrying over the complexities of the kinetic imagery in book 3, Álvarez and Granados reveal the kind of creative heights that the transportation and mobility of poetry between languages and cultural experiences can reach.

Notes

1. See Ernest Klein, *A Comprehensive Etymological Dictionary of the English Language*, vol. 1 (Amsterdam: Elsevier, 1966), 1640.

2. Susan Bassnett, *Translation* (London: Routledge), 3–4, emphasis mine.

3. See David Halliday, Robert Resnick, and Jearl Walker, *The Fundamentals of Physics*, vol. 1, especially chaps. 2, "Motion along a Straight Line," and 4, "Motion in Two and Three Dimensions" (New York: Wiley, 2014).

4. Indicative of this are, for instance, Milton's two versions of Psalm 114, itself a superb poetical piece on the phenomenon of cultural and geographical migration. In chapter 1 of this volume, John Rumrich, referencing said psalm, makes a case of the adjective/noun "Hebrew" being derived from a lexical item meaning "crossing over," or indeed "coming/going from outside." With respect to the journeying, or possible "foreignness," suggested by the demonym "Hebrew" in the Old Testament, see Gen. 14:13, as Rumrich advises, as well as Ex. 1:15, John 1:9, and Sam. 29:3.

5. For an overview of the more than twenty Hispanophone translations of *Paradise Lost*, see Angelica Duran, "*Paradise Lost* in Spanish Translation and as World Literature;" and Mario Murgia, "Either in Prose or Rhyme," in *Milton in Translation*, ed. Angelica Duran, Islam Issa, and Jonathan A. Olson (Oxford: Oxford University Press, 2017), 265–78 and 279–92, as well as "Milton in Revolutionary Hispanoamerica," in "Milton in the Americas," ed. Elizabeth Sauer and Angelica Duran, special issue, *Milton Studies* 58 (2017): 203–22.

6. "el asunto de que trata el poema es uno de los más misteriosos, delicados é importantes de nuestra religión cristiana, y por consiguiente expuesto á más equivocaciones y errores." Juan Escóiquiz, "*Prólogo*," in Milton and Escóiquiz, *El Paraíso perdido* (Barcelona: Biblioteca Salvatella, 1886), xi. The original orthography and punctuation are preserved throughout. All Spanish to English translations and English re-translations in this chapter are mine unless otherwise noted.

7. "Enfrentrado [*sic*] a la sádica tarea de convertirme en aquel mítico Procusto . . . , decidí respetar las exigencias métricas y el significado, y mantener . . . un difícil equilibrio que unas veces se salda a favor de las primeras y otras en beneficio del segundo." Milton and Enrique López Castellón, *El Paraíso perdido* (Madrid: Abada, 2005), 49.

8. Margaret Hoffman Kale, "Milton's 'Gums of Glutinous Heat': A Renaissance Theory of Movement," *Milton Quarterly* 29, no. 3 (October 1995): 89.

9. In chapter 2 of the present volume Sydney Bartlett makes a case of the relationship between physical movement and ideological choice in the epic.

10. Narration often takes precedence over description here but does not supersede it, since actions can only occur as verbal accounts of events taking place within the time-space of the narrative poem. In "On the Diegetic Functions of the Descriptive," Michael Riffaterre has stated that "no narrative can develop without using the descriptive mode"; Riffaterre, *Style* 20, no. 3 (Fall 1986), 281.

11. Christopher Ricks discusses and problematizes Donald Davie's use of lines 37 and 38 in book 3 of *Paradise Lost* to demonstrate how, in the epic, "syntax is employed so as to make the most of each word's eventfulness." Ricks points to the fact that the considerations by Davie serve to illustrate "the poet's realizing that language, unlike the pictorial arts, operates through time." Ricks also thinks of this as "a very useful insight into Milton's style" because it ultimately proves (against some of Davie's seemingly contradictory propositions) that some of the poet's stylistic peculiarities are but a means to achieve considerable "kinetic and dramatic effect." See Ricks, *Milton's Grand Style* (Oxford: Clarendon Press, 1963), 41–42.

12. Hoffman Kale, "Milton's 'Gums of Glutinous Heat,' " 12.

13. Paraphrasing Gérard Genette, Riffaterre has defined diegesis as follows: "By this term Plato and Aristotle designate a narration, but they use it both to specify the verbal equivalent of non-verbal events and the representation of verbal events: that is, the words uttered by characters, as an observer/narrator recounts them from his viewpoint and with the slant with which this viewpoint affects them, as opposed to words simply quoted verbatim"; Riffaterre, "On the Diegetic Functions of the *Descriptive*," 281.

14. For more on the implications of stillness and the nuanced uses of the word "still," as both adjective and adverb, in Milton's poetry in general, and *Paradise Lost* in particular, see chapter 1 by John Rumrich in this volume.

15. Maura Brady, "Space and the Persistence of Place in *Paradise Lost*," *Milton Quarterly* 41, no. 3 (October 2007): 173. The critics that Brady references are Jules David Law, Ken Hiltner, and John S. Tanner.

16. See Gordon Campbell and Thomas N. Corns, *John Milton. Life, Work, and Thought* (Oxford: Oxford University Press, 2008), 274.

17. For more on the relationship between motion and reference frame, see the Editors of Encyclopedia Britannica, s.v. "motion," *Encyclopedia Britannica*, August 22, 2022, https://www.britannica.com/science/motion -mechanics. For more on the relationship between the archfiend's sense of geographical orientation—or lack thereof—and the figure of God, see H. F. Robins, "Satan's Journey: Direction in *Paradise Lost*," *Journal of English and Germanic Philology* 60, no. 4 (October 1961): 699–711.

18. See chapter 11 by Marissa Greenberg in this volume, where she interrogates the presumption that walking is the normative state of pre- and postlapsarian humanity in Milton's epic and its adaptation in Alexis Smith's *Snake Path*.

19. Walter Clyde Curry, *Milton's Ontology, Cosmogony, and Physics* (Lexington: University of Kentucky Press, 1957), 157.

20. The role of the Spanish Inquisition in encumbering, on both sides of the Atlantic, the reception and translation of Milton's oeuvre, and *Paradise Lost* in particular, cannot be underestimated. As Angelica Duran has stated: "The institution succeeded in severely minimizing Hispanophone reception of Milton by curtailing its popularity when the general public still read epics, translated and otherwise. Additionally, it succeeded in constructing the narrow and plainly unattractive representation of Milton that pervades Hispanophone reception of Milton, different in both degree and kind from Anglophone reception"; Duran, "John Milton, Englishman," in *Reception: Texts, Readers, Audiences, History*, vol. 2 (2010): 25. See also Duran's *Milton among Spaniards* (Newark: Delaware University Press, 2020).

21. "No contento Milton con dar alegóricamente cuerpos á los Ángeles, se los atribuye efectivos, aunque etéreos y sútiles, cosa contraria á la doctrina católica, que los cree absolutamente incorpóreos; pero le ha sido indispensable esta ficción, pues sin ella, la composición de su obra era del todo imposible, ó en lugar de un poema, hubiera dado a luz un frio y exacto tratado de metafísica." Milton and Escóiquiz, "Prólogo" (Prologue), xiii.

22. "los lectores conocerán las dificultades que ha tenido que vencer el traductor, para hacer que con las paráfrasis que en algunos trozos han sido necesarias, no aparezcan estraños algunos episodios que sin estos requisitos parecerían inconducentes." Milton and Granados, "A los lectores" (To the readers), xix It is worthwhile pointing out that Granados was unaware of Escóiquiz's Miltonic endeavors. In fact, he thought that he had been the first poet ever to have translated the epic into Spanish, as he himself claims in his "Prologue" (iv).

23. Jeremy Munday uses the term "translatorial action" when he describes the theoretical approach to the practice of the German-born Finnish theoretician Justa Holz-Mänttäri. See Munday, *Introducing Translation Studies* (London: Routledge, 2001), particularly the chapter "Functional Theories of Translation."

24. The Italian poet Lorenzo Mancini had used the same stanza for his 1842 translation of *Paradise Lost*. See Daniele Borgogni, "'Censur'd to Be Much Inferiour': *Paradise Lost* and *Regained* in Italian," in Duran, Issa, and Olson, *Milton in Translation*, 231–48.

25. Jiří Levý, *The Art of Translation* (Amsterdam: John Benjamins, 2011), 189.

26. Frank L. Huntley, "A Justification of Milton's 'Paradise of Fools' (P.L. III, 431–499)," *ELH* 21, no. 2 (June 1954): 109.

27. "Defectos" and "los muchos episodios que [los críticos] dicen se hallan como agenos del poema." Milton and Granados, "Prólogo," xix.

CHAPTER 9

❧

Presencing the Author

Illustrations of Milton in
Hispanoamerican Publications

Angelica Duran

I was introduced to the poetry, prose, and figure of John Milton in the 1970s, when I was a child growing up in California, via two compendiums geared toward and popular with general Anglophone readers, and with obvious endurance: *The Harvard Classics: The Five-Foot Shelf of Books* (1902–10) and *101 Famous Poems with a Prose Supplement* (1929). Both are aimed toward, variously, the "cultivated man," "any intellectually ambitious American family," the "young reader," "young men and women whose education was cut short," and "souls, in these noise-tired times, that turn aside into unfrequented lanes, where the deep woods have harbored the fragrances of many a blossoming season."[1] In both collections Milton is but one of many predominantly male, canonical writers.[2]

Both US compendiums forefront the writers as much as their prefaces forefront readers. They do so, in part, by including visual illustrations. *The Harvard Classics* includes a single grayscale frontispiece for each volume: for example, in volume 40—*English Poetry 1, Chaucer to Gray*—the "Facsimile of the title-page of the First Folio Shakespeare dated 1623 From the original in Lenox Library, New York" with William Shakespeare's well-known engraved author portrait, and, in volume 3—*Bacon, Milton's Prose, Thos. Browne*—an author portrait of Thomas Browne, beneath which is a coat of arms and the handwritten "Your very wellwishing friend & servant Tho Browne."[3] Most germane to this study, volume 4—*Complete Poems in English: Milton*—includes as the frontispiece a photograph with the caption "Milton's Cottage,

233

Chalfont St. Giles, from the garden. The only house now standing in which Milton is known to have lived." Volume 4 organizes the poems to reflect Milton's biography: "POEMS WRITTEN AT SCHOOL AND AT COLLEGE, 1624–1632," "POEMS WRITTEN AT HORTON, 1632–1638," "POEMS WRITTEN DURING THE CIVIL WAR AND THE PROTECTORATE, 1642–1658," "PARADISE LOST, 1658–1663," "PARADISE REGAINED, 1665–1667," and "MILTON'S INTRODUCTION TO SAMSON AGONISTES" and "SAMSON AGONISTES, 1667–1671."[4]

The slim volume *101 Famous Poems* includes to the left of each title an oblong grayscale author portrait, author's date of birth and death, and in some cases brief information related to the text, author, or author portrait. In the 2010s when I revisited my home copy of the volume, I noted readily that the author portrait of Milton next to "Sonnet on His Blindness" is one that circulates widely, notably in Charles Knight's *The Gallery of Portraits* (1833), even though it is interpretive, just as is the title (fig. 9.1).[5]

By interpretive author portraits, I mean ones in which the author's physical features stray far enough from those in authentic author portraits to look like a different person or the same person at a different age. *101 Famous Poems* freely mixes authentic and interpretive author portraits, the former reflected in that of, for example, Maltbie Davenport Babcock, underneath which is a note that emphasizes its authenticity: "Photographed from portrait hanging in the lecture room of the Brick Presbyterian Church, New York, of which Dr. Babcock was formerly pastor."[6]

I revisited the illustrations in my beloved copies of these compendiums after returning from the first of my extended research trips in Hispanoamerican countries, since I was puzzled, first, by how persistently Milton's author portraits appear in Hispanophone translations of his works and other works that discuss him and, second, by the unique nature of some of those author portraits.[7] Some of the author portraits circulate widely in both Anglophone and Hispanophone works. Ubiquitous in Anglophone ones, as Nathalie Collé has explored, are copies of "the famous line engraving by William Faithorne, which represents the blind poet at the age of sixty-two and which was designed to serve as the frontispiece to Milton's *History of Britain, That Part Especially Now Call'd England* (1670)."[8] This elder Milton stares out at readers on the verso page facing the copy of the title page of *Paradise Lost* in Merritt Hughes's *The Complete Works and Essential Prose of John Milton* (1957), which was for decades the standard edition of Milton's works at US universities; the book jacket

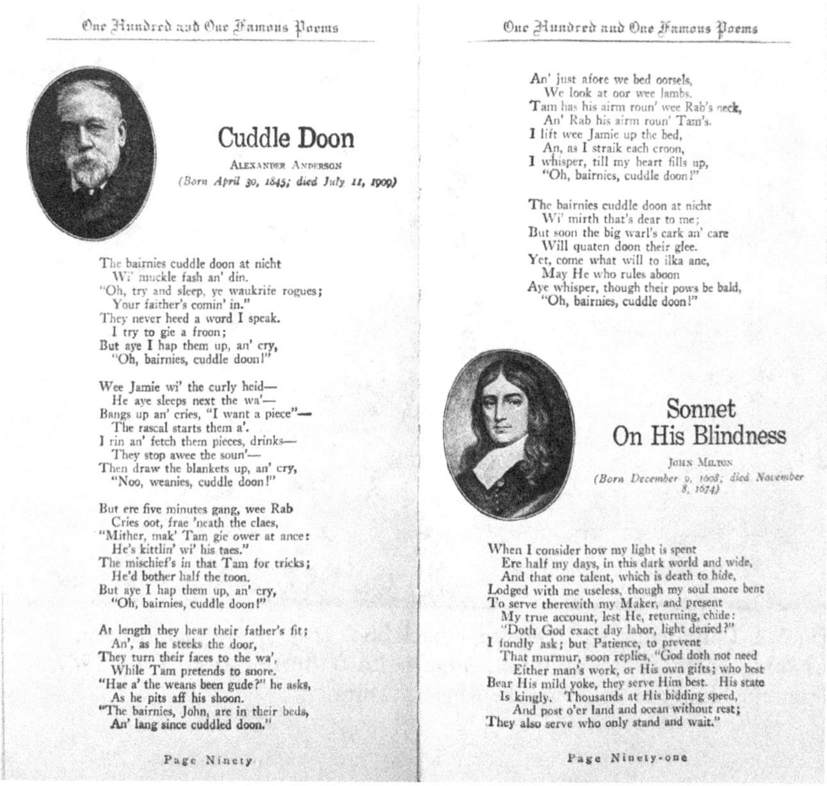
One Hundred and One Famous Poems

Cuddle Doon

Alexander Anderson
(Born April 30, 1845; died July 11, 1909)

The bairnies cuddle doon at nicht
Wi' muckle fash an' din.
"Oh, try and sleep, ye waukrife rogues;
Your faither's comin' in."
They never heed a word I speak.
I try to gie a froon;
But aye I hap them up, an' cry,
"Oh, bairnies, cuddle doon!"

Wee Jamie wi' the curly heid—
He aye sleeps next the wa'—
Bangs up an' cries, "I want a piece"—
The rascal starts them a'.
I rin an' fetch them pieces, drinks—
They stop awee the soun'—
Then draw the blankets up, an' cry,
"Noo, weanies, cuddle doon!"

But ere five minutes gang, wee Rab
Cries oot, frae 'neath the claes,
"Mither, mak' Tam gie ower at ance:
He's kittlin' wi' his taes."
The mischief's in that Tam for tricks;
He'd bother half the toon.
But aye I hap them up, an' cry,
"Oh, bairnies, cuddle doon!"

At length they hear their father's fit;
An', as he steeks the door,
They turn their faces to the wa',
While Tam pretends to snore.
"Hae a' the weans been gude?" he asks,
As he pits aff his shoon.
"The bairnies, John, are in their beds,
An' lang since cuddled doon."

Page Ninety

One Hundred and One Famous Poems

An' just afore we bed oorsels,
We look at oor wee lambs.
Tam has his airm roun' wee Rab's neck,
An' Rab his airm roun' Tam's.
I lift wee Jamie up the bed,
An, as I straik each croon,
I whisper, till my heart fills up,
"Oh, bairnies, cuddle doon!"

The bairnies cuddle doon at nicht
Wi' mirth that's dear to me;
But soon the big warl's cark an' care
Will quaten doon their glee.
Yet, come what will to ilka ane,
May He who rules aboon
Aye whisper, though their pows be bald,
"Oh, bairnies, cuddle doon!"

Sonnet On His Blindness

John Milton
(Born December 9, 1608; died November 8, 1674)

When I consider how my light is spent
Ere half my days, in this dark world and wide,
And that one talent, which is death to hide,
Lodged with me useless, though my soul more bent
To serve therewith my Maker, and present
My true account, lest He, returning, chide:
"Doth God exact day labor, light denied?"
I fondly ask; but Patience, to prevent
That murmur, soon replies, "God doth not need
Either man's work, or His own gifts; who best
Bear His mild yoke, they serve Him best. His state
Is kingly. Thousands at His bidding speed,
And post o'er land and ocean without rest;
They also serve who only stand and wait."

Page Ninety-one

Fig. 9.1. Unknown artist, author portrait of John Milton, grayscale, from *101 Famous Poems with a Prose Supplement* (Chicago: Cable Company, 1929), pp. 90–91. From the library of and photo by Angelica Duran.

of Barbara Lewalski's *The Life of John Milton* (2000); the web page of Gordon Campbell's entry on "John Milton" in the *Oxford Dictionary of National Biography* (2009); and the bottom left of the cover pages of the December issues of the scholarly journal *Milton Quarterly*.[9] In Hispanophone publications, the Faithorne, with Milton facing forward and slightly left rather than slightly right and hair a bit shorter, is displayed in a Hispanophone textbook about the Reformation and Counter-Reformation published in the 1990s in Cuba, for example.[10] The Milton author portrait in Knight's *The Gallery of Portraits* graces the center of the book cover and title page of the scholarly journal *Milton Studies*. Since the journal's book covers are brown-scale with black, Milton is rendered with hair color close to the auburn he is said to have had.[11]

Fig. 9.2. Unknown artist, color paperback book cover, from Juan Milton, *El Paraíso perdido* (John Milton, *Paradise Lost*) (Buenos Aires: TOR, 1957). From the library of and photo by Angelica Duran.

The distinctive nature of Milton's features and backgrounds that circulate in Hispanoamerican works can be best illustrated by the book cover of a paperback edition of *El Paraíso perdido* (*Paradise Lost*) published in 1957 in Argentina (fig. 9.2).[12] Taking up just a quarter of the colorful book cover, the author portrait is placed below a tunicked and white-winged angel Michael and left of the fallen Adam and Eve standing amid a tropical garden of Eden. This author portrait includes the high white collar from the Faithorne, as well as Milton's shoulder-length hair parted in the middle, though now black. The color of Michael's, Adam's, and Eve's hair is auburn, the hair color that early biographers ascribe to Milton—which is to say it is not a matter of a limited color palette that accounts for Milton's distinctively black hair. We thus have a case of the active practice of visual translation in which artists naturalize foreign authors.[13]

Also distinctive in the paperback's book cover is the background. Instructive here is the Marshall frontispiece, the "notoriously distorted engraved portrait" of Milton at the age of thirty-seven by William

Marshall, used in, according to Lewaski, "the original edition of *Poems of Mr. John Milton, both English and Latin* (1645)."[14] Its lack of verisimilitude provoked Milton to write a brief, cheeky Greek satire, "In effigiei eius sculptorem" (Against the Engraver of his Portrait), placed directly beneath the author portrait.[15] Some reader-viewers have conjectured that the Marshall frontispiece represents the companion poems *L'Allegro* and *Il Penseroso*: the background depicting the former with a "shepherd tell[ing] his tale / Under the hawthorn in the dale," and the foreground depicting the latter with Milton indoors in a "cell" who in old age attains "something like prophetic strain" (*L'Allegro*, 67–68; *Il Penseroso*, 169, 174).[16] This is to say that, although the verisimilitude to Milton's physical features is lacking, a sensitivity to his *Poems* as a whole may be on display.

What, then, can we make of the book cover of the 1957 *El Paraíso perdido*? Primarily, it is simply eye-catching for prospective book buyers. Also, as with the Marshall author portrait, it resonates with the book at hand, since the concluding scene of *Paradise Lost* is represented in the background. More particularly, the foliage, resembling that of the Americas, would generate a sense of affiliation from its Hispanoamerican reader-viewers. Finally, since this *El Paraíso perdido* possesses no other illustrations, the book cover as a whole and author portrait in particular essentially preside over the book, viewed glancingly at the very least every time reader-viewers pick it up—and the signs of use are clear on this copy.

These and other author portraits of Milton propel us to consider their uses and likely effects as they circulated—or to put this volume's title to work, *moved*—across time, languages, and borders, in general and specifically in Hispanophone books published in Hispanoamerica. I can in no way be comprehensive. Instead, I outline the illustrations of Milton made during his lifetime to show the instability and energies of such illustrations from the very onset, then move on to key illustrations of Milton in Hispanoamerican publications, where the hybridity specific to the region, mestizaje, is on full display.[17] What we find with the visually represented body of this world literature author alongside the textual body of his works in the Hispanoamerican network are repeated instantiations of a key characteristic of mestizaje drawn from its Indigenous American heritage: cultural cocreation, in the useful terms of Paula Gunn Allen, coming "from the position of creativity rather than from that of reactivity."[18]

Widely Circulating Milton Author Portraits

Three of the four portraits of Milton created during his lifetime are considered by and large authentic, as many art historians and literary historians have ably summarized: the one "now commonly attributed to the Dutch painter Cornelius Janssen (or Johnson), painted in 1618, when the boy was ten; the so-called Onslow portrait, representing Milton at the age of twenty-one, when he was a student at Cambridge"; and the Faithorne portrait, the only one that depicts Milton after he became blind at forty-five years old.[19] The most well-known anecdotal evidence that the Faithorne accurately depicts the older Milton's features is the story from roughly 1721, that Milton's youngest daughter Deborah remarked, upon seeing the portrait of her deceased father, "in a Transport,—'tis My Father, 'tis my Dear Father! I see him! 'tis Him! And then She put her Hands to several Parts of Her Face, 'tis the very Man! Here, Here"; this counterbalances the assessment by Elizabeth Minshull, Milton's third wife, who was dissatisfied with it and all others, saying that "the Pictures before his books are not *at all* like him," as Barbara Lewalski records.[20] Although created during Milton's lifetime, the Marshall frontispiece is deemed as an inaccurate representation of Milton's features.

All four of the author portraits have Milton facing forward and slightly right (from the viewers' perspective).[21] The Faithorne corroborates the assessment by Milton and his early biographers that he showed no obvious sign of blindness, like rolling eyes, decidedly skewed eyes, drooping eyelids, and cloudy irises that accompany some types of blindness.[22] It is worth noting, however, that the eyes are slightly askew in both the Onslow and Faithorne. Also, in contrast to the Marshall, the three authenticated portraits have single-color backgrounds and depict only Milton's head to just below the shoulders, thus calling attention to the facial features, hair, and upper-torso clothing. This contrasts, for example, the dreaming John Bunyan down to his waist reclining on his left hand and arm in the frontispiece of *The Pilgrim's Progress* (1678).[23] As such, the authenticated author portraits of Milton promote a view of an author involved in the *vita contemplativa*—the head figured as a primary site of imagination, speculation, and reflection— more than the *vita activa*, figured more greatly with the entire body.

The interpretive author portrait in Knight's *The Gallery of Portraits* re-creates a middle-aged Milton, which draws from the Onslow and Faithorne, just as forensic specialists might re-create renderings of probable current likenesses using digital technology on old photographs of young people. It also straightens the eyes, thus making a striking visual statement next to the title given to Milton's sonnet in *101 Famous Poems*, "On His Blindness": blind authors can look just like full-sighted ones.[24] This visual translation naturalizes blindness, akin to the naturalizing of the foreign author Milton on the book cover of *El Paraíso perdido*, previously discussed (fig. 9.2).

It must be noted that these widely circulating author portraits necessarily signal foreign transmission when they appear in publications from outside England and the erstwhile British Empire.[25] We get a sense of literary networks developing within obstacle-ridden internationalism to a broad if uneven globalization with the first publication of the Hispanophone translation of *Paradise Lost* (Ghent, 1868) by Colombian Aníbal Galindo and its republication (Bogotá, Colombia, 2002). The 1868 *El Paraíso perdido*, with the epic in English on verso pages and Spanish on recto pages, possesses no illustrations. It is no wonder given the great difficulties of publishing this edition at all, as we can derive from Galindo's gracious explanation of the typographical errors that riddle the edition, due to his having to copyedit from Paris while he was carrying out his duties as "Secretario de la Legacion de Colombia en Inglaterra y Francia" (Secretary of the Colombian Embassy in England and France). In his dedication to the major Colombian *letrado* (learned or educated person) José María Vergara y Vergara, Galindo expresses the sense of urgency to make Milton's epic available to Hispanophone readers, because it serves the "ilustración y virtudes" (enlightenment and virtues) of the dedicatee and, by extension, other Hispanophone readers.[26] The 2002 republication of Galindo's Hispanophone translation, with no English on facing pages, by Panamericana Editorial includes a copy of the Knight's *The Gallery of Portraits* interpretive author portrait on the plain back cover fold-in and a few of the fifty grayscale engravings by France's Gustave Doré (ca. 1866), which are likely the most widely circulating illustrations of *Paradise Lost* across the globe.[27] The Doré illustrations first appeared in two bicentenary editions of an Anglophone *Paradise Lost*, one deluxe, neither with an author portrait. The Colombian republication is thus a clear case of *mestizaje*, drawing together literary and visual artists from diverse eras and locales, from home and abroad.

The author portrait of Milton that serves as the frontispiece of *El Paraíso recobrado* (*Paradise Regained*; 1889), translated by Mexico's Julio Montés de Ocá, is also an interpretive one that has circulated widely since at least the 1830s in Anglophone, Francophone, and perhaps other translations of Milton's works (fig. 9.3).[28] This author

Fig. 9.3. Unknown artist, author portrait of John Milton, grayscale, from *El Paraíso recobrado* (*Paradise Regained*) (Mexico City: Tipografia "La Provincia," 1889), frontispiece. Photo by Angelica Duran.

portrait combines with the "Prólogo" to imply (wrongly) that Milton was middle-aged, rather than older, when he published *Paradise Regain'd* (1674), an implication only augmented by its brown tinge, which renders Milton's hair auburn. The author portrait with its plain background is one of only two illustrations in the elegantly sparse *El Paraíso recobrado*, the other being an unattributed illustration of Jesus and Satan in "Canto IV" (book 4).[29] The author portrait draws out the spectral presence of an important literary figure or author-function, for readers aware of the growing canon of world literature, and of the originating human behind the linguistically mediated work at hand, for all its readers. The author portrait's current state of being very light—which could be how it appeared originally or has become after more than a century—only adds to its spectral nature. Indeed, the one-page "Prólogo" and seven pages of endnotes are equally light in regard to "Juan Milton"—as his name is Spanished on the two title pages—certainly no mention or overt visual indication of his blindness. I am reminded that, as a child poring over the interpretive author portrait from Knight's *The Gallery of Portraits* next to "On His Blindness" in *101 Famous Poems*, I conjectured that the human creator of the poem had been born blind or had become blind by his early adulthood.

Overall, these widely circulating author portraits combine with the translated verbal texts which they accompany to situate Hispanoamerican readers in Western and increasingly global cultural circuits. At times, these visual texts serve, as they do in Anglophone editions of Milton's works, simply to humanize the work of great world literature as the product of a fellow human from days gone by, though marked as historically other by the consistent early modern clothing. At other times, the visual context is decidedly affiliative, actively positioning Milton within a Hispanoamerican text and context through particular visual details.

Hispanoamerican Milton Author Portraits

Complementary to these widely circulating Milton author portraits are new interpretive author portraits that have not gained currency outside of Hispanoamerica, including full-body renderings of Milton.[30] Two Milton author portraits, published in Mexico roughly a century apart, manifest the participation yet independence of the Mexican press within the world literature circuit. The author portraits in *La Ilustración mexicana* (*The Mexican Enlightenment*; 1852) (fig. 9.4) and *El Paraíso perdido* (1967) (fig. 9.5) include many markers of major Milton author portraits: a high white collar and shoulder-length hair parted down the middle against a plain background, though facing forward and slightly left rather than slightly right. The former even replicates the slightly skewed eyes.

Fig. 9.4. José Decaen (attributed), author portrait of John Milton, grayscale, from *La Ilustración mexicana* (1852), facing page 72. Courtesy of Hemeroteca Nacional de México, Biblioteca Nacional de México. Photo by Gabriela Villanueva Noriega.

Fig. 9.5. Unknown artist, author portrait of John Milton, grayscale, from John Milton, *El Paraíso perdido*, trans. Juan Escóiquiz and unknown adapter (Mexico City: Editorial Nacional, 1967), frontispiece. Photo by Angelica Duran.

The backgrounds of these Hispanoamerican Milton author portraits are sparse but significant. Beneath both are Anglophone versions of Milton's first name *John* rather than the Hispanophone *Juan*. This readily underscores his Englishness. We must be cautious about attributing any general motive or effect in the use of "John Milton" in Hispanophone texts, even when the same texts Hispanicize other foreign names. We do well to consider the regular designation in Anglophone texts of Spain's Miguel de Cervantes, a mishmash that avoids Englishing the first name of the author of *Don Quixote* (1605) to Michael but that drops the second surname so commonly used in Hispanophone names—here Saavedra.[31] In the 702-page volume 3 of *La Ilustración mexicana*, thirteen of the twenty-six laminate inserts contain personal names: Eastern names and their descriptors are in

Spanish, as with "Nassar-Eddin, Schah de Persia," "Mirza-Taghi-Khan, Primer ministro del Schah," and "Zingha"[32]; and all Western European names, except Milton's, are Spanished, as with "Juan Calvino," "De Lamartine," "Rubéns," and "Alfredo Crowquill."[33] Yet, volume 1, for example, retains "John Campbell."[34]

The handwritten signature used for Milton's Anglophone name under the author portrait in *La Ilustración mexicana* works much as does the handwritten message and signature under the author portrait of Thomas Browne in *The Harvard Classics*, previously mentioned, to signal authenticity. This authenticating element signals a shared humanity greater than that signaled by typeface.[35] José Decaen's interpretive author portrait with the handwritten signature buttresses the emphasis on Aristotelian ethos, derived from present or implied human speakers or agents, in the corresponding nine-page entry "Milton" by Francisco Zarco Mateos, "one of the prominent figures involved in the outlining" of Mexico's Constitution of 1857.[36] Zarco describes Milton as a beleaguered human being who remained resilient amid the "tantas pesares" (many obstacles) that he overcame to publish *Paradise Lost*: "enfermedades" (illnesses) including blindness, the death of two wives, and "mayor aislamiento" (major isolation) due to Restoration politics. Zarco reminds us that Milton was a father when he mentions the "hermosos cuadros que pintan á Milton rodeado de sus hijas" (beautiful paintings that picture Milton surrounded by his daughters).[37]

Zarco's description accrues poignancy for readers who know of Zarco's many personal, medical, and political obstacles through his early death of tuberculosis shortly after his fortieth birthday in 1869.[38] Indeed, the human condition figured in *La Ilustración mexicana* resonates with the historical context and human agents related to the author portrait. The history of the Marshall frontispiece is again instructive. Lewalski has called attention to Milton's "comment in the *Pro Se Defensio* (1655) stating that he had bowed to the 'suggestion and solicitation of a bookseller' and allowed himself 'to be crudely engraved by an unskillful engraver because there was no other in the city at that time.'"[39] Analogous matters of available human resources and individual artistic talent bear on the interpretive author portrait in *La Ilustración mexicana*, although resulting from esteem rather than in contempt. While the Milton author portrait lacks any express reference to the artists or engravers, we can attribute it to Decaen with some confidence by the presence of references to only "Decaen" and the similar style in all the other grayscale laminate inserts.[40] Further, the Mexican publisher Ignacio Cumplido, one of the most famous in

244   Presencing the Author

Hispanoamerican history and the first to publish a Hispanoamerican translation of *Paradise Lost* (unillustrated) in 1858, repeatedly relied on Decaen in this and many other publications for the practical know-how, cultural capital, and unique aesthetic talent that he brought with him from Europe to his adopted homeland.[41] As Montserrat Gali Boadella demonstrates in her survey of printing in post–Independence Mexico (1821), Decaen was one of the French immigrants who constituted "el monopolio decidido de los litógrafos franceses entre 1835 y 1850" (the decided monopoly of French lithographers between 1835 and 1850).[42] Itself in political turmoil, Mexico benefited from a wave of French immigrants precipitated by France's greater political instability.

The inclusion of an entry on "Milton" in *La Ilustración mexicana* at all, then with an author portrait that is the first of the few laminate inserts in volume 3, invites us to ask, how does Milton fit into the eclectic volume and the five-volume set as a whole? The answer can be gleaned from Zarco's entry, which draws out parallels between the historical moment of crisis in Milton's homeland, "Inglaterra en el siglo XVII durante la larga revolucion" (England in the seventeenth century during its long revolution), and in Zarco and his original readers' homeland of nineteenth-century Mexico.[43] Zarco explains Mexico's political instability as negatively impacting his own current scholarship:

> Los límites que debe tener este escrito y las circunstancias en que nos encontramos no nos permiten darle toda la estension que deseáramos, ni recurrir á las autoridades de los críticos, ni á citas que solo pueden hacerse cuando por algunos dias puede uno encerrarse en una biblioteca, en que encuentre todo lo que busque, lo cual es demasiado dificil. Las opiniones que emitamos no estarán, pues, fundadas en autoridades estrañas y serán solo el resultado de la impresion que en nuestro ánimo han producido las bellezas de Milton que durante muchos años nos han servido de consuelo y de recreo.

> (The limitations of this writing and the circumstances in which we find ourselves do not permit that we give it the extent that we would like, nor to take recourse to the authority of critics, nor citations that can be made only by spending some days shut up in a library, to find all that one seeks, which is very difficult. The opinions we state will not be, thus, founded on foreign

Angelica Duran   *245*

authorities and will be solely the result of the impression left on my/our soul by the beauties of Milton that have served me/us over many years as consolation and recreation.)[44]

Zarco describes the encouragement he has found in Milton's ability to shoulder through similarly difficult times to create works of enduring value. He does so in the hopes of encouraging the next generation of Mexicans, but really all "humanidad" (humanity), to experience it as well:

> Nuestro ánimo ha sido llamar la atencion de la juventud estudiosa hácia las obras de Milton, y para que puedan sentir y apreciar el efecto de los rasgos mas bellos es preciso que los estudien en el original [. . .]. El Paraíso es el poema en que se canta el asunto mas sublime que interesar pueda á la humanidad, está fundado en las luminosas verdades del cristianismo, y engalanado con todas las gracias y adornos que puede producir una imaginacion eschuberante y ardiente.

> (Our aim has been to draw attention to studious youths toward Milton's works and, so that they can feel and appreciate the effect of the most beautiful traits, it is exigent that they study them in the original [. . .]. The *Paradise* is the poem in which the most sublime theme that can interest humanity is sung; it is founded on the luminous truths of Christianity and embellished with all the graces and adornments that an exuberant and zealous imagination can produce.)[45]

A pithy indicator that Zarco had read Milton's works in their original English—that is, that he practiced what he preached—is his use of the Anglophone "Paradise regained" amid his otherwise uniform Hispanophone references to *El Paraíso perdido* and *El Paraíso recobrado*.[46] This (intentional?) slip combines with his learned footnotes about the quality of available Francophone, Hispanophone, and Lusophone translations to show the good effects of studiousness.[47]

The early placement of Zarco's Milton entry, showcased with the Decaen interpretive author portrait and handwritten signature, serves to reanimate the figure of Milton in the subsequent remarks about him in the rest of volume 3. In the Hispanophone translation of the essay "El civilizador" (The Civilizer) by "A[lphonse] de Lamartine," we find the French philosopher proposing that es suficiente un corto número de personages bien escogidos para que pasen ante la vist[a] y la imaginacion de las masas todos los tiempos conocidos. Suponed que teneis la facultad de exhumar solo y hablarles un momento en su idioma á las figuras históricas, confusas y diversas que vamos á recordaros al caso, y que las clasificais despues cada una por su fecha y por su gerarquía en los siglos para formar con ellas eslabon por eslabon, la larga cadena de los tiempos y de las cosas.

(a small number of well-selected figures are sufficient to bring before the eyes and imagination all the masses known throughout time. Suppose that you have the power of calling them alone and talking with these historical figures for a moment in their languages, confused and diverse whom we are going to remind you of, as cases in point, and you can classify each one later by their date and their rank in the centuries to form with them link by link a large chain of time and of facts.)[48]

Milton is the fifty-second of the geographically and historically wide-ranging list of 121 such "well-selected figures" that Zarco then provides, starting with "Móises" and "Homero" and ending with "Juana de Arco" and "Tácito, &c., &c., &c."[49]

In another essay by Zarco in volume 3, "De la protección de la literatura" (Of the Protection of Literature), Milton emerges again: "Mientras en la Inglaterra alcanzaban gracias y mercedes los poetastros que corrompian el lenguaje y ponian en boga las alusiones obscenas, Milton, pobre y abandonado, producia el *Paraiso perdido*" (While poetasters who corrupted the language and put obscenities in vogue were thanked and attained favor in England, Milton, poor and abandoned, produced *Paradise Lost*).[50] This assessment doubles as self-encouragement and encouragement for fellow Mexicans who would advance Mexican letters as part of world literature. Zarco elsewhere calls in early modern Spaniards Cervantes and Francisco Gómez de Quevedo y Santibáñez Villegas, as well as French and Italian writers, as examples of great writers who produced their works without court or governmental support:

preciso es reconocer que el genio no necessita de la proteccion ni del amparo del poder, sino que por el contrario se eleva, se engrandece y se purifica en las luchas que tiene que sostener, y que la persecucion ó el abandono, son el crisol que mas le

conviene para adquirir ese brillo esplendente, que nada empaña
ni oscurece.

(it is necessary to recall that genius does not need the protection or shelter of power, but rather on the contrary is elevated,
enlarged, and purified through the battles it has to undergo; and
that persecution and abandonment are the crucible that best
suits it to acquire that splendid brilliance that nothing tarnishes
or darkens.)[51]

Zarco reaches beyond his own linguistic and national spheres as he
seeks to inspire readers to refine their own sensibilities and writings, in
consonance with *The Harvard Classics* and *101 Famous Poems.*

In another essay in volume 3, "Viaje del Nevado de Toluca" (Voyage to the Snow-Covered Mountain of Toluca), Zarco's contemporary
José María Heredia affiliates with writers faraway in time and place
when witnessing his homeland. He describes the Toluca volcano west-
southwest of Mexico City as an "horno inmenso que realizó en otros
dias el tartaro de Virgilio y el infierno de Milton" (immense oven that
in other days was realized in Virgil's Tartarus and Milton's Hell).[52]
Heredia might have read Milton's Hell in an Anglophone *Paradise
Lost*, as Zarco recommends, or in any one of the many Hispanophone,
Francophone, or Italophone translations that circulated in nineteenth-
century Mexico. Heredia would have had access to not only Milton's
works but also the figure of Milton. For example, volume 3 includes
a Hispanophone translation of Thomas Gray's English poem "Elegy
Written in a Country Churchyard," "Elegía," with its famous reference
to "Some mute inglorious Milton" ("Algun callado Milton, mas sin
fama").[53]

The other derivative author portrait of Milton, with closed eyes (fig.
9.5), appears in the opening paratexts of two different Hispanophone
translations of *Paradise Lost* published by the Mexican press Editorial
Nacional in 1951 and 1967. My focus is on the latter because of my
greater access to it and given its special status as a tercentenary edition.[54]
We witness with this edition not the constrained bricolage Claude Lévi-
Strauss describes of "savage" cultures but rather mestizaje, which casts
"[Mexico's] history as an epic tale of nation" and perhaps even region,
"forged precisely from the encounter of civilizations," with Europe and
Africa primarily, but also Asia, variously celebratory, angry, or elegiac.
The 1967 *El Paraíso perdido* represents human agents mingling, as it
combines Milton's innovative seventeenth-century English verbal art,

248   Presencing the Author

Doré's nineteenth-century European visual art, and vibrant twentieth-century Mexican modern art.[55]

The opening paratext advertises that this edition "Contiene 41 láminas de Gustavo Doré y 23 a todo color de Miguel Fernández de Lara" (Contains 41 laminates by Gustave Doré and 23 in full color by Miguel Fernández de Lara).[56] The illustrations consist of thirty-six of the fifty grayscale Doré illustrations; twenty-four rather than twenty-three illustrations in the vibrantly colored chromolithography genre, or *cromo*, popular in Mexico, by the little-known Mexican artist Fernández de Lara; and five additional grayscale illustrations that the press might have ascribed to Doré—which would result in the advertised "41"—but are not by Doré. These five are the author portrait and four others featuring full-body illustrations of Milton situated in English settings.

The first (fig. 9.6), "Reconciliación de Milton con su esposa" (Reconciliation of Milton with his wife) of a slim, dark-haired Milton standing on the left with a kneeling Mary Powell Milton on the right, their right hands joined, illustrates the scene "en la casa de uno de sus amigos" (in the house of one of his [Milton's] friends) described on the facing page in the four-page "Biografía."[57] The second (fig. 9.7), "Milton dictando su poema á sus hijas" (Milton dictating his poem to his daughters), is again a domestic scene but this time outdoors. This Milton has closed eyes, indicating blindness like the author portrait. The other facial features, however, bear little resemblance to the author portrait. As in the first illustration in the "Biografía," Milton is again standing, as is one of his daughters, though the other daughter is seated with pen in hand; and it too illustrates the description on the facing page, that, though he experienced "ceguera, trabajaba de continuo, auxiliado de sus hijas de su primer matrimonio, que le servían de amanuenses y le leían cuantos libros tenia necesidad de consultar" (blindness, he worked continuously, aided by his daughters from his first marriage, who served him as amanuenses and read him the many books he needed to consult).[58] Here, his right hand is raised, bent from the wrist as if conducting his musical verse. Both domestic scenes are oft-told and oft-illustrated. Thus, these illustrations in this Mexican publication are squarely within a worldwide cultural circuit.[59]

The last two illustrations reside in the six-page translator's prologue, focused on translational matters and the poem's narrative, and do not correspond with the descriptions on facing pages, as to be expected. They instead illustrate descriptions from the preceding short biography. In "Milton secretario de Cromwell" (Milton, secretary

Figs. 9.6 and 9.7. Unknown artist, "Reconciliación de Milton con su esposa" and "Milton dictando su poema a sus hijas," grayscale, from John Milton, *El Paraíso perdido* (1967), facing pages VI and VIII. Photos by Angelica Duran.

to Cromwell), Milton again bears little resemblance to the author portrait; the lips are slightly petulant and his hair is curlier than in authentic author portraits, with a stray curl gracing his forehead (fig. 9.8). Milton stands jauntily with his right hand near the hilt of his sword hanging on his hip and his left hand grasping a rolled document, while Cromwell, with a slight scowl, sits. Cromwell joins Milton in his sartorial choice of a high white collar. The final illustration (fig. 9.9), "Milton enfermo" (Milton sick), figures a Milton with a much more receding hairline than in the Faithorne—other derivative copies depict a receding hairline.[60] On his deathbed, Milton is at last freed of the ubiquitous high white collar. He is instead wearing a nightshirt and blanket; and, rather than standing, he reclines on his bed, with a young woman—his third wife Elizabeth Minshull or a servant—standing at the foot of his bed.[61] As in the other illustrations, Milton's mouth is closed, indicating his silence or a pause. In this last illustration his left hand is raised slightly as if he still has so much more to say, an interpretation buttressed by the books and pages strewn on the floor nearby.

Figs. 9.8 and 9.9. Unknown artist, "Milton secretario de Cromwell" and "Milton enfermo," grayscale, from John Milton, *El Paraíso perdido* (1967), facing pages XII and XIV. Photos by Angelica Duran.

These four illustrations, placed shortly after the author portrait and before the verbal text of *El Paraíso perdido*, draw readers' attention to the primary human agent behind what is shown to be a work that has been transmitted through many hands from an originating human source. The settings of the illustrations tether him to a specific temporal and national space, even as they untie him from any single identity—he is friend, husband, politician, patriarch—or a sole type of environment—workplace, home, or the natural world, each of which will be so stunningly, verbally depicted in the epic that the readers of the edition have "all before them" (*PL*, 12.646).

Milton's cameo appearances in *La Ilustración mexicana* and as the sociable "Genius of the shore" ("Lycidas," 183) of readers' engagement with *El Paraíso perdido*, in its opening paratexts, clearly display the fulsome if disjointed timeframes and aesthetics that mark the modernity into which Mexico and all American nations emerged. Their unique characteristics reflect Hispanoamerica's trademark mestizaje: in *La Ilustración mexicana* the ready collaboration with recent European, specifically French, immigrants; in *El Paraíso perdido* the Doré illustrations created the century before and in Europe, but still of great, and perhaps ever-increasing, importance combined with the new, Hispanoamerican illustrations by Fernández de Lara and the unknown artist(s).

Conclusion

My primary aim and pleasure in reading literary texts is in understanding what and how they mean. Attending to book illustrations of Milton enables us to recuperate and perhaps experience the human relations that are, for many, foundational in the import and importation of literary texts. We know that many written works have oral and social beginnings and afterlives, not just in ancient times but also, for example, in the early modern English bookstores where a reader would read aloud books and pamphlets to auditors; in the many homes where evening family circles fostered cultural literacy; and perhaps most germane, with Milton reading aloud throughout his adult life: the "dictation, some part, from time to time, of a Tractate which he thought fit to collect from the ablest of Divines" to the students in the homeschool he oversaw in his thirties; the political correspondence he composed and delivered to amanuenses in his role as Secretary of Foreign Tongues in the Interregnum government in his forties; then his use of "whatever hand came next," his family and friends, to write down his late masterpieces during the Restoration in his fifties and sixties.[62] Illustrations of Milton in works about and by him, in their original languages and in translation, invoke yet another instance and kind of the social, one that Gordon Teskey describes aptly in *Delirious Milton: The Fate of the Poet in Modernity*: "We think of the speech as a *presencing* of the speaking self to itself, in a state that is prior to writing and even opposed to it."[63] In this light, the author portraits and illustrations in the Hispanoamerican books discussed presence Milton's speech acts, especially with their focus on the head and hands, both associated with verbal transmission, as well as in the full-body representations.[64]

It is through illustrated editions of Milton's works and compendiums, at times with presencing author portraits, that many reader-viewers have been introduced to and have experienced Milton's works and legend, as I was in my Hispanoamerican household in California in the 1970s. Correlatively, it is through illustrated and translated editions that his works have moved into the realm of world literature rather

252   Presencing the Author

than simply English literature. Milton's represented embodiment—as male, as conspicuously or inconspicuously disabled, as variously European in general or English in particular, as lone author or companionate government official and family member—provides multidimensionality to world literature and to authorship. Milton's works and image establish a relationship between Milton, the myriad of artists and publishing agents from diverse sites who have dedicated their energies and resources to his works, and reader-viewers, fulfilling Milton's desire to leave "something so written to aftertimes, as they should not willingly let it die."[65] Each of these human elements, in turn, constitute part of an ever-changing literary canon, whether it be part of a global cultural circuit or a regional, linguistic, or national-cultural tradition.

We have more than three centuries of clear indications that Milton's poetic imagination has communicated to writers across time and space, through their allusions, imitations, translations, and other literary works. So, too, to visual artists, as evidenced by the Hispanoamerican illustrators of Milton and his works, only a few of which I have discussed here. Whatever the quality of those illustrations, as measured by verisimilitude or artistic acumen, and whether they evince mostly the sharp colors and flora so often associated with Latin America or mostly international and global elements, they call us to consider what has interested creative readers in the past about Milton and other authors, as well as to consider our own agency as readers and cocreators of their afterlives whatever our locales.

Notes

1. Charles Eliot, ed., *The Harvard Classics* (New York: P. F. Collier and Son, 1902–10), quotations at 50:3, 50:3, 50:7, 50:8; Roy Cook, ed., *101 Famous Poems with a Prose Supplement* (Chicago: Cable Company, 1929), n.p.

2. Women authors in *The Harvard Classics* include Jane Austen, Elizabeth Barrett Browning, and George Sand (Amantine Lucile Aurore Dupin). Of the seventy-one writers in *101 Famous Poems*, the ten women authors are Elizabeth Barrett Browning, Alice Cary, Mary Mapes Dodge, "George Eliot (Mary Ann Evans)," Mary Howitt, Lucy Larcom, Winifred M. Letts, Edna St. Vincent Millay, Ella Wheeler Wilcox, and Eva Rose York; Cook, *101 Famous Poems*, 137.

3. Eliot, *Harvard Classics*, 40:n.p., 40:spine; 3:spine. Milton's prose works in volume 3 are *Areopagitica* and *Tractate on Education*. Other frontispieces in the *Harvard Classics* forefront nonhuman or nonhumanizing elements, as in volume 29—*Voyage of the Beagle: Darwin*—with the frontispiece of "*Amblyrynchus Demarlii: A species of Lizard found on some of the Islands of the Galapagos Archipelago*"; Eliot, *Harvard Classics*, 29:n.p.

4. Eliot, *Harvard Classics*, 4:spine, 4:n.p., 4:1–2. An illustration of "Milton's Cottage, Chalfont St Giles" also appears in Barbara Lewalski, *The Life*

of John Milton (Malden, MA: Blackwell, 2000), plate 14, facing page 334, and as the frontispiece by the Spanish artist Gregorio Prieto in John Milton and Gregorio Prieto, *Milton: El Paraíso perdido: Dibujos de Gregorio Prieto para El Paraíso perdido de Milton* (Madrid: Arte Bibliogfilia, 1972), n.p.

5. Charles Knight, *The Gallery of Portraits*, vol. 1 (London: Charles Knight, 1833), facing page 42. "Sonnet 19: When I Consider" does not directly mention visual impairment, yet Milton's late-onset blindness has led to the common retitling of this sonnet. For its impact of this sonnet on Helen Keller and her activism for the blind community, see Duran, "The Blind Leading the Blind and Sighted: John Milton and Helen Keller," in *Milton in Popular Culture*, ed. Laura L. Knoppers and Gregory M. Colón Semenza (New York: Palgrave Macmillan, 2006), 187–98. Special thanks to Beverley Sherry for advising me on the Knight's Gallery author portrait. For major Milton author portraits, see George Charles Williamson, *Milton Tercentenary* (Cambridge: Clay at the University Press, 1908); and Leo Miller, "Milton's Portraits: An Impartial Inquiry into their Authentication," special issue, *Milton Quarterly* (1976): 1–43.

6. Cook, *101 Famous Poems*, 37. Special thanks to Joseph Wittreich for helping me determine the best descriptive terminology for various author illustrations.

7. The first publications of the Hispanophone translations of *Paradise Lost* by Mexico's Francisco Granados Maldonado and Colombia's Enrique Álvarez Bonilla, which Mario Murgia discusses in chapter 8 of this volume, possess no illustrations of any kind.

8. Nathalie Collé, "Author Portraits of Milton, Authorship, and Canonization," in *Global Milton and Visual Art*, ed. Angelica Duran and Mario Murgia (Lanham, MD: Lexington Books, 2021), 141–64.

9. Merritt Y. Hughes, ed., *The Complete Poems and Major Prose of John Milton* (Indianapolis: Odyssey Press, 1957), 206; Lewalski, *Life of John Milton*, book jacket; Gordon Campbell, "John Milton (1608–1674)," *Oxford Dictionary of National Biography*, last modified 2009, https://www.oxforddnb.com/; and *Milton Quarterly*, https://onlinelibrary.wiley.com/journal/1094348x, cover.

10. Walter Goetz, *Reforma y Contra-reforma* (Madrid: Espasa-Calpe, 1975). In addition to the derivative Faithorne author portrait, the selections from the Hispanophone translation of *Paradise Lost* in this work are interspersed with illustrations by Gustave Doré and William Blake.

11. *Milton Studies*, https://www.psupress.org/books/titles/978-0-8207-0705-1.html, book cover and title page. Milton's hair has drawn the attention of, among others, John Keats in "Lines on Seeing a Lock of Milton's Hair" (written 1818; published 1893); James Henry Leigh Hunt in "To Robert Batty, M.D., on His Giving Me a Lock of Milton's Hair" (1818); and Jayne Lewis, "A Lock of Thy Bright Hair," *Humanities* 4 (2015): 797–817.

12. Among the many well-researched and delightful syntheses of Milton author portraits, see especially John Martin, *The Portrait of John Milton* (Princeton, NJ: Princeton University Library, 1961). All Spanish to English translations are my own, unless otherwise stated, and all transcriptions of the Spanish originals maintain their orthographical features.

13. The 1736 edition of Paolo Rolli's Italian translation, *Il Paradiso perduto*, for example, has a dashing author portrait of "Giovanni Milton."

14. Lewalski, *Life of John Milton*, 226.

15. John Hale's English translation indicates the disapproval; John Hale, "Milton's Greek Epigram," *Milton Quarterly* 16, no. 1 (1982): 8–9.

16. Joseph Wittreich, email message to author, June 19, 2020. For other conjectures, see Emma Depledge, John Garrison, and Marissa Nicosia, introduction to *Making Milton: Print, Authorship, Afterlives* (Oxford: Oxford University Press, 2021), 1–14.

17. I use the term "mestizaje" well aware of its fraught nature. See Antonio Cornejo Polar, "*Mestizaje* and Hybridity," in *The Latin American Cultural Studies Reader*, ed. Ana del Sarto, Alicia Ríos, and Abril Trigo (Durham, NC: Duke University Press, 2004), 760–64; and Philip Swanson, *The Companion to Latin American Studies* (London: Routledge, 2014).

18. Paula Gunn Allen, "Border Studies," in *The Ethnic Canon: Histories, Institutions, and Interventions*, ed. David Palumbo-Liu (Minneapolis: University of Minnesota Press, 1995), 41. This can and should be fruitfully combined with Gordon Teskey's convincing argument about "delirious Milton," that "the creative artist communicates creativity to us so that we feel creative in return"; Teskey, *Delirious Milton* (Cambridge, MA: Harvard University Press, 2006), 32.

19. Collé, "Author Portraits of Milton, Authorship, and Canonization," in *Global Milton and Visual Art*, 143. For digital images of all four portraits, see *John Milton* (ca. 1629) by an unknown artist (NPG 4222), *John Milton* (1618) after Cornelius Johnson (Cornelius Janssen van Ceulen) (NPG D38831), *John Milton* (1645) by William Marshall (NPG D5262), and *John Milton* (1670) by William Faithorne (NPG 610), National Portrait Gallery, London, last modified 2022, https://www.npg.org.uk/.

20. Lewalski, *Life of John Milton*, 694n33; Helen Darbishire, *Early Lives* (London: Constable, 1932), 3.

21. Laura Knoppers refers to a much less common profile view of a Milton author portrait from a "unique 1680 copy" of "the 1645 poems"; John Milton, *Complete Works of John Milton, Volume II*, ed. Laura Knoppers (Oxford: Oxford University Press, 2008), lx, lxii.

22. For a brief, informative survey and interpretation of Milton's blindness, see John Rumrich, "The Cause and Effect of Milton's Blindness," *Texas Studies in Literature and Language* 61, no. 2 (2019): 95–115.

23. For author portraits of John Bunyan in a variety of media, see Nathalie Collé-Bak, "Bunyan's Pilgrims on Canvas, on Stage, in the Cellar, and in the Art Gallery," *Bunyan Studies* 15 (2011): 112–28, and Nathalie Collé, "'[W]hen Thou Dost Anneal in Glasse Thy Storie,'" *Bunyan Studies* 22 (2018): 84–113. For a visual representation of Bunyan made during his lifetime in a painting rather than book illustration, see *John Bunyan* (1684) by Thomas Sadler (NPG1311), National Portrait Gallery, London.

24. By contrast, the full-body painting of a sitting Milton with whitened eyes in the painting by Henry Fuseli, *Milton Dictating to His Daughter* (1794), highlights the blindness of the older blind Milton. See https://www.artic.edu/artworks/44739/milton-dictating-to-his-daughter.

25. For author portraits and illustrations in key Hispanophone translations of *Paradise Lost* from Spain, many of which circulated in Hispanoamerica, see Angelica Duran, *Milton among Spaniards* (Newark: University of Delaware Press, 2020).

26. John Milton, *El Paraíso perdido* (1868), trans. Aníbal Galindo (Ghent: Imprenta de Eug. Vanderhaegen, 1868), title page, vii. Vergara y Vergara voices his appreciation of the translation by calling it an "obra clásica" by "Doctor Galindo"; José María Vergara y Vergara, *Artículos literarios* (London: Juan M. Fonnegra, 1885), 256.

27. For more on the global circulation of Doré's illustrations of *Paradise Lost*, see Angelica Duran and Mario Murgia, "An Introduction, Things Visible," Hiroko Sano, "Doré's *Paradise Lost* and *Ukiyo-e* Prints," and Ana Elena González-Treviño, "*Paradise Lost* in Music Videos," in Duran and Murgia, *Global Milton and Visual Art*, 3–19, 75–88, and 117–38, respectively.

28. Special thanks to Joseph Wittreich for information on early versions of this interpretive Milton author portrait. The photo, taken in March 2020, is of the copy of *El Paraíso recobrado* at the Perry-Castaneda Library at the University of Texas at Austin.

29. John Milton, *El Paraíso recobrado*, trans. Julio Montés de Ocá (Mexico City: Tipografia "La Provincia," 1889), facing page 32.

30. Full-body renderings of Milton are common in paintings and other media beyond books. For a prefatory book illustration emphasizing that the image is a textual importation of a *cuadro* (painting), see after Mihály Munkácsy, *Milton, dictando á sus hijas el PARAISO PERDIDO* [*Milton Dictating "Paradise Lost" to his Daughters*] (1877)," on the publisher webpage for *Global Milton and Visual Art*, Features tab, web fig. 6C, https://rowman.com /ISBN/9781793617064/Global-Milton-and-Visual-Art. The frontispiece of the fourteenth edition of the Tonson *Paradise Lost* is a full-body rendering of Milton, flanked by Homer and Virgil, with a winged angel flying overhead and John Dryden's "Epigram on Milton" (1688) below the illustration; I am grateful to Milton's Cottage for access to their copy of this edition.

31. For author name usage in the Ibero-Spanish context, see Duran, *Milton among Spaniards*, 154–55, 159–61.

32. *La Ilustración mexicana* (Mexico City: Ignacio Cumplido, 1851–55), vol. 3 facing pages 184a, 184b, and 360.

33. *La Ilustración mexicana*, vol. 3 facing pages 156, 230, 444, and 664.

34. *La Ilustración mexicana*, vol. 1 facing page 172.

35. For the reception of italics as approximations of handwriting, see Paul C. Gutjhar and Megan Benton, *Illuminating Letters: Typography and Literary Interpretation* (Amherst: University of Massachusetts Press, 2001).

36. Gabriela Villanueva Noriega, "How Milton's Rebel Angels Landed in Nineteenth-Century Mexico," in Duran and Murgia, *Global Milton and Visual Art*, 247–66.

37. Zarco, in *La Ilustración mexicana*, 3:78.

38. For Zarco's health issues and his correspondence with Mexican President Benito Juárez, see José Santos Valdés, *Francisco Zarco Mateos* (Torreon, Mexico: Imprenta Mayagoitia, 1979).

39. Lewalski, *Life of John Milton*, 200. See also John Milton, *Complete Prose Works*, ed. Don M. Wolfe et al. (New Haven, CT: Yale University Press, 1953–82), 4:750–51.

40. Volume 3 possesses seventeen grayscale laminate inserts that share artistic features and refer to the surname "Decaen" and six that have no artist, engraver, or lithographer name. The two color-laminate inserts refer to another lithographer and bear a distinct appearance.

41. The translator of the 1858 *El Paraíso perdido* is the Mexican poet and politician Francisco Granados Maldonado. For more on Maldonado, as well as Galindo discussed earlier, see Mario Murgia, "Either in Prose or Rhyme," in *Milton in Translation*, ed. Angelica Duran, Islam Issa, and Jonathan R. Olson (Oxford: Oxford University Press, 2017), 279–92.

42. Montserrat Gali Boadella, "Artistas y artesanos franceses en el México independiente" (French Artists and Artisans in Independent Mexico), *Amérique Latine Histoire et Mémoire Online* 17 (2009): para. 37, https://journals.openedition.org/alhim/3180. Some indication that Decaen was incorporated into Mexican society is the varied use of his French names Joseph Antoine and Hispanophoned José Antonio and José A.

43. Zarco, in *La Ilustración mexicana*, 3:72.

44. Zarco, in *La Ilustración mexicana*, 3:73.

45. Zarco, in *La Ilustración mexicana*, 3:78–79.

46. Zarco, in *La Ilustración mexicana*, 3:79.

47. Zarco, in *La Ilustración mexicana*, 3:78.

48. Alphonse de Lamartine and unknown translator, in *La Ilustración mexicana*, 3:486.

49. Lamartine and unknown translator, in *La Ilustración mexicana*, 3:486–87.

50. Zarco, in *La Ilustración mexicana*, 3:601.

51. Zarco, in *La Ilustración mexicana*, 3:601.

52. José María Heredia, in *La Ilustración mexicana*, 3:619.

53. Thomas Gray, "Elegy Written in a Country Churchyard" (London: Castell Bros., [ca. 1887]), line 17; Thomas Gray and unknown translator, in *La Ilustración mexicana*, 3:641.

54. Special thanks to Mario Murgia for access to his 1951 copy and to Mario Murgia and Luis Bermilla for confirming in 2019 that Editorial Nacional is defunct.

55. The 1951 edition is the Hispanophone translation by Spain's Dionisio Sanjuan (orig. 1868), and the 1967 by Spain's Juan Escóiquiz (orig. 1812). For the Doré and Fernández de Lara illustrations, as well as the collaborative Hispanophone translation, in the 1967 *El Paraíso perdido*, see Angelica Duran, "Dore's Illustrations with *Cromos* in *El Paraíso perdido*," in Duran and Murgia, *Global Milton and Visual Art*, 96–115. For bricolage, see Ian Buchanan, *A Dictionary of Critical Theory*, last modified 2022, https://www.oxfordreference.com/. For mestizaje, see R. Douglas Cope, "Mestizaje," in David Carrasco, *Oxford Encyclopedia of Mesoamerican Culture* (New York: Oxford University Press, 2001), 291–96.

56. John Milton, *El Paraíso perdido* (1967), trans. Juan Escóiquiz and unknown adapter (Mexico City: Editorial Nacional, 1967), [IV].

57. Milton, *El Paraíso perdido* (1967), trans. Escóiquiz and unknown adapter, facing page VI, VI.

58. Milton, *El Paraíso perdido* (1967), trans. Escóiquiz and unknown adapter, VIII.

59. For visual representations of Milton dictating, see Anna Zsófia Kovács, "Milton Dictating to his Daughters: Varieties on a Theme from Füssli to Munkáscy," in *Milton through the Centuries*, ed. Gábor Ittzés and Miklós Péti (Budapest: L'Hartmattan, 2012), 322–37; and Angelica Duran, "John Milton and Disabilities Studies in Literature Courses," *Journal of Literary and Cultural Disability Studies* 6, no. 3 (2012): 327–39.

60. Examples include the bust *John Milton* (NPG 3781) by unknown artist, National Portrait Gallery, London.

61. Lewalski records Elizabeth Fisher as the maidservant in the Milton household in Milton's final days; Lewalski, *Life of John Milton*, 537.

62. Darbishire, *Early Lives*, 62, 73. For the handwriting of amanuenses, see William Poole's part 1 in John Milton, *The Complete Works of John Milton: Volume XI*, ed. William Poole (Oxford: Oxford University Press, 2008).

63. Teskey, *Delirious Milton*, 46.

64. For the author portrait as "suspended between two extremes: On the one hand, it tends towards likeness, and on the other, toward strangeness. On the one hand, it identifies, on the other, it distances," see Jean-Luc Nancy, *Portrait*, trans. Sarah Clift and Simon Sparks (New York: Fordham University Press, 2018), [vii].

65. John Milton, *The Reason of Church Government*, book 2 (1642), *JMRR*. Instrumental in my approach to and the very social context of Milton's works highlighted in this chapter is Bruno Latour, *Reassembling the Social* (Oxford: Oxford University Press, 2007).

CHAPTER 10

◠

Moved and Surprised by White Sin

Milton's Satanic Influence in Part 1 of
Pauline E. Hopkins's *Hagar's Daughter*

Reginald A. Wilburn

Novels of racial passing make inward moves on numerous readers by exposing audiences to the hell of living in a racist society where mixed-race characters of African descent are devalued as unworthy of equal citizenship rights. To explore and examine the range of reader-response techniques for producing these inward effects on readers is to cultivate a deeper appreciation for the numerous ways Milton's writing cause a variety of bodies to move with hell-raising urgency. Pauline E. Hopkins exposes this dynamic by addressing institutional racism as affronts to Black people's humanity in her serialized novel *Hagar's Daughter: A Story of Southern Caste Prejudice*. Published on the journalistic pages of the *Coloured American Magazine*—"America's first black literary periodical"—from March 1901 to March 1902, *Hagar's Daughter* draws on Milton's *Paradise Lost* to surprise (white) readers with the moral sins of white supremacist culture.[1]

Throughout the expositional stages of part 1 of the novel, Hopkins preaches a gospel of Black revolt by railing against the racism perpetrated against Black citizens in the antebellum United States. To expose the nation's historical turpitude, Hopkins adopts numerous storytelling devices, in particular the narrative of racial passing. Able to migrate across the color line because of their skin complexions, some of Hopkins's Black characters pursue transgressive routes toward a racial freedom denied them because of their race. If Milton's monist vitalism ascribes active movement to the embodied soul, as Rachel Trubowitz and Marissa Greenberg astutely argue in the introduction to this

259

volume, Hopkins's novel of racial passing provides a premiere example that evidences how this dynamic moves surprisingly across the annals of literary history. One notices these traces of Milton's monist sensibilities manifesting in the fictional lives of Eve's filial daughters in African American literature beginning in the late nineteenth century. *Hagar's Daughter* is part of this tradition. At the center of Hopkins's intertext of satanic influence is a Black Eve who, as a rewriting of the first mother of *Paradise Lost*, offers a poetic expression of certain Black women's existential travails at the dawn of the twentieth century. To contemporary readers open to being surprised by literary sins of white racism, Hopkins's Miltonic novel offers a chance to be moved in body, mind, and soul toward an elevated and embodied consciousness of human equality regardless of gender or race.

Contextualizing *Hagar's Daughter*

One of the more pronounced narrative devices Hopkins employs is raising Miltonic Hell. Cleverly appropriating lines, figures, and motifs from *Paradise Lost*, Hopkins not only shows the antebellum United States to be hellish for Black Americans but also extends Milton's influence to the twentieth-century African American novel. Preaching from Milton's epic as a type of secular-sacred intertext, Hopkins's novel moves receptions of *Paradise Lost* across literary history in ways that universalize it for Black and white audiences, yet with some major contextual divergences. Elizabeth McHenry, discussing the significance of nineteenth-century periodicals and African American literary societies for Black American audiences, offers notable insights concerning the value associated with these cultural institutions. As she shows, "newspapers were the primary sites of publication and sources of literary reading for African Americans in the nineteenth century."[2] By publishing *Hagar's Daughter* in the *Coloured American Magazine*, Hopkins signals that her literary project aims to meet the specific cultural needs of Black reading audiences. These needs included exposing Black audiences to the great works of the canon as a cultural backdrop for understanding the peculiar complexities associated with living in the United States while Black and Othered. The literary aim of the *Coloured American*, as explained in the May 1900 inaugural issue, was to promote "the higher culture of Religion, Literature, Science, Music, and Art of the Negro, universally."[3] By publishing works like *Hagar's Daughter*, the magazine likewise moved readers from either side of the color line to adopt different interpretive positionalities. As Mikko Tuhkanen asserts, Hopkins used this venue as an opportunity to "repeatedly admonish her readers to recognize the reincarnation of slavery's white supremacist ideology in the turn-of-the-century efforts at black disenfranchisement and the rise of racial violence."[4] In this regard, Hopkins's affective and cognitive moves on readers benefit from the author's selective decisions to appropriate particularized aspects of Milton's *Paradise Lost*. More than a century later, Hopkins's Miltonic serializing of plot continues to move audiences to adopt one of at least two interpretive perspectives: readers may affirm the interpretive righteousness of God as a storytelling device for espousing equal rights of Black citizenship; or they may be moved to condemn those whose immoral ideologies of racist cant ignominiously mark them as fallen and belonging to the devil's party, possibly without even knowing it. These Miltonic moves occur via a storytelling method wherein Hopkins shows signs of reveling in Milton by surprising new generations of astute intertextual readers.

Part 1 of the novel initiates the practice of moving readers with surprise through Hopkins's several appropriations from *Paradise Lost*. In addition to direct and allusive references, Hopkins also takes cues from *Paradise Lost* via its mode of Miltonic reader-response.[5] This mode works to surprise fallen audiences before exalting them to states of spiritual righteousness in matters pertaining to Black racial injustice. Not unlike the "Heav'nly Muse" (*PL*, 1.6) that Milton's epic voice petitions at the opening of *Paradise Lost*, Hopkins's narrator adopts an affective aesthetic that proves suitable to instructing and inspiring fallen readers of her times. That is, like Milton's epic narrator, Hopkins's narrator shows signs of aiming to "Illumin" (*PL*, 1.23) that which proves spiritually dark in the hearts and minds of fallen (white) readers. Illuminating these inward regions of readers' bodies and souls holds potential for "rais[ing] and support[ing]" (*PL*, 1.23) whatever might be regarded as depraved and low among Christian audiences who know the well justified ways of God.

Hagar's Daughter moves by the spirit of what can be regarded as an (in)visible strain of Miltonic influence. This strain of intertextual influence registers what has escaped detection by a majority of critics for more than a century. In other words, Milton has been lying hidden in plain sight relative to existing citational practices in scholarship. Throughout *Hagar's Daughter*, this (in)visibility of presence and influence moves across the textual body of Hopkins's novelistic text to tell a fictional migration story of racial passing across the color line. Told in two parts, these seemingly disjointed stories of racial passing focus on the lives of a series of differentiated yet interrelated characters. Novels of racial passing typically chronicle the tragic downfall and outcomes of certain disadvantaged African American characters possessing the fairest of phenotypical hues. Forces and stressors of racism pose problems for exceptionally fair and Black characters, who sometimes feel compelled to move down, along, or across the rigidly defined color line of their times by assuming white identities.

While a majority of Africanist characters know they are Black at the exposition stage of plot, others, like Hopkins's protagonist in part 1 of *Hagar's Daughter*, metaphorically fall into a knowledge of their Blackness belatedly, often in moments of terror-stricken surprise. Part of the terror that these tragic mulatta characters feel involves bearing the burden of having to live "under a regime of white supremacist ideology" that no longer affords them the entitlements of a social privilege they once enjoyed.[6] Regardless of the racial understandings characters like Hagar may have of themselves at a novel's exposition, their dilemma tends to motivate them to move fugitively across the color line. But these migrations seldom prove successful. Too often, tragic mulattas die by the denouement. These tragic endings ultimately mock the fugitive enterprise of daring to escape into whiteness while making distinct cognitive moves on the minds of fallen readers.

Hopkins's Bookmarking of Milton

Hopkins's Hagar figures as a symbolic variation of the tragic mulatta character in part 1 of the serial novel. Emily Clark explains the particularized dilemmas tragic mulatta characters endure in novels of racial passing. Such characters, she notes, are "sometimes enslaved, sometimes free, but always doomed by [their] racial liminality, which denies [them] a niche in a rigidly biracial world."[7] For Allyson Hobbs, racial passing symbolically connotes "an exile, sometimes chosen, sometimes not."[8] Crossing boundaries of race in this manner, Hobbs observes, constitutes one's "anxious decision to turn . . . back on a black racial identity and to claim to belong to a group to which one was not legally assigned."[9] Revelations of these characters' true, albeit socially constructed, racial identities often surprise readers. This affective reader-response aesthetic has potential for yielding audiences a much truer knowledge of the fictions associated with race as biologically determinable. These truer insights especially benefit from the

Miltonic surprises engineered by gifted and talented authors, like Hopkins, whose strategic use of satanic figures also are grounded in a poetics saturated with allusions to or echoes of Miltonic fallenness.

Hopkins surprises Miltonic readers with an interpoetic flair of satanic design too difficult for them to overlook or disregard. The earliest trace of Milton's (in)visible influential presence in the novel surfaces in an early chapter from part 1 after Hopkins has oriented readers to a setting rife with satanic hostility. Furthermore, this setting induces readers into a satanic orientation of expositional fallenness. A demonic setting augments this reader-response experience by prompting allusive recollections of Hell in book 1 of *Paradise Lost*. After appropriating a brief passage from book 1 of Milton's epic (*PL*, 1.752–57), Hopkins begins allusively troping with other satanic figures from the poem. Each subsequent allusion to the epic further places and rounds readers in a Miltonic state of mind. Collectively, they function as intertextual bookmarks of Black enlightenment that keep observant readers alert to the various ways Milton's influential presence moves across the literary body of Hopkins's text and on the minds, hearts, and souls of her readers as well.

Karla F. C. Holloway adopts the term "bookmark" to refer to an interpretive phenomenon for assessing influence in the African American literary tradition. Holloway notes the important "associations between texts and bodies" as instructional for the story "about black folk and reading that hasn't yet made it to our library shelves."[10] What Holloway identifies as a "missing text" in assessments of Black authors and the works they compose ultimately reveals an enlightened epistemology concerning literary influence. This missing text, she continues, "pronounce[s] some message about the one who carries" a given book either in public or privately.[11] Ignoring it amounts to overlooking the indelible imprints bookmarks are known to impress on the minds of reading authors. In part 1 of *Hagar's Daughter*, Milton's (in)visible influence not only strengthens Hopkins's role in this story by strengthening her intertextual engagement with the literary canon but also emphasizes the terrors associated with racial passing. Hopkins exposes these terrors on at least three interpretive grounds of Miltonic contention in the first section of the novel: setting, characterization, and diction.[12] Constructing her text on these Miltonic grounds can lead to elevating the consciousness of readers about the "deeply political and resonantly personal" roles bookmarks play in culturally evaluating and interpreting Black-authored works influenced by any number of literary traditions.[13]

Hopkins first bookmarks *Hagar's Daughter* with *Paradise Lost* by rewinding the plot back three decades and grounding the setting of the novel as analogous to Milton's Hell. The opening chapters of the novel "offer a microcosm of Hell," as Lois Brown explains.[14] Brown also accounts for Hopkins's decision to orient readers to a fallen US landscape by predating the historical present by forty years. According to Brown, Hopkins's "narrative incursions into the past" affirmed her "unwavering belief that such cultural study was vital to American social redemption."[15] Similarly, Colleen C. O'Brien avers that Hopkins "revisits the antebellum and Reconstruction periods to demand civil rights for African Americans during the Nadir."[16] Both critics' evaluative assessments of Hopkins's use of historical setting provide insightful contexts concerning the symbolic significance of the story's setting, which opens in 1860 and within a politically contentious area of South Carolina just before the start of the American Civil War. Hopkins's narrator explains the tyrannical context of this symbolic setting, noting that during this period "nothing short of a miracle could preserve the union of states so proudly proclaimed by the signers of the Declaration of Independence."[17] The temporal setting amplifies the tyrannical contexts associated with this debauched southern climate in which "the proslavery Democracy was drunk with rage at the prospect of losing control of the situation" (*Hagar's*, 3). This climate also proves hostile to Black people, since it entails "a system of mob-law and terrorism against all sympathizers with the despised party" of proslavery agitators (*Hagar's*, 4). The narrator further explains this system was inaugurated to the Negro's disadvantage. Blacks in the region "felt . . . no safety . . . beneath the Stars and Stripes, and, so feeling, sacrificed [their] home[s] and personal effects and fled to Canada" (*Hagar's*, 4). Descriptions like these depict a landscape of fallenness socially positioned on the verge of chaos, horror, and mutiny.

Threats of rebellion reign to so high a degree that even the spirit of heroic activism is mocked. Set at a historical moment of increasing antislavery agitation, the narrative description of the times reveals a nation headed for ruin. Chapter 1 of *Hagar's Daughter* is set in the South Carolina legislature. Hopkins's narrator describes how "debate in the Senate became fiery and dangerous as the crisis" of the slavery question gained preeminence among legislators (*Hagar's*, 6). In keeping with traditions of Black Miltonic reception in African American literature, Hopkins's narrative of the proceedings brings to mind the "congressional similes" in Frederick Douglass's *Narrative* and Sutton E. Griggs's appropriation of the Milton's epic near the end of

Imperium in Imperio.[18] At chapter's end, Hopkins's narrator apprises readers that Abraham Lincoln is elected president, which serves as "the signal for secession" and causes the southern landscape to "let loose the dogs of war" (*Hagar's*, 7). Chapter 2 meets the interpoetic challenge of accurately describing the southern landscape as hellish in design by appropriating Satan's poetry from *Paradise Lost*.[19] The chaos brought about by Abraham Lincoln's election and South Carolina's subsequent decision to secede from the Union evokes the satanic spirit of Milton's infernal council in book 2 of *Paradise Lost*. The streets resound with parading bands and "barrelhead orations from excited orators with more zeal than worth" (*Hagar's*, 7–8), even as slave traders, leading "gangs of slaves chained together like helpless animals destined for the slaughter-house . . . , [pause] in their hurried journey to participate in the festivities which ushered in the birth of the glorious Confederate States of America" (*Hagar's*, 8).[20] Yet ultimately, as Hopkins's narrator reveals, "Words cannot describe the scene" of villainy (*Hagar's*, 8). Only Milton's epic seems capable of accurately characterizing the landscape with the vividness Hopkins's storytelling prowess demands.

To compensate for this lack of descriptive accuracy, Hopkins bookmarks the novel with uncited quotations from *Paradise Lost*. This intertextual borrowing verbally paints the hellish scene of satanic fallenness Hopkins wishes readers to keenly visualize. It also requires readers to access and tap into a kind of "domain-specific knowledge" grounded in an interpretive recollection of the Hell Milton re-creates in his original poem.[21] For instance, Hopkins alludes to the rebel angels' debate in the "spacious hall" of Pandemonium, with its "Doric pillars overlaid / With golden architrave" (*PL*, 1.762, 714–15), when her narrator describes the riotous meeting of "leading Southern politicians" in a "magnificent hall of the St. Charles Hotel," a "vast hall . . . filled with tables which spread their snow-white wings to receive the glittering mass of glass, plate and flowers" (*Hagar's*, 13). Brown's literary biography of Hopkins, which offers the only discussion to date of Hopkins's engagement with Milton in *Hagar's Daughter*, identifies several incidents in the novel as Miltonic, including the episode at the St. Charles Hotel. Brown's assessment that the southern legislators' meeting is modeled "on the gathering in *Paradise Lost* where Satan convenes his fallen angels" is strengthened when Hopkins describes the series of seditious orators and their raucous audience, all calling for the continuation of slavery, as "Pandemonium" (*Hagar's*, 18).[22] In the inaugural speech delivered in this southern hellish capital, the

Honorable Robert Toombs sounds like Milton's seditious angels when he calls on his crew to "rive [their antagonists] from the temple of liberty, or pull down its pillars and involve him in a common ruin" (*Hagar's*, 14).[23] Toombs continues to rail against the federal government, which he charges has passed "into the traitorous hands of the black Republican party," and vows to "conquer" and "subdue" "these demons in human form" (*Hagar's*, 15). Next, Jefferson Davis, whom the narrator introduces as "the savior of the South," addresses the raucous audience as an "assembly of patriots" who will "lead the march of the gallant band who will give us the liberty we crave" (*Hagar's*, 16). His seditious advocacy echoes "the role that Milton gives to Satan as an equivalent or narrative double of the Son."[24] In total, eight orators address the legislators, each advocating his respective support of slavery, rebellion, and secession from the Union, in a litany of demonic speakers evocative of the debate in Milton's Hell.[25] Hopkins's catalog of "epic villains" and their infernal ideologies pave the way for more intense intertextual engagements with *Paradise Lost* as the satanic plot continues to unfold.[26]

Bookmarking her novel with this Miltonic framing device facilitates Hopkins's efforts to make greater cognitive and affective moves on readers. Her most astute intertextual readers will find themselves primed and moved to witness Milton's allusive presence continually reverberating throughout the remainder of the expositional plot. They also will feel the shifts in narrative style that emphasize Hopkins's use of satanic characterization. Moreover, as Brown remarks, Hopkins extends her tropological practice of Miltonic engagement by using numerous "references to Hell and to the fall of Satan to segue into the introductions of the novel's primary villains."[27] These satanic introductions not only instigate inward moves on the hearts and minds of readers but also cause the novel's first Eve-like protagonist to migrate along and across the color line to tragic depths of social degradation. Hopkins's trio of villains—St. Clair, Isaac, and Ellis—contribute to Hagar's metaphorical fallenness as a by-product of the novelist's "intricate character development."[28] Their presence and impact on the plot subsequently render Hagar in the intertextual image of a racially re-created variation of Milton's Eve.

St. Clair Enson qualifies as Hopkins's premiere villain in part 1 of the novel. The narrator's myriad satanic epithets make it intertextually clear that St. Clair is analogous to Milton's Satan as an expression of a modern "antebellum devil."[29] He is "wild and self-willed," "a terror to the God-fearing community where he lived," and possesses "the diabolical beauty of Satan himself" (*Hagar's*, 20–21). The twinning of these poetic conceits—Satan's diabolical energy and his prefallen beauty—amounts to a poetic act of "satanic creation," for St. Clair, like Milton's infernal hero, dares to "re-create himself in a different image" of self-authored begottenness.[30] Along this axis of Miltonic poetics, Hopkins's St. Clair also echoes Milton's "Artificer of fraud" by committing infernal deeds while "under saintly show" (*PL*, 4.121–22). Readers encounter St. Clair at a moment when he finds himself in dire economic straits. When he learns that his older brother Ellis is betrothed and therefore set to secure their family's wealth, St. Clair resolves to return home to "see this fair woman who had come to blast his hopes and steal his patrimony for her children" (*Hagar's*, 23). The satanic tenor of this decision is driven home by Isaac, St. Clair's slave. As St. Clair considers his return, Isaac astutely reads his face, which "grew black with a frown of rage that for the time completely spoiled the beauty women raved over" (*Hagar's*, 23) in a manner similar to Satan's shifting countenance at the opening of book 4 of *Paradise Lost*. In fact, Isaac, remarking to himself in Black dialect, declares: "Marse St. Clair never look dat a way widout de debbil himself am broked loose" (*Hagar's*, 24). These demonic associations add greater satanic dimension to Hopkins's strategy of characterizing St. Clair as an echoic composite of Milton's Satan. Equally important, Isaac can so readily identify St. Clair's demonic nature because he too closely resembles his owner's character himself. As the narrator explains, "one might have seen the lurking deviltry of a spirit kindred to his [Isaac's] master's" (*Hagar's*, 28). As the phrase "spirit kindred" suggests, theirs constitutes a relationship bound by poetic fallenness with St. Clair functioning as a satanic origin or author of Isaac's own devilish character.

Hopkins's emphasis on Isaac's and St. Clair's demonic dispositions occurs at thematic variance with the introduction of Hopkins's first Eve-like protagonist in chapter 4. Hagar is eighteen years of age when readers first encounter her character. According to the plot, she returns home to the Maryland setting after "a four year's sojourn at the North in a young ladies' seminary" (*Hagar's*, 32). A woman seminarian, Hagar enters the plot as a kind of supernal antithesis to St. Clair's and Isaac's devilish characters. Chapter 4 also introduces audiences to St. Clair's brother, Ellis. Hagar and Ellis meet, are smitten by one another, and experience a budding romance. Their romance moves readers to see both characters as allusive reincarnations of Adam and Eve in Paradise. Interestingly, Hopkins constructs Hagar's Eve-like character by relying upon white beauty norms. Hopkins employs this construction as a poetic strategy for tricking unsuspecting readers into believing Hagar is white. Surprising readers through this trickster method registers as a variation of Milton's poetry that causes audiences to fall via errors of racial interpretation.

Surprised into White Sin

Ellis falls by his own errors of racial interpretation upon seeing Hagar initially. Hagar's face "haunt[s]" Ellis even as he imagines possessing it (*Hagar's*, 35). Recalling her physical beauty in a narrative form reminiscent of a poetic blazon, Ellis describes Hagar's

> pure creamy skin, the curved crimson lips ready to smile,—lips sweet and firm,—the broad, low brow, and great, lustrous, long-lashed eyes of brilliant black—soft as velvet, and full of light with the earnest, cloudless gaze of childhood; and there was heart and soul and mind in this countenance of a mere girl. Such beauty as this was a perpetual delight to feast the eyes and charm the senses—aye, to witch a man's heart from him; for here there was not only the glory of form and tints, but more besides,—heart that could throb, soul that could aspire, mind that could think. (*Hagar's*, 35)

This passage, especially its references to "pure creamy skin . . . full of light," leads readers to assume Hagar is white. In the absence of any additional context cues to the contrary, such an interpretation of Hagar's characterization seems logical. Yet, and as Martha Cutter argues elsewhere, "someone who appears to be a 'good reader' may be fooled by racial ideologies and generic conventions that he or she takes for granted."[31] Indeed, women possessing beauty like Hagar's have long been valorized in Western literature for meeting standards of whiteness. This history clarifies the playful deceit of Hopkins's decision to withhold the Eve-like protagonist's Black racial identity from unsuspecting readers.

This narrative tactic facilitates a central strategy of surprising readers about the instability of race and the flawed certitudes and disadvantaged suppositions that epistemologies of ignorance advance—a strategy that anticipates Stanley Fish's reader-response theory concerning *Paradise Lost* and its affective impact on fallen readers. Anticipating Fish's belief that "the only defense against verbal manipulation (or appearances) is a commitment that stands above the evidence of things that are seen," Ellis's blazon offers a lesson in reading race with greater critical awareness.[32] Readers, should they initially err by believing Hagar is white, fall by being less attuned to those errors in language operations that falsely signify race through visual cues alone. Hopkins's unfolding plot soon exposes that such orientations to the fictions represented in language can prove flawed, limiting, or fallen as is the case when initially misinterpreting Hagar's racial identity. If, throughout *Surprised by Sin*, Fish justifies Milton's purpose in *Paradise Lost* as that of educating "the reader to an awareness of his position and responsibilities as a fallen man," Hopkins re-creates this dynamic by inducing audiences to misinterpret Hagar as white.[33]

Chapter 4 primarily "explores a Southern paradise that is akin to Eden," whereas the next two chapters emphasize what Brown recognizes as "incursions into this earthly heaven by devilish forces."[34] Not long after Ellis's blazon, Hopkins presents Hagar in a manner reminiscent of Milton's Eve. When Hagar leaves the house "for the shadow of the trees," for example, she reclines and "let[s] down the long braids of her hair" which fall "over the sides of the hammock and [sweep] the top of the long, soft grass" (*Hagar's*, 36). Like Milton's Eve, who "tresses wore / Disheveld, but in wanton ringlets wav'd" (*PL*, 4.305–6), which Stephen Dobranski has discussed at length, Hagar possesses a lengthy skein of hair that seems to join her with the paradisal landscape.[35] Hopkins enhances this Miltonic recall by describing Hagar and Ellis as "favor[ing] children of the gods all that long, happy summer" (*Hagar's*, 39), an allusion to Milton's description of Adam and Eve: in "their looks divine / The image of their glorious Maker shone" (*PL*, 4.291–92), and "the goodliest man of men since borne / His Sons, the fairest of her Daughters *Eve*" (*PL*, 4.324–25). The chapter concludes with Hagar and Ellis as a married couple. When Hagar gives birth to their first child, a daughter, Ellis esteems her as a "picture of sweet womanhood," as "Eve's perfect daughter" (*Hagar's*, 46), in blunt reprise of the divine first mother in *Paradise Lost*.

This estate of matrimonial paradise erodes in subsequent chapters, however, because of the demonic interference of St. Clair and Isaac. Isaac arrives at the married couple's home, his shadow falling "across the doorsill" (*Hagar's*, 41). He is followed by his enslaver, the very mention of whose return to Enson Hall casts "the first shadow" to befall the newlywed couple "since the beginning of their honeymoon" (*Hagar's*, 47). St. Clair arrives at Hagar and Ellis's home accompanied by yet another demonic accomplice, the slave trader Mr. Walker.

270   Moved and Surprised by White Sin

Their arrival at Enson Hall sets Hopkins's satanic plot into acceler-
ated motion. Of particular note, through Walker, readers learn Hagar
indeed is Black and a former slave. The novel suggests she has forgotten this critical aspect of her past, and the revelation causes Hopkins's
Eve-like daughter to move fugitively along the color line with urgent
expediency and, presumably, to her death.

With St. Clair in attendance, Walker explains to Ellis that roughly
fourteen years prior he "bought a slave child from a man in St. Louis"
(*Hagar's*, 52). He subsequently loaned her to a white friend on account
of "not being able to find a ready sale" for the slave girl due to her
white complexion (*Hagar's*, 52). Walker asserts his understanding that
his former slave presently resides at the Enson estate, the friend having
"passed" the girl "off on the community here as their own" (*Hagar's*,
53). Even as Walker explains that he has come to reclaim his "stolen
property," he exclaims to Ellis a shocking accusation: "and you have
married her" (*Hagar's*, 53; original emphasis).

During this conversation, which upends the dialogue between Adam
and "*Raphael*, the sociable Spirit" (*PL*, 5.221) in books 5–8 of Milton's epic, Hagar descends the stairs and enters the living room. Walker
reminds Hagar of her childhood experience of being bought by him
and lent to the Sargeants. She "hears the course laugh of the rough,
brutal slave trader," scans the room to search Ellis's face, and then
shrieks and sinks "fainting to the floor" (*Hagar's*, 54). Walker's surprising revelation thus not only undermines the Edenic existence of
marital bliss Hagar recently knew but also induces Hopkins's Eve-like
daughter's physical fall and her descent into temporary madness. Both
results plunge Hagar into states of satanic anguish that are anchored
allusively on the demonic grounds of Milton's Hell.

Hopkins's readers experience metaphorical fallenness alongside
Hagar when they too are surprised by the revelation that she is Black
and a slave, not a whitened version of Milton's Eve of *Paradise Lost*.
In this way, Hopkins "worries" the figure of Milton's Eve, translating
its appropriation in an interpoetic manner evocative of the intertextual technique Cheryl Wall attributes to a certain sisterhood of African
American women writers.[36] The concept of "worrying the line," as
examined by Wall, refers to genealogical "re-visions" of texts and figures
produced by African American women writers who focus on "points of
intersection between trajectories of metaphorical lineage and literary
tradition."[37] When artistic wordsmiths create literature with an atten-
tiveness to these powers of signification, they engage in a sophisticated
elaboration of language as a prized currency of culture. This literary

Reginald A. Wilburn 271

currency bonds Black women writers into an Africanist sisterhood. Wall, appropriating the musical term of Black expressivity, theorizes the concept of worrying the line to announce and document "metaphors of kinship" that illustrate Black women's familial relations to one another.[38] Her theory also bonds different groups of Black women writers across the annals of time via their various techniques of "revis[ing] and subvert[ing] the conventions of the genres they appropriate."[39] These re-visions often also "rewrite canonical texts in order to give voice to stories those texts did not imagine."[40] Hopkins participates in this dynamic practice through her Eve-like characterizations of Hagar, worrying a distinct (color) line in Miltonic tradition that has yet to be theorized fully in relation to African American fiction by Black women.

Worrying this line in African American women's writing promises to move readers by surprising them with the fallenness inherent in a cultural language and a literary tradition that define, signify, and interpret race with interpretive commands of accuracy. Hopkins's revelation that Hagar is Black creates a "duh" or an "a ha" moment for readers of Milton's epic as well. With no racial cues to contradict a reading of Adam and Eve in *Paradise Lost* as anything but white, it seems illogical to conceive Milton's portrayal of the first parents as racial Others. Receptions of Milton's Eve as white seem likely, particularly considering the epic writer wrote to dignify his country at a time when his nation continued investing in the transatlantic slave trade. And, as a white Christ survives as an orthodox image of the messiah in post-Reformation English Christianity, how could that interpretive dynamic work differently relative to Milton's canonical portrayals of Adam and Eve in his epic? Hopkins, by worrying the line of tradition with respect to iconic biblical figures, surprises readers by rendering some of her Black characters with the fairest of skin tones as slightly darker versions of the Eve he re-creates in *Paradise Lost*. This narrative technique seems designed to lead readers to adopt flawed interpretations of Hopkins's characters. When readers fall by the sins of these flawed interpretations, their errors ultimately reveal the fictions of race and the fallen stories people sometimes tell about certain moving bodies that hegemonic culture too often has deemed and defined as inferior.

Miltonic Movements in *Hagar's Daughter*

After surprising readers about the fictions of race that sometimes cause Black bodies to move across the color line, Hopkins advances the plot by bookmarking the novel with additional allusions to *Paradise Lost*. Several paragraphs subsequent to Hagar's fainting spell, Walker demands six thousand dollars from Ellis in payment for Hagar and the couple's infant daughter. Although Ellis pays the requested amount and the Enson home resumes the sanctity of quietude it once possessed, "happiness," according to the narrator, "fled forever" (*Hagar's*, 56). The concluding chapters of part 1 of *Hagar's Daughter* (chaps. 6–8) constitute a satanic exposition full of intertextual allusions to Milton's epic.

One passage in particular metaphorically characterizes Hagar's response to the knowledge of her Black racial identity as a condition suggestive of satanic fallenness. Aunt Henny discovers Hagar "crouched upon the floor . . . , writhing and screaming" (*Hagar's*, 57), a frenzied state of shock and madness that recalls Satan's "internal hell as a dynamic state" of discomfort.[41] Yet Hagar's mental woes and bodily fits evince a "sutur[ing of] madness and blackness together" that Therí Pickens theorizes as "black madness/mad blackness."[42] Pickens's theory usefully dismantles "ideological constructions of white supremacy where blackness is considered synonymous with madness or the prerequisite for creating madness."[43] In an earlier passage from book 1 of *Paradise Lost*, for instance, Milton's epic narrator describes the devils' hellish suffering as "Regions of sorrow, doleful shades, where peace / And rest can never dwell, hope never comes" (*PL*, 1.65–66). Beelzebub, too, describes Hell as a "gloomy deep" (*PL*, 1.152). These poetic snippets suggest that Milton's Hell serves as a triggering geographical site for Milton's devils. This sorrowful and doleful region causes Milton's devils to experience feelings akin to posttraumatic stress. Hagar likewise experiences bouts of (di)stress. For instance, in recalling her childhood past, she ruminates on the thought of her enslaved mother, "wonder[ing] that the very thought did not strike her dead" (*Hagar's*, 57). Thereafter, Hagar contemplates "the black abyss into which the day's events had hurled her, leaving her there to grovel and suffer the tortures of the damned" (*Hagar's*, 57). This passage characterizes Hagar's fall into the knowledge of her racial identity as synonymous with being hurled into an abyss of black hellishness. It also strengthens Hopkins's bookmarking engagement with Milton's satanic epic by implying Hagar is doomed to an existence of hellish enslavement along and within the color line of Black racial identity. Hagar's hellish enslavement performs an intertextual reprise of an early moment in book 1 of Milton's epic.

According to the epic narrator's reading of the satanic landscape in *Paradise Lost*, "Eternal Justice had prepared" Hell "For those rebellious" denizens who languish in "their prison ordained / In utter darkness, [with] their portion set / As far removed from God and light of heav'n" (*PL,* 1.70–73). Hagar experiences an equally horrid form of satanic abjection upon understanding herself as tragically Black in a world that demonizes her as a racial outcast unworthy of equal citizenship rights. Fallen metaphorically by standards of whiteness, Hagar is cognizant that her skin tone mocks her existence. Nor will it save her in this fallen world. Relative to "her education, beauty, [and] refinement," Hagar queries, "what did they profit her now?" (*Hagar's,* 57). These thoughts of woe and desolation explain why Hagar, like Satan and his fallen angelic peers at the opening of book 1, lie prone in servile defeat, "crouched still lower in the dust of utter humiliation" (*Hagar's,* 57). Interestingly, Hagar and Milton's devils share the despair of being crouched in hellish abjection. Hopkins's diction and the extent to which she characterizes her protagonist's hellish psychological sufferings combine to strengthen symbolic ties between both literary works.

Hagar undergoes a fit of "black madness/mad blackness" shortly after musing on her lamentable condition as a degraded and enslaved Black subject. Examining "her features in the mirror," she becomes horrified by her reflection (*Hagar's,* 57). "Even to her prejudiced eyes," the narrator relates, Hagar remains unable to observe "a trace of the despised chattel" that the social customs of her time ascribe to those with Black skin tones (*Hagar's,* 57). In maddened disgust, she shatters the mirror with a single blow, and as it splinters into "a thousand tiny particles," she considers the frenzied conflict of having to "expect [Ellis] to forget all his prejudices, which were also her own" (*Hagar's,* 58). Only that morning Hagar was Ellis's wife. But in an instantaneous moment, Walker's racial revelations legally work to define this fair and Black daughter of Eve as Ellis's matrimonial "slave, his concubine!"—a redefinition that resonates with the "horrible fatality that had named her Hagar" (*Hagar's,* 58). This cruel poetic irony instigates Hopkins's interpoetic decision to bookmark Hagar's fallen state with *Paradise Lost* by appropriating lines of blank verse reminiscent of Milton's "grand" literary style.[44]

In the midst of her maddened frenzy, Hagar suddenly remembers she is named after the biblical character whose tragic story appears in Genesis 16:1–16 and again in Genesis 21:9–21. Names and naming are especially significant to this portion of Genesis: affirming the covenant with Abram and Sarai, God renames them Abraham and Sarah (Gen. 17:5, 15). Framing this narrative of origins—Christian exegesis interprets Jesus as the fulfillment of Abraham and Sarah's genealogical and covenantal union—is the story of the Hebrew couple's "Egyptian" (Gen. 16:1) bondswoman, Hagar. In naming her Eve-like protagonist

Hagar, Hopkins draws on this biblical story as a racial-cultural analog to African American experience. The result is to surprise readers with the roots of white sin in the foundational narratives of Christianity. Hopkins's Hagar, like Black readers of the novel at the time it appeared in the *Coloured American*, knows too well the injurious impact of racist ideologies that, despite the official end of slavery in the United States, restrict Black peoples' freedoms and especially Black women's rights of citizenship. For these reasons one is apt to find different African American authors troping with the biblical Hagar as an interpoetic expression of Black female subjectivity.[45]

Hopkins, like numerous African American writers, tropes with this tradition by assigning her Eve-like protagonist the name of her biblical precursor and namesake in Genesis. In doing so, Hopkins performs a comparative raced reading of biblical scripture that is two-toned in its symbolic appropriation of Milton's Eve. On the one hand, Hopkins's Hagar bears an intertextual resemblance to the first mother in *Paradise Lost* simply because chapter 3 of the novel describes her as a perfect, white, and narcissistic reflection of Eve in a literary work already bookmarked with Milton's epic. On the other hand, Hopkins's protagonist, in addition to being aware of her biblical namesake, also performs her intellectual cognizance of the sorrows associated with her forerunner in scriptural tradition. This recognition generates a subsequent recall of *Paradise Lost* within a turn-of-the-century work of serialized fiction that Milton criticism deserves to be cognizant of.

In the same novelistic passage where Hagar laments her woeful association with her Egyptian precursor from Genesis, she remembers a poem about the biblical slave by Eliza Jane Poitevent Holbrook Nicholson. A poet, journalist, and subsequent editor of her deceased husband's newspaper, the *New Orleans Picayune*, Nicholson published two poems that retell stories about heroic women from the Bible. Her poem "Hagar" takes the viewpoint of the Egyptian slave.[46] Hagar castigates Abraham for banishing her to the wilderness and refusing to leave Sarah, even as she champions her love and servitude to Abraham. Rather than pandering to a disposition of pitiful sentiment, that is, Hagar expresses resilience. Nicholson's poem culminates in a stanza that expresses Hagar's defiance of the god that the biblical couple serve:

> Farewell! I go, but Egypt's mighty gods
> Will go with me, and my avengers be.
> And in whatever distant land your god,
> Your cruel god of Israel, is known,

Reginald A. Wilburn

> There, too, the wrongs that you have done this day
> To Hagar and your first-born,
> Shall waken and uncoil themselves, and hiss
> Like adders at the name of Abraham. (quoted in *Hagar's*, 58)

Because Nicholson innovates the retelling of the biblical story in a poetic form of blank verse, when Hopkins's Hagar recalls it, *Hagar's Daughter* registers another intertextual bookmark wherein Milton's influential presence becomes visible. Indeed, Hopkins's appropriation of Nicholson's "Hagar" represents a triple-stranded type of Miltonic bookmark. First, the literary event of appropriation simultaneously supplies alert readers a "missing text" of influence, a kind that Holloway has theorized as "calling attention to [twentieth-century African American authors'] accomplished mastery of books."[47] Inasmuch as this type of bookmarking recognizes Hopkins's mastery of literary text, the signifier likewise reveals the author's protagonist as equally gifted in belles lettres. Second, because Nicholson composes her biblical poem in lines of unrhymed blank verse, her style of versification instantly implicates Milton as a source of influence. Joseph Wittreich argues Milton lent to Western literary tradition a new respect for the poetic rhythm of unrhymed blank verse. He also contends that "by the third decade of the eighteenth century, blank verse became established as 'the idiom of opposition' in English poetry."[48] Portraying Hagar as a kind of heroic outcast and rebel against Abraham's God inflects this instance of storytelling with greater Miltonic resonance. Third, Nicholson adopts this literary form in a work proclaiming the dissident sentiments of an enslaved Egyptian woman. By railing against the god of her enslavers, Nicholson's Hagar equally registers as both a feminist outcast and a rebellious Eve.

Hopkins's appropriation of Nicholson's poem bookmarks her serialized novel with Milton in other allusive ways. Borrowing the final eight lines of Nicholson's poem amplifies the tenor of rebellious, self-willed fallenness expressed in the peroration of the appropriated literary work. On the one hand, these lines convey the biblical Hagar's resolve to follow her Hebrew enslavers to "whatever distant lands [their] god . . . is known." On the other hand, Nicholson's Hagar refuses to worship their "cruel god." Instead, she will continue serving her Egyptian gods while vowing to spread a gospel of rebellion against her enslavement and her son's disenfranchisement. As Nicholson's Hagar proclaims, she will shout the wrongs of her oppressors until they "waken and uncoil . . . and hiss / Like adders" at the very mention of the Hebrew patriarch's name. The serpentine allusions used in this line privilege satanic sedition against the Hebrews and their deity. Nicholson's Hagar proclaims this seditious gospel in satanic language where, as Danielle St. Hilaire theorizes, meaning resides in "the positive expression of a negative relationship."[49] Speaking in the satanic tongues of fallen angels, Nicholson's Hagar preaches a racial gospel of Black revolt while energizing the narrative moment of Miltonic appropriation in Hopkins's novel.

Other Miltonic bookmarks surface in subsequent paragraphs, contributing to Hopkins's aesthetic of making cognitive and affective moves on readers' bodies. These engagements with Milton continue to surprise readers with the characters' satanic fallenness. In one instance Ellis bangs on Hagar's door and she admits him with a physical expression of abject lowliness: "overpowered" by, and laden in, "bitter shame, Hagar shrinks from Ellis' sight . . . with clasped hands and hanging head" (Hagar's, 59). As Hagar comports herself as "a slave before her master," Ellis groans and observes to himself, "How changed, too . . . a blight had even fallen upon her glorious beauty" (Hagar's, 59), a resounding echo of Satan's words to Beelzebub: "But O how fall'n! how chang'd / From him, who in the happy Realms of Light / Cloth'd with transcendent brightness didst out-shine / Myriads though bright" (PL, 1.84–87). Emphasizing the white sin embedded in this appropriation of Paradise Lost, Hopkins's narrator explains: "He who had always upheld the institution as a God-given principle of humanity and Christianity, suddenly beheld his idol, stripped of its gilded trappings, in all its filthiness. Then in his heart he cursed slavery" (Hagar's, 59).

Hopkins's most astute intertextual readers will interpret almost instantly that these sentiments expose Ellis as being moved on and by a Miltonic spirit of satanic recognizance. That is, Hagar's ontological transformation from a perfect Eve-like daughter to an enslaved subject correlates with the bookmarks that Ellis's own understandings of Milton's poem have left on his intellectual powers of intertextual recall, perception, and interpoetic application. Surprised by Hagar's metamorphosis, Ellis interprets what he sees through a snippet of Milton's familiar epic. This satanic recall also produces the intertextual effect of equating Hagar and her fallen condition with Milton's devils. As a result of these intertextual associations, Ellis sees his enslaved wife anew: no longer "Eve's perfect daughter" (Hagar's, 46), Hagar now resembles the first mother's fallen image. This change in Ellis's opinion of Hagar reveals his own fallen attitudes about Black racial identity. It also exposes the grave material implications for racially informed readings of Hagar's body and other Eve-like daughters in Black literary tradition, who, through no fault of their own, suffer the injustice of being labeled as metaphorically fallen. Mikko Tuhkanen argues that Hagar finds herself "in the dark abyss of invisible blackness after her unconscious passing has been read by the slave trader Walker."[50] This relocation from paradise to abyss registers her abject status, but it also compels her to act. As part 1 of *Hagar's Daughter* moves toward its conclusion, Hagar moves with expedient urgency relative to her new positionality as a Black woman.

The three concluding chapters to part 1 of *Hagar's Daughter* chronicle Hagar's fugitive movements across and along the color line. When Ellis renews his "devot[ion]" to Hagar, the couple plans to remarry and flee to Europe, far away from the "shame of public ostracism and condemnation" in the southern United States where news of their miscegenous "sin in innocence—if sin it be"—will surely become public (*Hagar's*, 60–61). Ellis departs to settle these affairs, leaving Hagar in "an agony of hope and fear" (*Hagar's*, 62). At this point in the plot, St. Clair returns in the form of an origin story. St. Clair, the reader is surprised to learn, is the product of a rape committed on a human woman by a devil (*Hagar's*, 63–64). Even as this origin story recalls the incestuous violence of Satan, Sin, and Death in book 3 of *Paradise Lost*, it reveals the similarly demonic roots of white racism. As Aunt Henny relays, the devil rapes St. Clair's mother because Uncle Ned, a slave and conjure man, made a deal with him: to prevent getting whipped by an overseer, Uncle Ned promises to serve alongside the devil, including arranging rape. Poetically authorized by the sins of slavery, St. Clair naturally manifests as a filial progeny of the satanic vices that give him demonic beingness in the fictional world created by Hopkins in her novel of racial passing.

St. Clair's backstory serves other functions relative to Hopkins's designs of satanic storytelling. Beyond offering a rationale for St. Clair's satanic personality, it allows narrative time for Ellis to conduct business affairs associated with the fugitive plan of escape he devises for his family's benefit. But his plans do not materialize. Ellis is found dead near the wharf at the edge of the garden where St. Clair was conceived. The mysterious nature of Ellis's death makes it easy for St. Clair to seduce members of the community into believing his brother, unable to cope with the realities of his wife's and daughter's racial identities, committed suicide.

But Hagar is unconvinced, and after Ellis's funeral and burial, she descends from her bedroom and accuses St. Clair of her husband's murder. St. Clair "recoil[s]" from Hagar's accusation as she continues to berate him and his "twin demon" Walker, who "brought home the story that broke [her husband's] heart" (*Hagar's*, 70). In response to Hagar's satanic allegations, St. Clair grants Walker permission to sell her and her infant into slavery at the slave market on the grounds of the nation's capital. Once transported there and on the night before she is to be sold, Hagar escapes and makes her way "to the forests of Arlington Heights" in nearby Virginia (*Hagar's*, 73–74). Her route takes her across a bridge, and when she notices that pursuers await her on either end, Hagar casts her eyes to heaven, springs over the bridge's railing, and sinks beneath the rolling dark waters below.

Part 1 of *Hagar's Daughter* concludes with this tragic ending. In part 2, without mentioning the immediate aftermath of Hagar's perilous jump or referencing her by name for more than twenty-five chapters, Hopkins tells an entirely new story about the lives of elite white Washingtonians, or so we are led to believe. This seemingly unrelated narrative leaves audiences suspended in a state of animated fallenness. Milton's Satan knows this feeling all too well, of course. Only toward the end of part 2 of *Hagar's Daughter* does Hopkins settle readers—albeit on new grounds of contention—when she reveals three of her major women characters are Black and passing as white in the elite social circles of Washington, DC. Most surprising, two of these women are none other than Hagar, who goes by the name Estelle, and her daughter Jewel. Neither character knows the true nature of their filial bonds with one another for most of part 2 of the novel. Yet Hagar, having moved across the racial color line and changed her name, reclaims her status as a type of perfect daughter of Eve. At the same time, as Estelle, which name, like her daughter's, evokes the starry brightness of Lucifer, embodies the fallen knowledge of her Blackness. And this fallen knowledge leads Hopkins once again to "change / [Her novel's] Notes to Tragic" (*PL*, 9.5–6): *Hagar's Daughter* ends with readers learning of Jewel's death.

Throughout the two parts of *Hagar's Daughter*, Hopkins remains steadfastly devoted to telling migration stories about race and the color line that her characters move along and pass over. Possessing Miltonic mastery, Hopkins bookmarks her fictional work of racial passing with *Paradise Lost*. Her translation of Milton's satanic epic across space and time works to convey the tragic perils confronting fair complexioned Black women whose white and unsuspecting paramours regard them as "perfect" (*Hagar's*, 43) Eve-like daughters. More than cheap poetic novelty, Hopkins's literary strategy works to surprise readers by the sins of white racism. These sins, as racial passing novels characteristically show, lead certain Black characters and especially Black women characters to affective and physical movement in an effort to (re)claim their freedom and personhood. The tragic ends that these characters meet acknowledge for (Black) readers of the *Coloured American Magazine* the hellish setting that proves so hostile to Eve's Black daughters in African American literary tradition. Just as importantly, they work to move today's (white) readers toward the self-reflection and enlightenment ascribed to Milton's epic—cognitive and spiritual effects that are still necessary to achieve racial and gender justice at the present time.

Notes

1. Lois Brown, *Pauline Elizabeth Hopkins: Black Daughter of the Revolution* (Chapel Hill: University of North Carolina Press, 2008), 2.

2. Elizabeth McHenry, *Forgotten Readers: Recovering the Lost History of African American Literary Societies* (Durham: Duke University Press, 2002), 12.

3. "Announcement," *Coloured American Magazine* 1, no. 1 (May 1900): n.p.

4. Mikko Tuhkanen, "'Out of Joint': Passing, Haunting, and the Time of Slavery in *Hagar's Daughter*," *American Literature* 79, no. 2 (2007): 337.

5. Appropriations of Milton also surface in several of Hopkins's nonfictional writings in the *Coloured American Magazine*. Combined, these journalistic writings evidence a knowledge and command of Milton exceeding beyond that of a simplistic signifier of Hopkins's imaginative fancy. Rather, they attest that she wrote herself in good literary company with the likes of David Walker, Frederick Douglass, William Wells Brown, Frances Harper, and Anna Julia Cooper.

6. Gary L. Lemons, "Skinwalking and Color Linecrossing: Teaching Writing Against Racism," in *Race in the College Classroom: Pedagogy and Politics*, ed. Bonnie TuSmith and Maureen T. Reddy (New Brunswick, NJ: Rutgers University Press, 2002), 279.

7. Emily Clark, "The Tragic Mulatto and Passing," in *The Palgrave Handbook of the Southern Gothic*, ed. Susan Castillo Street and Charles L. Crow (London: Palgrave Macmillan, 2016), 260.

8. Allyson Hobbs, *A Chosen Exile: A History of Racial Passing in American Life* (Cambridge, MA: Harvard University Press, 2014), 4.

9. Hobbs, *A Chosen Exile*, 5.

10. Karla F. C. Holloway, *BookMarks: Reading in Black and White: A Memoir* (New Brunswick, NJ: Rutgers University Press, 2006), 4.

11. Holloway, *BookMarks*, 6.

12. For discussion of the grounds of Miltonic contention, readers may wish to consult Mark R. Kelley, Michael Lieb, and John T. Shawcross, eds., *Milton and the Grounds of Contention* (Pittsburgh: Duquesne University Press, 2003); and Reginald A. Wilburn, *Preaching the Gospel of Black Revolt: Appropriating Milton in Early African American Literature* (Pittsburgh: Duquesne University Press, 2014).

13. Holloway, *BookMarks*, 7.

14. L. Brown, *Pauline Elizabeth Hopkins*, 326.

15. L. Brown, *Pauline Elizabeth Hopkins*, 326.

16. Colleen C. O'Brien, "Race-ing Toward Civilization: Sexual Slavery and Nativism in the Novels of Pauline Elizabeth Hopkins and Alice Wellington Rollins," *Legacy* 20, no. 1/2 (2003): 119.

17. Pauline Hopkins, *Hagar's Daughter: A Story of Southern Caste Prejudice*, in *The Magazine Novels of Pauline Hopkins*, introduction by Hazel V. Carby (New York: Oxford University Press, 1988), 3. Hereafter cited in text as *Hagar's* and followed by page number.

18. See Wilburn, *Preaching the Gospel*, 163, 313. Frederick Douglass, *Narrative of the Life of Frederick Douglass, an American Slave, Written by Himself*, edited by William L. Andrews and Williams S. McFeely (New York: Norton, 1997), 32; Sutton E. Griggs, *Imperium in Imperio* (New York: Modern Library, 2003), 133.

19. Consult Neil Forsyth's foundational *The Satanic Epic* (Princeton, NJ: Princeton University Press, 2003) on Satan's "extremely important role" throughout *Paradise Lost* (17).

20. This appropriation affirms Hazel V. Carby's argument that *Hagar's Daughter* constitutes a text where the author represents the world "through individual white villains who symbolized the power of white society to oppress and embodied greed and rapaciousness"; Carby, *Reconstructing Womanhood: The Emergence of the Afro-American Woman Novelist* (Oxford: Oxford University Press, 1987), 146.

21. Patrick Colm Hogan, *Cognitive Science, Literature, and the Arts: A Guide for Humanists* (New York: Routledge, 2003), 123.

22. L. Brown, *Pauline Elizabeth Hopkins*, 337.

23. The language of pulling down pillars and involving in common ruin is clearly an allusion to Milton's *Samson Agonistes*, as well.

24. Forsyth, *Satanic Epic*, 13.

25. L. Brown likewise interprets this collection of "proslavery characters" as allusive recreations of "Satan and his chief associates"; Brown, *Pauline Elizabeth Hopkins*, 332.

26. L. Brown, *Pauline Elizabeth Hopkins*, 332.

27. L. Brown, *Pauline Elizabeth Hopkins*, 331.

28. L. Brown, *Pauline Elizabeth Hopkins*, 363.

29. L. Brown, *Pauline Elizabeth Hopkins*, 351.

30. Danielle A. St. Hilaire, *Satan's Poetry: Fallenness and Poetic Tradition in Paradise Lost* (Pittsburgh: Duquesne University Press, 2012), 18.

31. Martha J. Cutter, "An Intricate Act of Passing: Strategies of Racial and Textual Subversion in Charles Chesnutt's 'The Passing of Grandison,'" *CEA Critic* 70, no. 2 (Winter 2008): 54.

32. Stanley Fish, *Surprised by Sin: The Reader in* Paradise Lost, 2nd ed. (Cambridge, MA: Harvard University Press, 1997), 21.

33. Fish, *Surprised by Sin*, 1.

34. L. Brown, *Pauline Elizabeth Hopkins*, 326.

35. Stephen Dobranski, "Clustering and Curling Locks: The Matter of Hair in *Paradise Lost*," *PMLA* 125, no. 2 (March 2010): 337–53, 512.

36. Cheryl Wall, *Worrying the Line: Black Women Writers, Lineage, and Literary Tradition* (New Brunswick, NJ: Rutgers University Press, 2005).

37. Wall, *Worrying the Line*, 8–9.

38. Wall, *Worrying the Line*, 12.

39. Wall, *Worrying the Line*, 13.

40. Wall, *Worrying the Line*, 13.

41. See Marissa Greenberg and Rachel Trubowitz's introduction to this volume, 4. In other words, Hagar's crouched and writhing manner metaphorically aligns her with Satan's serpentine nature. As such, Hopkins cleverly alludes to Hagar's condition of satanic fallenness as an embodied echo of the hellish degradation she suffers upon learning she is Black, enslaved, and not white.

42. Therí Alyce Pickens, *Black Madness :: Mad Blackness* (Durham, NC: Duke University Press, 2019), 4.

43. Pickens, *Black Madness*, 4.

44. Christopher Ricks, *Milton's Grand Style* (Oxford: Clarendon Press, 1963).

45. Delores S. Williams theorizes the reception of the biblical Hagar in African American culture in terms of a rich "liberation tradition of African-American biblical appropriation"; Williams, *Sisters in the Wilderness: The Challenge of Womanist God-Talk* (Maryknoll, NY: Orbis Books, 1993), 2. L. Brown concurs, noting Hagar's biblical tale proves "relevant" "since after Eve . . . [she] suffered one of the notable and early exiles reported in the Old Testament"; Brown, *Pauline Elizabeth Hopkins*, 360.

46. Eliza Poitevent Nicholson, "Hagar," *The Cosmopolitan* (November 1893) is reproduced in appendix D: The Figure of Hagar in Pauline Elizabeth Hopkins, in *Hagar's Daughter: A Story of Southern Caste Prejudice*, ed. John Cullen Gruesser and Alisha R. Knight (Petersborough, Ontario: Broadview, 2021), 295–99.

47. Holloway, *BookMarks*, 13.

48. Joseph Wittreich, *Why Milton Matters: A New Preface to His Writings* (New York: Palgrave Macmillan, 2006), 95, quoting Nicholas von Maltzahn, "'Acts of Kind Service': Milton and the Patriot Literature of Empire," in *Milton and the Imperial Vision*, ed. Balachandra Rajan and Elizabeth Sauer (Pittsburgh: Duquesne University Press, 1999), 248. The brevity of Nicholson's blank verse poem on a religious subject also invites comparison between "Hagar" and *Paradise Regained*, which Barbara Keifer Lewalski identified as a "brief biblical epic"; *Milton's Brief Epic: The Genre, Meaning, and Art of Paradise Regained* (Providence, RI: Brown University Press, 1966), 324–32.

49. St. Hilaire, *Satan's Poetry*, 65.

50. Tuhkanen, "Out of Joint," 347.

CHAPTER 11

∽

Snaking the Path

Disability, Pedagogy, Justice

Marissa Greenberg

Reparative Miltonic Pedagogies

In a brilliant essay on teaching *Paradise Lost* in prison, scholar and activist Sarah Higinbotham makes the case for a "pedagogy of repair."[1] Beginning with Milton's claim in *Of Education* (1644) that "the end of learning is to repair the ruins of our first parents," Higinbotham expounds the various ways that "to repair" signifies in Milton's epic before showing its operations in her prison classroom.[2] To repair in Miltonic contexts means more than simply "to fix." As Higinbotham wryly points out, "Milton's claim that education will repair the ruins from the Fall is radical, even unreasonable, if by 'repair' he means to restore straightforwardly to a previous state."[3] Instead, it indicates a range of processes including return to a place, as in repatriation, and of a relationship, as in the re-pairing of Adam and Eve.[4] But whether material, spatial, or interpersonal, Miltonic repair indicates transformation.[5] Like the reconstruction of the ship of Theseus, or Miranda's return to "a brave new world," the repair of Eden's ruins yields something at once familiar and strange (*The Tempest*, 5.1.217).[6] At the heart of Milton's theory and practice of education, then, is a principle of ontological and epistemological change. Even when physical movement is circumscribed, as in a prison, reparative pedagogy offers the prospect of progressive motion. Throughout his writings, in fact, Milton promotes education not for its promise to restore humanity to an Edenic "happy State" but for its capacity to move us toward "A Paradise within . . . , happier farr" (*PL*, 1.29, 12.587).[7]

283

For Milton reparative pedagogy is a monist project inseparable from political and religious revolution. He pursues these interlocking goals throughout his career. From *Of Education* to *Paradise Lost*, Milton returns time and again to food and knowledge as synonymous consumables capable of energizing change. Milton addresses *Of Education* to Samuel Hartlib, a prominent figure among a pan-European cohort of educational reformers inspired by the theories of John Amos Comenius.[8] By advocating for a humanist approach to learning, Milton pushes back against scholasticism and its reliance on custom. He disparages Cambridge University dons for dishing out an "asinine feast of sowthistles and brambles" that leaves students capable of nothing more than regurgitating dogma and licking the soles of authority (*Of Education*). By contrast, students in Milton's ideal classroom consume a nourishing and substantive diet of textual study, practical tutorials, and physical training that prepares them for political debate and theological inquiry. The same year as he publishes *Of Education*, Milton advocates for a more capacious if no less ambitious reformation in *Areopagitica*. In addition to promiscuous reading of books published without state censorship, Milton promotes London as a vast classroom filled with all sorts of learning opportunities, including instrumental music and pictorial images, neoclassical architecture and new-fangled apparel, mixed "conversation" and motley "company" (*Areo.*) He admits that these other sources of knowledge, like unlicensed books, may "corrupt the mind"; but for this very reason, Milton deems them necessary to the formation of mindful citizens and Christians. "I cannot praise a fugitive and cloister'd virtue, unexercis'd & unbreath'd," Milton writes, again denouncing passive adherence to tradition, because "that which purifies us is trial, and trial is by what is contrary" (*Areo.*). Anything that exercises the faculties of reason and choice becomes a potential source of edification.[9] To illustrate this claim, Milton again uses food imagery. Citing the apostle Paul, Milton asserts that "To the pure, all things are pure, not only meats and drinks, but all kinde of knowledge whether of good or evill; the knowledge cannot defile, nor consequently the books, if the will and conscience be not defil'd" (*Areo.*). The connection between food and knowledge reaches an apex in *Paradise Lost*, of course. Raphael's account of digestion and ontological evolution in book 5 and Adam and Eve's experience of eating and epistemological change in books 9 and 10 reveal a robust monism. As in his prose tracts, in *Paradise Lost* food is not simply a metaphor for Milton's recommended regime of divine directives, heavenly narratives, earthly labors, and unrepeatable trials.[10] Instead, it is of a piece with Milton's

Marissa Greenberg

revolutionary approach to education as a complexly embodied "experience" (*PL,* 8.190) that transforms individuals and institutions.[11]

Yet reparative pedagogy is not the same for every body [*sic*]. The form, speed, and direction of its movement adapt to the diversity of learners. As Ryan Hackenbracht, Karra Riley, and Philippa Earle have demonstrated, for example, both pedestrian and passionate motions are constitutive of self-knowledge in Milton's epic and brief epic.[12] The monist philosophy underlying them may be familiar to today's students from epistemologies far removed from Miltonic literature. Embodied, dynamic modes of knowledge may be found all over the world, and many precede colonialism or respond to the violent imposition of imperial epistemes, including Christianity and Cartesian science. In the US Southwest where I teach, for example, Indigenous and Latinx epistemologies value nonbinary, relational, and embodied ways of knowing and being, such as dreams and borders, that collaborate with one another and with linguistic and narrative modes in the lived practices of meaning and world making.[13] In *Paradise Lost,* as I will demonstrate, Milton proposes a complementary epistemology of bodyminds that moves from materially circumscribed ways of knowing to fuller, more complex ways of being in—and thus making meaning through—the world. Margaret Price, a leading scholar in feminist disability studies, defines *bodymind* as "a sociopolitically constituted and material entity that emerges through both structural (power- and violence-laden) contexts and also individual (specific) experience."[14] This definition is useful to Milton scholar-teachers because it weaves a monistic thread from Milton's commitment to educational reform to today's social justice–oriented pedagogies. Vital to the movement for social justice in higher education is acknowledging the historical devaluation of diverse theories of knowledge and the systemic oppression of underrepresented minority students as epistemologically deficient. It also insists on the restoration of diverse epistemologies by affirming how marginalized students acquire and practice knowledge. Teaching Milton monistically likewise extends beyond showing bodyminds in his poetry and prose to authorizing students' bodyminds as sources of knowledge and inquiry.[15]

In this essay I point to Milton's monism as both subject and method of reparative pedagogy. I argue that the doctrine of "one . . . matter all" (*PL,* 5.472) demands that we reckon with what it means for students to move through a ruined world often hostile to different ways of knowing and being. I demonstrate this connection through an examination of disabled bodies and their movements in *Paradise Lost* and their adaptation in Alexis Smith's *Snake Path* (1992). The choice to focus on disabled bodies and their movements is motivated in part by the attention afforded in the epic to visual impairment as at once a mode of and a limitation to embodied knowledge. Milton was blind when he composed *Paradise Lost*, of course, and blindness is a prevalent theme throughout his late poetry. Scholars have begun to unpack the aesthetic and political significance of visual impairment in Milton's writings. Citing Tobin Siebers's notion of complex embodiment in *Disability Theory*, Amrita Dhar demonstrates a "blind language" in Milton's sonnets that "[recognizes and recovers] the importance of differently-abled creative aptitudes and conditions such as those negotiated by Milton."[16] Steven Swarbrick mounts a similar argument in response to modernist disparagements of Milton's visual images in *Paradise Lost*. Milton marshals blindness as "an active or creative force" within a "prosthetic economy," Swarbrick argues, especially in books 11 and 12: here, a heavenly unction enables Adam to see the future, but for the reader who remains blind to Michael's visions, it figures Milton's accommodating poetic images that are eventually replaced by auditory and tactile prostheses.[17] According to these scholars, Milton's poetics does not represent blindness as inhibiting knowledge, let alone requiring a cure. Quite the opposite: it presents disability as an epistemology that facilitates reparative education.

Examining the combination of visual and narrative media in books 11 and 12 of *Paradise Lost*, Ryan Netzley proposes that for Milton "learning from history entails more than learning its lessons, laws, and even its final causes and aims"; the poet also "attempt[s] to push learners beyond such a scripted discovery, toward a conception of freedom that would reside outside of conflicts over choice and determinism, and instead be truly creative."[18] Netzley frames this pedagogy in terms of the "possibility that . . . we might actually learn how to act, without a pattern, map, or rule to guide us."[19] In Netzley's pedagogy of historical possibility, I discern resonance with what disability scholars, artists, and activists call *crip time*. In one of the most influential meditations on the phrase, Petra Kuppers defines crip time as "the traces of temporal shifting" in the lives of many disabled people.[20] These shifts may be understood as empowering, liberatory, even redemptive. As Alison Kafer writes: "Rather than bend disabled bodies and minds to meet the clock, crip time bends the clock to meet disabled bodies and minds."[21] Or they may register pain and loss that resist control. Parsing these experiences, Ellen Samuels writes about how disability not only shifts time but also may actually break it:

> *Crip time is broken time.* It requires us to break in our bodies
> and minds to new rhythms, new patterns of thinking and feeling
> and moving through the world. It forces us to take breaks, even
> when we don't want to, even when we want to keep going, to
> move ahead. It insists that we listen to our bodyminds *so* closely,
> *so* attentively, in a culture that tells us to divide the two and push
> the body away from us while also pushing it beyond its limits.[22]

Writing from the perspectives of Milton studies and disability studies, respectively, Netzley and Samuels both describe disruptions of normative temporality as sources of knowledge. Such crip epistemology is synonymous with not only monist philosophy but also reparative pedagogy for Milton. I argue, first, in *Paradise Lost* Milton generates transformative models of being and knowing through the movements of disabled bodies and, second, we must do the same in our Milton classrooms.

By attuning ourselves and our students to crip epistemology in *Paradise Lost*, we create opportunities for recognition and affirmation of the full diversity of human bodyminds.[23] In a memorable articulation of disability as an identity, Tobin Siebers writes that "disability is the other other that helps make otherness imaginable."[24] Yet those who identify as women, people of color, and/or LGBTQ, like people with disabilities, also know from experience how "we are simply not 'in' a world that is separate from ourselves. Rather, we allow a world to be by our very presence and through our physical bodies."[25] Milton evokes this monist episteme in *Paradise Lost* by presenting disability as a condition of meaning making and knowledge acquisition—in a word, education—in a fallen world.

This crip knowledge is also evident in Alexis Smith's *Snake Path*, a late twentieth-century art installation that adapts Milton's epic in and through a public university campus. Snaking the path of Smith's installation, like reading *Paradise Lost*, generates epistemologies of embodiment and its intersectional relationship to structures of power and privilege, including in higher education. Prominent within a colonial curriculum, Milton's poetry and prose have been used to perpetuate myths about literary value and pedagogical validity: what bodies of work get taught, how, and to whom. *Paradise Lost* introduces method and means to the pursuit of epistemic justice that embraces a diversity of ways of knowing and being.[26] If Milton's "great Argument" is to "assert Eternal Providence / And justifie the ways of God to men" (*PL*, 1.24–26), the larger argument of this essay is that we

288   Snaking the Path

as scholar-teachers of Milton must, first, name the unearned privilege
of normative bodies, motions, and epistemes in Milton's epic and our
readings of it and, second, authorize and advocate for different experiences of embodied movement as sources of literary and sociopolitical
knowledge for a new generation of Milton scholars.[27] To put my argument in its most revolutionary terms, we must repair our pedagogy so
students may repair their world.[28]

Disability and Accommodation in *Paradise Lost*

A close reading of *Paradise Lost* confirms Angelica Duran's
description of Milton's approach to teaching as multimodal and
"accommodat[ing . . .] the abilities of students."[29] In this context the
metalanguage of disability in the epic's opening books is a bit surprising.[30] In books 1 and 2 Milton presents Satan's movements as difficult
and encumbered. Rising from the burning lake, Satan uses his spear
as a cane: "He walked with [it] to support uneasy steps" (*PL*, 1.295).
The poet-speaker credits Satan's need for a prosthetic third leg to Hell's
uneven landscape, "the burning marl, not like those steps / On heav-
en's azure" (*PL*, 1.295–96). Yet Satan's unsteady movement, like his
diminished light and scarred face (*PL*, 1.591–601), exceeds geographical location.[31] It conditions his every interaction with the worlds of
Milton's poem:

> horror and doubt distract
> His troubl'd thoughts, and from the bottom stirr
> The Hell within him, for within him Hell
> He brings, and round about him, nor from Hell
> One step no more then from himself can fly
> By change of place[.] (*PL*, 4.18–23)

These famous lines extend Satan's loss of ease from his steps to his
thoughts and, through intertextual allusion to Christopher Marlowe's
Doctor Faustus, make clear the entanglement of Satan's physical and
mental troubles with his spiritual ones. A similar dis-ease characterizes
Satan's "solitary flight" out of Hell: "He som times / . . . scours the right
hand coast, som times the left" (*PL*, 2.632–33). Although "scours"
denotes haste (Satan "Puts on swift wings"; *PL*, 2.631), use of the
word to mean lawless street violence, such as rioting, would appear in
print within a few years of *Paradise Lost*'s publication (*OED*). Even as

Satan's journey in book 2 draws on ancient and early modern imagery of global adventure, it also enacts the criminal pathology frequently associated with human bodies that move differently through the world.[32] Disobedience and despair become inseparable from disability.

An obvious counterpoint to Satan's disabled bodymind is Adam and Eve's "nobler shape erect . . . Godlike erect" (*PL,* 4.288–89). Here Adam and Eve's moral rectitude, their obedience to the divine in whose image they are created, is indistinguishable from their upright posture. So too their bodily motions through Paradise offer a stark contrast to Satan's uneasy steps in Hell and unruly flight through Hell and Chaos:

> So hand in hand they passd, the lovliest pair
> That ever since in loves imbraces met,
> *Adam* the goodliest man of men since borne
> His Sons, the fairest of her Daughters *Eve.* (*PL,* 4.321–24)

Twice more in book 4 Adam and Eve's movements are described in similar terms: "So passd on" and "Thus . . . pass'd / On" (*PL,* 4.319, 689–90). In all three instances adverbs indicate transitions through time ("So" and "Thus") and space ("on").[33] Adam and Eve's movements connect not only prelapsarian moments and Edenic places but also other bodily motions: standing, sitting, and reclining (*PL,* 4.326, 327, 330). These activities, which follow the "toil / Of their sweet Gardning labour," are presented in terms of "ease / More easie" (*PL,* 4.327–30). The reader may justly conclude that Adam and Eve "passd" with easy ease, as well.[34]

Identifying Milton's metalanguage of disability is necessary to naming ableism in *Paradise Lost.* However, it is not enough; in the modern-day university, unlike in Milton's Eden, naming is not the same as knowing. We, with our perceived and real dominion over our classrooms, must also call out our participation in the poem's bias. Milton makes little reference to the exact mode of Adam and Eve's passing, yet readers tend to presume that they walk.[35] To demonstrate this presumption, it is instructive to return to Adam and Eve's introduction in terms of their "nobler shape erect . . . Godlike erect." Of this phrase the editors of *The John Milton Reading Room* observe: "Milton repeats the word, 'erect,' as if standing erect were as much, or more, a matter of nobility and godlikeness as it is simply a matter of walking on two, rather than four, legs." The editors correctly point out the anthropocentrism in Milton's verse. In doing so, however, they replicate its ableism. If the ability to walk on two legs is sign and symptom of godly humanity, other modes of moving through the world—with no legs (a wheelchair) or four legs (crutches) or more (a service animal)—become other and less than human, whether bestial or demonic. Fostering ableist reading practices are other associations between dominant identities and godliness. Again, in Adam and Eve's introduction to the poem, the "imbraces" of this "lovliest pair" indicate heterosexual union; "man of men" elevates cisgender male identity; Eve's "fair[ness]," like her "golden tresses" (*PL,* 4.305), denotes racial whiteness; and the proximity of homophones "Godlike" and "goodliest" reinforce the Christian supremacy at the epic's core. When bundled with these dominant identities—privileged in Milton's world and in many of his current-day readers' worlds—is it any surprise that students and teachers alike often assume "passd" denotes nondisabled movement and specifically unencumbered, unaccommodated walking?

Calling out these assumptions, and their basis in structures of privilege, creates the conditions for a more authentically inclusive pedagogy. Not only does it acknowledge historical systemic inequities on our campuses and in our curricula; it also welcomes explicitly students' diverse backgrounds and experiences into the classroom. It may take a student familiar with their institution's procedures for requesting accommodation, for example, to recognize universal design of a sort when Adam observes that their midday "walks . . . require" (*PL,* 4.627) removal of "Blossoms" and "Gumms . . . if [he and Eve] mean to tread with ease" (*PL,* 4.630, 632).[36] Here Milton seems to portray Eden rather than Adam and Eve as the source of dis-ease.[37] In a manner similar to modern social models of disability, the unfallen world of *Paradise Lost* locates barriers to access in the environment rather than the individual. Yet this is not the attitude that many students encounter on university and college campuses, let alone in the world at large, where the presumption that the "problem" of inaccessibility lies in the bodymind of the disabled student. So too for students who navigate the world with wheelchairs, crutches, or service animals, Adam and Eve's entrance "hand in hand" may indicate not simply mutual affection but also prosthetic-like support. This reading is evident at the end of *Paradise Lost* when Adam and Eve leave Eden "hand in hand with wandering steps and slow" (*PL,* 12.648). Their uncertainty and pace are due, in part, to the loss of Paradise's familiar "Walks" and "foot step-trace" (*PL,* 11.270, 329)—a scenario uniquely accessible to students with agoraphobia or obsessive-compulsive disorders, for instance. Indeed, it may take students accustomed to making "thir solitary way" (*PL,* 12.649) through unfamiliar and unwelcoming built and social environments to imagine the role of accommodation so early in Milton's epic. Similarly, students whose sexual orientation, gender identity, and/or gender expression (SOGIE) do not conform to hetero- and/or cisgender normativities might add that Adam and Eve's easy movements in book 4 replicate heterosexual privilege. For these students to pass hand in hand with same-sex partners is to refuse to pass in another sense of the word and to incur the risks of physical and verbal assault.[38] Similar dangers face students walking while Black, a woman, Muslim, or transgender.[39] Traditional Milton scholarship and pedagogy may take Adam and Eve's entrance to the epic as indicative of godly, able-bodied, and thus normative movement; but for many of today's students, easy passage is far from the norm. We must acknowledge these embodied realities as valid and valued interpretive frames for students' study of *Paradise Lost*.

In doing so, our Milton classrooms become laboratories for epistemic justice. By taking a monistic approach to disabled moving bodies in *Paradise Lost*, we invite students to bring their embodied ways of knowing and being to their Milton studies. A worldview of "one matter . . . all" sets in motion a diversity of interpretive paths—as diverse as the students in our classrooms—through Milton's English Christian epic. We cannot undo the deeply embedded structures of power and privilege in academia, let alone society at large; nor can literature alone heal the harms done by institutions of higher learning, including participation in the slave trade and settler colonialism. But we can practice a reparative pedagogy that meaningfully includes all bodyminds in pursuit of epistemic and social justice.

Crip Knowledge in *Paradise Lost* and *Snake Path*

Snake Path—Alexis Smith's late-twentieth-century adaptation of *Paradise Lost*—enacts the centrality of embodied movement in Milton's pedagogy of repair as well as the authority ascribed to particular kinds of bodies and motions in the modern academy.[40] More than simply a shorthand for the role of moving bodies in Milton's theory of education and knowledge, *Snake Path* reframes the question "How can education be reparative?" in terms of "What are the lived realities of today's students?" The monism of Smith's primary intertext informs her art, as well, inviting a reinterpretation of *Snake Path* and *Paradise Lost* in relation to the identity politics of the twenty-first-century academy.

Built in 1992, Smith's permanent art installation in the Stuart Collection on the campus of University of California, San Diego, features a 560-foot-long, ten-foot-wide slate and concrete path in the shape of a serpent. Its tail points in the direction of the open plain of Warren Mall, the university's science and engineering hub, and its tongue flicks toward the Tree of Knowledge–like architecture of Geisel Library, named in 1995 in honor of Theodor and Audrey Geisel (a.k.a., Dr. Seuss and his wife).[41] The serpent's body wraps around a miniature garden with a marble bench on which is carved a quotation from Thomas Gray's "Ode on a Distant Prospect of Eton College" (1742; pub. 1747):

> Yet ah! why should they know their fate?
> Since sorrow never comes too late,
> And happiness too swiftly flies.
> Thought would destroy their paradise.
> No more; where ignorance is bliss,
> 'Tis folly to be wise.[42]

Also along the path is an oversized library book sculpted out of granite. A call number carved along its spine and a quotation on one facade— "And wilt thou not be loathe to leave this Paradise, but shalt possess a Paradise within thee, happier far" [*sic*]—identify the monolith as a representation of Milton's *Paradise Lost*.

Snake Path points up the urgency of monist approaches to teaching Milton. More specifically, Smith's installation elicits a moving meditation on human variation and its relationship to learning.[43] Smith's choice of location between the university's main library and laboratories reflects a Miltonic understanding of a well-rounded education: extended engagement with repositories of established knowledge, or "great books," as well as varied opportunities for experiential and experimental learning—a combination of knowledge acquisition, application, evaluation, and creation familiar to users of Bloom's taxonomy.[44] *Snake Path* itself is not a conventional research space but a *kairotic space*. Margaret Price defines kairotic space "as the less formal, often unnoticed, areas of academe where knowledge is produced and power is exchanged."[45] These spaces include campus environments that are more or less welcoming to, let alone secure for, students who do not hold dominant identity positions. As an interactive public art installation on the campus of a state university, *Snake Path* reflects on the role of embodied movement in histories of exclusion from higher

Marissa Greenberg 293

education and in the pursuit of a more diverse, inclusive, and just academy.

Among the earliest and most influential studies of *Snake Path* is Wendy Furman-Adams and Virginia James Tufte's examination of artistic interpretations of humanity's fall in *Paradise Lost*. Like other twentieth-century women's "re-visions of [Milton's] poem," Furman-Adams and Tufte argue, *Snake Path* demonstrates an interest in "redemption, or at least . . . transformation."[46]

> Through her *Snake Path* project at the University of California, [Smith] has sought—*literally*—to lead a large viewing and reading public, albeit on a variety of levels, to what she sees as the poet's central insight about life: an insight about innocence and its loss, but especially about the compensations of life as a responsible and educated adult in the world as it is. Her work, finally, is not an image, or a series of images, but *literally a journey*—out of the Eden of innocence to what, she hopes, will prove to be something better.[47]

The "literal[ism]" of Smith's installation as Miltonic pedagogy appears to falter when Furman-Adams and Tufte turn to the embodied experience of each "journey." *Snake Path* "moves the walker on—not too steeply, but steadily uphill," according to Furman-Adams and Tufte. But students move along a much more "difficult path" when they pursue higher education's "complex intellectual and emotional journey of oscillating loss and restoration."[48] The dissolution of monist correspondence into symbolism—the physical journey is *like* (because easier than) the intellectual and emotional one—is rooted, I propose, in an ableist interpretation of *Snake Path*. The description of Smith's installation as "mov[ing] the walker on" assumes nondisabled student bodies.[49] The physical ability to make steady progress uphill figures for cognitive normativity and mental health that enable steady progress to graduation. This connection becomes more explicit in a note glossing the more "difficult path" of higher education: "Anyone involved in college teaching knows how common is this failure of nerve—this terror of new knowledge—how crippling it can be (especially, perhaps, for first-generation collegians)."[50] Notwithstanding its sensitivity to the challenges facing first-generation students, a majority of whom are people of color or from low-income families, this note taps into the metalanguage of disability that we saw in the opening books of *Paradise Lost*.[51] The student who stalls in their education journey is "crippled"; their "failure of nerve" is neither physiological (electrochemical signals) nor psychological (mental illness) but constitutional: they lack commitment, drive, chutzpah. Returning to the assumptive walker moving on *Snake Path*, we find an interpretive equivalence between nondisabled student bodies and academic success stories.

At first blush, Smith's design endorses this interpretation by excluding disabled bodies from moving on *Snake Path*. Shortly after its installation, a critic observed "that the path's crowned back and the steep grade do not allow access for some with disabilities."[52] Yet I would argue that *Snake Path* is not unconscious of or without purpose in its frustration of easy passage. The bench in the miniature garden welcomes not only leisurely walkers but also anyone who needs to pause in their progress and take rest: travelers who use braces, crutches, or other prostheses, or suffer chronic pain, or are pregnant, for example. Such rest does not constitute lack of movement; rather, it is motion with a velocity of zero that, in Milton's writings, is repeatedly portrayed as a precondition of godly service.[53] Through its bench *Snake Path* confronts the notion that progress necessitates motion at a constant velocity toward a predetermined destination. In place of this socio-institutional ideal, *Snake Path* promotes crip epistemologies. Lost time and bodily suffering are the subjects of Gray's "Ode," the concluding lines of which are carved into the bench on *Snake Path*. Gray's poet-speaker gazes on his childhood school where he was "A stranger yet to pain!" The boys whom he watches racing and playing remain insensible to the loss of "buxom health" that awaits them—a loss alternatively physical ("cheer of vigour"), mental ("fur[ious] Passions"; e.g., depression), and sensorial ("slow-consuming Age"). The visual artist Riva Lehrer puts this sentiment in blunter if no less eloquent terms: "'disability' includes everything that befalls the human body."[54] If a traveler along *Snake Path* does not need to use its bench now, more likely than not they will require its accommodation in the future.

The diverse ways in which disability manifests point up one problem with a universalist approach to disability. Even individuals with seemingly identical diagnoses or impairments experience their disability in different ways, often due to environmental contexts and intersecting identities. Just as importantly, the prospect of disability in their future does not tend to inspire nondisabled people toward justice. Bill Hughes advocates against a universalistic approach, arguing that "no matter how much we go on about a common humanity, in everyday life the negative ontology of disability and the particularities of prejudice and oppression tend to reassert themselves."[55] When examined through the social justice of disability model, in fact, insistence on the shared vulnerability of the human bodymind invalidates disability as an identity, obfuscates the dehumanization and discrimination that disabled people experience, and denies the intersectionality of disability and other marginalized positionalities. Acknowledging the "ubiquity of human misery" does not alter perceptions and projections of normativity; rather, as Hughes points out, it perpetuates binaries—abled and disabled, valid and invalid, good and evil, human and monster—by fostering underlying fears about the instability of nondisabled embodiment, including frailty, loss of autonomy, and death.[56] But if a universalistic approach to disability ends up authorizing a normative, ableist ontology, a justice-based approach can support the development of a positive disability identity rooted in the unique epistemologies that disabled bodyminds make possible. Admittedly, because disability breaks quotidian routines, or *how* we know, and their attendant epistemologies, or *what* we know, it generates a "terror of new knowledge" such as Furman-Adams and Tufte ascribe to higher education. Whether or not users take advantage of the accommodation afforded by *Snake Path*'s bench, its presence, and the inscription in its stone of Gray's universalist "Ode," confront users with the ontological validity and epistemological authority of broken motion along Smith's snaking path.

If Smith's Romantic intertext points to the human suffering that requires breaks as we move through the world, her Miltonic one points to human breakage as the precondition for repair in and of the world. Adam and Eve utterly and completely break God's creation in book 9 of *Paradise Lost*. The Fall introduces seasonal change, inclement weather, predatory violence, and of course death to the earth. It also leads to humanity's expulsion from Paradise. The unfamiliar world beyond the garden gates is a source of sorrow and fear for Adam and Eve. So how may Michael claim, in lines quoted on *Snake Path*'s monolithic stone text, that they "wilt though not be loath / To leave this Paradise, but shalt possess / A Paradise within thee, happier farr" (*PL*, 12.585–87)? The answer to this question lies in the terrifying yet reparative pedagogy of crip knowledge. Just as Milton rejects explanations of his blindness as divine punishment, he does not present human disability as a source for despair.[57] Instead, fallen bodyminds move through the world in new ways that necessitate and occasion new ways of learning.

The connection between moving bodies and crip knowledge in *Snake Path* becomes clearer when we examine pre- and postlapsarian pedagogies in *Paradise Lost*. Before the Fall Adam and Eve's formal education, like all their movements, is characterized by ease. Raphael's prelapsarian history lesson takes place during Adam and Eve's midday retirement from labor (*PL,* 5.229–33). Sitting in shady comfort with food and drink at hand, the sociable angel engages Adam in conversation and accommodates his heavenly narrative to "human sense" (*PL,* 5.572). Learning becomes considerably more difficult after the Fall. The militant Michael directs Adam uphill before beginning his history lesson. "Ascend / This Hill," Michael commands (*PL,* 11.366–367); "Ascend, I follow thee, safe Guide, the path / Thou lead'st me," Adam concedes (*PL,* 11.371–72); and "So both ascend" (*PL,* 11.376). Milton's repetition of "ascend" creates a loose climax scheme that prepares the reader for the journey upward—a journey that Milton does not describe. Immediately after stating that man and angel "both ascend," the poet implies that they arrive at their destination:

> It was a hill
> Of Paradise the highest, from whose top
> The Hemisphere of Earth in cleerest Ken
> Stretcht out to amplest reach of prospect lay. (*PL*, 11.377–80)

At first blush, the absence of any description of Adam's and Michael's ascent suggests that the archangel "set[s]" Adam atop the hill, just as Satan would "Our second Adam" (*PL,* 11.382–83). Indicating otherwise is the catalog of locales visible from the hill's top (*PL,* 11.385–411). These twenty-five lines of cartographic survey introduce a literal pause in the epic narrative. Even as the prospect may be breathtaking, its dilation opens space-time within the poem for Adam to catch his breath, as it were, after the rigors of ascent.

The limits of Adam's—and all of humanity's—fallen body continue to emerge as Michael's lesson begins. To enable Adam to "behold" (*PL,* 11.423) principal events in Christian history, Michael administers a purgative that forces Adam to sink down, eyes closed, in a trance (*PL,* 11.419–20). With the archangel's (literally) helping "hand," Adam "Soon" recovers his upright, attentive position (*PL,* 11.421–22). Then, he bears eye- and earwitness to the manifold "suff'rings" of humanity listed in Gray's "Ode": murder, ambition, poverty, environmental disaster, and old age. During this historical survey Adam does not move from Michael's hilltop classroom. Yet the motion proves no less exhausting for being cognitive and temporal rather than physical and spatial. The bodily effort demanded by Michael's lesson becomes evident at the beginning of book 12:

> As one who in his journey bates at Noone,
> Though bent on speed, so heer the Archangel paus'd
> Betwixt the world destroy'd and world restor'd,
> If *Adam* aught perhaps might interpose;
> Then with transition sweet new Speech resumes. (*PL*, 12.1–5)

These lines, added to the 1674 edition of *Paradise Lost*, "[strive] to replicate the experience it means to transmit."[58] Like the metareceptivity of Adam's "astonied" body (*PL*, 9.890), which Ross Lerner shows manifests in "the petrification of the verse" in books 11 and 12, Michael's pause and Adam's silence enact the experience of teaching and learning.[59] This experience is best described in terms of Adam's exhaustion, not disinterest; as Michael acknowledges, his multimodal instruction "Must needs impaire and wearie human sense" (*PL*, 12.10). Adam's experience, moreover, "appeals to readerly sympathy by standing in for readerly experience."[60] The introduction of a break into *Paradise Lost*'s material text and historical narrative, like the inclusion of a bench in Smith's *Snake Path*, registers the lived reality of disability for students of Milton's epic as well as within it.

Whereas Adam's history lesson alerts readers of *Paradise Lost* to crip time as the new normal, so to speak, Eve's taps into alternative forms of embodied knowledge—forms that resonate as much with Indigenous, Latinx, and Black Feminist epistemologies as with Milton's monism and remind us of the critical intersectionality of disability and other identities. When Eve meets up with Adam in book 12, she explains: "Whence thou returnst, and whither wentst, I know" (*PL*, 12.610). In this line "returnst" poetically precedes what it chronologically follows—namely, "wentst." What Eve "know[s]" from her divinely inspired dream is neither teleological nor typological history, although like Adam she commands now greater understanding of the protoevangelium. Instead, she appears to reject normative temporalities of movement. This new knowledge is exactly what the pair needs as their exile approaches. Indeed, the pattern of "returnst" and "wentst" reappears as Adam and Eve exit Eden: "They looking back . . . beheld / Of Paradise, so late thir happie seat":

> Som natural tears they drop'd, but wip'd them soon;
> The World was all before them, where to choose
> Thir place of rest, and Providence thir guide:
> They hand in hand with wandring steps and slow,
> Through *Eden* took thir solitarie way. (*PL*, 12.641–49)

Return is not an option for Adam and Eve; they must progress through Eden and into the world. Their passage will not be easy, and no "place of rest" will be provided to them. Yet they are not without accommodation: Adam and Eve have one another to support their faltering steps and Providence to guide them. This freedom of movement may be a source of sorrow, even terror, but it is the consequence of breaking normative patterns and creating innovative ones.

Adam and Eve's respective educations in books 11 and 12 thus prepare them "To leave this Paradise" in possession of "A Paradise within." These lines, carved on Smith's monolith of *Paradise Lost*, as previously mentioned, confront travelers when they ascend *Snake Path* and to anyone descending who looks back on the installation.[61] In corresponding rhythm with Adam's ascent in book 11, he and Michael "descend the hill" in book 12 (*PL,* 12.606; also *PL,* 12.588 and 12.607). The final descent includes Eve as well:

> In either hand the hastning Angel caught
> Our lingring Parents, and to th' Eastern Gate
> Led them direct, and down the Cliff as fast
> To the subjected Plaine[.] (*PL,* 12.637–40)

This movement precedes Adam and Eve "looking back" before they take "thir solitary way."[62] In a similar fashion *Snake Path* invites a backward glance in anticipation of going forward. This encounter with nonlinear, broken time works in tandem with the installation's undulating, graded route and its accommodating bench. *Snake Path* creates a temporal, physical, and cognitive experience that, like *Paradise Lost,* registers the variation of human knowledge in the monist connection between transformative learning and embodied movement.

Just as the intertexts in Smith's *Snake Path* present paradise as a geographical place (Eton, Eden) and a state of mind ("ignorance," grace), they register change as a result of moving bodily through the world. How can we bring this monism into our Milton classrooms to foster students' creation of new knowledge? Behind this local question are larger, systemic issues in higher education. What kinds of bodies and motions do institutions, instructors, and students include and exclude? Where and when do differently moving bodies become perceived as incompatible with academic progress? How can embodied movement feature in social justice–oriented policies and pedagogies? To begin tackling these questions, let us consider what a Milton classroom is—both in *Paradise Lost* and at our colleges and universities.

Inclusive Milton Classrooms

In an influential reading of *Paradise Lost*, John Gillies argues that Milton uses the word "room" to designate neither space nor place but the conditions governing embodied experience. "The Miltonic room," Gillies writes, "is an environment with built-in predispositions that are alternatively cosmic, physical, metaphysical, moral, emotional, and spiritual. It is the sum of possibilities within which a given life form . . . might thrive or wither."[63] This conception of room allows us at once to bear witness to what is baked into the learning environments at many of our institutions, even as it invites us to design rooms that temporarily disrupt those foundations. Indeed, according to Gillies's reading, room is a noun expressive of the material and immaterial circumstances of living and a verb that designates potentially transformative experiences. This understanding of room captures both a student's individual, multifaceted embodiment and their interaction with learning environments. It counteracts the fantasy that students (or teachers, for that matter) can leave their selves, including their biases, at the door when entering the Milton classroom. But it also catalyzes pedagogical practices that resist the violence of oppression by creating rooms inclusive of diverse bodyminds.

Creating such rooms means teaching in ways that invite students to perceive how "their lives and backgrounds are reflected in the curriculum and in classroom conversations."[64] This kind of "reality pedagogy," as Christopher Emdin dubs it, fosters students' personally meaningful engagement with educational content.[65] Meeting students where they are does not require an abandonment of formalist or historicist methodologies. Ayanna Thompson and Laura Turchi inspired a generation of scholar-teachers in early modern English literature to develop culturally responsive pedagogies that foster students' discovery of "divergent paths to knowledge" about sixteenth- and seventeenth-century texts and contexts.[66] So even as we make Milton's poetry relevant to students' embodied identities and lived experiences, we would do well to heed Doug Eskew's precept to teach it "with a good deal of its alienating features intact."[67] Unflinching presentation of Milton's linguistic, cultural, and political difference also refuses to perpetuate the academic disenfranchisement of Black, Brown, Indigenous, and lower-class white students by denying them access to complex or otherwise challenging literature and critical methods.[68] Ideally, then, our teaching will bring Milton's poetry to today's students without diminishing the distance between them. This approach makes possible "apprehensive readings" that, as Ruben Espinosa explains, "resist the tendency to locate in similitude . . . only a positive valence instead of the stifling nature that such similitude encourages."[69] It also establishes a foundation for students' encounters with difference in the world around them. In the dynamic motion between their real sense of otherness and the otherness of early modern English literature, students undertake their own movement along the snaking path of reparative pedagogy.

Milton scholar-teachers are actively developing strategies and tactics for creating Milton classrooms that focus on students' lived experiences and embodied identities. Two articles published in 2012 present curricula in which students dialogue with artists toward personally meaningful and academically rigorous interpretations of *Paradise Lost*. Angelica Duran shares scaffolded lesson plans for using illustrations of "blind Milton" in undergraduate and graduate Milton courses. These illustrations give students an "immediate experience of collaboration and interdependence," Duran argues, in the artistic object (such as portraits of Milton that include human and nonhuman prostheses, like amanuenses and a cane) and in the academic process (including the lesson itself which privileges students without visual impairments and who can more easily analyze images).[70] Also teaching with visual art, Wendy Furman-Adams describes using artistic interpretations of *Paradise Lost*, including *Snake Path*, as part of a pedagogy that "challeng[es] students to arrive at 're-visions' of their own, in their effort to understand this most complex and multivalent of poems."[71] Both Duran and Furman-Adams demonstrate ways to engage students with Milton's writings within a complex ecology of bodies and/in motion.[72]

In my own Milton classroom I put rooming into practice through a teaching and learning strategy called *caucusing*. Developed in collaboration with Elizabeth Williamson, caucusing is a social justice–oriented pedagogy in which students self-identify with and move among a range of affinity discussion groups.[73] Foregrounding at different moments their positionalities of race and ethnicity, sex and gender, religion, and disability, students read Milton's writings through a number of epistemological lenses, both individually and collectively, before bringing them together in intersectional analysis. By grounding students' encounters with *Paradise Lost* in their embodied identities, caucusing calls on us to design rooms that

1. acknowledge the impact of students' individual and shared experiences of moving in the world on their understanding of and responses to Milton's epic;

2. authorize those embodied experiences as both sources of knowledge about and methods of making knowledge from *Paradise Lost*;
3. welcome students' productive disruption of conventional methods of literary analysis, cultural critique, and institutional authority;
4. and develop new patterns of interaction between students and between them and the literary text, including multimodal and intermedial speech and writing.

Even as caucusing calls us on to be designers, we too move in and among these rooms. As academic professionals and unique persons, we would be remiss to indulge fantasies of instructional neutrality. Our institutional power and cultural biases cannot be dropped at the doors and log-on pages of our in-person and virtual classrooms. Commitment to a pedagogy of repair thus demands humility and bravery. For many of us, this means owning up to unearned privilege as nondisabled or nondisabled passing. This acknowledgment cannot be tacit. We must make clear to students our awareness of our own positionalities and their role in how we read and teach Milton. We must also be explicit about our expectations for inclusivity in our classrooms. Following policy with practice, we may create authentically just learning environments for historically excluded students and model equity for traditionally privileged students. In these ways, caucusing offers another meaningful response to the urgent call for equity and inclusion in premodern literary studies. And if we are successful, we may foster a new generation of Milton scholar-teachers who are both representative of and responsive to diversity in higher education.

A pedagogy of repair may not be suitable to all instructors at all career stages and all institutions. Some students remain committed to a myth of a prophetic Milton whose Christian teachings are the sole aim of their study. When invited to nonuniversalist interpretations of Milton's poetry, these students may seek to expose (as if we were hiding) and discredit instructors. Their efforts may be wittingly or unwittingly aided by institutional administrations and leadership afraid to support social justice–oriented instructors out of fear of negative media and its impact on donors. Especially nontenure-track and untenured-term faculty put their jobs on the line when they bring to their classrooms what I am describing as an authentically monist approach to teaching Milton. This situation is especially dire for instructors whose positionalities make them particularly vulnerable to the pressures and precarities of a career in higher education. Yet none of us is immune from socially conservative organizations committed to destroying so-called liberal or activist faculty or from a broader public suspicious of or even hostile to politics in the literature classroom. For those of us who can, however, I believe that teaching Milton today requires us to mobilize knowledge generated by a new generation of bodyminds and honed through diversity, oppression, and activism as a means of repair. Such embodied motions are tantamount to our and our students' historical moment, its political movements, and its calls for progress. They cannot be absent from our Milton pedagogy without doing a disservice to our students and our field.

Notes

1. Sarah Higinbotham, "Education as Repair: *Paradise Lost* in Prison," in *To Repair the Ruins: Reading Milton*, ed. Mary C. Fenton and Louis Schwartz (Pittsburgh: Duquesne University Press, 2012), 358. I am grateful to Katherine Gillen, Sarah Higinbotham, my coeditor Rachel Trubowitz, and two anonymous reviewers for their vital feedback and invaluable support at various stages of this chapter's evolution.

2. Milton, *Of Education*, quoted in S. Higinbotham, "Education as Repair," 339.

3. S. Higinbotham, "Education as Repair," 341; cf. David Hawkes and Joe Lockard, "Samson on the Yard: Teaching Milton's *Samson Agonistes* in an Arizona Prison," *Milton Quarterly* 54, no. 3 (2020): 167–83, which oversimplifies S. Higinbotham's reading by eliding its emphasis on the choice of incarcerated students to be in the classroom.

4. On the role of education in S. Higinbotham's students' return to their communities, see Charles Tarwater Jr., "The Mind Oppressed: Recidivism as a Learned Behavior," *Wake Forest Journal of Law and Policy* 6, no. 2 (2016): 357–69; and David Evan, "The Elevating Connection of Higher Education in Prison: An Incarcerated Student's Perspective," *Critical Education* 9, no. 11 (2018): 1–14, https://doi.org/10.14288/ce.v9i11.186318.

5. For evocations of transformation, see S. Higinbotham, "Education as Repair," 355 and 358.

6. As Prospero wryly points out to his daughter, the "goodly creatures" of men are only "new to [her]" (*The Tempest*, 5.1.216, 219). Scholars have long cited Shakespeare's *The Tempest* as a source for Milton's *Mask*, but recent research indicates considerably more extensive engagement with Shakespeare's plays throughout Milton's career; see Claire M. L. Bourne and Jason Scott-Warren, "'thy unvalued Booke': John Milton's Copy of the Shakespeare First Folio," *Milton Quarterly* 56, no. 1–2 (March–May 2022): 1–85, https://doi.org/10.1111/milt.12418. Although the literature on the ship of Theseus is beyond the scope of this essay, my reference here draws on Thomas Hobbes's take on the ancient paradox; see Constantin Lupașcu, "In the Mind of Theseus or Hobbes and the Paradox of the Second Ship," *Annals of Philosophy, Social & Human Disciplines* 2 (2019): 5–17.

7. On Adam and Eve's "happy State," consult chapter 2 by Sydney Bartlett in this volume.

8. On Milton's relationship to theories propounded by the Hartlib Circle, see, among others, Oliver Morley Ainsworth, ed., *Milton on Education: The Tractate on Education* (New Haven, CT: Yale University Press, 1928); Barbara K. Lewalski, "Milton and the Hartlib Circle: Educational Projects and Epic Paideia," in *Literary Milton: Text, Pretext, Context*, ed. Diana Benet and Michael Lieb (Pittsburgh: Duquesne University Press, 1994), 202–19; and, of particular relevance to the present study, Matthew Ritger, "Milton and the Literary Workhouse," *Milton Studies* 63, no. 2 (2021): 294–327.

9. A similar logic plays out in *L'Allegro* and *Il Penseroso*. In this pair of poems, which themselves model literary imitation, allusion, and debate as pedagogical methods, the speakers teach readers about the relative merits of "mirth" and "melancholy" by relaying the sensorial experiences that each affords, from raucous rustic feasts and popular stage comedies to ascetic monasticism and ecstatic ecclesiastical music. For another reading of movement in these poems, consult chapter 1 by John Rumrich in this volume.

10. On labor and trial as sources of knowledge, see Joanna Picciotto, *Labors of Innocence in Early Modern England* (Cambridge, MA: Harvard University Press, 2010), and Debapriya Sarkar, "'Sad Experiment' in *Paradise Lost*: Epic Knowledge and Evental Poetics," *Exemplaria* 26, no. 4 (2014): 368–88, https://doi.org/10.1179/1041257314Z.000000000593. Learners, like eaters, in *Paradise Lost* include not only Adam and Eve but also the angels: Uriel learns hypocrisy and Abdiel's loyalty is tested through Satan's dissimulations, and although the heavenly forces know God's omnipotence, they are taught this lesson through the 'lived' experience of war and the Son's necessary triumph over Satan and his army.

11. Sharon Achinstein, *Milton and the Revolutionary Reader* (Princeton, NJ: Princeton University Press, 1994).

12. Ryan Hackenbracht, "Milton on the Move: Walking and Self-Knowledge in *Paradise Lost*," in *Milton, Materialism, and Embodiment: One First Matter All*, ed. Kevin J. Donovan and Thomas Festa (Pittsburgh: Duquesne University Press, 2017), 59–80; Karra G. Riley, "Milton, the Passions, and the Knowing Body," *The Seventeenth Century* 35, no. 1 (2020): 31–53; and Philippa Earle, "'Till Body Up to Spirit Work': Maimonidean Prophecy and Monistic Sublimation in *Paradise Regained*," *Milton Studies* 62, no. 1 (2020): 159–89, https://doi.org/10.5325/miltonstudies.62.1.0159. We see a more youthful Milton grappling with the implications of interconnection in A Masque; see Beth Bradburn, "Bodily Metaphor and Moral Agency in *A Masque*: A Cognitive Approach," *Milton Studies* 48 (2004): 19–34.

13. This essay does not present opportunity to explore fully, let alone to cite sufficiently, the wealth of scholarship on Indigenous and Latinx epistemologies—not to mention Black Feminist epistemology, which has been crucial to bringing embodied modes of knowledge to more mainstream (i.e., white, Eurocentric, patriarchal) academic discourse. My brief comments here are most directly indebted to Margaret Kovach, *Indigenous Methodologies: Characteristics, Conversations and Contexts* (Toronto: University of Toronto Press, 2009); and Gloria Anzaldùa, *Borderlands/La Frontera: The New Mestiza* (San Francisco: Spinsters/Aunt Lute, 1987).

14. Margaret Price, "The Bodymind Problem and the Possibilities of Pain," in "New Conversations in Feminist Disability Studies," special issue, *Hypatia* 30, no. 1 (Winter 2015): 271.

15. This essay amplifies calls for teaching social justice in premodern literary studies as a counterpart to greater diversity and inclusion in the field of Milton studies: see, e.g., Hillary Eklund and Wendy Beth Hyman, eds, *Teaching Social Justice Through Shakespeare: Why Renaissance Literature Matters Now* (Edinburgh: Edinburgh University Press, 2019); Sharon Achinstein, "'Here at least / We shall be free': The Places of English Renaissance Literature," in "The State of Renaissance Studies II," special issue, *English Literary Renaissance* 50, no. 1 (2019): 1–7; and Reginald A. Wilburn, "Getting 'Uppity' with Milton; or Because My Mom Politely Asked: 'Was Milton Racist?,'" in "Milton Today, Part I," special issue, *Milton Studies* 62, no. 2 (2020): 266–79.

16. Amrita Dhar, "Toward Blind Language: John Milton Writing, 1648–1656," *Milton Studies* 60, nos. 1–2 (2018): 76, https://doi.org/10.5325/miltonstudies.60.1–2.2018.0075.

17. Steven Swarbrick, "Object-Oriented Disability: The Prosthetic Image in *Paradise Lost*," *Journal of Narrative Theory* 49, no. 3 (2019): 326 and 339, https://doi.org/10.1353/jnt.2019.0014.

18. Ryan Netzley, "Learning from History: Empiricism, Likeness, and Liberty in *Paradise Lost*, Books 11–12," in *Milton's Modernities: Poetry, Philosophy, and History from the Seventeenth Century to the Present*, ed. Feisal G. Mohamed and Patrick Fadely (Evanston, IL: Northwestern University Press, 2017), 88–89.

19. Netzley, "Learning from History," 93.

20. Petra Kuppers, "Crip Time," *Tikkun* 29, no. 4 (2014): 29.

21. Alison Kafer, *Feminist, Queer, Crip* (Bloomington: Indiana University Press, 2013), 27.

22. Ellen Samuels, "Six Ways of Looking at Crip Time," *Disability Studies Quarterly* 37, no. 3 (2017): n.p., original emphases.

23. "Crip theory" emerged at the juncture of Disability and Queer Studies; consult, among others, Kafer, *Feminist, Queer, Crip*; and Robert McRuer, *Crip Theory: Cultural Signs of Queerness and Disability* (New York: New York University Press, 2006). Although in this chapter I focus on disabled bodies and their movement in Milton's epic, my larger goal is to advocate for a reparative pedagogy that addresses historical systems and lived experiences of stigmatization and oppression, and supports activism in and beyond our classrooms, tied to compulsory normative embodiments, including but not limited to gender expression and sexual orientation.

24. Tobin Siebers, *Disability Theory* (Ann Arbor: University of Michigan Press, 2008), 48. Here Siebers also points to a central tenet of social justice movements in and beyond the classroom—namely, intersectionality.

25. Patrick Bracken and Philip Thomas, "Time To Move Beyond the Mind-Body Split: The 'Mind' Is Not Inside But 'Out There' in the Social World," *British Medical Journal* 325, no. 7378 (Dec. 21–28, 2002): 1434.

26. On epistemic justice, consult Miranda Fricker, *Epistemic Injustice: Power and the Ethics of Knowing* (New York: Oxford University Press, 2007). A foundational essay on the marginalization of alternative epistemologies in academia and its relationship to embodied identity, lived experience, and

intersecting oppressions is Patricia Hill Collins, "Black Feminist Epistemology," in *Black Feminist Thought: Knowledge, Consciousness, and the Politics of Empowerment*, 2nd ed. (New York: Routledge, 2000), 251–71.

27. Paralleling demographic changes in the United States population, more students from racial and ethnic minorities are pursuing higher education, and currently women constitute the majority of undergraduates in the United States. Lorelle L. Espinosa, Jonathan M. Turk, Morgan Taylor, and Hollie M. Chessman, *Race and Ethnicity in Higher Education: A Status Report*, "Chapter 1: Population Trends and Educational Attainment" and "Chapter 3: Enrollment in Undergraduate Education," *American Council in Education*, February 2019. www.equityinhighered.org.

28. Here I am indebted to Sarita Cannon, " 'Do I Remain a Revolutionary?': Intellectual and Emotional Risk in the Literature Classroom," *MELUS* 42, no. 4 (December 2017): 37–59.

29. Angelica Duran, "A Multi-Modal Teaching Tool: A(n Obstacle) Course in *Paradise Lost*," *Studies in Medieval and Renaissance Teaching* 24, no. 2 (2017): 131. Note that modern-day educators will likely reject Milton's exact methods, including an exclusively Western canon and corporal punishment.

30. I am inspired here by Wilburn's reading of race in *Paradise Lost*, which draws on Elizabeth Higinbotham's definition of a "metalanguage of race" as a " 'global sign' . . . [that] speaks about and lends meaning to a host of terms and expressions, to myriad aspects of life that would otherwise fall outside the referential domain of race"; Wilburn, "Getting 'Uppity' with Milton," 267, quoting E. Higinbotham.

31. In chapter 8 in this volume, Mario Murgia offers an alternative reading of Satan's "uneasy steps" (*PL*, 1.295).

32. Given prevalent racial and religious prejudices in the twenty-first-century United States, this moment might be understood by students in the United States in terms of state violence against Blacks and Muslims under the guise of law and security. So too premodern English literature frequently reflects cultural prejudices by portraying nonwhite, non-Christian "Others" as criminals. Academic discourse has yet to acknowledge fully the extent to which moral and medical models shaped premodern attitudes toward disability that associated disabled bodyminds with pathology. Simply put, the dominant understanding of impairment, whether congenital or as a result of accident, war, or other trauma, was as both cause of and punishment for violation of divine order. What premodern racism and ableism share is a monist sense of body and spirit. For a promising practical approach to teaching the intersection of disability and race in the Milton (or poetry or theory) classroom, consult Amrita Dhar, "When They Consider How Their Light Is Spent: On Intersectional Race and Disability Theories in the Classroom," in *Race in the European Renaissance: A Classroom Guide*, ed. Anna Wainwright and Matthieu Chapman (Tempe: Arizona Center for Medieval and Renaissance Studies Press, 2023), 161–83.

33. The *OED* cites *A Mask*—"Yea there, where very desolation dwells . . . She may passe on with unblench't majestie" (428, 430)—to illustrate the meaning of "pass on": "to continue in one's actions; to continue, advance, or persist; to proceed to a further stage, progress" (*OED*).

34. Book 2 foretells Sin and Death's construction of "a Bridge . . . by which the Spirits perverse / With easie intercourse pass to and fro" (*PL,* 2.1028–31). This travesty of the movement of unfallen "Angels to and fro / Pass[ing] frequent" on the stairs between Heaven and Earth becomes even clearer after humanity's fall when the hellish bridge is built: "a passage broad, / Smooth, easie, inoffensive" (*PL,* 3.533–34; 10.304–05).

35. In book 4 walking per se is attributed to the angels, both fallen and unfallen (*PL,* 4.528, 677, 685), but not to humans.

36. "Universal design" was coined in 1989 by architect Ron Mace but has since been adapted to numerous disciplines, including pedagogy.

37. Here "walks" is at once action/noun and activity/verb. Supporting a reading of "walks" as a noun is Uriel's and Adam's subsequent usage (*PL,* 4.586; also 8.305, 528) and the revision of Adam's "walk" to "walks" in book 4 of the 1674 printing of *Paradise Lost.* The latter, however, like the singular "walk" in the epic's 1667 printing, may also function as a synonym of "to tread" or, in the manner of a gerund, "the act of walking."

38. For an overview of the term, consult Linda Schlossberg, "Passing," in *The Wiley Blackwell Encyclopedia of Gender and Sexuality Studies,* ed. Nancy A. Naples (Malden, MA: Wiley-Blackwell, 2016), 1–2. In chapter 10 in this volume, Reginald Wilburn examines Milton's "(in)visible influence" on Pauline Hopkins's narrative of racial passing in *Hagar's Daughter.*

39. This is a necessarily incomplete list of identities that have been historically and continue to be targets of state and popular violence in the United States and around the world.

40. A description and images of Alexis Smith, *Snake Path* (1992), are available on the Stuart Collection, https://stuartcollection.ucsd.edu/artist/smith -a.html.

41. A thematic map of the campus, showing the proximity of these built structures, is available at https://maps.ucsd.edu/map/default.htm. In 2021 Dr. Seuss Enterprises announced that it would stop publishing six of Dr. Seuss's books for their culturally insensitive and harmful depictions of people of color. Even as this decision spurred conservative diatribes against "cancel culture," it led many critics and scholars to point out the importance of re-visioning literature and its legacies for social justice.

42. Gray's poem in its entirety may be accessed on the Poetry Foundation website: https://www.poetryfoundation.org/poems/44301/ode-on-a-distant -prospect-of-eton-college.

43. Here I consciously adapt Wendy Furman-Adams's description of *Snake Path* as "elicit[ing] a walking meditation on the nature of Paradise and its relationship to learning"; Furman-Adams, "Milton and the Visual Arts," in *Milton in Context,* ed. Stephen B. Dobranski (Cambridge: Cambridge University Press, 2010), 208.

44. Readers unfamiliar with Bloom's taxonomy may wish to consult "What is Bloom's Taxonomy," *Bloom's Taxonomy,* https://bloomstaxonomy.net/.

45. Margaret Price, *Mad at School: Rhetorics of Mental Disability and Academic Life* (Ann Arbor: University of Michigan Press, 2011), 21.

46. Wendy Furman-Adams and Virginia James Tufte, "'Pleasing was his shape, / And lovely': The Serpent with Eve and Adam in Art Before Milton

and in Re-visions by Three Twentieth-Century Women," *Milton Studies* 37 (1999): 90 and 94.

47. Furman-Adams and Tufte, "Pleasing was his shape," 129, emphases added.

48. Furman-Adams and Tufte, "Pleasing was his shape," 131.

49. This same assumption is evident in Furman-Adams's most recent examination of *Snake Path*: "readers literally walk uphill," pass the nine-foot monolith of *Paradise Lost*, and on to the mini-garden with its bench, where these "walkers" may sit but then "must rise from the bench and continue the path, . . . mov[ing] steadily uphill." Wendy Furman-Adams, "Other Eyes: Women Artists Rewriting *Paradise Lost*," in *Women (Re)Writing Milton*, ed. Mandy Green and Sharihan Al-Akhras (New York: Routledge, 2021), 263–64.

50. Furman-Adams and Tufte, "Pleasing was his shape," 140n50.

51. In the almost quarter century since Furman-Adams and Tufte's article, the "terror of new knowledge" has arguably shifted from first-generation college students, many of whom are people of color or from low-income families and who, as Kyle Grady explains, "recognize that their insight could prove essential to opening up new and under-explored territory" to children of college graduates, often white and beneficiaries of familial wealth, who are not only taught but also tutored to succeed on standardized tests that (ironically) fail to develop independent critical thinking skills; Grady, " 'The Miseducation of Irie Jones': Representation and Identification in the Shakespeare Classroom," *Early Modern Culture* 14 (2019): 29, https://tigerprints.clemson.edu /emc/vol14/iss1/3/. Also consult David P. Haney, "Supporting First-Generation Students' Spirit of Engagement," *Inside Higher Ed*, November 6, 2020, https://www.insidehighered.com/views/2020/11/06/colleges-should-tap-first -generation-students-spirit-academic-and-civic-engagement; and Vernon G. Smith and Antonia Szymanski, "Critical Thinking: More Than Test Scores," *NCPEA International Journal of Educational Leadership Preparation* 8, no. 2 (2013): 16–25.

52. Margaret Stevens, "Paradise Built," *Landscape Architecture* 83 (1993): 24. A connection may be made to *Snake Path* within the Stuart Collection, a site-specific assemblage that is a product of artists "sitting, watching, and walking around"; Rick Kennedy, "Lying in Plain Sight," *Boom: A Journal of California* 6, no. 4 (2016): 76.

53. For more on Miltonic motion with a velocity of zero, consult Rachel Trubowitz's chapter 4 in this volume.

54. Riva Lehrer, *Golem Girl: A Memoir* (New York: One World, 2020), 303.

55. Bill Hughes, "Being Disabled: Towards a Critical Social Ontology for Disability Studies," *Disability & Society* 22, no. 7 (2007): 678, https://doi.org /10.1080/09687590701659527.

56. Hughes is responding to and quoting from Bryan S. Turner, "Biology, Vulnerability and Politics," in *Debating Biology: Sociological Reflections on Health Medicine and Society*, ed. S. Williams, L. Birke, and G. Bendelow (London: Routledge, 2003), 271–82, quote 276.

57. Angelica Duran, "The Blind Bard, According to John Milton and His Contemporaries," *Mosaic: A Journal for the Interdisciplinary Study of*

Literature 46, no. 3 (2013): 141–57, https://doi.org/10.1353/mos.2013.0031. Cf. John Rumrich and Stephen M. Fallon, introduction to *Immortality and the Body in the Age of Milton* (Cambridge: Cambridge University Press, 2018), where the editors point to Milton's rendition in his *Commonplace Book* of John Chrysostom's *Twelfth Homily on Genesis* to argue that, for Milton, "in comparison with subline angelic subsistence the human body may be felt as a normative disability—and bodily existence as a kind of debasement that the soul must strive to overcome of transform. But it is a humiliation that permits humanity 'to surpass even the angels' " (12).

58. Ross Lerner, "The Astonied Body in *Paradise Lost*," *ELH* 87, no. 2 (2020): 448.

59. Lerner, "Astonied Body," 448. Most anyone who has been in a synchronous teaching and learning environment can imagine the "Heav'nly instructor" (*PL*, 11.871), although eager to proceed with his lesson, pausing in expectation of a question or a comment. They will also recognize the silence that often follows these unstructured pauses before the instructor starts up again.

60. Lerner, "Astonied Body," 447.

61. By using the language of "looking back," I am not simply echoing Milton's phrasing but also pointing out how *Snake Path*, even as it calls attention to different experiences of embodied movement, may be complicit in ableism—here, privileging visually unimpaired travelers.

62. Compare my reading in "Milton Much Revolving," in "Milton and Periodization," ed. Rachel Trubowitz, special issue, *Modern Language Quarterly* 78, no. 3 (2017): 388.

63. John Gillies, "Space and Place in *Paradise Lost*," *ELH* 74 (2007): 40.

64. Chris Emdin, "Teaching Isn't about Managing Behavior; It's about Reaching Students Where They Really Are," *The Atlantic*, July 24, 2020, https://www.theatlantic.com/education/archive/2020/07/reality-pedagogy-teaching-form-protest/614554/.

65. Emdin, "Teaching Isn't about Managing Behavior."

66. Ayanna Thompson and Laura Turchi, *Teaching Shakespeare with Purpose: A Student-Centred Approach* (London: Bloomsbury, 2016), 5.

67. Doug Eskew, "Shakespeare, Alienation, and the Working-Class Student," in *Shakespeare and the 99%: Literary Studies, The Profession, and the Production of Inequity*, ed. Sharon O'Dair and Timothy Francisco (Cham, Switzerland: Palgrave Macmillan, 2019), 48.

68. Eskew, "Shakespeare, Alienation"; and S. Higinbotham, "Education as Repair," esp. 348.

69. Ruben Espinosa, "Stranger Shakespeare," *Shakespeare Quarterly* 67, no. 1 (2016): 61, https://doi.org/10.1353/shq.2016.0012.

70. Angelica Duran, "John Milton and Disability Studies in Literature Courses," Comment from the Field, *Journal of Literary & Cultural Disability Studies* 6, no. 3 (2012): 330, https://doi.org/10.3828/jlcds.2012.26.

71. Wendy Furman-Adams, "Visualizing *Paradise Lost*: Artists Teaching Milton," in *Approaches to Teaching Milton's Paradise Lost*, ed. Peter C. Herman (New York: MLA, 2012), 136. Regarding *Snake Path*, Furman-Adams argues that Smith's installation reflects the artist's own efforts to repair the ruins, including a loss of "human mutuality" (132).

72. Duran takes this pedagogy further in "a multi-modal though primarily physically active kinesthetic pedagogical tool for [developing critical thinking] with *Paradise Lost*"; Duran, "A Multi-Modal Teaching Tool," 126. Three appendixes guide instructors through execution of this curriculum, which features teamwork; use of physical places, activities, and objects as mnemonic devices; and tools for understanding literary structures (chronology, linguistic relations) as entry points for meaning making; Duran, "A Multi-Modal Teaching Tool," esp. 136.

73. Marissa Greenberg and Elizabeth Williamson, "Caucusing in the Classroom," in *Teaching Literature in the Online Classroom*, ed. John Miller and Julie Wilhelm (New York: MLA, 2022), 125–39.

AFTERWORD

Moving in and with Milton

Stephen M. Fallon

"*E pur si muove*," Galileo muttered in 1633 to his inquisitors, so the legend goes, after recanting under pressure his claim that the Earth moved around the sun. This was five years before Milton visited him and nearly a dozen before Milton lionized the natural philosopher in *Areopagitica*. "And yet it moves." One might say the same of the status of matter in seventeenth-century England and Italy, as the ancient unchanging superlunary world and the inertness of merely passive matter gave way to the incessant motion of modern matter: the cosmic motion of Galileo's rotating Earth, the perpetual self-motion of Margaret Cavendish's vitalist matter, and the morally driven motion of Milton's animist materialist creatures up toward or down away from God. Milton's works, as has become increasingly clear and as this volume confirms, carry traces of the new philosophy of the seventeenth century.

This collection brings together essays on the intersections of monism, vitalism, and motion in Milton and the early modern world, and on the movement of Milton's vital and vitalist works as they are received through time and space. The essays paint a rich portrait of Milton's writings in relation to his contemporaries' meditations on celestial and terrestrial movements, to diaspora and colonization, and to the proliferating byways of Milton's reception history. Together, the authors weave a tapestry of various motions, literal and metaphorical, apparent and occult, "Cycle and Epicycle, Orb in Orb" (*PL*, 8.84).

A critical contribution of this volume is its contributors' explorations of the implications of Milton's monism, which I have labeled *animist materialism,* for motion. Milton's animist materialism is a variety of substance monism, holding as it does that all existents, including souls and angels, are composed of what Milton calls "one first matter

311

312   Afterword

all" (*PL,* 5.472), a matter with extension and mass rather than Aristotle's formless and qualityless *prima materia.* Before and in tandem with a turn to Galileo's revision of Aristotle, though, we must attend—as do contributors to this volume—to the theological bases of Milton's monism. As Ryan Hackenbracht observes in Tennyson's poetry, Milton's animist materialism was not always understood in relation to, let alone in sync with, scientific thinking. Theologically speaking Milton's monism is compatible with moral dualism; Paul's flesh and spirit are moral rather than ontological categories. His *flesh* is not the body but fallen human nature, and the *spirit* is not an incorporeal soul but the influence of and adherence to the divine. Milton's insistence, through the mouth of Raphael in *Paradise Lost,* that "if not deprav'd from good," one grows "more refin'd, more spiritous, and pure, / As neerer to [God] plac't or nearer tending / . . . / Till body up to spirit work" (*PL,* 5.471, 475–78) has as its corollary that, if depraved from good, one becomes less refined and less spiritous, that is, more grossly and less tenuously corporeal. This reverse trajectory we can observe in the rebellious Satan and his followers as they descend the ontological ladder in the War in Heaven ("though Spirits of purest light, / Purest at first, now gross by sinning grown"; *PL,* 6.660–61) or in Adam's newly gross state after his sin makes him unfit to remain in Paradise ("Those pure immortal Elements that know / No gross, no unharmoneous mixture foule, / Eject him tainted now, and purge him off / As a distemper, gross to aire as gross"; *PL,* 11.50–53). While one might sniff out dualism from these passages, the fact that virtuous creatures can see their bodies "turn all to spirit" and that conversely one can descend into more clotted grossness is possible only because the ontological spectrum between spirit and body is not dualistically divided at any point. The engine for movement along this monist spectrum is the very Pauline dualism that is sometimes adduced as evidence against Milton's monism. In her chapter on *Samson Agonistes* Achsah Guibbory demonstrates the implications of Paul's bifurcation of flesh and spirit for the historical movements of Jews across geographical and religious borders. Drawing on contemporary disability studies in her essay in this volume, Marissa Greenberg examines disabled bodies in motion in *Paradise Lost* and its adaptation as evidence of Milton's monist approach to learning for all kinds of bodyminds. These scholars' considerations of embodied difference as at once an invitation to and a limit on political, social, and spiritual motions puts new pressure on our understanding of the kinetics of Milton's monism.

Stephen M. Fallon

As several of the essays in this volume make clear, Galileo's revolutionary work on motion provides a lens for understanding movement and stasis in Milton's works and world. Challenging the Aristotelian position that rest is the natural state of sublunary matter and that a constant external force is required to keep an object in motion, Galileo argued that all objects move uniformly in constant velocity in the absence of external forces, and that apparently stationary objects are in fact moving at a constant velocity of zero miles per hour. The purported stillness or rest of sublunary objects becomes a matter of relative motion, a question of the frame of reference that in their essays in this volume John Rumrich takes up in relation to stillness in Milton's early poetry and Sydney Bartlett in her consideration of pre- and postlapsarian "state[s]." Galileo's insight was the death knell of the centuries-old belief in the radical division between sublunary and superlunary worlds, prompting speculation about the continuity between terrestrial and celestial worlds and opening a door between Earth and the heavens. In *Paradise Lost* Milton walks through that door in peregrinations through chaos and cosmos. Raphael's holding out the possibility that Adam's and Eve's bodies might "wingd ascend" and "in Heav'nly Paradises dwell" (*PL,* 5.498, 500), as Erin Webster demonstrates, participates in seventeenth-century speculation, sparked by Galilean cosmology, on travel to other worlds.

If Galileo argued that apparently still or resting bodies are moving with a constant velocity of zero, Margaret Cavendish argued that every macroscopic body is made up of myriad bodies all in motion. For Cavendish, material bodies do not merely have the power to move themselves and initiate motion, motion is the constant state of material bodies. While sharing with Thomas Hobbes the principle that everything that is, is material, and that events in the world, including mental events, are explicable in terms of matter in motion, she emphatically rejects the view that parts of matter are moved, passively, by collision with other moving parts of matter. In Cavendish's unusual view, nature (i.e., everything that is, except for God) is one infinite body of living and moving matter. Each parcel of the one moving infinite matter is self-moving. To take the classical example of the billiard ball, Cavendish maintains that a stationary ball moves when coming into contact with a moving ball not because motion is transferred from one colliding ball to another, but because the parts of the stationary ball *perceive* the motion of approaching ball, and then actively *pattern* their motions in response. Moreover, while a stationary ball does not appear to move in relation to its surroundings, it is itself composed of smaller parts constantly in motion among themselves. All matter moves itself. And Cavendish argues not merely that motion and knowledge are characteristic of matter, but that they are the same thing:

> no motion can be without perception, because every part or particle of nature, as it is self-moving, so it is also self-knowing and perceptive; *for matter, self-motion, knowledge and perception, are all but one thing*, and no more differing nor separable from each other, then body, place, magnitude, colour and figure.[1]

Cavendish's bodies organize and move themselves. Her picture is one of the constant motion characterizing even apparently stationary objects.

Cavendish is an instructive example of one end of a monist materialist spectrum, with her strong vitalist conception that every parcel of matter, however small and apparently inert, is alive, active, and free. Hobbes, with his universal mechanist monism, his denial of freedom of the will, and his assertion that "*conceptions* . . . are nothing *really*, but *motion* in some internal substance of the *head*," lies at the spectrum's other end.[2] For Milton, like Cavendish, life and motion are not accounted for by complex organizations of passive parcels of body; matter itself can be instinct with life and activity, and that which might conventionally be seen as inorganic and inert can move itself. In Angelica Duran's and Mario Murgia's essays on Hispanoamerican author portraits and translations, respectively, we find something analogous to this Miltonic and Cavendishian vitalism, as ostensibly nonliving bodies—here, books with printed images and text—move across space and time and, as a result of their motions, move viewers and readers.

If Galileo's redefinition of apparently resting bodies opened the door between sublunary and superlunary worlds, Milton's and Cavendish's animist materialisms opened the door between physical and mental states and actions. Thoughts, including moral choices, are not the product of an immaterial soul but of the material body-soul. To think one's way into this perspective, one has to leave behind the belief that expressions such as "inner turmoil" or being "transported by rage," as Satan is when Milton's God sees him journeying through chaos (cf. *PL*, 4.16–19, 3.80–81), are merely metaphorical rather than literal. Mental motions, as this volume richly illustrates, are physical and spatial motions as well. The same self-moving vitalism, the meeting and union of the intellectual and the material, informs another apparently merely metaphorical description of books in *Areopagitica*:

Stephen M. Fallon

> Books are not absolutely dead things, but doe contain a potencie
> of life in them to be as active as that soule was whose prog-
> eny they are; nay they do preserve as in a violl [i.e., vial] the
> purest efficacie and extraction of that living intellect that bred
> them . . . [A] good Booke is the pretious life-blood of a master
> spirit, imbalm'd and treasur'd up on purpose to a life beyond
> life. (*Areo.*)

Milton here expresses a belief, embodied also in the description in his 1630 "On Shakespear" of the force of the dead Shakespeare enter-ing and dominating the reader's imagination by means of his printed works, that books carry the vital presence of an author in a way that a tomb cannot. As John Rumrich explains, "Milton's metaphors, arising from the perspective of a vitalist monist who understood all creation as substantially unified and deriving from a single matrix of divine origin, possesses more ontological heft than is generally recognized. He does not typically trade in *mere* metaphor."[3] The animation of books is not limited to Milton's own writings, of course, but extends to their afterlives as adaptation. Essays by Jennifer Wallace and Reginald A. Wilburn explore novels in which the bodies of Milton's disinterred corpse and enslaved Black women, respectively, are shown both full of and generative of life. Here as throughout this volume, and as Rachel Trubowitz argues potently in her chapter, Milton's moving bodies are always and already the vital matter of science, religion, and politics.

Several of the essays in this volume draw on the new Galilean under-standing of motion as including stillness and on animist monism's erasure of the lines between thought and body and between spatial orientation and moral states. But the volume's meditations on motion move beyond and outside the implications of substance monism and Galilean physics. We see in Erin Webster's chapter, to take one exam-ple, a motion that disrupts, avant la lettre, a Hegelian conception of the end of history. If Hegel in *The Philosophy of History* imagined history beginning in the East and ending, with the concrete manifesta-tion of the Spirit, in modern Protestant Germany, Webster traces an arc from an Eden in the East through a (pristine or spoiled?) Eden in the Americas to a potentially infinite series of superlunary Edens. That which would spell the end of historical motion gives way to infinite possibilities of motion.

In these pages John Rumrich discovers stillness in Milton's poetry, from his early psalm translations to his great epic and dramatic trag-edy, while Sydney Bartlett shows how motion is a constant in Milton's political prose and poetry, as he advocates moving forward to republican freedom and admonishes creeping backward to monarchy. Ryan Hackenbracht in turn finds Milton moving through Tennyson, and in Reginald A. Wilburn's chapter we see *Paradise Lost* moving through *Hagar's Daughter*. Rachel Trubowitz measures movement in sacred time in her reading of *Samson Agonistes* as advancing from ethnic hostility to (exclusive) universalism, and Achsah Guibbory offers us a Milton moving between potential philosemitism and actual antisemitism. Mario Murgia and Angelica Duran plot motion across national and ethnic boundaries, as Milton's writings traverse borders and languages, both remaining the same and adapting to cultural contexts unfamiliar and even hostile. Jennifer Wallace recounts how preparing to write *Digging Up Milton* sent her moving physically through today's London, historically through the London of the late eighteenth and nineteenth centuries, and in literary terms through and across genres. In a call for movement as change in the way we will teach Milton in the future, Marissa Greenberg finds inspiration in the static motion of a three-dimensional landscape sculpture at the University of California, San Diego.

Milton, when viewed from outside, can seem the prime candidate for the deadest, whitest, and most male of the dead white males. In this volume, which moves with assurance inside Milton and his works, we see the opposite of ossification. Milton's world, his works, and his legacy are in constant motion. There is no dead, inert matter in the universe that he imagines and realizes in his poetry: the cosmos is a living, breathing, gendered organism. While in his greatest poem, *Paradise Lost*, Milton looks back to understand how his world came to be, he ends with forward motion, as Adam and Eve, however "wandring [their] steps and slow," are offered as models for us to make and remake our worlds (*PL,* 12.648). The invitation has been taken up countless times in the 350 years since the publication of the twelve-book second edition. And it has moved around not only the Anglophone world but also across linguistic borders, translated into at least fifty-seven languages, including Albanian, Bengali, Estonian, Faroese, Hebrew, Icelandic, Manx, Tamil, Tongan, and Urdu.[4] Readers have been drawn to the beauty of Milton's creations and moved by his calls to action. The moving Milton captured in this volume is a revolutionary mover at a revolutionary time as well as an author calling us to revolutions of our own.

Stephen M. Fallon   *317*

Notes

1. Margaret Cavendish, *Observations upon Experimental Philosophy*, ed. Eileen O'Neill, Cambridge Texts in the History of Philosophy (Cambridge: Cambridge University Press, 2001), 113, emphasis added.

2. Thomas Hobbes, *Tripos; in Three Discourses*, "I. Human Nature, or the Fundamental Elements of Policy," chap. 7, part 1, in *The English Works of Thomas Hobbes of Malmesbury*, 11 vols., ed. William Molesworth (London: John Bohn, 1840), 4:31, original emphasis.

3. John Rumrich, "Flesh Made Word: Pneumatology and Miltonic Textuality," in *Immortality and the Body in the Age of Milton*, ed. John Rumrich and Stephen M. Fallon (Cambridge: Cambridge University Press, 2018), 139–52, quote 140.

4. *Milton in Translation*, ed. Angelica Duran, Islam Issa, and Jonathan R. Olson (Oxford: Oxford University Press, 2017), 6.

CONTRIBUTORS

Sydney Bartlett is an independent scholar and lives in California.

Angelica Duran is a professor of English, comparative literature, and religious studies at Purdue University. She is the author of *The Age of Milton and the Scientific Revolution* (Pittsburgh: Duquesne University Press, 2007), *Milton among Spaniards* (Newark: University of Delaware Press, 2020), and more than sixty journal articles and scholarly chapters.

Steve Fallon is Cavanaugh Professor of the Humanities Emeritus at the University of Notre Dame. He is the author of *Milton among the Philosophers: Poetry and Materialism in Seventeenth Century England* (Ithaca, NY: Cornell University Press, 1991) and *Milton's Peculiar Grace: Self-Representation and Authority* (Ithaca, NY: Cornell University Press, 2007), as well as a coeditor of *Modern Library's Complete Poetry and Essential Prose of John Milton* (2007).

Marissa Greenberg is an associate professor of English at the University of New Mexico and author of *Metropolitan Tragedy: Genre, Justice, and the City in Early Modern England* (Toronto: University of Toronto Press, 2015).

Achsah Guibbory is a professor of English at Barnard College and has published extensively on the seventeenth century. *Christian Identity, Jews, and Israel in Seventeenth-Century England* (Oxford: Oxford University Press, 2010) was supported by a Guggenheim fellowship and won the John Shawcross Award from the Milton Society of America.

Ryan Hackenbracht is an associate professor of English at Texas Tech University and the author of *National Reckonings: The Last Judgment and Literature in Milton's England* (Ithaca, NY: Cornell University Press, 2019).

Mario Murgia is a poet, essayist, and professor of English at the National Autonomous University of Mexico (UNAM). Murgia is the author of *Versos escritos en agua: La influencia de Paradise Lost en Byron, Keats y Shelley* (Lines Writ in Water: The Influence of Paradise Lost on Byron, Keats and Shelley) (UNAM, 2017) and *Singularly Remote: Essays on Poetries* (MadHat Press, 2018).

John Rumrich is Celanese Centennial Professor at the University of Texas, Austin. He is the author of *Milton Unbound* (Cambridge: Cambridge University Press, 1996) and coeditor of *The Norton Critical Edition of British Poetry, 1603–60* (Ithaca, NY: W.W. Norton, 2006).

320 Contributors

Rachel Trubowitz is a professor of English at the University of New Hampshire, Durham. She is the author of *Nation and Nurture in Seventeenth-Century Literature* (Oxford: Oxford University Press, 2012) and numerous scholarly articles.

Jennifer Wallace is Harris Fellow and Director of Studies in English and Comparative Literature at Peterhouse, University of Cambridge. Her publications include *Shelley and Greece: Rethinking Romantic Hellenism* (Basingstoke, UK: Palgrave Macmillan 1997), *Digging the Dirt: The Archaeological Imagination* (London: Duckworth, 2004), *The Cambridge Introduction to Tragedy* (Cambridge: Cambridge University Press, 2007), and *Tragedy since 9/11: Reading a World out of Joint* (London: Bloomsbury, 2019). Her novel, *Digging Up Milton*, was published in 2015 by Cillian Press.

Erin Webster is an associate professor of English at William & Mary and author of *The Curious Eye: Optics and Imaginative Literature in Seventeenth-Century England* (Oxford: Oxford University Press, 2020).

Reginald A. Wilburn is University Professor at Texas Christian University, where he serves as the associate provost for Undergraduate Affairs. He is the author of *Preaching the Gospel of Black Revolt: Appropriating Milton in Early African American Literature* (University Park: Pennsylvania State University Press, 2014).

INDEX

Page numbers for illustrations are in italic. Works are by John Milton unless otherwise noted.

101 Famous Poems (Cook, ed.), 233–35, *235*, 238–41, 246–47, 252n1

ableism. *See under* disability
Abraham (biblical figure), 25–27, 44n7, 101, 134
Achinstein, Sharon, 50–51, 68n15
Adam and Eve. See under *Paradise Lost*, main characters in
Aeneid (Virgil), 50, 182, 198
African American culture: biblical adaptation in, 144–45, 281n45; Hagar's legacy of (*see under* Hagar); literary periodicals' role in, 259–61, 279, 279n5; Milton's influence on, 11, 14, 144–45, 259–60
African continent: envisioned as extraterrestrial realm, 83, 91–93; Ethiopian or Ottoman empires in, 93; Eurocentric conceptions of, 129, 247–48; Moors from, complexion or religion of, 129; as pictured on world maps, 75–78
Africans or African Americans. *See* Black people
afterlife, the: agnostic vs. conditional views of, 202–4; of authors and books, 17n19, 251–52, 314–15; Calvinist understandings of, 153, 202–3; in Christianity, 94–95, 205–6; for humans or other species, 183–93. *See also* borders: of life vs. death
Alfred, Lord Tennyson. *See* Tennyson, Alfred
Allen, Paula Gunn, 237, 254n18
Álvarez Bonilla, Enrique, 215, 226–30, 253n7
American continent: as earthly location of Paradise, 71–95; European colonization of, 9–10, 72–75, 92–93; Indigenous inhabitants of (*see*

Amerindians); as pictured on world maps, 72–74, 80–81; temporality of as New World, 71–72, 78–80, 82
Amerindians: Columbus's first impressions of, 71–92; creation story challenged by, 79–80, 185; Eurocentric conceptions of, 6–7, 185–86; prelapsarian state of (*see* prelapsarian state: of the Americas); premodern civilizations of, 85, 93; on religious conversion of, 142–43; treated as primitive, 71–78, 87, 247–48; viewed as lost tribes of Israel, 80, 132, 135, 142–43
angels: agility and swiftness of, 217, 223–24; expulsion of, from Heaven, 104–12; Milton's portrayal of, 40–41, 222–25
Anglo-Judaeus, The (Hughes), 129–30, 133
animation: of humans or animals, 44, 184–90, 220–22; of ideas or imagination in print, 17n19, 251–52, 314–15; of inert objects, 6–7, 17n19, 24, 28; of walls or other borders, 105–12. *See also* author portraits: aura of authors in; presencing
"Another on the Same," 32–33
Antoine, Joseph (José Antonio). *See* Decaen, José
apocalypse: of the English nation, 168–69; of humankind or the world, 193–98, 284–85; pre- vs. post-, 113–15, 118, 199
Apology for Smectymnuus, An, 55
Areopagitica: anti-Catholicism of, 10–11, 150; creeping or wandering movements in, 54–57, 64–65; flowing of truth and virtue in, 6–7, 17n17; Galileo lauded in, 9, 310–11; Romantic reception of, 162; treatment of reformation in, 284

321

322   Index

Aristotle: on agency, narrative, and time,
   32–3, 117, 231n11, 231n13, 243;
   on enslavement, 86; on motion, vs.
   Galileo, 3, 9, 12, 105–7, 111–12; on
   the sub- and superlunary, 107
Asian continent: as earthly location of
   Paradise, 71–79, 82–83, 87, 92–93,
   96n11; empires in, 92–93; envisioned
   as the East, 83–84, 127–28; mistaken
   for America, 78; people of or
   descended from, 127, 131, 242–43,
   247–48; as pictured on world maps,
   72, 82–83, 87, 92–93
Atabalipa, 85, 93
Augustine, Saint, 158n39, 188–89, 221
author portraits: aura of authors in,
   233–34, 240–41, 243–45, 250;
   cultural hybridity of, 232–52; as
   literary interpretation, 236–37, 251–
   52; of Milton or his life (see Milton,
   portraits of); simulation of Milton's
   signatures in, 234, 245–46; taming
   of the unfamiliar in, 235–37, 238–
   39, 241–47. See also afterlife, the: of
   authors and books

Bartlett, Sydney, 13, 17n13, 29
Bassnett, Susan, 213–14
Bergerac, Cyrano de, 72, 95n4
Black people: animus toward (see
   racism); enslavement of (see
   enslavement); Hagar, close
   identification with (see Hagar: legacy
   of); literature or culture of (see
   African American culture); resurgence
   of violence against, 127–28
Blake, William: as character in historical
   fiction, 178n37; The First Book of
   Urizen, 163; The Marriage of Heaven
   and Hell, 162–64; Milton (poem),
   168–69; Paradise Lost, illustrations
   for, 164, 253n10
Bloom, Howard, 183, 306n44
bodies: dynamic states of, 4, 105; fluids
   or humors of, 10, 19n33; represented
   in literary works (see imagery);
   motions in or movements of (see
   movement); vs. souls (see monism).
   See also embodiment; immixing
   (comingling)
Bonilla, Enrique Álvarez. See Álvarez
   Bonilla, Enrique
Book of Mormon, The (Smith), 142–43

borders: of abled vs. disabled people (see
   under disability; embodiment); of
   active vs. contemplative life, 29–30,
   238; of animal vs. human, 157n25,
   184–85, 194–98, 202–4, 288–89; of
   empiricism vs. theology, 204, 220–21;
   of fact vs. fiction, 173–75; of human
   remains vs. literary relics, 159–62,
   164–66, 174. 182–83, 204–5; of life
   vs. death, 117–18, 159–76, 185–
   202; of past vs. present (see time);
   of pre-social vs. social, 111–12; of
   rich vs. poor, 165–66, 169–70, 173;
   surveillance and policing of, 103–4;
   as trope in Paradise Lost, 104–12
borders, crossing or trespass of, 101–4,
   114–20, 247–48. See also flowing;
   passing; wandering
borders, fixed vs. fluid views of, 99–100,
   105, 109–12, 118, 299–300
boundarylessness: of death, 101–3, 112–
   21; of divinity (see God [Christian]:
   all-ness of); of eternity, 114–15
Browne, Thomas, 233–34, 243
Browning, Robert Barrett, 182–83
Bunyan, John, 238–39, 254n23
Burns, Robert, 164, 178n33
Byron, Lord (George Gordon), 172–73,
   179n52

Caleb Williams (W. Godwin), 170–71
Calvin, John: and Judaism, sermons on,
   148–49; on predestination, 153, 202–
   3; on renunciation, 225–26
carrying (passing on): as teaching or
   translating, 213–16, 230n4, 305n33
cartography: of the Earth (see world
   maps); of medieval Europe, 100–101;
   of Milton's London, 167–68; of the
   Moon, 81–83, 94–95
Castellón, Enrique López. See López
   Castellón, Enrique
Catholics: Hispanoamerican, 11,
   14, 215–16; Protestants on (see
   Protestants: anti-Catholicism of);
   racialization of, 10–11, 129
Cavendish, Margaret, 311, 313–14
censorship, 6–7, 51–56, 162–63, 215,
   284
Chambers, Robert, 183–85, 208n24,
   210n60
Charles I or II, 48–57, 67, 131–32, 150–
   54, 162

Index

Chernaik, Warren, 131–32, 157n32
Christianity: antisemitic tropes in, 129–30, 134–55; beliefs concerning Jews or Judaism (*see* Calvin, John: and Judaism, sermons on; Milton, John, religious contexts); bifurcation from Judaism, 101–4, 113–18, 128–30, 134–46, 150–55; conception of freedom as contingent on (*see* liberty: as uniquely Christian); creation story of (*see under* Amerindians; Paradise); early ties of to Hellenism and Judaism, 44n7, 121–2n6; legacy of racism owing to, 129–32, 142–45, 259–60, 289–90, 305n32; as universal religion, 103–4, 118–22n6, 144–54
Christianity, kinds of: Calvinism, 148–53, 202–3, 225–26; deism, 130, 150–55; Presbyterianism, 52–53; Protestantism (*see* Protestants); Roman Catholicism (*see* Catholics)
Civil War (English), 49–50, 131, 162, 243–47. *See also* Cromwell, Oliver; Commonwealth, the
clockwork: vs. crip time, 286–87, 297, 306n36; in Heaven vs. Hell (see under *Paradise Lost*, settings in); as spiritual time, 38–40
Clymer, Lorna, 164–65
Coleridge, Samuel Taylor, 170–71
colonization: of the Americas, 9–10, 71–75, 80–85, 93, 289; of other planets, 82–83, 95–96
Commonwealth, the: readmission of Jews into, 10, 68n21; stability of as state, 56–57, 68–69n22; viewed as Eden, 48–49, 53–57, 62–67, 132
Comus. See Maske Presented at Ludlow Castle, A
Confessions (Augustine), 158n39, 188–89, 221
Confessions of a Justified Sinner (Hogg). *See* Hogg, James
Copernicus, Nicolaus, 3, 15–16n2, 108–9, 222–23
Cowper, William, 175–76
creeping, 54–58, 68n17
crip: epistemology of, 285–88, 291–95, 304n23; mobility of, 286–94, 306n37; temporality of, 38–40, 286–87, 297, 306n36 (*see also under* time)
Cromwell, Oliver, 14, 48–49, 127–33, 248–49, *250*

Dante, 183, 191, 192, 204
Darwin, Charles: fondness of for *Paradise Lost*, 182–83; on species, mutability or origins of, 185, 193–94, 203; Tennyson, as advocate of, 183–86, 193–94, 204–5 (*see also* Tennyson, Alfred: "By an Evolutionist")
David (biblical figure), 140–41, 147–49, 187
Day, Aidan, 183–84
Decaen, José. See *La Ilustración mexicana*
De Doctrina Christiana. See Treatise on Christian Doctrine, A
Defensio pro Populo Anglicano, 162
Descartes, René. *See* monism: vs. Cartesian dualism
descent: of Adam and Eve (*see* Fall, the); of human species, 185, 193–94, 203; into the underworld, 193–98, 227–28
Deuteronomy, 115–16 123–24n25, 131, 147
Dhar, Amrita, 286, 305n32
Digging Up Milton (Wallace), 14, 160–62, 168–76
disability: and ablism, experiential harm from, 295, 305n32; affinity through, as solidarity, 243, 250, 294–95, 307–8n57; in all humans compared to angels (*see* embodiment: of angels); clockwork vs. crip time of (*see* crip: temporality of); environment surrounding as integral to, 294–95, 299–300; immobility owing to, 286, 288–89, 308n61; metalanguage of, 288–90, 293; as source of knowledge (*see* crip: epistemology of); systemic oppression based on, 285, 294–95, 304n23, 305n32; universalist approaches misapplied to, 295–96
Discovery of a New World in the Moone, The (Wilkins), 72, 81, 94n6
divine will. *See* God: divine will of, vs. chance
Doctrine and Discipline of Divorce, The, 68n19, 145
Donne, John, 81, 203
Doré, Gustave, 239, 247–48, 250–51, 253n10, 256n55.
dualism. *See under* monism
Duran, Angelica, 10–11, 14, 232n20, 308n72

Earle, Philippa, 16n10, 139, 285
early modern studies. *See under* Milton, scholarship on
education. *See* reparative pedagogy
Eikonoklastes, 17, 56–59, 167
Einstein, Albert, 33–38
Elegy III (On the Death of the Bishop of Winchester), 206
"Elegy Written in a Country Churchyard" (Gray). *See* Gray, Thomas
Eliot, John, 80, 142
Eliot, T. S., 181, 207n2
El Paraíso perdido: cultural hybridity in, 11–15, 214–16, 223–52; translations of, 239, 243–44, 255n26, 256n41, 256n55 (*For specific translators, see* Álvarez Bonilla, Enrique [Colombia, 1896]; Doré, Gustave; Escóiquiz, Juan [Spanish, 1886, rev. ed. 1967]; *for illustrators, see* Blake, William; Galindo, Aníbal [Colombia, 1868]; Granados Maldonado, Francisco [Mexico, 1858]; Lara, Miguel Fernández de; López Castellón, Enrique [Spain, 2005]; Sanjuan, Dionisio [Spain, 1868])
El Paraíso perdido (Argentinean ed.,1957): cover of with Milton portrait overlay, 236–37, *236*, 239; frontispiece with Marshall variant, 236–38, 243
El Paraíso perdido (Colombian ed., 1868, rev. 2002): with illustrations by Doré, Blake, and others, 235, 239, 247–48, 250–51, 253n10, 256n55; with Knight's *Gallery* portrait (Galindo trans., 2002), 239, 255n26
El Paraíso perdido (Mexican ed., 1975). See *Reforma y Contra-reforma*
El Paraíso perdido (Mexican ed., 1951, 1967): illustrations in, of Milton with Cromwell or family (1967 ed., trans. Escóiquiz), 247–51, *249*, *250*; portrait in, of Milton with closed eyes (Faithorne variant), 235–37, 241–43, *242*, 247–48, 256n55
El Paraíso recobrado, 239–41, *240*, 245
embodiment: of angels, 217, 223–24, 306n35, 307–8n57; of authors through books (*see* animation: of ideas or imagination in print); of the circumcised vs. uncircumcised,

112–14, 118, 129, 141–51; environment surrounding as integral to, 294–95, 299–300; as experiential wisdom, 259–60, 284–301, 304–5n26; gendered or sexualized, 127–28, 268–71, 287–91, 304n23; of mind or soul, 259–60, 284–95, 300–1, 304–5n26; normalization of, 267–68, 287–88, 290–95
England: anti-Catholicism of (*see under* Protestants); Eden as allegorical for, 51–59; imagined racial lineage of, 142–43; on Jews and Judaism (*see under* Jews)
enslavement: of African people, 143–45; of biblical Jews, 135–37, 140–44; of non-Christians (*see* liberty: as uniquely Christian)
"Epigram on Milton" (Dryden), 255n30
epistemic justice. *See under* reparative pedagogy
*Epitaphium Damoni*s, 40–41
Escóiquiz, Juan, 214–25, 232n22, 242, 256n55
Eurocentrism: in speculations on, Africa or Asia, 129, 247–48; the Americas or Amerindians, 6–7, 71–95, 185–865; inhabitants of other worlds, 72–75, 80–84; other planets (*see under* the Moon); the primitive, 87, 247–48, S71–78
Evans, John Martin, 74, 80, 84, 89
Exodus: as migration narrative, 25–27, 44n7, 136, 144–45
expulsion: Adam and Eve from Eden, 101, 104–12, 172; of Jews from England, 150–55; natural vs. divine, 109–10, 124n29; of Satan from Heaven, 4–6, 87, 92, 149, 219–20
extraterrestrial realms. *See under* worlds

Fabian, Johannes, 71–72
Faithorne, William, Sr., portraits of: 1670 original, with late-life Milton after onset of blindness, 234, 237–38, 249; 1833 version, widely circulated, 234–35, *235*, 237–41, 253n5; 1951 variant, with Milton's eyes closed, 235–37, *236*, 239, 241–43, 253n10; 1957 version, overlay on book cover illustrating garden scene, 236–37, *236* (*for detail, see under* El Paraíso perdido)

Index

Fall, the: of Adam and Eve, 51–62, 170–76, 216–20, 283–84; of Amerindians, 79–80, 86–87; of the body, from agility into frailty, 294–98; of humanity or world writ large, 23, 52–62; of Satan, or the Son, 4–6, 87, 92, 134–50, 219–20; of students, from learning, 135, 138, 146–48, 284–93

Fall, the, as symbol: of lost innocence, 65–67, 79–86, 93–95, 170–71, 219–20; of revolutionary France, 170–71

Fall, the, in women's art or novels: critical reprises of (see *Digging Up Milton* [Wallace]; *Hagar's Daughter* [Hopkins]; *Snake Path* [Smith, 1992])

Fallon, Stephen M., 7–8, 17n16, 68n20, 139, 308n57

fetishism, 159–62, 164–65, 174

Fish, Stanley, 7, 106

flowing, 99–100, 289–90

free verse, as freedom of movement, 50, 214, 224–25

Freud, Sigmund, 28, 117

Furman-Adams, Wendy, 293–95, 300, 306n43, 307n49, 307n51

Fuseli, Henry: *Milton Dictating to His Daughter* (painting), 163–64, 177n15, 254n24; "Milton Gallery" (exhibit, 1799), 177n15

Gali Boadella, Montserrat, 244, 256n42

Galilei, Galileo: allusions to in Milton's works, 9, 34, 90; Aristotle or Newton compared with, 9–12, 34–36, 105–7, 111–12, 121n2; astronomical discoveries of, 72–73, 80–81, 90; experiments of on gravity, 34–36, 45n16, 105–7, 111–12; hailed as new Columbus, 81–86, 96n24; hypothesis on the law of inertia (see stasis: as zero-velocity motion); kinematics in theories of, 100, 310–11

Galindo, Aníbal, 239, 255n26

Gallery of Portraits, The (Knight, ed.), 234–35, 238–41, 253n5

Garden of Eden. See under *Paradise Lost*, settings in

Gentiles (term), 112–14, 123–24n25, 136–41, 146

Gervase of Ebstorf. *See* world maps: *Mappa Mundi* (Ebstorf, ca. 1235)

Gilbert, William, 82–83, 97n33

God (Christian): all-ness of, 8, 103–4, 118, 220–23; beneficence of, 5–6, 121–22n6, 137, 153, 157–88; as creator or father, 104, 184, 188; divine will of, vs. chance, 4–5, 109–10; dynamic stillness of, 8, 27–28, 33, 109–10; Hebrews, treatment of, 25–26; sanctioning transgressions of Samson, 115–16; temporal accommodation of, 23–24, 38–44, 198, 221

Goethe, Johann Wolfgang von: influence of on Tennyson, 183, 189–93, 210n47; mutability in works of, 191–92; as poet-scientist, 209–10n46

Granados Maldonado, Francisco, 215, 223–30, 232n22, 253n7, 256n41

Grant, Elizabeth, 160–61, 166–75

Gray, Thomas: "Elegy Written in a Country Churchyard," 247; "Ode on a Distant Prospect of Eton College," 292, 294–97

Greenberg, Marissa, 11, 15, 108–9, 259–60

Guibbory, Achsah, 9–10, 14, 25, 68n21, 103, 118

Guillory, John, 119, 123n24

Hackenbracht, Ryan, 5, 8, 13, 285, 312, 316

Hagar: dual relevance of, in biblical traditions, 144, 281n45; enslavement of offspring of, 273–78; legacy of, 144–45

"Hagar" (Nicholson), 144–45, 157n31, 281n46, 281n48

Hagar's Daughter (Hopkins): audience of, canon expanded through, 260–61; as biblical appropriation, 262, 273–75; Black women foregrounded in, 260, 271, 274, 278–79; mobilization of reader affect in, 259–63, 273–74; as selective intertext of *Paradise Lost*, 260–76, 279n5; title character of, as Black Eve, 160, 261–66

Hagar's Daughter (Hopkins), tropes in: Miltonic Hell, 259–66, 270–79, 281n41; mulatta figure, 262–63; racial passing, 259–63, 277–79; satanic figures, 262–68, 272–73, 276–79; the Fall, 261–73

Hallam, Arthur Henry (A. H. H.). See *In Memoriam, A. H. H.*

Index

Harvard Classics, The (Eliot, ed.), 233–34, 252n2
Haskin, Dayton, 118, 120–21
Hebrews (book of), 101, 122n7
heliocentrism. *See* motion (physics): of Earth around sun
Heng, Geraldine, 20n41, 129
Herbert, George, 186–87, 209n32
heroism, 115–16, 119
Hesperian Gardens, 73, 75, 90–91, 93–94. *See also* Paradise
heterosexism, 290–91
Hevelius, Johannes, 83–84
Higinbotham, Sarah, 283, 302n3
Hill, Christopher, 49–50, 67
Hispanoamericans: literary culture and modernity of, 213–14, 239–47, 250; Milton's reception from, 11, 214–16, 223–30, 232n20, 239–52
History of Britain, The, 234–34
Hobbes, Thomas, 283, 302n6, 313–14
Hobbs, Allyson, 262–63
Hoffman Kale, Margaret, 216, 219
Hogg, James, 164, 173–74, 179n57
Homer, 19–20n37, 50, 166–67, 255n30
Hope of Israel, The (Menasseh), 127, 129, 132–34, 141–42
Hopkins, Pauline E. See *Hagar's Daughter* (Hopkins)
horror, confrontations with, 101–2, 115–18, 161–65, 179n55, 273
Hughes, Bill, 294–95, 307n56
Hughes, Merritt Y., 67n4, 157n25, 234–35
Hughes, William, 129–30, 133
humoral tradition. *See* bodies: fluids or humors of
Huxley, Thomas, 184–85, 203–4

idolatry, 137–38, 141–42, 160, 164, 174
Il Paradiso perduto, 254n13
Il Penseroso and *L'Allegro*: illustrations for, 237; Melancholy and Mirth in, 26–27, 28–32, 41, 303n9
imagery: aural or auditory, 40, 218, 246–47; of corporality, 224–25; delirious or vertiginous, 7, 117–18, 125n33, 226–27; of light and dark, 3, 26–46; of mountains, 3–4, 24–25, 37
Il Penseroso and *L'Allegro*, kinetic: cosmological, 3–4; of food and digestion, 99–100, 138–39, 284–85, 303n9; of the landscape, 24; in

Paradise Lost, 26–46, 105, 110–11, 214–30; of spiritual conditions, 32
immixing (comingling), 101–3, 112–21, 121n5, 152–53
Indigenous people. *See* Amerindians
"In effigiei eius sculptorem" (Against the Engraver of His Portrait), 237, 254n15
In Memoriam, A. H. H. (Tennyson): composition of, 183, 189, 210n60; Goethe's or Milton's influence on, 14, 46n26, 181–206; Orphic descent in, 193–98; as scientific epic, and spiritual test, 183–86, 198–202, 208n16, 210n60
innocence. *See under* Fall, the
intersectionality, 287–88, 294–300, 304n24

Janssen (or Johnson), Cornelius. *See* Milton, John, portraits of: in early life
Jessey, Henry, 129–33
Jews: antisemitic tropes concerning, 129–30, 134–55; debates regarding English resettlement of, 68n21, 127–30, 149–55; diasporic condition of, 10, 104, 127–30, 132–34, 230n4; racialization of, 10–11, 20n41, 128–29, 230n4; violence against, resurgence of, 127–28, 130–31, 305n32; white privilege afforded or denied to, 155n4
Jews, religion of: Amerindians viewed as lost tribes of, 80, 132, 135, 140–50; Christianity's selective appropriation of, 25, 131–34; considered as part of universal religion, 103–4, 118–22n6, 144–54; debates on conversion or redemption from, 113, 130–35, 140–50, 152–54; as disqualification for freedom (*see* liberty: as uniquely Christian); laws of, on marriage and divorce, 123–24n25; status of, as chosen people, 25–26: vs. Gentiles, 112–14, 123–24n25, 136–41, 146
Job (book of), 136–37, 153, 156n24
John Milton Reading Room, The (*JMRR*), 15, 289–90
Joshua (book of), 144–45
Judges (book of), 118, 123–24n25

Kafer, Alison, 286–87, 304n23
Kale, Margaret Hoffman. *See* Hoffman Kale, Margaret

Index 327

Keats, John, 165–67, 178n33
Kepler, Johannes, 10, 81–82, 96n24
Kerrigan, William, 45n20, 68n20
kinematics, 100–101, 111–12. *See also*
kinopolitics
King, Martin Luther, Jr., 144–45
kinopolitics, 47–67, 99–101, 109–10,
215–16; in *Paradise Lost*, 99–121. *See
also* kinematics

La Ilustración mexicana: essays
commenting on Milton, 243–47,
255n38 (*see also* Zarco Mateos,
Francisco); portrait in, by Decaen
(1852), with simulation of Milton's
signature, 241–45, 242, 250–51,
256n40, 256n42
L'Allegro. See *Il Penseroso* and *L'Allegro*
Lamarck, Jean-Baptiste, 183, 185
Lamartine, Alphonse de, 242–43, 245–46
Lara, Miguel Fernández de, 241, 248,
250–51
Latinx or Latin Americans. *See*
Hispanoamericans
Lerner, Ross, 297, 308n59
Lévi-Strauss, Claude, 247–48
Levý, Jiří, 226–27
Lewalski, Barbara Keifer: on Milton's
life, 67n4, 235–43, 252–53n4,
257n61; on Milton's works, 50, 67n4,
136–37, 156n24, 281n48
liberty: as exercise of reason, 56–57,
153–55; as freedom of movement,
220, 222–23; as free will, 5–6, 161,
220, 222–23; as uniquely Christian,
130–32, 143–49, 154–55
Lizzie. *See* Grant, Elizabeth
Loewenstein, David, 50, 113
López Castellón, Enrique, 215
Lucretius, 184–86, 196
Luke (gospel), 120, 134–36, 143–47, 202
Luxon, Thomas, 16n3, 53, 97n47
"Lycidas," 206, 225–26, 250–51

Maldonado, Francisco Granados. *See*
Granados Maldonado, Francisco
Man in the Moone, The (F. Godwin), 72
mappae mundi. See under world maps
Marlowe, Christopher, 28, 288
marriage: discord in, 47, 63–65; as divine
indulgence, 28–29, 94; prohibitions
on outside social group, 152–53,
259–60; sanctioned as transgression

for Samson, 115–17, 122n9, 123–
24n25, 124n26, 130–50
Marriage of Heaven and Hell, The
(Blake), 162–64
Marshall, William. *See under* Milton,
John, portraits of
Mask Presented at Ludlow Castle, A,
31–37, 139, 190, 216, 219, 303n12,
305n33
Masson, David, 190–91
Mateos, Francisco Zarco. *See* Zarco
Mateos, Francisco
McHenry, Elizabeth, 259–60
mechanism. *See* vitalism: vs. materialism
or mechanism
melancholy, 29–32, 39–40
Menasseh ben Israel, 127, 129, 132–34,
141–42
mestizaje, 152–53, 182–96, 237–39,
247–51, 254n17
Metamorphoses (Ovid), 182, 185–86,
192–96, 205–6
metaphysics vs. materialism, 32, 184,
223–24. *See also* monism; spirituality
vs. materiality
migration: across the globe, 9–10, 239;
of Adam and Eve from Paradise,
71–95, 101; of Hebrews from Egypt,
25–27, 134; hostility generated from,
127–28, 150–55, 243–44, 256n42.
See also borders, crossing or trespass
of; borders: surveillance and policing
of; translation: as cultural hybridity
millenarianism, 129–30, 133–35, 145,
150
Milton, John, body of: exhumation and
commodification of, 159–66, 178n37,
179n55, 182–83; portraiture of as
presencing, revivifying, 233–52;
self-representation of (*see* "When
I consider how my light is spent");
disabilities in, late-life blindness, 3,
14, 163, 243, 251–52, 253n5; lifelong
chronic illness, 11, 29, 243, 251–52
Milton, John, historical contexts:
censorship, writings against, 6–7, 54–
56, 151, 162, 284; French or Mexican
Revolutions, influence on, 162–66,
243–47; geocultural biases of, 72–73,
84–95 233; republicanism of, 48–67,
118, 129, 162–66, 243–47; role of
as Cromwell's secretary of foreign
tongues, 48–50, 129, 167, 251

328   Index

Milton, John, influences of: from biblical languages and scripture, 10–11, 24–27, 44n3, 131, 214–16; from classical authors, 19–20n37, 50, 166–67, 182; from Copernicus, 3–4, 15–16n2, 16n4; from Galileo, 9, 34, 90, 100, 104–12, 311–12; from Shakespeare, 166–67

Milton, John, influences on: African American culture, 11, 14, 144–45, 259–60; contemporary art and activism, 283–302; Hispanoamerican culture, 11, 214–30, 232n20, 239–52; the Romantic period, 14, 162–76, 179n57, 181–206, 295; the Victorian period, 14, 181–83, 189–90

Milton, John, kinetic sensibilities of: in his sense of souls as animated matter, 6–7, 17n19, 233–37, 245; in his sensory imagery of motion and movement, 4–5, 9, 184; in his stress on active reason and virtue, 6–7, 17n17, 286

Milton, John, life of: biographers on (*see* Lewalski, Barbara Keifer; Masson, David; Toland, John); family religion or marriages of, 25, 248–50; imagined racial lineage of, 190–91; residence of in London, 166–70

Milton, John, philosophies of: as animist materialist, 8, 17n19, 104–6, 184–93, 311–15; as monist, 48–60, 139, 190–91; as vitalist monist, 59–60, 259–60, 284–98, 311–15. *See also* monism; vitalism

Milton, John, portraits of: ailing in bed, *250*; with Cromwell while serving as secretary, 248–49, *250*; in early life (1618, 1629), 238–39; in *El Paraíso recobrado* (1889), 239–41, *240*; by Faithorne (1670), *235*, *236*, *242*; as "Giovanni" or "Juan" Milton, 235–37, *236*, 239, 254n13; with his daughter as visual interpreter (*see under* Fuseli, Henry); with his spouse and daughters, 247, 248–49, *249*; from Knight's *Gallery* (1833), 234–35, *235*, 238–39, 241; by Marshall (1645), 236–38, 243–44; Milton's country home, 233–34; Milton's satire of Marshall's portrait, 237, 254n15; on a paperback cover (Argentina, 1957), *236*

Milton, John, religious contexts: Calvinism, turn away from, 153–54; debates or tracts on theology, 10–11,

129–50, 153–54, 190–93; views on Jews and Judaism, 10–11, 103, 128–50, 153–54

Milton, John, scholarship on: early modern studies, inclusivity of, 283–302, 304n15, 305n27, 305n32; Milton studies, 4, 8, 12–15, 304–5n26, 304n15, 305n32; resources for (see *The John Milton Reading Room*); teaching of, misuses of Milton in traditional classrooms, 287–88; reparative strategies for, 299–302; students' sense of otherness as valuable in, 300, 305n29, 307n51. *See also under* reparative pedagogy

Milton, John, translations of: across the globe, 316; from biblical languages, 25, 190; of *Paradise Lost* (see *Paradise Lost*, translation challenges of); into Romance languages (see under *El Paraíso perdido*; *Il Paradiso perduto*; Mirabeau, Comte de)

Milton, John, works of: accessibility or availability of, 14, 290–91; canonization and popularization of, 215, 233–35, 252, 260–61, 287–88, 292; sublime aesthetic in, 45n20, 163–66, 181–83, 223–30, 247

Milton, John, works of, adapted or alluded to by others: *see* Blake, William; Burke, Edmund; Wordsworth, William; "Epigram on Milton" (Dryden); *Caleb Williams* (W. Godwin); *Digging Up Milton* (Wallace); Fuseli, Henry: "Milton Gallery"; *Hagar's Daughter* (Hopkins); *In Memoriam, A. H. H.* (Tennyson); *Snake Path* (Smith)

Milton, John, writings of. See *individual works*

"Milton: Alcaics." See Tennyson, Alfred

"Milton's Cottage," 233–34

Mirabeau, Comte de: *Sur la liberté de la presse*, 162; *Théorie de la royauté*, 162

monarchy, as original sin, 52–54

monism: on body as soul (primal matter), 8–9, 104, 216–25; on body/mind as non-binary (bodymind), 8–9, 294–95, 305n32, 311–15; on embodied consciousness, 259–60, 284–301, 304–5n26; on embodied spiritual consciousness, 260, 263–64, 273–74; ties of to vitalism, 8–9, 12–13, 17n19,

Index 329

259–60, 315; vs. Pauline dualism, 139–40, 284, 312; vs. Cartesian dualism, 4–10, 184–90, 216–17, 285, 312

Montés de Ocá, Julio, 239–40

Moon, the: imagined geographies of, 81–83, 94–95; telescopic observations of, 72–73, 80–81; territorial claims to (*see* colonization: of other planets)

moral laws: absolutism vs. relativism of, 28–29, 173–74, 202–4; as laws of physics, 4–5, 201–2. *See also* racism: as moral sin

Mosaic law, 101, 123n25, 132, 147–49

Moses (biblical figure), 113–15, 137, 145, 157n32

Moshenska, Joe, 9, 163

motion (physics): definition of, 213–14; of Earth around sun, 3, 15n1, 16n3, 36, 311; laws of, 33–34, 71–74, 80–81, 105–7; on particles (*see* kinematics); role of gravity in, 33–34, 105–8; subjective experience of, 33–38; time as measure of, 13, 32–37

motionists, 53

movement: aimless or labyrinthian, 41–42, 224; as constancy or corruptibility, 37, 183–95, 203–6, 217, 222–26; of emotions or empathy, 259–63, 273–74; mental or metaphysical, 16n6, 32, 215–19, 288–302, 308n61; musical, 5, 30, 40–43, 193–98, 218; of or within the body, 47–67, 99–100, 105, 215–16; poetics of, 28–30, 213–16; as recursive or regressive, 3, 15n1, 57–58; of the soul, 26, 205–6, 215–16; spatial or temporal (*see* migration; time); stability as form of, in self or state, 57–58. *See also* imagery; kinopolitics

movement, types of. *See* carrying; creeping; flowing; immixing; passing; presencing; repairing; resting; returning; rolling; stagnating; swaying; waiting; walking; wandering

mulatta figure. See under *Hagar's Daughter* (Hopkins), tropes in

Munday, Jeremy, 225, 232n23

Murgia, Mario, 8, 10–11

music. *See* movement: musical

Muslims, 10, 127, 155, 291, 305n32

Nail, Thomas, 14, 99–103, 109–12, 118, 121

nation-state, 10, 57—65, 99–104, 111–12, 118–21

Nativity Ode, 13, 27–28, 32, 37, 137

Naturam non pati senium (Nature is not subject to old age), 33

necromancy, 159–76, 194–95

neighborliness. *See* Protestants: as global community

Netzley, Ryan, 286–87

Neve, Philip, 159–68, 174–76

Newton, Isaac, 33–35, 100, 121n2

New World. *See under* American continent; Eurocentrism

Nicholson, Eliza Poitevent Holbrook. *See* "Hagar" (Nicholson)

Nyquist, Mary, 11, 87–88, 96n16, 157n28

Ocá, Julio Montés de, 238–40

Oedipus Rex (Sophocles), 117, 167

Of Education, 56–59, 283–84, 291

"On Time," 38–40, 45n22

Origen of Alexandria, 199, 201–2

original sin: of global conquest, 94–95; of the monarchy, 52–59. *See also* Fall, the

Orpheus, 30, 193–98

otherworldliness. *See* worldliness

Other Worlds (Bergerac), 72, 95n4

Ovid, 182, 185–86, 192–96, 205–6

Paradise: as earthly realm (*see* Hesperian Gardens); as envisioned in *Paradise Lost*, 71–92, 283, 289–92, 297–98; as extraterrestrial, 72–73, 83–95; as living present, 78–83, 91–95; migration of, from Asia to Americas, 71–83, 96n11; restoration of or return to, 199, 283. *See also* Fall, the; prelapsarian state

Paradise Lost: Americas represented in, 74, 85–95; border-crossing motif in, 104–12; cartography and cosmology of, 71–95, 221–24; change and creation in, 44, 189–90; Darwin's fondness for (*see under* Darwin, Charles); abled or disabled bodies in, 288–91, 304n23; as epic or tragedy, 50, 57, 170–76, 266, 278–79; gender and sexuality in, 289–91; historical contexts for, 48–67, 85, 190–91, 215; metaphysics in, 183–95, 203–6, 216–23; motion and movement in,

330 Index

Paradise Lost (*continued*)
3–9, 23–51, 105–7, 215–30, 288–98; panoramic views in, 181–82; "Paradise of Fools, 222, 228–29; salvation in, 5–6, 39, 79–95, 216–17, 225–26; *Samson Agonistes*, connection to, 18n22, 112–21; staging of reader affect in, 286; "The Ode [or Prayer] to Light," 3–6, 218–23, 226–27; time in and pace of, 38–44, 84–95, 217–18, 231n10; trope of wandering in, 59–67

Paradise Lost, Adam and Eve in: compared to Amerindians, 86; expulsion or migration of, 101, 109–12, 172; flowing, able-bodied movements of, 289–90; happy state of (*see* Paradise; prelapsarian state); on inhabitants of other worlds, 84, 89–91; Protestant heroism of, 189–90, 198; Eve's similarities to Mirth (see under *Il Penseroso* and *L'Allegro*); speculative kinship with (see *Hagar's Daughter* [Hopkins]: title character of, as Black Eve); trials in gullibility or virtue of, 42, 56, 59–62, 303n10

Paradise Lost, Raphael in: as historian and narrator, 104–7, 296, 312; on Adam's creation and offspring, 54, 63, 94–95, 189–92, 199–200; on angels, 41–43, 104–5; on possibility of other planets, 36–39, 72–75, 84–91; on salvation (*see* salvation: Christian); on War in Heaven, 24–25, 43, 84–91

Paradise Lost, Satan in: Abdiel's lesson to, 5, 16n9, 303n10; and/as the Jews, 146, 157n33; as corrupt or revolutionary figure, 55, 67n4, 162–63, 219–20, 228–29; as figure of disability and criminality, 288–89; damnation and expulsion of (*see also* the Fall: of Satan, or the Son); gaze of, 16n6, 42, 108–9, 201, 222; motions of, 4–6, 16n6, 88, 101–9; on other worlds, 90–92, 111, 222–23, 228–29; propulsive flight of, 16n6, 49, 60, 72–74, 106–8, 219–24; Romantic reinterpretation of, 171–72; stagnation of, 7, 39, 87–88, 217–18; view of Chaos, 105; vs. Satan in *Caleb Williams*, 170–71

Paradise Lost, other characters in: the angels, as guardians of borders, 110–11; dancing of, 40–42; Chaos: dynamic state of, 4–5, 42, 74; sublimity of, 27, 163–64; ties to God in infinity of, 27, 37–38; God, 8, 135, 187–88, 220–23; Michael, 62, 92–93, 101–13, 206; Sin, 39–40, 171, 306n34; the Son, 187, 196–98

Paradise Lost, published illustrations for: of censored materials (Boydell, 1794–7), 163–64, 177n15; in Spanish translations (*see* Blake, William; Doré, Gustave; *El Paraíso perdido*; *Reforma y Contra-reforma*)

Paradise Lost, settings in: Eden, as allegorical for England, 51–59; as site of conquest, 85; embodiment in, 5–6, 288–91, 304n23; expulsion from, 104–12, 172; flooding of, 110–12; in Romanticism, 171–73; natural wonders in, 182; Heaven and Hell, as material or spiritual realms, 184, 197, 219–20; contrasting temporalities of, 38–40; dynamic states of, 4–5, 38–39, 74, 173, 215–28; expulsion from and to, 101, 104–12; in Romantic era, 171–73; sublimity of, 163–64, 227–28, 247; war waged in, 23–25, 38–41; Tree of Knowledge, 47, 56, 61–64

Paradise Lost, translation challenges of: ideological registers, 215–16, 223–24, 228–29; kinetic imagery, 224–27; metaphysics, 223–30; poetic form, 214–16

Paradise Regain'd: on familial love, 120–21; publication history of, 239–40; Satan and the Son, portrayed in, 130, 134–50; Spanish translation of (see *El Paraíso recobrado*); stillness and duration in, 37–44

Paraphrase of Psalm 114, A, 24–28, 33, 37, 230n4

passing: gendered or sexual, 290–91; racial, 14–15, 259–63, 276–79; spatial (passing through or over), 25–27, 65–67, 134. *See also* borders: trespass or crossing of

Paul, Saint (the apostle): anti-Judaism of, 113, 128–30, 134–46; on body vs. soul (*see* monism: vs. Pauline dualism); on Christian liberty,

Index

154–55; on the resurrection, 197–99; on universal religion, 13–14, 103–20, 143–49, 199–200

Philistines, 101–3, 113–21

Plato, 203, 231n13

polygenism vs. monogenism, 192–93

prelapsarian state: of the Americas, 86–88, 91, 142–43; of the Ancients, 87; happiness in, 6, 17n13, 53, 62–65; from postlapsarian perspective, 215, 219–20, 295–96; as spiritual vs. sartorial nudity, 88

presencing, 12, 233–52

Price, Margaret, 285, 292

Private Memoirs and Confessions (Hogg). *See* Hogg, James

Protestants: Adam and Eve as heroes of, 198; anti-Catholicism of, 10–11, 127–55; clergy and doctrines of, 52–53, 101, 118; evangelism of as empire, 10, 87–88, 141–42; as global community, 101–2; view of other religions as in past, 54–57, 78–79, 84–95

Prynne, William, 129–30, 133–34, 152–53

Psalms (book of), 24–28, 33, 37, 76, 147, 230n4. See also *A Paraphrase of Psalm 114*

racial difference: as concept developed historically, 129, 155n4, 268–69, 305n32; as difference of religion (*see* Catholics: racialization of; Jews: racialization of); fragility or mutability of (*see* borders: fixed vs. fluid views of); freedom as contingent on, 154–55; as somatic, 129, 141, 185–86

racism: antisemitism compared with, 128–29, 155n4; biblical precedents for, 127–55; ethnic iconographies of, 128, 142–43; global metalanguage of, 305n30; as intersectional, 268–71, 287, 304–5n26; inward experience of, 259–79; as moral sin, 259, 268–71; against people of color, 10, 185–86, 259–62, 277–78; systemic oppression based on, 11–12, 259, 287–302, 305n32; in theories of social evolution, 127–29, 183–86, 208n24; violence based on, 260–61, 305n32, 306n41

Ready and Easy Way, The, 48–49, 51–66, 68n20, 132

Reason of Church Government, The, 4

redemption, 101–3, 114–20, 135–36, 140–50, 153–54

Reforma y Contra-reforma (Reformation and Counter-Reformation), 235–36, 253n10

religious differences: in Calvinism or Catholicism, vs. Protestantism, 131–49, 153–54, 202–16, 223–30; in circumcised vs. uncircumcised, 112–18, 129, 141–51; as somatic (*see* Catholics: racialization of; Jews: racialization of; African continent: Moors from, complexion or religion of)

reparative pedagogy: adaptability and diversity in, 286–302, 306n36, 307n51; both in and outside classroom, 283, 292–93, 299–302; as epistemic and social justice, 285, 287–88, 291–95, 304n15; importance of lived experience in (*see* embodiment: as experiential wisdom); as inclusive and non-binary, 285–87, 289–91, 295, 301–2; as transformative of mind and world, 283, 287–88, 304n23, 304n24

reparative pedagogy for Milton: *Paradise Lost* as model for, 283–87, 295–98; as project of national repair, 284–85; in the utopian classroom, 284, 305n4, 305n29. See also *Of Education*

resting: as element of crip time, 294; in physics, 107; as pre- or postlapsarian, 6, 17n14, 104, 221–22

returning, 3, 58–59, 284

revolutions: around the sun (*see under* motion [physics]); of governments (*see* Civil War; French Revolution); in interior states, 108–9

Ricks, Christopher, 191–92, 231n11

Riffaterre, Michael, 231n10, 231n13

Rogers, John, 5, 7–8, 109–10

rolling, 105–9

Romaine, William, 151–52

Roman empire, 93, 140

Romans (epistle of), 131, 134–40, 145–46, 149

Romanticism, 14, 162–76, 179n57, 181–206, 295

332 Index

Rosenblatt, Jason P., 119–20, 121–22n6, 124n31, 138
Rumrich, John: on animist materialism, 8–9, 12–13, 17n19, 315; on disability as human condition, 308n57; on Galileo and gravity, 107–8; on Jewish diaspora, 134, 230n4; on active stillness (*see under* stasis)

salvation: Christian, 101–2, 114–15; cosmic, 199–200, 202–4; of humans or animals, 201–2; through epic poetry, 195, 198–202
Samson Agonistes: Chorus in, 101, 112–16, 123n21, 124n27; classical influences of, 166–67; as epic or tragedy, 115–17, 121, 121n6, 166–67; immixing in, 101–3, 112–22n5, 144; Jews or Judaism in, 10–11, 121n5, 134–50, 316; Manoa and Dalila in, 101–4, 112, 115–21, 124n26, 125n37; proto-Christian title character of, 101, 104, 125n37; sanctioned transgression in, 115–17, 122n9, 123–24n25, 124n26, 130–50; and Shakespeare, 167
Samuels, Ellen, 286–87
Sanjuan, Dionisio, 247–48, 256n55
Sauer, Elizabeth, 10, 84–87
Saurat, Denis, 184. 189–90
Scafi, Alessandro, 75–79, 96n11
sciences: of astronomy or physics (*see* Copernicus, Nicolaus; Einstein, Albert; Galilei, Galileo; Newton, Issac); of biology (*see* Chambers, Robert; Darwin, Charles; Lamarck, Jean-Baptiste); poetics and poets of (*see* Goethe, Johann Wolfgang von; Lucretius; Milton; Ovid; Tennyson, Alfred; Virgil)
Second Defense, The, 48, 53–57, 65–66, 67n3, 131
Shakespeare, William: *As You Like It*, 32; author portraits of, 233–34; *Hamlet*, 28–29, 169–70; *King Lear*, 38; Mistress Quickly (character), 169–70; *The Tempest*, 32, 283, 302n6; vernacular of, 166–67
Short Demurrer to the Jewes (Prynne), 129–30, 133–34, 152–53
Shoulson, Jeffrey, 26, 44n7, 123n21, 136, 144–45, 184
Siebers, Tobin, 286–87, 304n24

slavery. *See* enslavement
Smith, Alexis. See *Snake Path* (Smith, 1992)
Snake Path (Smith, 1992), 15, 287–88, 291–98, 306n27
social Darwinism. *See* racism: in theories of social evolution
Sonnets: Sonnet 7, 33; Sonnet 19, 7, 9, 20n39, 33, 206, 241, 253n5; Sonnet 22, 11, 20n39
Spenser, Edmund, 19–20n37, 68n18
spirituality vs. materiality, 104, 138–39, 146, 183–206, 284, 312. *See also* monism
stasis: as active stillness, 6–9, 13, 23–44, 219, 313–15; as stability, in self or state, 23, 57–58, 217; as zero-velocity motion, 6, 23, 107–10, 294; vs. stagnation, 6–7, 87–88. *See also* resting
Stiles, Ezra, 142–43
stillness. *See* stasis
sublimity: in Burke and Kant, 163–66, 182; in Milton, 45n20, 163–66, 181–83, 223–30, 247
swaying, 68–69n22, 93

Taylor, Jesse Oak, 195–96
Tennyson, Alfred: on the afterlife, 181–89, 196–97, 201–6; "By an Evolutionist," 205–6; elegy for Alfred Henry Hallam (see *In Memoriam, A. H. H.*); "Lucretius," 206; on materialism and metaphysics, 182–83, 188–91, 203–5; "Milton: Alcaics," 181–83; as poet-scientist, 183–86, 201–2, 210n60 (*see also* Darwin, Charles: Tennyson as advocate of); religious faith and doubts of, 183–85, 198–206, 208n16; son on influences of, 191–92; on species extinction, 193–98; on transmutation of souls, 183–95, 203–6
Tenure of Kings and Magistrates, The, 52–59, 102–4, 131
Teskey, Gordon, 7, 115–18, 125n33, 251, 254n18
theology: Columbus's influence on, 73–79; Galileo's influence on, 6–10, 72–73
time: of antiquity or the East, vs. Europe, 82, 92–95; Aristotelian, 32–33; backward/forward orientations

Index

to, 15, 92–95, 112–19, 170–71, 204; of Catholicism or Judaism, vs. Protestantism, 54–57, 78–79, 84–95, 101–4, 118, 122n6; of Christian theology (*see under* afterlife, the); chronological and linear, vs. cyclic and eternal, 38, 113–15, 199, 204–5, 222; of crip time, vs. clockwork, 38–40, 286–87, 297, 306n36; of Eden in New World, 54, 78–80; of Providence, 23–24, 38–44, 119–20, 198, 221; as sacred, 117, 316

Toland, John, 14, 130, 150–55

tragedy: Aristotelian, 117; of mulatta figures (see under *Hagar's Daughter* [Hopkins], tropes in); of postlapsarian state (*see* apocalypse: pre- vs. post-; the Fall); in Romanticism, 170–76; vs. comedy, 56–57, 166, 169–70, 176, 303n9

transgression: sanctioning of, 115–16, 122n9, 123–24n25; as wandering, 47, 55–56, 62–67, 217; vs. normativity, 118–19

translation: difficulties in (see *Paradise Lost*, translation challenges of); as colonial resistance, 11, 229–30, 239, 247–48; as cultural hybridity, 13–14, 213–16, 223–52

Treatise on Christian Doctrine, A, 38, 139, 184, 189–91

Trubowitz, Rachel, 9–14, 26, 139, 144, 259–60

truth: as exercise of liberty, 17n17, 56–57, 153–55; personified as flowing, 6–7; relativist views of, 174–76

Tufte, Virginia James, 293–95, 307n51

Tuhkanen, Mikko, 261, 277

United States: antebellum period in, 259–62; antisemitic and racist violence in, 127–28, 155; border of with Mexico, 109, 120; civil rights movement of, 144–45; demographics of, 305n27

universalism, 199–200, 204, 260–61, 295

Van Langren, Michael Florent, 82–83

Vaughan, Henry, 199, 211n66

vernacular culture, 169–71, 173–75

Vestiges of the Natural History of Creation (Chambers), 183–85, 208n24, 210n60

Victorianism, 189–90

Virgil: as model for Milton, 166–67, 182–83; as poet of science, 185–86, 196–98; sublimity in works of, 247

vitalism: of the embodied soul (*see under* monism); vs. materialism or mechanism, 6–9, 32, 184–202, 259–60

waiting, as active virtue, 6–7, 17n17, 37, 136–39, 198. *See also* resting; stasis

walking: ableist assumptions about, 288–94, 306n37; of angels vs. humans, 217, 223–24, 306n35; as self-knowledge, 5, 16n10, 218, 287–88, 292

Wallace, Jennifer, 14, 160–62, 168–76

wandering, 4, 29, 69n24–26; as creativity, 182, 218; of Satan, 60–62; as transgression, 47, 55–62, 68n19, 289

Webster, Erin, 9–10, 13

Westall, Richard, 163–64

white supremacism, 127–28, 144, 155, 259–62, 272. *See also* racism

Wilburn, Reginald A., 11, 14, 144

Williamson, Elizabeth, 300–301

Wittreich, Joseph, 121–22n6, 237, 275

women: as authors, 233, 252n2; as mothers or forerunners, 259–79; as students of Milton, 287, 290–91, 304n23

Woodward, David, 73–74

Wordsworth, William, 169–72

worldliness: vs. inexperience (*see* Fall, the: of Adam and Eve); vs. otherworldliness, 89, 184, 216–24; vs. piety (*see* spirituality vs. materiality)

world maps: compared to medieval pictures, 73–74; Isidoran (T and O maps), 82–84; *Mappa Mundi* (Ebstorf, ca. 1235), 77, 78; *Mappa Mundi* (Psalter, ca. 1265), 76, 91; Paradise positioned on (*see* Paradise). *See also* cartography

worlds: extraterrestrial, 71–95, 311–12; inhabited or uninhabited, 72, 75, 79–83, 89; known and unknown (Old World / New World) (*see under* American continent; Eurocentrism); natural or supernatural, 28, 32, 57, 164–65; subterranean, 193–98

Zarco Mateos, Francisco, 243–47, 255n38